MW01232606

International Political Economy Series

Series Editor
Timothy M. Shaw
University of London
University of Massachusetts Boston, Boston, MA, USA
London, UK

The global political economy is in flux as a series of cumulative crises impacts its organization and governance. The IPE series has tracked its development in both analysis and structure over the last three decades. It has always had a concentration on the global South. Now the South increasingly challenges the North as the centre of development, also reflected in a growing number of submissions and publications on indebted Eurozone economies in Southern Europe. An indispensable resource for scholars and researchers, the series examines a variety of capitalisms and connections by focusing on emerging economies, companies and sectors, debates and policies. It informs diverse policy communities as the established trans-Atlantic North declines and 'the rest', especially the BRICS, rise.

More information about this series at
http://www.palgrave.com/gp/series/13996

Peter Arthur • Kobena T. Hanson
Korbla P. Puplampu
Editors

Disruptive Technologies, Innovation and Development in Africa

palgrave
macmillan

Editors
Peter Arthur
Department of Political Science
Dalhousie University
Halifax, NS, Canada

Kobena T. Hanson
African Development Bank
Abidjan, Côte D'Ivoire

Korbla P. Puplampu
Department of Sociology
Grant MacEwan University
Edmonton, AB, Canada

ISSN 2662-2483   ISSN 2662-2491 (electronic)
International Political Economy Series
ISBN 978-3-030-40649-3   ISBN 978-3-030-40647-9 (eBook)
https://doi.org/10.1007/978-3-030-40647-9

© The Editor(s) (if applicable) and The Author(s), under exclusive licence to Springer Nature Switzerland AG 2020
This work is subject to copyright. All rights are solely and exclusively licensed by the Publisher, whether the whole or part of the material is concerned, specifically the rights of translation, reprinting, reuse of illustrations, recitation, broadcasting, reproduction on microfilms or in any other physical way, and transmission or information storage and retrieval, electronic adaptation, computer software, or by similar or dissimilar methodology now known or hereafter developed.
The use of general descriptive names, registered names, trademarks, service marks, etc. in this publication does not imply, even in the absence of a specific statement, that such names are exempt from the relevant protective laws and regulations and therefore free for general use.
The publisher, the authors and the editors are safe to assume that the advice and information in this book are believed to be true and accurate at the date of publication. Neither the publisher nor the authors or the editors give a warranty, expressed or implied, with respect to the material contained herein or for any errors or omissions that may have been made. The publisher remains neutral with regard to jurisdictional claims in published maps and institutional affiliations.

This Palgrave Macmillan imprint is published by the registered company Springer Nature Switzerland AG.
The registered company address is: Gewerbestrasse 11, 6330 Cham, Switzerland

ACKNOWLEDGEMENTS

This publication reflects the culmination of discussions that started informally on the impact of disruptive innovation on the lives of everyday Africans, gradually morphing into if and how exactly these technologies were shaping lives, communities, and the continent. Our initial conversations took on more meaning, till the suggestion was floated as to why not write a book on this emerging issue.

Next came the roping in of potential contributors and we appreciate the ease and willingness with which almost everyone signed onto the project. Our shared commitment to the contribution to knowledge and Africa's transformation agenda brought us together to turn what started out as a chat on social media into a concrete knowledge product. We are particularly indebted to each contributor of the volume for taking time from their busy schedule to contribute a nuanced and insightful chapter on how disruptive innovations are shaping the African continent. Their commitment to the volume and the broader pursuit of knowledge that contributes to shaping the development landscape in Africa is inspiring. We are grateful for their contribution to this volume.

At Palgrave, our heartfelt thanks go to Tim Shaw (Series Editor) for his early encouragement and belief in the timeliness and pertinence of the topic and to Anca Pusca (Senior Editor) and Katelyn Zingg (Editorial Assistant) for their patience and clear guidance throughout the development of this volume. Appreciation likewise goes to the two anonymous reviewers whose invaluable feedback helped shape the quality and critical thoughts of the volume.

We also desire to acknowledge, with gratitude, the support and love of our families who had to endure our absences while we were editing the volume. Finally, while accepting culpability for all editorial slip-ups, the views expressed in this volume solely remain the exclusive responsibility of the individual contributors.

CONTENTS

NOTES ON CONTRIBUTORS

Nafisa A. Abdulhamid is a PhD candidate at Dalhousie University, Canada, and a doctoral fellow at the Centre for the Study of Security and Development. She is also a Glyn Berry scholar and a recipient of the Doris Boyle Graduate Prize and the Khalida Quraishi Memorial Graduate Award in Islamic Studies. Her research interests range from employing the constructivist notion of "communities of practice" to explore institutional practices, the discourse on the Responsibility to Protect (R2P), and commercialized micro-credit to a critical analysis of the Gender and Development (GAD) model.

Peter Arthur is Associate Professor of Political Science and International Development Studies at Dalhousie University, Canada. His research interests focus on sub-Saharan Africa, with an emphasis on the contribution of small-scale enterprises, new regionalism, capacity development, and postconflict reconstruction, the governance of oil, and natural resources management. His works have appeared in edited volumes and journals, including *Africa Today*, *African Studies Review*, *Commonwealth and Comparative Politics*, and *Journal of Contemporary African Studies*.

Joseph Baricako is an economist at the United Nations Economic Commission for Africa (UNECA) in Addis Ababa. Barikaco has contributed extensively in research and capacity building across the continent in several areas of economics, most importantly international economics, macroeconomics, economic geography, econometrics, regional integration, and trade. He has published in refereed journals as well as chapters in books.

George O. Essegbey is a former director of the Science and Technology Policy Research Institute of the Council for Scientific and Industrial Research (CSIR), Ghana, and a member of the Scientific Board of AfricaLics and Management Board of the African Technology Policy Studies. His research focuses on science and technology, policy research, innovation studies, new technologies, and climate change. He has published in journals such as *Technology and Investment* and *Tailoring Biotechnologies* and contributed chapters in edited volumes such as *Agribusiness and Innovation Systems in Africa*.

Kobena T. Hanson is Principal Evaluation Capacity Development Officer at the African Development Bank in Abidjan. Hanson's research focuses on capacity development, natural resource governance, regional development, and public policy. He has published in many peer-reviewed journals such as *Environment and Planning A, GeoJournal, Journal of African Development, African Geographical Review*, and *Africa Today*. He has edited and coedited several books, including *From Millennium Development Goals to Sustainable Development Goals: Rethinking African Development*.

Abbi M. Kedir is Associate Professor of International Business at the University of Sheffield, UK. He is an applied quantitative economist with vast experience in analyzing and modeling development issues with policy focus on economies of Africa. He has consulted for the World Bank and the UK Department for International Development (DFID). He has served as a government civil servant in Ethiopia (for 2 years in the 1990s) and as an economic affairs officer at the UNECA (2014–2015). Kedir has published extensively in his areas of research interest.

Euphrasie Kouame is a development economist and working as an inclusive finance specialist at the United Nations Capital Development Fund (UNCDF) based in Dakar. Her expertise includes project management; rural finance and multisectoral interventions to support SDGs; formulation of policy and strategic plan for delivery of financial services; market research to inform the design of innovative, responsible and more valuable formal financial services for the poor; scoping and segmentation for digital financial services; customer-centric product development; and process design. She has provided training and technical assistance to a variety of financial institutions, policy makers, and community-based organizations throughout the West and Central Africa.

Samuel M. Mugo is Associate Professor of Chemistry at Grant MacEwan University, Canada. Mugo's research is focused on developing smart polymer nanomaterials as molecular receptors for fabricating mobile chemical analytics platforms. His group has developed mobile sensors for use in precision agriculture, environmental monitoring, and noninvasive wearables for environmental, health, and wellness applications. The polymer nanomaterials developed in Mugo research group are also utilized for the encapsulation and controlled release of biopesticides and nutraceuticals. Mugo has published his research in several academic journals.

Benjamin Ofori-Amoah is Professor of Geography and Chair of the Department of Geography at Western Michigan University in Kalamazoo, Michigan, USA. Ofori-Amoah is an economic geographer and a regional planner with expertise in economic development, technological change, location analysis, urban and regional planning, and geographic information system (GIS) applications. His research focuses on the technological change and economic development of Africa, urban and regional planning in Africa, and local economic development with reference to America's small cities.

Joseph Oppong is Professor of Geography and Academic Associate Dean of the Robert Toulouse Graduate School at the University of North Texas (UNT) and Adjunct Professor of Public Health at the UNT Health Science Center in Fort Worth both in the USA. Oppong's research centers on the geography of disease and health services and seeks to answer the question: who is getting what disease, where, and why? He has served as Chair of the Health and Medical Geography Specialty Group and the Africa Specialty Group of the Association of American Geographers.

Korbla P. Puplampu is in the Department of Sociology at Grant MacEwan University, Canada. His research interests include the global restructuring of agriculture and higher education and transnational and global citizenship. Puplampu's articles have appeared in academic journals and has coedited and contributed to several books including *From Millennium Development Goals to Sustainable Development Goals: Rethinking African Development.*

Timothy M. Shaw has taught at Dalhousie University from 1971 to 2000 and directed the Pearson Institute, the International Development Studies department, and the Centre for Foreign Policy Studies. He has held visiting professorships in Denmark, Japan, Nigeria, South Africa, Uganda, UK, USA, Zambia, and Zimbabwe. Recently, Shaw directed the Institute of Commonwealth Studies at the University of London, the Institute of International Relations at the University of the West Indies in Trinidad and Tobago, and the Global Governance and Human Security program at University of Massachusetts Boston, where he continues to serve as a visiting professor. He is the editor of the International Political Economy (IPE) series for Palgrave Macmillan and Springer and the IPE of New Regionalisms series for Routledge.

Vanessa T. Tang is Lecturer in International Economics in the School of Accounting, Economics and Finance, University of KwaZulu-Natal (UKZN), South Africa. She has consulted for various organizations, including the African Capacity Building Foundation, the Institute of Natural Resources, and the KwaZulu-Natal Provincial Treasury. She is the principal UKZN investigator for the Network for Regional Integration Studies (NETRIS) and a coeditor of the *International Journal of African Integration*. Her research interests are economics of education, time series analysis, international trade, comparative regional integration, special economic zones, and the open economy pol-icy-making in the global South. She has published in journals such as *South African Journal of International Affairs* and *Investment Management and Financial Innovations* and contributed to several edited books.

ACRONYMS

AfCFTA	African Continental Free Trade Area
AI	Artificial Intelligence
AVU	African Virtual University
EAC	East African Community
EADD	East Africa Dairy Development project
EU	European Union
FDI	Foreign Direct Investment
FOCAC	Forum on China-Africa Cooperation
GVCs	Global Value Chains
ICTs	Information and Communication Technologies
IMF	International Monetary Fund
IoT	Internet of Things
IPE	International Political Economy
MDGs	Millennium Development Goals
MFIs	Microfinance Institutions
MMT	Mobile Money Transfer
MNO	Mobile Network Operators
MOOC	Massive Open Online Course
NERICA	New Rice for Africa initiative
OECD	Organisation for Economic Co-operation and Development
PIIGS	Portugal, Ireland, Italy, Greece, and Spain
PPPs	Public-Private Partnerships
PVs	Photovoltaic Systems
RECs	Regional Economic Communities
RFID	Radio-Frequency Identification
SDGs	Sustainable Development Goals
SME	Small and Medium-Sized Enterprise

SSC	South-South Cooperation
SoEs	State-Owned Enterprises
TOC	Transnational Organized Crime
UNCDF	United Nations Capital Development Fund
UNCTAD	United Nations Conference on Trade and Development
UNECA	United Nations Economic Commission for Africa
UNEP	United Nations Environment Programme
WBES	World Bank Enterprise Survey
WEF	World Economic Forum
WTO	World Trade Organization

LIST OF FIGURES

LIST OF TABLES

PART I

Disruptive Technologies and Africa: The Policy and Institutional Environment

Disruptive Technologies, Innovation and Transformation in Africa: The Present and Future

Korbla P. Puplampu, Kobena T. Hanson, and Peter Arthur

INTRODUCTION

One major contribution from modernization theorists to the development discourse is the role of technology. As a dynamic phenomenon, technology is crucial in social change and occupies a pivotal place in addressing

K. P. Puplampu (✉)
Department of Sociology, Grant MacEwan University,
Edmonton, AB, Canada
e-mail: puplampuk@macewan.ca

K. T. Hanson
African Development Bank, Abidjan, Côte D'Ivoire
e-mail: k.hanson@afdb.org

P. Arthur
Department of Political Science, Dalhousie University,
Halifax, NS, Canada
e-mail: peter.arthur@dal.ca

© The Author(s) 2020
P. Arthur et al. (eds.), *Disruptive Technologies, Innovation and Development in Africa*, International Political Economy Series,
https://doi.org/10.1007/978-3-030-40647-9_1

the African development agenda. It is therefore not surprising that both the United Nations-sanctioned Millennium Development Goals (MDGs) (2000–2015) and the ongoing Sustainable Development Goals (SDGs) (2015–2030) have stressed the role of technological changes in order to attain the respective goals. As the focus of current development programs, the integrative potential of technological advancements and the broader forces cannot be underestimated. Particularly, the dramatic breakthroughs in communication and information technologies (CITs) on the economy (the 'sharing economy') and the transformation of markets and financial transactions (M-Pesa) offer both opportunities and challenges in Africa's development process (Hanson et al. 2018; Wallis 2016; Saeed and Masakure 2015).

The practical implications of CITs for development have further coalesced around the concept of disruptive technologies. Schumpeter (1942:83), *Capitalism, Socialism and Democracy*, introduced the idea of the creative-destructive forces of capitalism as a system which "incessantly revolutionizes the economic structure from within, destroying the old [system and], creating a new one." Any new technological regime will engender innovative changes, which could give rise to positive and negative outcomes in the long run. Bringing the historical context of technology in social change to the contemporary era, the work of Clayton Christensen on disruptive technology is instructive. According to Christensen (1997), disruptive technology and innovation address how the relationship between a product or service and market can give rise to novel outcomes and in the process displace existing competitors (see also Christensen et al. 2015).

Today, disruptive technologies are changing the business environment and large well-established companies are finding it increasingly difficult to deal with powerful new technologies. Disruptive technologies have the potential to impact growth, employment and inequality by creating new markets and business practices, the need for new product infrastructure, and different labor skills. The pace at which technology is transforming our lives is exponential. Entire industries are disrupted as new business models emerge. Regulators, businesses and individuals alike must adapt, or risk becoming irrelevant. Therefore, while some may view the developing changes as a threat, others perceive the potential and harness the limitless possibilities.

Consequently, there is an ongoing African effort to review development planning visions and strategies, with a focus on technology, science and innovation revolving around digital communication (Choi et al. 2019; Pienaar and Beecher 2019; African Union et al. 2016; Yonazi et al. 2012). Several aspects of the attempts to make the required impact on African development are spurred by the twin and related issues of disruptive technologies and innovation (UNDP 2015). Two themes can be gleaned from the emerging studies on digitalization and the development possibilities in Africa. First, there is a consistent effort to focus on several areas of the African development plan, from agriculture to climate adaptation, education, conflict resolution, south-south cooperation and diversification of exports (Hanson et al. 2018). Second, digitalization has become a key driver of the development agenda (Choi et al. 2019).

This book examines how disruptive technologies and innovation underpin the attainment of a broader development agenda in Africa. Contributors show how distinctive forms of technological innovation can impact critical development processes. For example, disruptive technologies can deepen the ongoing democratic and governance waves in Africa, specifically in the area of contested elections. Similarly, innovations in agriculture, the environment and energy promote changes in value-chain agriculture, and the use of sensors to manage e-waste and sustainable energy conservation are also transforming established practices. Furthermore, the role of disruptive technologies and innovation in education, health, financial services and the nature of paid work cannot be ignored. Underpinning all the above changes is the determination to enhance and advance institutional effectiveness and governance and the move toward developing an infrastructure that can enhance the safety and well-being of citizens, improve service delivery and increase resource utilization and partnerships for development, all interconnected through the blossoming Internet of Things (IoT).

The contributors to this book, bearing in mind the complex relationship between disruptive technology and innovation, adopt various methodological approaches, ranging from case studies to comparative methods, to make contributions that shed new insights on our understanding of disruptive technologies and the African development program. The authors, drawing on their knowledge and understanding of Africa's use of technology, highlight what needs to be done to sustain the benefits of emerging diverse technologies. In addition to identifying and analyzing the role disruptive technologies or innovations currently at play in various areas in terms of threats, opportunities and possibilities, the chapters demonstrate cases of success and failure in terms of disruptive technologies and innovation, as well as present viable pathways and good-fit practices, drawing from proven cases or illustrations in both the global North and South, for sustainable outcomes in the African context.

Individually and collectively, the authors discuss and highlight the mechanisms and initiatives that contribute to the realization of the development goals of African countries, especially in a period where disruptive technologies are rapidly changing how things are done. As a result, this book represents one of the most recent systematic efforts to bring together dialogue on disruptive technologies in Africa and will be of particular use and benefit to an eclectic audience. Apart from being a useful base for both graduate and undergraduate students in understating how disruptive technology is shaping various aspects of lives in Africa, researchers, policy makers, private sector actors, development agencies and development practitioners, in Africa and beyond, will equally find the book of significance in their understanding of the role of disruptive technology on the development process.

Overview of the Chapters

Besides the introductory and concluding chapters, the book, anchored by disruptive technology and its implications for innovation, is organized around three main themes: rethinking politics, innovation and the environment; transformations in the socioeconomic sphere; and the changing nature of wealth creation. The African state, like many others, continues to feature in the development debate, even if its influence has changed significantly. One factor contesting state power is the emergency of a vibrant civil society and network under the broader notion of governance. With several African countries pursuing democratic elections, contestations over election results have affected state power. Technological changes make it possible to rethink the state's role when it comes to national election. Arthur, in Chap. 2, "Disruptive Technologies, Democracy, Governance, Technology and National Elections in Africa: Back to the Future?", explores and assesses the role of mobile technologies and other forms of social media platforms to check government activities and help improve the governance, electoral and democratic processes. Arthur's motivation is to examine the relationship between digital or mobile technology access and citizen mobilization and the implications for governance and democratic process, political communication, political accountability and electoral integrity among African countries. Drawing on examples from a number of African countries, the chapter argues that despite access to digital and disruptive mobile technologies improving governance, democratic and electoral processes, there are potential harmful effects and concerns with their use. The chapter therefore calls for better education of citizens in the use of digital technologies, as well as the establishment of strategies and policies, which will guide the use of digital and mobile technologies and social media in the political sphere.

A central aspect of disruptive technology is the possibility of innovation. Chapters 3 and 4 both address the role of innovation in agriculture and the environment, respectively. Puplampu and Essegbey, in Chap. 3, point out that agricultural research plays a major role in any system of agricultural development. It not only offers new knowledge to end users in production and marketing but also consumers. Innovation is concerned with new changes in agricultural development, either from agricultural research or in technology. The relationship between agricultural research and innovation has significant implications for value-chain development. With disruptive technology as the framework, this chapter examines the agricultural research and innovation landscape in Africa. Drawing on relevant illustrative material from other regions in the global South and discussing their relevance for the African context, the chapter pays attention to how disruptive technologies can deepen the role of value-chain development for production, marketing and consumption systems.

Scientific innovations, specifically smart sensors, are creatively addressing key global societal issues, from environmental pollution and mitigation, intelligent water and waste management, precision agriculture, public health and nutrition, and food safety to energy conservation and climate change. Smart sensors and their disruptive potential are integral to the African development agenda. Mugo and Puplampu, in Chap. 4, therefore explore the trends and prospects of integrated smart sensors in resource utilization and management of e-waste in the context of the disruptive technologies as well as bridge the economic gap between the global North and global South. The chapter also focuses on the innovation tangents driven by regional internationalization of technology and the capacity of universities to spearhead homegrown technological solutions.

In addition to innovations in the environment through sensors, there are global implications of the environment, the need for sustainable energy and the possibility of a green economy. Ofori-Amoah, in Chap. 5, takes on the role of disruptive technologies in sustainable energy generation in

Africa. Ofori-Amoah points out that technology is a two-edged sword—on the one hand, it can be a great transformer of society and allow society to achieve immense degree of economic advancement; on the other hand, it can be disastrous and threaten the very existence of society. This chapter examines the dichotomous nature of technology with respect to energy generation and its impact on African economies. By comparing the impact of energy generated from current traditional sources with that from non-traditional sources in terms of sustainability and economic development, the chapter offers significant insights into the potential of the green economy, its sustainability and contribution to an understanding of the role of technology in the energy-development nexus in Africa.

The second theme in the book is about transformations in the socioeconomic sphere. Broadly defined, the socioeconomic sphere involves the state of well-being, specifically the health care, the role of knowledge-producing institutions and finally financial mobilization and entrepreneurship. Oppong, in Chap. 6, notes that disruptive technologies such as e-health, Immunotherapy and Next-Gen Genomics have been touted as an important answer to Africa's health-care crisis, but their potential contribution has not been critically examined. Facing excessively high and worsening physician-to-population ratios, innovations that allow medical procedures to be completed in more convenient and less expensive settings by technicians and nurses instead of physicians and specialists could expand the reach of health-care services to the millions currently without access. Yet considerable challenges abound. Examining the promise and challenge of disruptive technologies in health care in Africa, Oppong argues that notwithstanding the potential, without a supportive environment and infrastructure including secure but accessible personal health data systems, the potential benefit is not achievable or sustainable. He concludes by outlining policy options for expanding geographic access to health through disruptive technologies across Africa.

In Chap. 7, Puplampu and Mugo focus on higher education in Africa, identifying and analyzing the extent to which the disruptive possibilities, specifically how the transformational possibilities of open innovation, online learning and curriculum reforms, can elevate human capital development and global citizenship. They argue that higher educational institutions are indispensable in developing the human capital needed for national development. African universities, like their counterparts worldwide, have been thrust into the unprecedented changes made possible by globalization and continue to make claims about their role in educating for global citizenship. For Puplampu and Mugo, a key component in university-society relations is knowledge production and its utilization in the development progress. The focus on knowledge production and utilization assumes some significance in view of the implications of higher education for the nature and organization of teaching, research and community engagement, human capital development and global citizenship.

The critical role of finance and its mobilization in entrepreneurship cannot be overemphasized. Technology has intensified the mobility of finance as a form of capital. Kouame and Kedir address disruptive financial technology (FinTech) and entrepreneurship in Burkina Faso in Chap. 8. They set to understand the demand side of financial inclusion in Burkina Faso, by investigating the role of disruptive FinTech (financial technology) in the process, and by focusing on mobile money transactions and the use of information and communication technology (ICT)-enabled payment and deposit system in Burkina Faso. Looking at the role of digital money on entrepreneurship matters greatly because self-employment is a sustainable route out of poverty. The study shows that use of mobile money technology is not necessarily for investment purposes since most of the current use of mobile money is for transaction payments (e.g. utility bills) and/or payment of fees (e.g. tuition fees).

The role of technology and the mobility of finance are also the focus of Abdulhamid's work in Chap. 9, which addresses mobile money and financial mobilization in Africa, asking whether the uptake of M-Pesa should be analyzed as a Kenyan solution to global financial exclusion. Abdulhamid contends that the current global financial markets are failing to include and meet the needs of a majority of sub-Saharan African societies, particularly those who reside in rural areas, resulting in the significant exclusion of adults from formal financial services. The chapter examines Kenya's experimentation with M-Pesa, a mobile money transfer (MMT) service, and its role in fostering financial inclusion and promoting socioeconomic development, for example, bridging the distances between urban and rural areas and the broader citizens. The chapter outlines MMT technology as an innovative and disruptive form of branchless banking and examines the specific factors that were responsible for its success in Kenya. Second, it analyzes the impact of M-Pesa on Kenyan farmers, with a focus on MMT service and food security. Abdulhamid concludes her chapter by evaluating whether the M-Pesa model can be replicated across the African continent as more countries attempt to enhance their citizens' access to financial services.

The third theme of the book is on the changing dynamics of wealth creation. Peter Arthur, in Chap. 10, on small- and medium-sized enterprises (SMEs), industrialization and disruptive technologies in Africa, indicates many African policymakers realize that ICTs can assist with their socioeconomic development efforts, especially in the case of SMEs. Policy makers see SMEs as playing a key role in job creation, innovative instruments for developing and promoting competitive small firms, and enhancing entrepreneurship. Drawing from several African countries, this chapter examines how SMEs can use ICTs as a tool to improve their business operations, initiate socioeconomic development and promote the industrialization process. Additionally, it interrogates the impact and extent to which government policies on technology enable or constrain the activities of SMEs. The chapter concludes by sketching appropriate technology policy measures, initiatives and a practical framework to ensure that SMEs contribute to the overall development and industrialization efforts in African countries.

In Chap. 11, Baricako and Kedir contribute to how privatization and investment policies can serve as a source of foreign direct investment (FDI) in Africa. The authors note that current policy focus on domestic resource mobilization (DRM) needs to be complemented with external resource transfer such as FDI because the latter is a major route for technological spillover and a key source of development finance. Many African countries have been opening their economies to various degrees since the late 1980s. There is an increasing trend in privatizing state enterprises in African countries and that is encouraging investment from emerging economies such as China, India and Turkey as well as from traditional development partners such as the Organization for Economic Cooperation and Development (OECD). The chapter also addresses how regional developments open economies further. For instance, major continental initiatives such as the Continental Free Trade Area (CFTA) and local policy reforms such as privatization are expected to strengthen trade and investment links of African nations among themselves and with the rest of the world. Countries are keen to mobilize development finance for transforming their economies and embark on industrialization. Using a longitudinal/panel data, this chapter discusses the current state and evolution of development finance such as inward foreign direct investment (IFDI) within the context of privatization and investment policies in Africa. It finally emphasizes the role of IFDI for employment and the transfer of technical and management know-how.

Hanson and Tang, in Chap. 12, focus on disruptive technologies and the services sector. They argue that the growth in digital technologies is influencing and fast transforming societies all over, and Africa is no exception. Digitization, IoT (Internet of Things), blockchain technology and related growth in mobile technologies are rapidly redefining the provision of services and wealth generation in Africa. Globally, the share of digital trade is sizeable, with an estimated 12% of the global goods trade happening via international electronic commerce, with much of it driven by platforms, such as Alibaba, Amazon, eBay and Flipkart. Digitization is also reinforcing a trend of 'servicification' (increased trade in services), whereby there is an increase in the use, produce and sale of services. Across Africa, the growth in Nollywood movies, music and international sourcing arrangements in global value chains (GVCs) are good examples. Relatedly, participation in international production, trade and investments is increasingly organized within GVCs, which are heterogeneous, and uneven across and within countries. In the emerging landscape, triggered by digital disruption, the relationship between increased openness to trade in goods and trade in services has become more complex, with limitless threats, possibilities and opportunities to expand and deepen trade, investment and innovation. Thus, interrogating the essence of the growing disruption to Africa's development trajectories, regionalization and wealth accumulation, this chapter illustrates how the continent can leverage emerging disruptive technologies to enhance its bulging regionalisms, wealth dynamics and transformation of its socioeconomic environment.

Hanson, in Chap. 13, addresses automation of knowledge work. Hanson indicates that in today's rapidly changing knowledge economy, motivated by disruptive technologies and innovation, the means of automation have grown, so too have the number of applications and markets that demand these technologies. Indeed, the growth in AI (artificial intelligence), coupled with machine learning, while transforming the workplace, also frees up the need for human labor. The resulting revised landscape has the potential to impact labor force patterns, employment and inequality by creating new markets and business practices, new product infrastructure and different labor skills. Against the backdrop of the debate about disruptive technologies as the key to economic rather than environmental disruption and the emergence of 'techpreneurs,' this chapter interrogates how African countries should plan to negotiate the threats, possibilities and opportunities of the rapid automation of knowledge. The analysis also delves into what the continent can learn from other regions to maximize the positive dividends of disruptive technologies. The concluding chapter, "Digital Transformation: A Connected and 'Disrupted' Africa," by Hanson, Shaw, Puplampu and Arthur weaves together the broad themes in the chapters by discussing lessons learned and highlighting the broader implications and significance of disruptive technologies and their place in the development process among African countries. It notes that to enhance the benefits of disruptive technologies, African countries must employ creative ways to sustain the gains that come with it and find ways of addressing some of the challenges that accompany the use of disruptive technologies.

CONCLUDING REMARKS

One of the main purposes of this volume, which contains a wide spectrum of competing and complementary paradigms, was to reveal the varying and rich views on disruptive technologies and add to the emerging literature on whether disruptive technologies are helping or undermining development processes on the African continent. Particularly, this publication brings together a mixture of perspectives and issues to enhance our understanding of the role of disruptive technologies and innovation in Africa and the related implications for the region's development prospects. Contributing authors, who make use of detailed case studies and comparative methods, outline and interrogate landscape of the policy and environment framework. The varied, yet interlinked, foci are compelling in its holistic presentation of Africa's development aspirations. It is therefore our view and hope that this publication, which should appeal to academics, researchers, policy makers and development practitioners, will offer a fresh wave of discussions and inquiry regarding the place of disruptive technology on various aspects of life and endeavors on the African continent.

REFERENCES

African Union, Economic Commission for Africa; African Development Bank and United Nations Development Programme (AU/ECA/AfDB and UNDP). (2016). *Mdgs to Agenda 2063/SDGs Transition Report 2016: Towards an Integrated and Coherent Approach to Sustainable Development in Africa*. Addis Ababa: AU/ECA/AfDB and UNDP.

Choi, J., Dutz, M., & Usman, Z. (2019). *The Future of Work in Africa Harnessing the Potential of Digital Technologies for All.* Washington, DC: World Bank.

Christensen, C. M. (1997). *The Innovator's Dilemma – When New Technologies Cause Great Firms to Fail.* Cambridge: Harvard University Press.

Christensen, C. M., Raynor, M., & Mcdonald, R. (2015). What Is Disruptive Innovation? *Harvard Business Review, 93*(12 December), 44–53.

Hanson, K. T., Puplampu, K. P., & Shaw, T. M. (Eds.). (2018). *From Millennium Development Goals to Sustainable Development Goals: Rethinking African Development.* Abingdon/New York: Routledge.

Pienaar, A., & Beecher, Z. (2019). *Unlocking the Potential of MobileTech in Africa: Tracking the Trends and Guiding Effective Strategy on Maximizing the Benefit of Mobile Tech.* Winter Series, Issue 119, Hoover Institution https://www.hoover.org/research/unlocking-potential-mobiletech-africa-tracking-trends-and-guiding-effective-strategy

Saeed, A. M., & Masakure, O. (2015). The paradox of broadband access in sub-Saharan Africa. In E. Shizha & D. Diallo (Eds.), *Africa in the Age of Globalisation: Perceptions, Misperceptions and Realities* (pp. 83–99). Burlington: Ashgate.

Schumpeter, J. A. (1994) [1942]. *Capitalism, Socialism and Democracy.* London: Routledge

United Nations Development Program (UNDP). (2015). *Sustainable Development Goals.* New York: UNDP.

Wallis, W. (2016). *Smart Africa: Smartphones Pave Way for Huge Opportunities.* Available at: www.ft.com/intl/cms/s/0/aba818a6-c392-11e5-808f-8231cd71622e.html#axzz3zRD581QC. Accessed 26 Jan 2019.

Yonazi, E., Kelly, T., Halewood, N., & Blackman, C. (Eds.). (2012). *The Transformational Use of Information and Communication Technologies in Africa, AfDB Temporary Relocation Agency.* Tunis: The World Bank and the African Development Bank, with the support of the African Union.

PART II

Rethinking Politics, Innovation and the Environment

Disruptive Technologies, Democracy, Governance and National Elections in Africa: Back to the Future?

Peter Arthur

INTRODUCTION

The last two decades have seen a wide range of new information and communication technologies (Icts) such as mobile telephony sweeping across the world and among African countries on an unprecedented scale. Kanyam, Kostandini and Ferreira (2017) have pointed out, sub-Saharan Africa (SSA) has been the world's fastest growing mobile region in terms of subscribers and mobile connections (i.e., subscriber identity module (SIM) cards) during the 2008–15 period. Gallowa, Mollel, Mgoma, Pima and Deogratias (2018) indicate that in Tanzania, for example, mobile phone use has been growing rapidly in the past decade, with ownership in the general population in 2015 running at 64% (31,900,000 users), compared to the 1% of the population with fixed telephone lines (150,000 users). Similarly, in South Africa, access to mobile phones is now well over

P. Arthur (✉)
Department of Political Science, Dalhousie University,
Halifax, NS, Canada
e-mail: peter.arthur@dal.ca

© The Author(s) 2020
P. Arthur et al. (eds.), *Disruptive Technologies, Innovation and Development in Africa*, International Political Economy Series,
https://doi.org/10.1007/978-3-030-40647-9_2

80% and is growing (Chuma 2014). Finally, Koi-Akrofi, Koi-Akrofi and Welbeck (2013) note that mobile subscription of 30,360,771 for 2014 represents a penetration rate of almost 113.37% of Ghana's population.

Despite their emergence and increasing usage, little is known about how digital and mobile technologies, social media, the Internet environment and other instruments of communication contribute decisively to the governance and consolidation of the democratic process, beyond issues of accountability and transparency. As Hermanns (2008: 75) argues, notwithstanding the growing influence of new ICTs, in particular mobile phone technology, "there are far fewer publications in the political science literature on the impact of mobile phone technology on politics and political behavior." Moreover, the available literature deals with the role of social media in Western democracies, with less emphasis on emerging democratic environments and developing countries (Wolfsfeld et al. 2013). Therefore, the question that arises then is: How can and does the increased use of digital and mobile technology and the concomitant social media platforms impact governance, democratic and electoral processes in developing countries?

Against the backdrop of their consequences still very much a point of debate, and the related lacuna concerning the lack of research on the developing world (Wolfsfeld et al. 2013), this chapter draws on the theory of disruptive technology and innovation pioneered by Christensen (1997, 2001) to analyze the extent to which new disruptive and digital technologies are being employed by a wide range of actors to ensure the promotion of effective elections, good governance and democracy among African countries. Specifically, this chapter has two main goals: assess and understand the role of digital and mobile phone technology and other forms of social media platforms in a watchdog capacity. It also examines the relationship between mobile technology access and citizen mobilization and the implications for governance and democratic process, political communication, political accountability and electoral integrity. This chapter thus offers a unique opportunity to generate better understanding of the mechanisms and processes by which the increased use of new media, which is communication using digital technologies such as the Internet and mobile telephony, can influence the governance and the democratic electoral process.

The chapter is structured as follows. The first section discusses the concept of disruptive technology and the place of social media in the governance and democratic processes of countries. The second section delves into the role of new media in Africa's democratic and governance landscape. The processes and means through which social media and disruptive technology have become avenues of citizen participation, as well as promoting good governance and holding government accountable in the political realm, are outlined and analyzed in the third section. The fourth section highlights the challenges and problems of employing digital and mobile technologies and social media in Africa's political landscape. The final section delineates the policy implications and challenges of disruptive technology and social media in Africa.

Conceptualizing Disruptive Technology: An Overview

Clayton M. Christensen (1997), in his best-selling book, *The Innovator's Dilemma: When New Technologies Cause Great Firms to Fail*, argued that new technology can be placed into two categories: sustaining and disruptive. While sustaining technology relies on incremental improvements to an already established technology, disruptive technology lacks refinement, often has performance problems because it is new, appeals to a limited audience and may not yet have a proven practical application. Disruptive technologies typically involve a high rate of technological change, broad potential scope of impact, large economic value that could be affected and substantial potential for disruptive economic impact. Disruptive technology also involves the process, whereby the established ways of doing things, especially in the realm of business, are challenged because of innovations driven by ICTs (Christensen 1997, 2001).

As Danneels (2004) points out, Christensen (1997) opined that even though disruptive technologies initially underperform established ones in serving the mainstream market, they eventually displace the established technologies. Initially, disruptive technologies do not satisfy the minimum requirements along the performance metric most valued by customers in the mainstream segment and thus are considered inappropriate by incumbents in the mainstream market for satisfying the needs of their customers. The products based on the disruptive technology initially only satisfy a niche market segment, which values dimensions of performance on which the disruptive technology does excel. Over time the disruptive technology improves to the point where it also can satisfy the requirements of the mainstream market (Danneels 2004).

Among the disruptive technological changes that we are witnessing in the contemporary era include the interrelated forms of digital ICT—the computer, the Internet, the mobile phone and countless innovative applications for them, including 'new social media' such as 'Facebook and Twitter' (Diamond 2010: 76). Social media tools such as Twitter and Facebook, as politically disruptive communication technologies, can be properly understood and appreciated only in comparison to the most politically significant technological innovations of the twentieth century, such as radio and television (Hong and Nadler 2012). Unlike traditional mass communication models where the source produces a message that is encoded in media, received by the receiver, and produces feedback, users of disruptive technologies communicate with each other both directly and through platforms, and the contents of those platforms are produced by a few other users (Humphreys 2016: 10). Particularly, information does not flow in one direction from sender to receiver. Rather, everyone is potentially a source, and everyone is potentially a receiver. Thus, the audience are not passive, are potentially much narrower, and have more ownership or control over messages and channels because of lower cost of producing and sharing information (Humphreys 2016). In sum, new technologies and social media appear able to provide groups with powerful, speedy and relatively low-cost tools for recruitment, fundraising, the distribution of information and images, collective discussions, and mobilization for action (Wolfsfeld et al. 2013).

New Media, Governance and Democracy in Africa

The period from the 1950s, when many African countries attained independence, until the 1990s was characterized by civilian governments interspersed with many military rulers. During this period, African governments perceived the media as part of the machinery of state to be deployed in facilitating the process of development and achieve national cohesion among otherwise disparate ethnic groups (Ocitti 1999). According to Ocitti (1999), the media was generally seen as serving and thus advancing and providing support to the policies of the ruling system, such that criticism of government policies was not taken lightly. Moreover, a combination of state-sponsored repressive policies against journalists, including cases in which journalists were killed, as well as political and economic instabilities, and the resultant self-imposed censorship by journalists themselves, and Africa's gradual economic downturn from the 1970s to the 1990s, grossly affected the freedom and quality of the media (Ocitti 1999).

However, the emergence of increasing democratic governance on the continent from the early 1990s led to the proliferation and expansion of the African media, predominantly the print media (Ocitti 1999). Also, the subsequent liberalization and deregulation of the media allowed private media, including private radio and FM stations, to enjoy greater freedom and compete with the state-owned media. Significantly, the transition to democratic rule in many African countries resulted in the active participation of citizens in the political process and a relatively independent traditional media (TV, radio and print) playing a critical watchdog role. While the transition to democratic rule after years of authoritarian and unconstitutional rule saw the traditional media play a greater role in politics, initially, excessive control of state-owned media meant that they were largely used as mouthpieces for propagating the agenda of incumbent governments. In other words, although involvement and participation were occurring, opposition political parties had to contend with the lack of resources to compete on an equal footing with incumbent governments, especially when it came to the issue of media access to communicate their political messages. The greater monopoly of media ownership and control meant that reportage was skewed in favor of incumbent governments, while perspectives of the opposition parties were often marginalized.

Nevertheless, over the last decade, the advantages that incumbent governments enjoyed because of their domination and control of state media have been drastically reduced because of a more open political system and the dramatic rise of new media, which have been aided by the increase in mobile telephony usage and Internet penetration. The growth in mobile and cellular phone usage and the accompanying new forms of media among several African countries have not only fundamentally altered the ways that governance is taking place, but also how political parties and politicians attempt to communicate their messages. The continuous growth in the use of mobile broadband, mobile Internet, mobile media and wireless technology devices (Goggin 2011) means that diverse types of new media (feeds or microblogs like Twitter, blogs, chatroom and social networking sites) (Humphreys 2016) can be employed by the government as well as political parties. This is because they can reach their audience in greater numbers and with greater speed (Gyampo 2017).

Given the increasing availability of new disruptive technology and new media, the ensuing sections examine how they are impacting the political landscape in African countries.

DEMOCRACY, GOVERNANCE AND NATIONAL ELECTIONS

Political Participation and Activism

One of the main themes that has emerged in the literature is how digital technologies and new media provide a very good platform to network and reach out to their target audience, connect with them directly and generate trust by listening to what they have to say (Taprial and Kanwar 2012). Humphreys (2016) has pointed out that social media tools like Facebook enhance political activism because of lower costs for organizing, publicizing and participating in protests and therefore make mobilization more efficient in terms of time and money. Social media helps coordinate efforts within and across different activist groups. It can also draw together publics and focus attention for an extended period. It is therefore unsurprising that a significant and powerful contribution of new media (web-based media and cellular phones) is that they are widely used by the citizens to facilitate the transmission of politically and economically relevant information for purposes of political activism. This use of new media is not adventitious because it is a fundamental necessity in this digital media environment, where information flow becomes multidimensional (Bokor 2014).

For Onyechi and Obono (2017), the barrier of distance is no longer tenable with social media platforms, which enable one to establish links with people all over the globe just at the click of a button. To Karolak (2018), social media were of primary importance in the protest movements on the ground and in the creation of a transnational wave of uprisings in the Middle East and North Africa (MENA) region, commonly referred to as the Arab Spring. Information sharing, citizen journalism, mobilization and protest coordination, facilitated by social media, were the key ingredients in the emergence and success of the Arab Spring uprisings. In addition, in Tunisia, activists used social media to establish initiatives such as, among others, drafting the constitution collaboratively, denouncing corruption through online and offline activism and monitoring the work of the elected politicians (Karolak 2018). In Kenya, Kirigha et al. (2018) also found that a majority of educated urban youth prefer to use Facebook to access political information. In addition, the users viewed social media as a free space where they could express their political views without censorship or regulation. As a result, as the use of social media increases, so does participation in politics, indicating a positive relationship between how youth use social media and their participation in politics.

Similarly, Onyechi's (2018) research, which focused on the relationship between students of Ibadan University in Nigeria and their participation in the 2015 elections, showed that students spent an average of seven hours browsing social media platforms to get information relating to the 2015 political campaign. A key finding from this work was that there was a significant relationship between social media exposure patterns and students' participation during the 2015 political campaigns. Examining the South African student-led campaign known as Rhodes Must Fall, commonly referred to simply as #RMF, Bosch (2017) argued that the youth are increasingly using social networking sites to develop a new biography of citizenship which is characterized by more individualized forms of activism. She noted that Twitter and other social media platforms afford youth an opportunity to participate in political discussions, as well as discussions of broader sociopolitical issues of relevance in contemporary South African society, reflecting a form of subactivism. Finally, Tettey (2017: 687) avers that because of disruptive technologies, it is getting increasingly easier to organize political events in Ghana at short notice because of the ability to send text messages to multiple individuals from one source, to generate a chain message that gets redistributed by connectors within particular network nodes, or to trigger voice messaging across a network of political party members.

Political Communication and Accountability

Hellstrom (2008) has argued that ICTs are important instruments for improving governance because they enhance accountability, openness, transparency and free flow of information among various government departments and institutions. The narrative sustains that the mobile phone also facilitates information diffusion between the government and citizens on the one hand and the direct participation of citizens in the making of decisions that affect their livelihoods on the other hand. Thus, consistent with the findings from existing research, disruptive technologies such as social media are used by government officials to communicate with citizens and the latter have expressed their opinions via these channels (Tettey

2017). For example, Dzisah (2018: 34) notes that in the run-up to the 2016 elections in Ghana, a video post on the official Facebook page of the presidential candidate for the National Democratic Congress (NDC), which was about the presidential candidate spending time with one of his Facebook friends, within the first four days of the post was viewed 155,000 times and shared 1127 times. This suggests that Ghanaian politicians as well as voters have embraced the idea of social media as a complementary and effective communication tool as well as a source of political information.

The increasing use of social media was also observed through the posts and tweets by Nana Akufo-Addo, the then presidential candidate for the National Patriotic Party (NPP). In fact, Opara (2017) points out that the Nana Akufo-Addo campaign had a team that aggressively used social media. With a 'Change' campaign slogan, the social media team churned out loads of well-thought-out content, which appealed to the Ghanaian voter demographic. Similarly, in Nigeria, Alhassan (2018) has pointed out that Twitter and Facebook were the major social media platforms used during the 2015 elections to activate online political discussions and engagement, improve citizens' political knowledge, as well as build and maintain social capital. The Muhammadu Buhari-led All Progressives Congress (APC), which was formed in 2013 in anticipation of the 2015 elections, and subsequently won the presidency over the incumbent, Goodluck Jonathan, came up with possible solutions to the security challenges confronting Nigeria by disseminating them through social media platforms such as Facebook and Twitter.

Political parties in many African countries have also employed social media to communicate respective party policies and positions on key socioeconomic and governance issues, discuss and solicit the voice of people on key and current issues, mobilize support and membership for the parties, and raise funds more effectively at great speed and to a larger audience at lower cost. Social media alters the rigid internal party systems by allowing a bottom-up decision-making process. Communicating party positions and policy prescriptions on social media is expected to educate people and elicit positive feedback (Gyampo 2017). Social networking sites (Facebook), cross-platform messaging and Voice over Internet Protocol (VoIP), (WhatsApp) and microblogging services (Twitter) are among the most popular social media platforms and have the propensity to positively induce political participation (Dzisah 2018). It is unsurprising that Gyampo (2017) notes that political parties have designated people whose mandate is to post party policies, manifestoes and positions on key socioeconomic and governance issues on these social media platforms. Such individuals are charged with the responsibility of constantly monitoring how people 'like' or express support for the posts on Facebook. Additionally, political parties in Ghana, for example, also use social media to discuss and solicit voice or opinion on key issues affecting the nation. Indeed, social media allows millions of political party supporters and the undecided voters to voice their views on all critical national issues under discussion.

Several studies have noted that the widespread use of mobile phones and social media in Ghana has also enabled users to express their support and outrage over issues taking place in the country and facilitated better access to, and more timely response from, state officials, who are now regularly called upon to address issues within very limited timelines (Gyampo 2017; Tettey 2017; Dzisah 2018). As Tettey (2017: 687) has pointed out, social media has not only resulted in an opportunity for the public to engage with these officials but also offered a chance for the views of government to be articulated or contested. There is a growing expectation on the part of public officials that they will be subject to open scrutiny and accountability in the full glare of the public. Thus, while politicians in Ghana use their Twitter feed to articulate their policies, "with smartphones, some citizens, particularly the urban elite and government officials, are able to access and/or post comments on Twitter, Facebook, and other social media" (Tettey 2017: 690), as part of the political participation process.

In fact, disruptive technologies such as mobile phone and social media platforms also constitute accountability technology, in that they provide efficient and powerful tools for transparency and monitoring. Digital cameras combined with sites such as YouTube create new possibilities for exposing and challenging abuses of power (Diamond 2010: 76). Thus, the sacrosanct of closed-door or personal conversations and the related distinction between the private and the public are undermined by conscious or inadvertent creation of digital registers. The resultant disclosures are, thus, not based on '(s)he said, (s)he said' allegations, but are supportable with incriminating evidence in the words and voice of the accused (Tettey 2017: 688). Ordinary citizens are also equipped with a technology that allows them to record events and incidents in ways that were, until recently, the preserve of professionals, while the technology also facilitates the documentation of corrupt behaviors. The sharing capabilities of convergent media platforms have facilitated citizens' ability to tell their version of events to audiences outside of their immediate circles, thereby inflecting political discourse and shaping perceptions and attitudes. Mobile phone images have been used to hold public servants and governmental officials for their actions or inactions (Tettey 2017: 688). Through social media, citizen journalism (news gathering and production by nonprofessionals) can report when the traditional media fail, when the media are strongly influenced or controlled by the state or those in power or when the media provide insufficient coverage of a story (Bertot et al. 2010).

Elections and Checks and Balances

Given that they enhance citizens' participation in governance, ensure government accountability and encourage political participation, free, fair and credible elections are one of the basic and crucial elements of democratic government and governance (Alhassan 2018). Unsurprisingly, a studied dimension of disruptive technologies is the key role they play as part of the electoral processes, good governance revolutions and the democratic changes sweeping the developing world, especially in the Middle East and Africa. Social media, as noted earlier, has been used by politicians during the electoral process to demonstrate beneficial personality traits, improve name recognition and promote their activities and issue positions (Stier et al. 2018).

While being employed by politicians during elections to disseminate their messages to the public, social media may also boost public trust in the electoral system since they serve as an effective tool for electoral scrutiny in digital election monitoring (Karolak 2018). Diamond (2010: 77) notes that across much of the world, and especially in Africa, the quest for accountability makes use of the simplest form of liberation technology: text messaging via mobile phone. Mobile phone networks have proven particularly useful in Africa since they can cover vast areas without requiring much in the way of physical facilities beyond some cell towers. Frontline SMS, which enables large-scale, two-way text messaging purely via mobile phones and other software, has been used over mobile phone networks to monitor national elections in Nigeria and Ghana (Diamond 2010: 77). In Nigeria, Olabamiji (2014) demonstrates how new media was used to collate feelings of the electorate, their prediction of election outcomes and their assessment of candidates' performances during political debates or rallies. Moreover, with increasing distrust of the existing systems of running elections, which contributes to a skepticism of the integrity of election outcomes, a significant manifestation of mobile phones' contribution to democratic process in Ghana is their use by ordinary citizens, elections observers, political party representatives and journalists to ensure the integrity of ballots (Tettey 2017).

Finally, one of the key benefits of disruptive technologies such as digital and biometric technology in elections in Africa is that it enhances the polling environment and makes the electoral commission more robust and efficient by generating greater clarity and transparency regarding election outcomes (Iwuoha 2018). Thus, in addition to having the ability to capture and manage voter information, another line of research indicates that disruptive technologies reduce the stress of registration and eliminates issues like multiple and ghost registrants who tend to vote and cast doubts over the integrity of results. For Piccolino (2015), aside from restoring the public's confidence in the electoral process, a recurrent argument for introducing disruptive technology is that it would not only reduce fraud and make elections 'cleaner,' but it would also make contested election results and electoral violence less likely. In fact, tech-based systems deployed by media houses and political parties during Ghana's 2016 elections enabled them to easily collect, collate and project the results of elections, thereby limiting the potential for manipulation of electoral results and other forms of electoral fraud. The oversight provided by this multiplicity of election monitors, and their ability to instantly share results using their mobile phones, as Tettey (2017: 690) argues, has helped to reduce instances and allegations of vote tampering, eliminated discrepancies between official and unofficial tallies, and promoted acceptance of election results, if not outcomes, thereby overcoming electoral challenges and disputes. It is because of its ability to be a check on the electoral process that in Uganda's 2016 elections, the authoritarian and 'electoral dictatorship' government of President Museveni, which has ruled for the last 30 years, shut down social media platforms on the day of the election (Abrahamsen and Bareebe 2016).

Disruptive New Media, Politics and Governance: The Challenges and Criticisms

The above discussions have shown that disruptive technology and prominent social media websites, including blogs, Facebook, Twitter, Snapchat, Instagram, WhatsApp and LinkedIn (Kaplan and Haenlein 2010; Kietzmann et al. 2011), are offering numerous possibilities for modern, meaningful and equal participation and for novel forms of transparency and accountability (Gyampo 2017). While many people are now resorting to the use of disruptive technologies like Twitter and Facebook in political activism and mobilization, they are not devoid of serious concerns and limitations. Apart from Internet connectivity facilitating digital censorship and the identification and arrest in authoritarian regimes of individuals critical of political power holders (Rød 2015), a critical limitation of social networking sites is the lack of quality and reliability. The use of anecdotal reports as evidence of what is happening in the broader society is a danger and concern when using social networking as the basis for political mobilization and activism. In fact, social media can serve as outlets through which 'fake news,' which is defined and conceptualized by Allcott and Gentzkow (2017) as intentionally and verifiably false news articles as well as distorted signals uncorrelated with the truth, can be delivered. Moreover, social media tends to create small, deeply polarized groups of individuals who will tend to believe everything they hear, no matter how divorced from reality, as well as help foster an environment that enables those who are bent on creating and sustaining a divided and polarized society to continue. Particularly, social media is gradually displacing print and broadcast media in influencing public opinion, and elected officials have increasingly turned to it to listen to and interact with their constituents. Because of that, trolls and bots, disguised as citizens, have become a weapon to shape online conversation. Manipulating information and fomenting polarization, these bots and trolls have succeeded in creating distrust and confusion in the political and democratic landscape of many countries (Omidyar 2018).

Thus, although much of the literature has been devoted to the positives of social media, on the other side of the equation lies the potentially harmful effects that the abuse of these platforms might cause to governance and the democratic processes. For example, Lutz and du Toit (2014) have pointed out that while social media sites such as Facebook, Twitter and YouTube have become global channels of communication and offer politicians a unique and powerful means to interact with the electorate, they also can become disruptive outcomes for democratic governance. Instead of publications on social media generating constructive feedbacks from supporters and nonsupporters, they sometimes result in insults, unhealthy arguments, less constructive criticisms and dangerous allegations by 'faceless people' (people who choose to hide their names and identities) (Gyampo 2017). Furthermore, the views solicited on social media tend to be overly partisan and based on emotional sentiments, which are often not backed by evidence-based research, logic and critical thinking (Gyampo 2017). By sowing seeds of chaos, confusion and prejudice, social media helps to undermine public accountability and spread authoritarianism throughout the world (Deibert 2019).

Furthermore, while proponents contend that social media makes the communication landscape and the knowledge produced more democratic, a further challenge has to do with the fact that the channels through which people communicate are still owned by companies (Humphreys 2016). Also, calling into question the liberation technology framework, which sees social media as providing advantages to challengers over incumbents and helping democracy flourish, Zeitzoff (2017) has pointed out that there is general discontent that it also makes the government's job of monitoring and disrupting collective action easier. Kaplan and Haenlein (2010) also argue that making use of social media in the political realm has the potential of not only undermining representative government but also creating 'depoliticization.' This is because people can organize themselves to plan activities directly instead of working through their elected governments and other official representatives. Such people who organize with social media may always feel unwilling to vote during elections, notwithstanding the strong views and opinions that they may express on social media platforms.

Also, although those who have computers and Internet communications find themselves better trained, better informed and better able to participate in democracy (Cooper 2002), ICT infrastructure and skills are very limited and mostly accessible to those in urban areas (Ali 2011). In many developing countries, Grossman, Humphreys and Sacramone-Lutz (2016) have noted that the aggregation of preferences is limited by the weakness of civil society organizations, labor unions and political parties. Potential preference aggregators, such as unions and nongovernment organizations (NGOs), tend to be in urban centers. Political parties may have a wider reach, but many are weakly institutionalized and lack resources and elite cohesion. The implications of these are that preferences of the wider public will not be reflected in policy choices and only those with access to mobile phone and social media platforms will be heard. It also means that such citizens' incentive to proactively reach out to politicians in order to articulate interests, needs and policy preferences is severely reduced or curtailed. With marginalized populations engaging in politics at relatively low rates, not only are their demands less likely to be addressed but also, as Grossman et al. (2016) have noted, they are less likely to be articulated in the first place. Thus, even when citizens have issues they want to raise, technological fixes to communication deficits can be easily undercut by structural weaknesses in political systems (Grossman et al. 2016).

Additionally, social media and cell phone-enabled political engagement has according to Tettey (2017) sometimes been used to whip up political sentiments in ways that have raised tensions and led to violence. In Nigeria, for example, Olabamiji (2014) has noted that nagging, venting of anger and expression of frustration are commonplace on the new media. Similarly, in Ghana, Tettey (2017) has pointed out that phone-ins to radio and television programs that make overt appeals to 'action' to 'defend' one's political or ethnic group are now very common. Thus, the consequence of social media and the mobile phone's capacity for swift group mobilization is the low threshold that has emerged for the intensification of conflict and for political fragmentation as groups ride on the raw emotions of the moment to seek redress or to exact their own forms of justice through collective action. Dzisah (2018: 44) raises similar concerns by indicating that there are fringe elements within Ghanaian society that use social media's interactive capacity to fan religious, political and ethnic tensions and insulting language, as well as engage in vulgarity, thereby creating the potential for violent confrontation. Social media can become an intolerable medium for the trading of insults and the launching of tirades against those who disagree with viewpoints expressed on such platforms. Also, when everyone participates in information gathering and dissemination or engages in citizen journalism, credibility can be seriously challenged (Humphreys 2016: 250). This is evidenced in the case of Ghana where Tettey (2017: 688) argues that the ease with which individuals can insert themselves into the public sphere through mobile telephony has resulted in a situation where the quality of political conversation sometimes descends to banality and offensive posturing, leading to appeals to broadcast outlets to cut off callers or use delayed broadcast technology to truncate contributions which incite or make unsubstantiated allegations that are likely to evoke panic, fear or violence.

Moreover, technological innovations such as biometric voter registration and identification machines, electronic results transmission, database management systems, optical scanning, block chains and digital networks have improved the quality of polls in African countries and thus reduced electoral disputes (Iwuoha 2018; Micheni and Murumba 2018). Despite that, Iwuoha (2018) has argued that rural communities in countries like Nigeria generally face social deficits such as the nonavailability of proper infrastructure and long distances between polling stations and their dwellings. For him, the lack of effective electrical power supply and Internet services impinge on the functioning of the biometric technology and other ICT components deployed during elections. Apart from this, there are concerns that malfunctioning of biometric identification machines and possibility of hacking of electoral transmission machines could facilitate the rigging of the electoral process and outcomes. For example, during Ghana's 2016 presidential elections, the Electoral Commission directed its staff to stop electronically transmitting the electoral results to the tallying centers because of concerns that the system had been hacked or compromised. Similarly, Kenya's 2017 presidential elections were annulled by the country's Supreme Court after allegations by the opposition, led by Raila Odinga, of hacking and other widespread irregularities in the electronic transmission of votes.

Finally, Ferrara (2015) has argued that due to a mixture of social and economic incentives, a lack of effective policies against misbehavior and insufficient technical solutions to timely detect and hinder improper use, social media have been recently characterized by widespread abuse as evidenced in the peddling of lies, the spreading of misinformation and defamation. This is very much evident in many African countries where social media has served as the platform for defamation of character, publication of lies, falsehoods and the spreading of information whose trustworthiness may be doubtful. The publication of lies and deception and the circulation of doctored tape recordings to malign people have the tendency to cause fear and panic among the general public as well as end up destroying reputations and damaging hard-won images (Gyampo 2017; Tettey 2017; Omidyar 2018). For example, according to Tettey (2017: 689), in May 2014, a leaked tape recording of a speech by Ghana's President Mahama to party faithful in Kumasi created the impression that the President derided members of the Asante ethnic group. The government denied that interpretation of the President's words, released what it claimed was the authentic recording, and accused his political opponents of doctoring the speech in order to disparage him and to create political resentment toward him and his government. Such real-life examples show how misinformation spreading are greatly magnified by the massive reach and pervasiveness of social media can do potential harm to people as well as undermine relations, both among publics and between publics.

DISRUPTIVE TECHNOLOGY IN POLITICS: THE WAY FORWARD

The changes in the political landscape as well as improvements in the technology, especially digital and mobile technology, have resulted in drastic changes in democratic politics and political communication in African countries. The media landscape has been transformed by the rise of disruptive technologies in the form of web and Internet access and access of information through computers and now increasingly through mobile phones. Disruptive technologies have lessened the power of incumbents to control media; the new web-enabled communication infrastructure has made possible the broadening of the public sphere, encouraging public participation in news, with nontraditional journalistic platforms becoming important sites for 'alternative' journalism (Ogola 2015). For Wasserman (2011: 153), citizen journalism, where citizens use mobile phones and social media to produce content for mainstream media, has given citizens 'voice' by allowing them to rationally transmit their views and become represented in mainstream channels, transgress mainstream norms and practices and actively enter political life on their own terms. Also, the uptick in citizen journalism has contributed to holding government officials accountable for their policies and actions, as well as increasing political engagement and activism.

Notwithstanding these, the level of political participation and communication using digital and mobile phone and social media is constrained by the lack of access to the necessary infrastructure as well as by the fact that only the urban-based elites can make use of it. While the use of new digital technologies provides essential services to assist democratic governance in African countries, sub-Saharan Africa still lags in terms of Internet penetration. In Africa, it is estimated that 412,150,114 people use the Internet as of December 2017, with a penetration rate of 32% (Dzisah 2018). Given that Internet infrastructure in many African countries is costly and slow, it is crucial to develop policies and programs designed to bridge the global digital inequalities (Ali 2011; Castells 2002). This will help ensure that groups and individuals whose voices were previously marginalized in the political arena have the space and agency to express themselves and have their voices heard. As Bertot et al. (2010) state, it is important to both use technologies that are widely deployed to provide a broad base of technology access, but there is also often a substantial need to provide technological training, in particular, the spread of digital literacy, and engage in usability, functionality and accessibility testing to ensure the broadest ability to participate in e-government services and resources.

Furthermore, under old and traditional media, ownership and libel laws were put in place in many countries to respectively prevent media concentration and encourage diversity in the ownership, as well as protect people from having their lives ruined or reputation significantly destroyed because of false statements. It is in this regard that the rise of new media has resulted in attempts to similarly regulate it by ensuring that social media companies, for example, remove phony social media accounts and fake content, and are also held accountable for what appears on their platforms. Additionally, the increasing concern with privacy intrusion of citizens has led to temptations by governments throughout the world to regulate and impose restrictions on Internet and social media companies for them to be better stewards of their platforms. There are also calls for measures to restrict web-tracking and personal-data surveillance of users by social media companies, which is often used to target advertisements (Deibert 2019).

Finally, there is the free and open source software (F/OSS) movement in the United States and Europe, which according to Coleman (2012) engages in hacking and sees its activities as refusing restrictive intellectual protections, as well as part of the broader efforts toward open source, free speech, transparency and cultural articulation of liberalism in society. Notwithstanding the views of the F/OSS movement, strengthening the defenses of election infrastructure against hacking in African countries is a step in the right direction. By upgrading electoral databases, replacing voting machines that are considered vulnerable to hacking, and having a legal regime governing cybersecurity and hacking, which Kenya, for example, has, many African countries believe issues relating to the potential hacking and manipulation of elections can be addressed. In Kenya, the 2018 computer and cybercrime law that mandates severe punishment for a set of cyber-related offenses, including unauthorized access to or interference with computer systems by third parties, intentional unauthorized infiltration of a computer system and unauthorized interception of transmission of data over a telecommunications system, is seen as a deterrent for hackers. In 2008, Ghana passed the Electronic Transactions Act (Act 772), which provides for the regulation of electronic communications and related transactions, criminalized computer hacking and gave police officers more latitude in the pursuit of suspected cybercriminals. Additionally, as part of a Revised National Cybersecurity Strategy, not only is a cybersecurity law being developed, but moreover, Ghana's 2019 budget made provision for the establishment of a National Cybersecurity Authority (NCSA) to oversee cybersecurity, especially the protection of Critical National Information Infrastructure (CNII) in line with global trends and best practices. All these are aimed at ensuring that there are clear and explicit laws, policies and guidelines that establish expectations and the consequences of misuse of disruptive technologies and electronic communications.

Conclusion

The last two decades have seen rapid technological changes that are having a profound impact on governance and democratic processes. Particularly, one wonders what the specific implications of disruptive technologies like digital and mobile phone and social media platforms are having on the process of democratization, electoral processes and governance in general. This chapter offered insights into the role and impact of disruptive technologies and social media on the governance and democratic process among African countries. Modern disruptive technologies made possible through mobile telephony and Internet are actively empowering citizens and enabling them to engage in the political system, as well as helping to hold governments accountable, and consolidating the democratic process in Africa. Although not a silver bullet to consolidate the democratic process, their contribution to political communication as well as the promotion of accountability and governance cannot be underestimated. The combination of social media, web-enabled technologies, mobile technologies, transparency policy initiatives and citizen's desire for open and transparent government are fomenting a new age of opportunity that has the potential to create open, transparent, efficient, effective and user-centered ICT-enabled services (Bertot et al. 2010: 268). Social media introduce substantial and pervasive changes to communication between organizations, communities and individuals. This presents an enormous challenge for firms, as many established management methods are ill-suited to deal with customers who no longer want to be talked at; instead, customers want firms to listen, appropriately engage and respond (Kietzmann et al. 2011). The portability, accessibility (by those who can afford) and smartness of smartphones always make it easier for many people across the globe to use social media for all manner of purposes almost in their daily lives (Gyampo 2017). Although contributing to the improvements in the democratic process and the concomitant electoral system in many parts of Africa, several teething problems exist with the use of disruptive technologies. It is in this regard that outside of measures and policies to improve access and increase Internet penetration among African countries, issues relating to defamation and misinformation through disruptive technologies need to be addressed through education, as well as laws and regulations to guide their use.

References

Abrahamsen, R., & Bareebe, G. (2016). Uganda's 2016 Elections: Not Even Faking It Anymore. *African Affairs, 115*(461), 751–765.

Alhassan, A. A. (2018). The Role and Use of Social Media in Elections Campaigns and Voting Behavior in Nigeria: An Analysis of 2015 Presidential Election. *International Journal of Recent Innovations in Academic Research, 2*(6), 117–129.

Ali, A. H. (2011). The Power of Social Media in Developing Nations: New Tools for Closing the Global Digital Divide and Beyond. *Harvard Human Rights Journal, 24*, 185–219.

Allcott, H., & Gentzkow, M. (2017). Social Media and Fake News in the 2016 Election. *Journal of Economic Perspectives, 31*(2), 211–236.

Bertot, J. C., Jaeger, P. T., & Grimes, J. M. (2010). Using ICTs to Create a Culture of Transparency: E-Government and Social Media as Openness and Anti-corruption Tools for Societies. *Government Information Quarterly, 27*, 264–271.

Bokor, M. (2014). New Media and Democratization in Ghana: An Impetus for Political Activism. *Net Journal of Social Sciences, 2*(1), 1–16.

Bosch, T. (2017). Twitter Activism and Youth in South Africa: The Case of #RhodesMustFall. *Information, Communication & Society, 20*(2), 221–232.

Castells, M. (2002). *The Internet Galaxy: Reflections on the Internet, Business, and Society*. Oxford: University Press on Demand.

Christensen, C. (1997). *The Innovator's Dilemma: When New Technologies Cause Great Firms to Fail*. Harvard: Harvard University Press.

Christensen, C. (2001). Assessing Your Organization's Innovation Capabilities. *Executive Forum, 81*(2), 27–37.

Chuma, W. (2014). The Social Meanings of Mobile Phones Among South Africa's 'Digital Natives': A Case Study. *Media, Culture & Society, 36*(3), 1–11.

Coleman, G. (2012). *Coding Freedom: The Ethics and Aesthetics of Hacking*. Princeton: Princeton University Press.

Cooper, M. (2002). Inequality in the Digital Society: Why the Digital Divide Deserves All the Attention It Gets. *Cardozo Arts & Entertainment Law Journal, 20*(1), 73–134.

Danneels, E. (2004). Disruptive Technology Reconsidered A Critique and Research Agenda. *Journal of Product Innovative Management, 21*(4), 246–258.

Deibert, D. (2019). The Road to Digital Unfreedom: Three Painful Truths About Social Media. *Journal of Democracy, 30*(1), 25–39.

Diamond, L. (2010). Liberation Technology. *Journal of Democracy, 21*(3), 69–83.

Dzisah, W. (2018). Social Media and Elections in Ghana: Enhancing Democratic Participation. *African Journalism Studies, 39*(1), 27–47.

Ferrara, E. (2015). *Manipulation and Abuse on Social Media*. Available at https://arxiv.org/pdf/1503.03752.pdf. Accessed 3 May 2019.

Gallowa, D., Mollel, A., Mgoma, S., Pima, M., & Deogratias, E. (2018). Mobile Phone Use in Two Secondary Schools in Tanzania. *Education and Information Technologies, 23*(1), 73–92.

Goggin, G. (2011). Ubiquitous Apps: Politics of Openness in Global Mobile Cultures. *Digital Creativity, 22*(3), 148–159.

Grossman, G., Humphreys, M., & Sacramone-Lutz, G. (2016). *Information Technology and Political Engagement: Mixed Evidence from Uganda*. Available at: https://www.researchgate.net/profile/Guy_Grossman/publication/303818782_Information_Technology_and_Political_Engagement_Mixed_Evidence_from_Uganda/links/580bc6aa08aecba93500d11b/Information-Technology-and-Political-Engagement-Mixed-Evidence-from-Uganda.pdf. Accessed 7 May 2019.

Gyampo, R. E. V. (2017). Social Media, Traditional Media and Party Politics in Ghana. *Africa Review*. https://doi.org/10.1080/09744053.2017.1329806.

Hellstrom, J. (2008). *Mobile Phones for Good Governance–Challenges and Way Forward*. Stockholm University/UPGRAID. Available at: http://www.w3.org/2008/10/MW4D_WS/papers/hellstrom_gov.pdf. Accessed 20 Apr 2019.

Hermanns, H. (2008). Mobile Democracy: Mobile Phones as Democratic Tools. *Politics, 28*(2), 74–82.

Hong, S., & Nadler, D. (2012). Which Candidates Do the Public Discuss Online in an Election Campaign?: The Use of Social Media by 2012 Presidential Candidates and Its Impact on Candidate Salience. *Government Information Quarterly, 29*, 455–461.

Humphreys, A. (2016). *Social Media: Enduring Principles.* New York: Oxford University Press.

Iwuoha, V. C. (2018). ICT and Elections in Nigeria: Rural Dynamics of Biometric Voting Technology Adoption. *Africa Spectrum, 53*(3), 89–113.

Kanyam, D. A., Kostandini, G., & Ferreira, S. (2017). The Mobile Phone Revolution: Have Mobile Phones and the Internet Reduced Corruption in Sub-Saharan Africa? *World Development, 99,* 271–284.

Kaplan, A. M., & Haenlein, M. (2010). Users of the World, Unite! The Challenges and Opportunities of Social Media. *Business Horizons, 53*(1), 59–68.

Karolak, M. (2018). Social Media in Democratic Transitions and Consolidations: What Can We Learn from the Case of Tunisia? *The Journal of North African Studies.* https://doi.org/10.1080/13629387.2018.1482535.

Kietzmann, H. J., Hermkens, K., McCarthy, I. P., & Silvestre, B. (2011). Social Media? Get Serious! Understanding the Functional Building Blocks of Social Media. *Business Horizons, 54*(3), 241–251.

Kirigha, J. M., Mukhongo, L. L., & Masinde, R. (2018). Beyond Web 2.0. Social Media and Urban Educated Youths Participation in Kenyan Politics. In *Media Influence: Breakthroughs in Research and Practice* (pp. 176–193). Hershey: IGI Global.

Koi-Akrofi, G. Y., Koi-Akrofi, J., & Welbeck, J. N. (2013). Relationship Marketing Tactics and Customer Loyalty: A Case Study of the Mobile Telecommunications Industry in Ghana. *Asian Journal of Business Management, 5*(1), 77–92.

Lutz, B., & du Toit, P. (2014). *Defining Democracy in a Digital Age: Political Support on Social Media.* London: Palgrave Macmillan. https://doi.org/10.1057/9781137496195.

Micheni, E., & Murumba, J. (2018). *The Role of ICT in Electoral Processes: Case of Kenya.* IST-Africa Week Conference (IST-Africa).

Ocitti, J. (1999). *Media and Democracy in Africa: Mutual Political Bedfellows or Implacable Arch-Foes.* https://programs.wcfia.harvard.edu/files/fellows/files/ocitti.pdf. Accessed 27 Mar 2019.

Ogola, G. (2015). Social Media as a Heteroglossic Discursive Space and Kenya's Emergent Alternative/Citizen Experiment. *African Journalism Studies, 36*(4), 66–81.

Olabamiji, O. M. (2014). Use and Misuse of the New Media for Political Communication in Nigeria's 4th Republic. *Developing Country Studies, 4*(2). Available at http://citeseerx.ist.psu.edu/viewdoc/download?doi=10.1.1.818.1362&rep=rep1&type=pdf. Accessed 3 May 2019.

Omidyar, P. (2018). 6 Ways Social Media Has Become a Direct Threat to Democracy. *New Perspectives Quarterly, 35*(1), 42–45.

Onyechi, N. J. (2018). Taking Their Destiny in Their Hands: Social Media, Youth Participation and the 2015 Campaign in Nigeria. *African Journalism Studies, 39*(1), 69–89.

Onyechi, N. J., & Obono, K. (2017). Communication and Peace Building: The 2015 Presidential Elections in Nigeria. *Africology: The Journal of Pan African Studies, 10*(7), 22–35.

Opara, C. (2017). *How Social Media Played a Role in Ghana's 2016 Elections.* Available at: http://www.signalng.com/op-unedited-social-media-played-role-ghanas-2016-elections-chris-opara/. Accessed 4 June 2019.

Piccolino, G. (2015). *What Other African Elections Tell Us About Nigeria's Bet on Biometrics.* Available at: https://www.washingtonpost.com/news/monkey-cage/wp/2015/03/10/what-other-african-elections-tell-us-about-nigerias-bet-onbiometrics/?utm_term=.b79ed20588be. Accessed 30 May 2019.

Rød, E. G. (2015). Empowering Activists or Autocrats? The Internet in Authoritarian Regimes. *Journal of Peace Research, 52*(3), 338–351.

Stier, S., Bleier, A., Lietz, H., & Strohmaier, M. (2018). Election Campaigning on Social Media: Politicians, Audiences and the Mediation of Political Communication on Facebook and Twitter. *Political Communication, 35*(1), 50–74.

Taprial, V., & Kanwar, P. (2012). *Understanding Social Media.* London: Ventus Publishing.

Tettey, W. J. (2017). Mobile Telephony and Democracy in Ghana: Interrogating the Changing Ecology of Citizen Engagement and Political Communication. *Telecommunications Policy, 41*(7-8), 685–694.

Wasserman, H. (2011). Mobile Phones, Popular Media, and Everyday African Democracy: Transmissions and Transgressions. *Popular Communication: The International Journal of Media and Culture, 9*(2), 146–158.

Wolfsfeld, G., Segev, E., & Sheafer, T. (2013). Social Media and the Arab Spring: Politics Comes First. *The International Journal of Press/Politics, 18*(2), 115–137.

Zeitzoff, T. (2017). How Social Media Is Changing Conflict. *Journal of Conflict Resolution, 20*(10), 1–22.

CHAPTER 3

Agricultural Research and Innovation: Disruptive Technologies and Value-Chain Development in Africa

Korbla P. Puplampu and George O. Essegbey

INTRODUCTION

African agriculture continues to play significant direct and indirect roles in social development, but the sector is also confronted with numerous and persistent problems. Although agricultural systems have been able to boost the production of certain crops, mostly for export agriculture, the production of local food crops still experience significant postharvest losses culminating in poor market performance for farmers. Poor market performance, in a context of increasing urbanization and the need for increasing food production, has worrisome implications for sociopolitical

K. P. Puplampu (✉)
Department of Sociology, Grant MacEwan University,
Edmonton, AB, Canada
e-mail: puplampuk@macewan.ca

G. O. Essegbey
Science and Technology Policy Research Institute, Council for Scientific and
Industrial Research, Accra, Ghana

© The Author(s) 2020
P. Arthur et al. (eds.), *Disruptive Technologies, Innovation and
Development in Africa*, International Political Economy Series,
https://doi.org/10.1007/978-3-030-40647-9_3

order. In response, the African Union Agenda 2063 stressed the need for continental food security and also declared 2014 the Year of Agriculture, a declaration that reinforced the broader 2003 Comprehensive Africa Agriculture Development Programme (CAADP) (NEPAD 2003). At the global level, the United Nation's Millennium Development Goals (MDGs) (2000–2015) and the current Sustainable Development Goals (SDGs) (2015–2030) have both reiterated the need for major changes, often with multilateral specialized agencies (World Bank 2019a; FAO 2017a; UNDP 2003, 2015). For instance, SDG 1 (to end poverty in all its forms everywhere), SDG 2 (to end hunger, achieve food security and improve nutrition and promote sustainable agriculture), SDG 9 (industry, innovation and infrastructure), SDG 16 (peace, justice and strong institutions) and SDG 17 (strengthen the means of implementation and revitalize the global partnership for sustainable development) are significant to African agricultural development (UNDP 2015).

One recurring theme from the continental and global agricultural plans is a renewed emphasis on the role of science, technology and innovation in pushing the frontiers of the continental transformation agenda, particularly in terms of agribusiness, agricultural research and innovation (World Bank 2012, 2013; ACBF 2017). This is because agricultural research and innovation are critical components of the institutional system required and necessary to generate and disseminate the knowledge for agricultural development. Agricultural research plays a major role in any system and across the agricultural value chain. It offers new knowledge to end users in production and marketing and subsequently innovative products for consumers. Innovation is the use of knowledge to bring about scientific and technological applications to improve socioeconomic activities where such applications are new in the context of usage (Fu et al. 2014). With regard to agricultural systems, the use of new knowledge is particularly critical in agricultural research and development (R&D), and therefore there is the concept of National Agricultural Research System (NARS), which underscores the importance of knowledge acquisition, generation, application and dissemination.

One aspect of the African agricultural system that could benefit the most from agricultural research and innovation and agribusiness is the value chain, both at the local and global levels (FAO 2017b; World Bank 2019a; Malabo Montpellier Panel 2018; Larsen et al. 2009; Toenniesse et al. 2008). For example, the FAO-sponsored Regional Initiative on Value Chain Development is consistent with the African Union framework and policy guidelines such the CAADP and the 2014 Malabo Implementation Strategy and Roadmap. As AU (2018) shows, while Rwanda, Mali, Morocco and Mauritius have made significant progress on CAADP implementation goals, Sudan, Sierra Leone and Tunisia have not made significant progress. An important piece to spur progress and an essential cog when it comes to the value-chain matrix is communication and information technologies (ICTs). The African Union Summit of ICT Ministers in Addis Ababa echoed the critical place of ICTs in African agricultural development (Yonazi et al. 2012).

There are emerging studies on agricultural research and innovation in value-chain dimensions in other parts of the global South including the African situation (Gereffi 2014; Webber and Labaste 2010). Most of these studies examine different dimensions of the agricultural research and innovation plus value-chain environment, but without specific attention to the policy and institutional framework governing research and innovation. This chapter builds on previous studies while paying attention to the policy and institutional underpinnings for value chain, agricultural research and innovation in Africa against the backdrop of disruptive technology. We analyze how disruptive technologies can deepen the role of value-chain development for production, marketing and consumption systems, drawing on relevant illustrative material from other parts of the global South and discussing their relevance for the African context.

The chapter is organized as follows. The first section will present a theoretical overview of disruptive technology and value-chain agriculture. The second section will survey the agricultural research and innovation environment in Africa and isolate selected agricultural sectors integrating disruptive technology into their operations. The third section will analyze how the relationship between disruptive technology and innovation impacts value-chain and agricultural development before proceeding to conclusion and the way forward.

Disruptive Technology and Value-Chain Agriculture: A Theoretical Framework

Technology and technological changes have been part of agricultural systems since the beginning of time. From horse-drawn carriages to agricultural mechanization and genetically modified seeds, technological changes have led to increases in productivity, improved marketing for consumers to embrace new agricultural products. In contemporary times, the Green

Revolution in India and other Asian countries in the 1960s demonstrated how technology, within the relevant context, can bring about agricultural development (Patel 2013; Hazell 2009). More recent technological strides, for example, in genomics, have also transformed agricultural systems (Phillips 2008; Takeda and Matsuoka 2008).

One novel idea in the ongoing discourse on technology and society is the theory of disruptive technology. Pioneered by Christensen (1997), disruptive technology is an innovative process whereby novel products come on stream due to changes in technology and market processes by specific actors. Implied in the theory are several propositions and possibilities. The first is its entrepreneurial ethos and how prospective owners of capital can employ it to improve their economic activities. Second, as a process-laden theory, it can take any business onto a higher trajectory of productivity and market performance. For example, it makes it easier "to support financial inclusion and female financial empowerment ... [and is] an important avenue for creating market access" (Ndung'u 2018: 84). The theory can be applied to any sector of the economy, from small-scale to medium- and large-scale agricultural producers (Evans 2018a; King 2017). Finally, the theory is contingent on technological improvements in communication, such as smartphones, global positioning systems, satellite imagery, data transmission and artificial intelligence, in sum, the Internet of Things (IoT) (Evans 2018b, c; Hanson and Puplampu 2018).

IoT revolve around "a global infrastructure for the information society, enabling advanced services by interconnecting (physical and virtual) things based on existing and evolving interoperable information and communication technologies" (cited in ITU and Cisco 2016: 10). IoT is therefore a system in which "items in the physical world, and sensors within or attached to those items, are connected to the Internet via wireless and wired Internet connections" (Ndubuaku and Okereafor 2015: 23). In the emerging ecosystem, farmers can use their smartphones and relevant data to manage the application of fertilizer, the frequency and rate of water flows in irrigation projects in crop production, the amount of and how often to feed and manage the growth of livestock in a way to optimize productivity as well as check market prices and plan on the best time to harvest or move outputs to market (King 2017). Distributors and consumers would also be better informed about product quality through traceability and product code scans (World Bank 2019b). These are the tenets of digital agriculture, precision or smart agriculture, linking actors at different stages in the agricultural system in areas such as climate change, food security and sustainable livelihoods.

Smart agricultural systems give rise to "increasing efficiency of inputs such as labour, seeds, and fertilizers, to increase food security" (Lalitha et al. 2018: 7410). Hence, smart technologies are critical in crop production and livestock through improvements in weather forecasting, soil conditions, information sharing and the storage, through processing techniques that enhance productivity, distribution and the quality of food (Evans 2018a, b, c; King 2017). Simply put, digital agriculture makes it possible to leverage a range of services to the agricultural sector, therefore the renewal and promise of agricultural innovation platforms (AIP), agribusiness and value-chain agriculture (Greenville et al. 2019; Malabo Montpellier Panel 2018; Schaffnit-Chatterjee 2014; World Bank 2013, 2019a; Webber and Labaste 2010).

Agricultural innovation platforms (AIP) go beyond the traditional approach in agricultural research and the dissemination of research to involve all actors in the agricultural sector. AIP emphasizes several issues: greater participation by all agricultural actors (knowledge institutions, private sector, civil society and farmers' organizations), technology adoption and adaptation, and interactive and dynamic relations, hence a more inclusive process (Reardon et al. 2019; Tomich et al. 2019; Kim et al. 2009). The AIP approach dovetails into agribusiness and value-chain agriculture in profound ways. The central core of agribusiness is agricultural production and the supply of inputs. However, since production is never complete until marketing and consumption take place, agribusiness expands the length and breadth of agricultural organization and aligns with value-chain agriculture (Greenville et al. 2019; Schaffnit-Chatterjee 2014; Webber and Labaste 2010).

Value chain is about how agricultural actors "seek to capture and describe the complex interactions of firms and processes that are needed to create and deliver products to end users" (Webber and Labaste 2010: 9). It includes vertical and horizontal links and in-between processes with the sole aim to increase the value of a product or service. At each stage in the chain, the objective is to enhance the value of an agricultural produce or service, turning it into a high-value commodity or service "through the different phases of production (involving a combination of physical transformation and the input of various producer services), delivery to final consumers, and final disposal after use" (Hellin and Meijer 2006: 4).

One significant dimension of the value chain in agriculture is agro-processing, which addresses the perennial problems of postharvest losses and quality control. Take the case of contract farming and smallholder producers confronted with demands on quality control in order to enhance market accessibility in a global context and distribution at the national level (Reardon et al. 2019; de Janvry and Sadoulet 2019). Value chain can operate from the local and national to the regional and global levels and, because of the presence of multiple actors and activities, can engender improvements in the living conditions of actors in the agricultural sector from farm and nonfarm income sources (Moseley 2015).

The global South is home to various IoT-enabled smart agriculture schemes that demonstrate the relationship between disruptive technology and value-chain agriculture. In the Latin American subregion, the certified green coffee program in Nicaragua was instrumental in poverty-reduction schemes for smallholder famers, just as it was the case for potato farmers in Bolivia, Ecuador and Peru (Cavatassi et al. 2011; Donovan and Poole 2014; Thiele et al. 2011; Devaux et al. 2009). Several Asian countries are also harvesting the possibilities of smart agriculture. China, for example, has vigorously pursued various information-based applications from "greenhouse remote monitoring, automatic drip irrigation, and milk source safety information management to enhance agricultural production" (ITU and Cisco 2016: 33).

In India, the Nano Ganesh project, with a focus on providing small-scale farmers with a tool to remotely control their irrigation pumps, has eased burdens on time, labor and fuel consumption (Sylvester 2015). The Indian Space Research Organization (ISRO) has developed crop insurance technology using geoinformatics systems like geographical information system, global positioning system and android-based smartphone to advance yield estimation and the required planning for crop insurance (Lalitha et al. 2018). The transformation of beef-cattle production and marketing in Vietnam was a huge boost for the incomes of small-scale farmers (Stür et al. 2013).

With the changing technological landscape, digital agriculture, via mobile phones, and the IoT are increasingly assuming a pivotal role in value-chain agriculture. However, IoT and value-chain engagements in African agriculture, as in other places, require a policy and institutional framework, the capacity of the agricultural research and innovation system. The next section, in broad strokes, will outline the agricultural research and innovation landscape in Africa and isolate selected cases of smart or digital agriculture.

The Agricultural Research and Innovation Landscape in Africa: An Overview

The African Union, in line with the continent-wide initiatives, under the former New Partnership for Africa's Development (NEPAD), now the African Union Development Agency-led (AUDA) Comprehensive Africa Agriculture Development Programme (CAADP), designated the Forum for Agricultural Research in Africa (FARA) as the institutional body for harnessing and investing in research and technological investment for agriculture (NEPAD 2003: 17). FARA (2015: 7) is charged with incorporating "emerging sciences, technology and risk mitigation to generate enabling policies and institutions required for the sustainable implementation of programmes for African agricultural innovation." FARA works through and with national, regional and global agricultural research institutions in generating knowledge for all actors in the agricultural sector.

Agricultural research, whether at the basic or applied level, is about generating and disseminating knowledge to farmers and other agricultural actors. This model, in the context of CGIAR in the 1970s, was to utilize knowledge generated in the global North for the benefit of agriculture in the global South (Lele 2004). In its historical incarnation, there was a heavy presence of state-run institutions directly or indirectly related to the agricultural sector and the research focused mostly on technical solutions. Agricultural knowledge from this system was applied or adapted for agricultural systems through national or regional agricultural systems and extension services (Biggs 1990). With the onset of the African agricultural crises in the 1980s, the limitations of the existing model became obvious. For example, extension services, amidst resource constrains, must make difficult decisions on which farmers deserved the most support attention, those in export agriculture or those producing to supplement local or national food production needs (FAO 2017a).

Another fundamental problem was the assumption that knowledge only flowed from agricultural experts to farmers and other agricultural actors, as end users, and not vice versa, an assumption that undermines any path to sustainable agriculture (Barbier and Elzen 2012). Agricultural research to be able to address the needs of actors in the agricultural sector must also reorient and listen to the end users, thus the increasing relevance of agricultural research systems that are organized around the principles of innovation and sensitive to the imperatives in value-chain agriculture. The essential feature of agricultural innovation is that it is concerned with changes in production, marketing and consumption that may or may not be driven purely by research. According to the World Bank (2012: 2), innovation is the "process by which individuals or organizations master and implement the design and production of goods and services that are new to them, irrespective of whether they are new to their competitors, their country, or the world." Innovation is nonlinear and "stimulated by the interaction of individuals and organizations with diverse – often conflicting – stakes in the management of scarce resources of the governance of productive processes" (Devaux et al. 2018: 101).

Disruptive technology, agribusiness and value-chain agriculture can transform African agriculture, particularly in areas such as improvements in market access, eliminate the problems of weak physical infrastructure such as roads and railways which present difficulties to farmers and distributors alike in moving agricultural goods. Technological changes can also address the challenges in the nexus between agriculture and climate change, and finally improve the quality of agricultural produce and products for consumers, making it possible for farmers to diversify and become competitive in the national, regional and global value-chain operations. As part of a diversification and enhancing exports, cassava, maize, sunflowers and banana have been the focus of value-chain programs in Ghana, Kenya, Tanzania and Uganda, respectively (Essegbey 2009; Odame et al. 2009; Mpagalile et al. 2009; Kibwika et al. 2009). Digital platforms like Esoko (West and East Africa), DrumNet (Kenya) and Sissili Vala Kori (Burkina Faso) have been on the frontlines in providing ICT-enabled services to farmers (Yonazi et al. 2012). Esoko, for example, is providing agricultural market information, including real-time prices of agricultural commodities on the respective markets, weather forecasts, opportunities for connecting to buyers, cash transfers and input subsidies in countries such as Ghana, Tanzania, Malawi and Burkina Faso. Syngenta Foundation launched the Kilimo Salama (Safe Farming) weather index project in Kenya in 2009 (Lalitha et al. 2018; ITU and Cisco 2016). The project, a crop insurance program, uses solar-powered weather stations to collect weather information to process claims by farmers; claims are often paid using mobile payment platforms like M-Pesa.

Asenso-Okyere and Mekonnen (2012) document how mobile phones and the Internet have been critical in the innovation and dissemination of information to farmers in several African countries. For example, the Ethiopian Commodity Exchange (ECX) uses short message systems (SMS) and phone calls to help farmers with price data from different markets in the country. Farmers in Senegal also benefited from the activities of the Market Information Systems and Traders' Organization in West African and other private sector actors to exchange market information online and SMS, while Cargill, an agro-based company, purchased and paid cocoa farmers in Ghana through digitized procurement systems and mobile money services provided by companies like MTN and Tigo. Digitalization and financial inclusion constitute an "enabler of development, a supporter of progress, and a powerful tool to achieve the Sustainable Development Goals" (Ndung'u 2018: 85) in Ghana and other African countries. In addition to digital payments, it is common knowledge that small-scale farmers in Africa require financial commitments that are tailor made for the vagaries of agricultural income. The One Acre Fund, operating in East Africa, is one facility that specifically caters to the needs of small-scale farmers, providing farmers with high-quality farm inputs like improved seeds and a convenient distribution of the inputs (Ndung'u 2018: 87). The program also offers farmers with loans with flexible repayment options that are scheduled on M-Pesa, the pioneering financial services in Kenya. The flexibility of the credit system "allows farmers to closely match repayments to cash flow and reduce pressure on household finances" (Ndung'u 2018: 87).

The use of digital financial services and the relationship between mobile phones and mobile money in value-chain agriculture have been the source of several studies (Evans 2018a, b, 2019; Asongu and Nwachukwu 2016). The principles of the Ethiopian Commodity Exchange are also present in the TradeNet platform in Ghana (Lalitha et al. 2018; Addo 2016). The TradeNet is a trading platform that uses mobile phones and the Internet to connect traders and farmers with market information via SMS in real time. Evans (2018a: 79), drawing on the transformation potential of the Internet, argues that "connectivity using mobile phone is an opportunity that the farmer in any rural area could explore to improve financial inclusion and communication with the outside world."

One essential aspect of mobile phone and digital agriculture is the knowledge base of farmers. Owusu, Yankson and Frimpong's (2017) work on the gender dimensions of farmers' knowledge of mobile telephone and agricultural marketing development is instructive. With empirical data from smallholder farmers, the study stresses how mobile phone "bridges the gap between production and consumption centres, as it eliminates gaps that would have persisted due to the existence of deplorable road conditions and high transport cost" (Owusu et al. 2017: 47). In Ethiopia and Mozambique, value chain and innovation systems have improved production of livestock by small-scale farmers (Swaans et al. 2014; Ayele et al. 2012). The Namibia livestock traceability system also makes it possible to maximize the value chain of the industry, because it is possible to expand the scope and depth of livestock and improve the lives of several actors in the entire livestock industry (Yonazi et al. 2012: 46). In tea plantations in Rwanda, solar-powered panels have provided data transmitted wireless using radio frequency identification (RFID) tags to monitor soil moisture, carbon and other gases. Egypt has also embarked on ICT-managed schemes aimed at "improving the management of irrigation and drainage and increasing the efficiency of irrigated agriculture water use and services" (Yonazi et al. 2012: 47).

Rice production has benefited from research and innovation. One main problem in the value chain of the rice industry is low rice yield due to, among other factors, seed varieties, therefore the compelling reason for the development and dissemination of rice varieties that can stand stress and easily adapt to the respective agro-climatic regions (Arounaa et al. 2017). Research and development of better rice varieties, in addition to other policy changes, have been at the heart of two main projects: first, the Africa Rice Center and the New Rice for Africa (NERICA) project and, second, the Bill and Melinda Gates Foundation (BMGF) Rice Value Chain (Diakité et al. 2019; Diagne et al. 2011). The high dependence and cost of imported rice culminated in the New Rice for Africa (NERICA) (Diagne et al. 2011; Dalohoun et al. 2009). NERICA was developed in 1994 "through perseverance and the use of biotechnology tools such as anther culture and embryo rescue techniques" (Diagne et al. 2011: 255).

Several African countries from Burkina Faso, Gambia and Ghana to Uganda have subsequently adopted NERICA varieties (Diagne et al. 2011). Ghana, for example, launched NEWEST, a variety of rice modified for nitrogen and water efficiency as well as salt tolerance (Puplampu and Essegbey 2018: 64). Value-chain approaches have also been utilized in tackling risk management and climate variability and systems of rice intensification in Madagascar and Mozambique (Nyasimi et al. 2014). The next section will focus on livestock projects in selected African countries to contextualize the different aspects, possibilities and potential of disruptive technology and value-chain agriculture.

Animal Production and Value-Chain Agriculture

Dairy products in Kenya and Rwanda have been the beneficiaries of IoT-enabled disruptive and innovative management systems (ITU and Cisco 2016: 33; Kilelu et al. 2013; Swaans et al. 2013). However, the East African Dairy Development (EADD) project and the poultry industry in Mozambique are valuable examples for agricultural research, innovation and value-chain initiatives (Bah and Gajigo 2019; Omondi et al. 2017; Swaans et al. 2014; Firetail 2013). The EADD project, another beneficiary of the Bill and Melinda Gates Foundation (BMGF), began in 2008 with the stated aim to improve the region's milk production, an essential animal protein in Kenya, Uganda and Rwanda. The EADD was designed with the idea of integrating all the relevant actors in the industry, from cattle producers, mostly smallholder farmers, institutions in animal husbandry, marketing and diary farmers' associations with the sole objective to deal with capacity problems for cattle farmers, extension services and agricultural research institutions as well as signals for the milk market (Omondi et al. 2017; Firetail 2013).

In Kenya, the EADD projects are located in several districts within the Rift Valley and Central Province, with four hubs in total and over 120,000 registered farmers by 2012, while, in Uganda, projects are located in several districts in Central Uganda, which also had four hubs and over 45,000 registered farmers by 2012 (Firetail 2013: 13). The hub model is a systems approach to agricultural organization (Firetail 2013). In the case of EADD, the implementation structure at the regional hub was made up of the five main consortium partners—Heifer International (lead), TechnoServe, African Breeding Services, International Agroforestry Center and the International Livestock Research Institute. At the national and regional levels, apart from the International Livestock Research Institute, all the other consortium partners are present in the cluster. The hub model at the ground level, presided over by the Dairy Farmer Business Association, had lines of communication with EADD regional offices and milk processors and is directly working with a range of actors—bulking and chilling, transporters and registered farmers, particularly the active ones. The hubs are either farmer-owned or managed through dairy farmer producer organizations, with specific lines of work within each hub, for instance, pure processor linkage (direct sale to large milk processors) approach and mixed linkage (sales to others, including large milk processors) approach (Omondi et al. 2017: 588).

Mozambique's poultry industry, in addition to seafood, is integral to the production of animal protein and the source of income. A viable poultry industry for most rural residents "can increase their resilience by reducing their vulnerability to rainfall and other shocks … [and] also contribute to food security – an important factor given that the prevalence of malnutrition in the country, which affects 40% of children under 5 years" (Bah and Gajigo 2019: 4). The key question has been how to ensure the industry rose up to the challenges in the quantity and quality of jobs and products in the light of difficulties in access to finance and other key inputs such as "feed for chicken producers, seeds and fertilizers for grain producers, and machinery for chicken processors, among others" (Bah and Gajigo 2019: 4). There are also regional pressures on the poultry industry from South Africa, Zambia and Zimbabwe and global players like Brazil. The main actors in Mozambique's value chain are hatcheries, grain producers, feed processors, poultry producers, abattoirs, distributors and veterinary (Bah and Gajigo 2019: 5).

Disruptive Technology, Innovation, Value-Chain and Agricultural Development in Africa

According to Puplampu and Essegbey (2018: 65), "the blight of African agriculture is not the paucity of policies or institutions. The problem remains desirable policy and institutional outcomes in the face of available resources, because political commitment, although necessary, is not a sufficient condition." Indeed, the need to pay attention to policy and institutional capacity imperatives and outcomes cannot be overstated if disruptive technologies are expected to deepen the role of value-chain development for production, marketing and consumption systems. The analysis of the ongoing agricultural projects or initiatives will focus on three main themes.

The first theme is the genesis of each project, particularly the funding source. African agricultural planning and initiatives are mostly driven by donor funding, and the on folding dynamics with respect to disruptive technology and value chain reflect a continuation of the region's historical agricultural development nature (Puplampu and Essegbey 2018: 61–65).

Both the EADD project and the African rice projects are donor-driven. The difficulties of donor-driven agricultural development are well known, so the question is how African policy makers organize their national resources and priorities when it comes to the agricultural sector. Put differently, disruptive technology and value-chain agriculture would require well-resourced structure and institutions to make the desired impact to agriculture and subsequently society in general. This is because there is overwhelming evidence that when resources and reorientation are present in agricultural research and innovation systems, there have been tangible contributions as was the case of NERICA.

NERICA was possible because of the reconfiguration of the agricultural research system, bringing in a key innovation of farmer involvement in the methodology of the NERICA research project (FARA 2015). There are several lessons that can be gleaned from the NERICA research program. First, it is a concrete evidence of the capabilities of a well-resourced African agricultural research institution, especially the ability to liaise with research institutes in a global context. The Africa Rice Center was part of the broader CIGAR system. The second lesson is to reiterate the extent to which a change in research orientation, in this case the choice of a methodology, can create a platform for and gave credence to the role of farmers as co-knowledge creators in agricultural research (Kilelu et al. 2013). The above two lessons were noticeable in several value-chain projects and studies across the African continent (Trendov et al. 2019; AGRA 2018). The place of farmers, the primary site for agricultural production, requires a fundamental rethinking in the policy and institutional framework of African agriculture in an era of disruptive technology.

The rethinking begins with the role of the state in agricultural marketing, even though the restructuring of agricultural markets in Africa since the 1980s has provided mixed outcomes in terms of market reforms. African agriculture, like that in other parts of the world, has been subject to significant restructuring due to globalization of agriculture and its theoretical requirement for a minimal role of the state in agricultural organization (Cooksey 2011). The theoretical argument notwithstanding, the African state, like others, continues to assume a role in agriculture, especially in setting the policy and institutional framework (Puplampu and Essegbey 2018; Puplampu 2014).

One area of the policy and institutional framework is that the historical split between large-scale and small-scale farmers in Africa, in which the former was in the production of export agriculture and the latter producing for the local market, is no longer tenable under digital agriculture (AGRA 2017). This is because technology serves the role of an 'equalizer of sorts' for farmers, because regardless of their classification by policy makers, farmers in either case can engage in digital agriculture. In the historical context, state agricultural policy mistakenly undermined the smallholders and their ability to serve as a catalyst for agricultural transformation in Africa (AGRA 2018). Coffee producers, regardless of size, in Rwanda with improvements in quality and the certification process and cassava producers, mostly smallholders, in Ghana, can break through into competitive external markets (Lynam and Theus 2009; Essegbey 2009).

A second theme is the nature and role of agricultural actors, particularly private actors such as nongovernmental organizations (NGOs), considering the changing role of the state in African agriculture (Puplampu 2014). The state continues to have an influential role, even if not a powerful one in the agricultural sector in several, if not all, African countries. The state therefore must work with public and private actors, from the national to the global framework, to establish a policy environment that can create the synergies required for successful outcomes. The successful outcomes of disruptive and innovation in the EADD and coffee value chain in Rwanda had to do with the participation of all, and not only one, nongovernmental organizations, because the proliferation of NGOs has led to what Lynam and Theus (2009: 21) refer to as all the "necessary links throughout the rest of the value chain." These necessary links, with required feedback loops, are active parts in the innovation system (Trendov et al. 2019).

A third theme is the regional dimensions of digital agriculture and value chain. By its nature, agricultural research and innovation are expensive, and because it is prone to the free-rider problem, the state, by default, assumes some interest in the public interest implications of agricultural research and innovation. Furthermore, the same crop can be produced across several countries. Hence, in order to address the free-rider aspects of agriculture and smart agriculture, a regional approach has the potential to maximize the agricultural value-chain. The EADD, for example, aligns quite well with the East African Community (EAC), a regional economic community made up of Burundi, Kenya, Tanzania, Rwanda and Uganda (Puplampu 2015). Indeed, with EADD expected to commence operations in Tanzania, part of the EAC and Ethiopia (Common Market for Eastern and Southern Africa (COMESA)), regional integration would deepen the value chain of the milk industry in the region.

However, the state of the infrastructure is an important feature for any success of regional economic communities. Take the case of the cashew industry in Mozambique (Große-Rüschkamp and Seelige 2010; Hanlon 2000, 2001). Mozambique, a member of the Southern Africa Development Community (SADC), is also an instrumental partner in the Maputo Development Corridor (MDC), which links Mozambique and South Africa (Puplampu 2015). MDC created a platform for private sector participation in the mobility of goods and services through the corridor and presented a value-chain aspect for cashew nut and other economic activities in both Mozambique and South Africa and other countries within the SADC zone. The general point is that African agricultural policies and institutions, when political leaders and policy makers prioritize and invest in them, are capable of innovation and can innovate. This is because agricultural innovation and value-chain developments require considerable changes in the resource regime to perform at a sustainable level.

Conclusion and the Way Forward

This chapter examined the agricultural research and innovation landscape in Africa in a context of disruptive technology and value-chain agricultural development. The key question is the policy and institutional regime as well as resource conditions that would enable disruptive technology and value-chain agriculture to make the necessary impact and shore up the development of the region. There are several worthwhile initiatives on disruptive technology and value chain with enormous potential for the future of agriculture in Africa. These initiatives, in crops and livestock, have established the possibilities if the necessary and sufficient conditions are in place. It is increasingly clear that enacting policies and establishing institutions, as standalone entities, are not enough. Policies and institutions require a lot more to make a meaningful contribution to and benefit from disruptive technology and value-chain agriculture. This is particularly crucial given the challenges to effectively attain the vision of CAADP.

The study underscores several factors working together to bring about the necessary changes for successful outcomes in digital agriculture, the latest phase of African agriculture. These factors range from the sociopolitical context of technology, hard and soft issues of infrastructure in Africa, priorities for planning and investment to the structure of global relations and locale of Africa. Technology, as well we all know, is a not a disembodied entity and not neutral, and it must be situated in a social context. This context defines and, in turn, shapes the success or failure of any technology. Thus, on one hand, it is gratifying that many African countries have embraced agribusiness, value chain and the possibilities of disruptive technology to agricultural organization, with a specific objective on improving quality along the value chain. On the other hand, as Puplampu and Essegbey (2018: 61) argue,

> quality should be an integral part of the entire value chain, enlarging the range of beneficiaries to include smallholder farmers and a more strategic role of the state in forging innovation, particularly through public-private partnerships [is a useful reminder]. The policy dilemma … would be how to manage these challenges with prioritization and investment of available resources.

There are several missing links that should command the attention of political leaders and policy makers. While not new, the following are worth mentioning once again, if only to jolt the memory of political leaders, policy makers, private sector actors and regional and multilateral institutions within and beyond the African continent.

First, disruptive technology and the related trends about smart agriculture are not substitutes for capable policy and institutions, because IoT do not constitute the magic bullet for African agriculture. As forms of technology, they are only valuable in a given context. An important context here is both the hardware and the software, the former being the state of equipment, including physical infrastructure and the latter providing the social environment, specifically laws and other regulatory requirements. Although there is a verifiable mobile phone penetration in Africa, costs and reliability of network continue to be problems. Issues in the Internet ecology would have to be addressed in order to deepen the access of IoT-relevant actors in the agricultural sector.

Second, agricultural organizations, particularly those in production, must articulate what they want when it comes to democratic governance and other relevant aspects of farmers' experiences (IFAD 2018). Farmers, like any social group in a democratic society, need to raise and bring their level of organizational and political savvy to the contemporary age. They need to be able to extend their utilization of ICTs from agricultural production into the realm of competitive agricultural politics. They could use the various contemporary media platforms to engage with political leaders and policy makers. That requires farmers' organizations to be better organized, staking a claim that, for example, reminding political leaders they would have to eat, more so, eat what is grown at the local and national levels. As such, political leaders need to better focus on addressing the structural impediments in agricultural research and innovation. With the refrain that they feed citizens, agricultural leaders can bring sustained pressure on political leaders to address their needs.

Third, domestic sources of resources, including human and financial capital, must be mobilized for national development (ACBF 2015). The often-invoked mantra that African countries do not have enough and necessary resources for national and eventually continental development and for that matter must continue to depend on external sources of resources for development rings hollow and passé. While no society has ever developed without some type of assistance from external sources, no society also has developed solely by relying on internal sources. This is the reason for African countries to put their internal policy and institutional systems on sound footing so that they can better integrate external resources into a viable development agenda for the continent, assuming their policy objectives under the highly touted African Union Agenda 2063 do not become another mirage created by politicians lacking any, but surely in need of, transformative leadership qualities (ACBF 2019).

References

Addo, A. A. (2016). Explaining 'Irrationalities' of It-Enabled Change in a Developing Country Bureaucracy: The Case of Ghana's Tradenet. *Electronic Journal of Information Systems in Developing Countries, 77*(6), 1–22.

Africa Capacity Building Foundation (ACBF). (2015). *Africa Capacity Report 2015 – Capacity Imperatives for Domestic Resource Mobilization in Africa.* Harare: ACBF.

Africa Capacity Building Foundation (ACBF). (2017). *Africa Capacity Report 2017 – Building Capacity in Science, Technology and Innovation for Africa's Transformation.* Harare: ACBF.

Africa Capacity Building Foundation (ACBF). (2019). *Africa Capacity Report 2019 – Fostering Transformative Leadership for Africa's Development.* Harare: ACBF.

African Union (AU). (2018). *Inaugural Biennial Review Report of the African Union Commission on the Implementation of the Malabo Declaration on Accelerated Agricultural Growth and Transformation for Shared prosperity and*

Improved Livelihoods – The 2017 Report to the January 2018 Assembly. Addis Abba: African Union (Department of Rural Economy and Agriculture)

Alliance for a Green Revolution in Africa (AGRA). (2017). *Africa Agriculture Status Report: The Business of Smallholder Agriculture in Sub-Saharan Africa.* (Issue 5). Nairobi: Alliance for a Green Revolution in Africa (AGRA).

Alliance for a Green Revolution in Africa (AGRA). (2018). *Africa Agriculture Status Report: Catalyzing Government Capacity to Drive Agricultural Transformation.* (Issue 6). Nairobi: Alliance for a Green Revolution in Africa (AGRA).

Arounaa, A., Lokossoub, J. C., Wopereisc, M. C. S., Bruce-Oliverd, S., & Roy-Macauleyd, H. (2017). Contribution of Improved Rice Varieties to Poverty Reduction and Food Security in Sub-Saharan Africa. *Global Food Security, 14*, 54–60.

Asenso-Okyere, K., & Mekonnen, D. A. (2012). *The Importance of ICTs in the Provision of Information for Improving Agricultural Productivity and Rural Incomes in Africa.* African Human Development Report. UNDP Sponsored Research Series.

Asongu, S. A., & Nwachukwu, J. C. (2016). The Role of Governance in Mobile Phones for Inclusive Human Development in Sub-Saharan Africa. *Technovation, 55*, 1–13.

Ayele, S., Duncan, A., Larbi, A., & Khanh, T. T. (2012). Enhancing Innovation in Livestock Value Chains Through Networks: Lessons from Fodder Innovation Case Studies in Developing Countries. *Science and Public Policy, 39*(2012), 333–346. https://doi.org/10.1093/scipol/scs022.

Bah, E., & Gajigo, O. (2019). *Improving the Poultry Value Chain in Mozambique, Working Paper Series No 309.* African Development Bank, Abidjan, Côte d'Ivoire.

Barbier M., & Elzen, B. (Eds.). (2012). *System Innovations, Knowledge Regimes, and Design Practices Towards Transitions for Sustainable Agriculture.* Inra [online], posted online November 20, 2012. http://www4.inra.fr/sad_eng/Publications2/Free-ebooks/System-Innovations-for-Sustainable-Agriculture

Biggs, S. (1990). A Multiple Source of Innovation Model of Agricultural Research and Technology Promotion. *World Development, 18*(11), 1481–1490.

Cavatassi, R., González-Flores, M., Winters, P., Andrade-Piedra, J., Espinosa, P., & Thiele, G. (2011). Linking Smallholders to the New Agricultural Economy: The Case of the plataformas de concertación in Ecuador. *Journal of Development Studies, 47*(10), 1545–1573.

Christensen, C. (1997). *The Innovator's Dilemma: When New Technologies Cause Great Firms to Fall.* Boston: Harvard Business School Press.

Cooksey, B. (2011). Marketing Reform? The Rise and Fall of Agricultural Liberalisation in Tanzania. *Development Policy Review, 29*(Supplement), S57–S81.

Dalohoun, D. N., Hall, A., & Mele, P. V. (2009). Entrepreneurship as Driver of a 'Self-Organizing System of Innovation': The Case of NERICA in Benin. *International Journal of Technology Management and Sustainable Development*, *8*(2), 87–101.

de Janvry, A., & Sadoulet, E. (2019). *Agricultural Value Chain Development and Smallholder Competitiveness*. https://hal.archives-ouvertes.fr/hal-02069504

Devaux, A., Horton, D., Velasco, C., Thiele, G., López, G., Bernet, T., Reinoso, I., & Ordinola, M. (2009). Collective Action for Market Chain Innovation in the Andes. *Food Policy, 34*(1), 31–38.

Devaux, A., Torero, M., Donovan, J., & Horton, D. (2018). Agricultural Innovation and Inclusive Value-Chain Development: A Review. *Journal of Agribusiness in Developing and Emerging Economies, 8*(1), 99–123. https://doi.org/10.1108/JADEE-06-2017-0065.

Diagne, A., Gnonna, S.-K., Wopereis, M., & Akintayo, I. (2011). Increasing Rice Productivity and Strengthening Food Security Through New Rice for Africa (NERICA). In P. Chuhan-Pole & M. Angwafo (Eds.), *Yes Africa Can: Success Stories from a Dynamic Continent* (pp. 253–267). Washington, DC: World Bank.

Diakité, S., Cook, D., White, P., & Jaeger, P. (2019). Overview of the Rice Value Chain in Burkina Faso, Ghana, Mali, Nigeria, Ethiopia, Tanzania, and Uganda [Version 1; Not Peer Reviewed]. *Gates Open Research, 3*, 34. (document). https://doi.org/10.21955/gatesopenres.1114914.1.

Donovan, J., & Poole, N. (2014). Changing Asset Endowments and Smallholder Participation in Higher Value Markets: Evidence from Certified Coffee Producers in Nicaragua. *Food Policy, 44*, 1–13.

Essegbey, G. O. (2009). Ghana: Cassava, Cocoa, and Poultry. In K. Larsen, R. Kim, & F. Theus (Eds.), *Agribusiness and Innovation Systems in Africa*. Washington, DC: World Bank.

Evans, O. (2018a). Digital Agriculture: Mobile Phones, Internet & Agricultural Development in Africa. *Actual Problems of Economics, 7–8*, 205–206. https://mpra.ub.uni-muenchen.de/90359/. MPRA Paper No. 90359.

Evans, O. (2018b). Connecting the Poor: The Internet, Mobile Phones and Financial Inclusion in Africa. *Digital Policy, Regulation and Governance*. https://doi.org/10.1108/DPRG-04-2018-0018

Evans, O. (2018c). Repositioning for Increased Digital Dividends: Internet Usage and Economic Wellbeing in Sub-Saharan Africa. *Journal of Global Information Technology Management, 22*(1), 47–70.

Evans, O. (2019). Digital Politics: Internet and Democracy in Africa. *Journal of Economic Studies, 46*(1), 169–191.

Firetail. (2013). *East Africa Diary Development Project Evaluation – Final Report*. http://www.firetail.co.uk

Food and Agricultural Organization (FAO). (2017a). *The Future of Food and Agriculture – Trends and Challenges*. Rome: FAO.

Food and Agricultural Organization (FAO). (2017b). *Sustainable Production Intensification and Value Chain Development in Africa*. Accra: FAO Regional Office for Africa.

Forum for Agricultural Research in Africa (FARA). (2015). *Seeding Science for the Transformation of African Agriculture*. Accra: FARA Annual Report.

Fu, X., Zanello, G., Essegbey, G. O., Hou, J., & Mohnen, P. (2014). *Innovation in Low Income Countries: A Survey Report, Technology and Management Centre for Development (TMCD)*. Oxford: University of Oxford.

Gereffi, G. (2014). Global Value Chains in a Post-Washington Consensus World. *Review of International Political Economy, 21*(1), 9–37. https://doi.org/10.1 080/09692290.2012.756414.

Greenville, J., Kawasaki, K., & Jouanjean, M. (2019). *Value Adding Pathways in Agriculture and Food Trade: The Role of GVCs and Services* (OECD Food, Agriculture and Fisheries Papers, No. 123). Paris: OECD Publishing. https://doi.org/10.1787/bb8bb93d-en.

Große-Rüschkamp, A., & Seelige, K. (2010). *Analysis of the Cashew Value Chain in Mozambique*. Accra: Africa Cashew Initiative by Deutsche Gesellschaft für.

Hanlon, J. (2000). Power Without Responsibility: The World Bank and Mozambican Cashew Nuts. *Review of African Political Economy, 27*(83), 29–45.

Hanlon, J. (2001). Mozambique Wins Long Battle Over Cashew Nuts and Sugar. *Review of African Political Economy, 83*, 29–45.

Hanson, K., & Puplampu, K. P. (2018). The Internet of Things and Sharing Economy: Harnessing the Possibilities for Africa's Sustainable Development Goals. In K. Hanson, K. P. Puplampu, & T. M. Shaw (Eds.), *From Millennium Development Goals to Sustainable Development Goals: Rethinking African Development* (pp. 133–151). Abingdon/New York: Routledge.

Hazell, P. (2009, November). *The Asian Green Revolution*. IFPRI Discussion Paper 00911.

Hellin, J., & Meijer, M. (2006). *Guidelines for Value Chain Analysis*. Rome: Food and Agriculture Organization of the United Nations (FAO).

International Fund for Agricultural Development (IFAD). (2018). *Farmers' Organizations in Africa*. Rome: International Fund for Agricultural Development.

ITU (International Telecommunication Union) and Cisco. (2016). *Harnessing the Internet of Things for Global Development*. Geneva: ITU. www.itu.int/en/action/broadband/Documents/Harnessing-IoT-Global Development.pdf.

Kibwika, P., Kyazze, F. B., & Musoke, M. N. (2009). Uganda: Fish, Bananas, and Vegetables. In K. Larsen, R. Kim, & F. Theus (Eds.), *Agribusiness and Innovation Systems in Africa*. Washington, DC: World Bank.

Kilelu, C., Klerkx, L., & Leeuwis, C. (2013). Unraveling the Role of Innovation Platforms in Supporting Co-evolution of Innovation: Contributions and

Tensions in a Smallholder Dairy Development Programme. *Agricultural Systems, 118*, 65–77.

Kim, R., Larsen, K., & Theus, F. (2009). Introduction and Main Messages. In K. Larsen, R. Kim, & F. Theus (Eds.), *Agribusiness and Innovation Systems in Africa*. Washington, DC: World Bank.

King, A. (2017). The Future of Agriculture. *Nature, 544*, S21–S23.

Lalitha, A., Babu, S., & Purnima, K. S. (2018). Internet of Things: Applications to Developing Countries Agriculture Sector. *International Journal of Agriculture Sciences, 10*(20), 7410–7413.

Larsen, K., Kim, R., & Theus, F. (Eds.). (2009). *Agribusiness and Innovation Systems in Africa*. Washington, DC: World Bank.

Lele, U. (2004). *The CGIAR at 31: An Independent Meta-Evaluation of the Consultative Group on International Agricultural Research*. Washington, DC: World Bank.

Lynam, J., & Theus, F. (2009). Value Chains, Innovation, and Public Policies in African Agriculture: A Synthesis of Four Country Studies. In K. Larsen, R. Kim, & F. Theus (Eds.), *Agribusiness and Innovation Systems in Africa*. Washington, DC: World Bank.

Malabo Montpellier Panel. (2018, June). *Mechanized: Transforming Africa's Agriculture Value Chains*. Dakar.

Moseley, W. G. (2015). Regional Value Chains and Productivity Enhancement. In K. T. Hanson (Ed.), *Contemporary Regional Development in Africa* (pp. 181–200). Surrey: Ashgate Publishing.

Mpagalile, J., Ishengoma, R., & Gillah, P. (2009). Tanzania: Sunflower, Cassava, and Diary. In K. Larsen, R. Kim, & F. Theus (Eds.), *Agribusiness and Innovation Systems in Africa*. Washington, DC: World Bank.

Ndubuaku, M., & Okereafor, D. T. (2015, November 4–7). *Internet of Things for Africa: Challenges and Opportunities*. 2015 International Conference on Cyberspace Governance, Abuja.

Ndung'u, N. (2018). New Frontiers in Africa's Digital Potential. In *Harnessing Africa's Digital Potential: New Tools for a New Age – Foresight Africa Report*. Washington, DC: Africa Growth Initiative at Brookings.

New Partnership for Africa Development (NEPAD). (2003). *Comprehensive Africa Agriculture Development Programme*. Midrand: New Partnership for Africa Development.

Nyasimi, M., Amwata, D., Hove, L., Kinyangi, J., & Wamukoya, G. (2014). *Evidence of Impact: Climate-Smart Agriculture in Africa* (CCAFS Working Paper no. 86). Copenhagen, Denmark: CGIAR Research Program on Climate Change, Agriculture and Food Security (CCAFS).

Odame, H., Musyoka, P., & Kere, J. (2009). Kenya: Maize, Tomato, and Diary. In K. Larsen, R. Kim, & F. Theus (Eds.), *Agribusiness and Innovation Systems in Africa*. Washington, DC: World Bank.

Omondi, I., Rao, E. J. O., Karimov, A. A., & Baltenweck, I. (2017). Processor Linkages and Farm Household Productivity: Evidence from Diary Hubs in East Africa. *Agribusiness, 33*(4), 586–599.

Owusu, A. B., Yankson, P. W. K., & Frimpong, S. (2017). Smallholder Farmers' Knowledge of Mobile Telephone Use: Gender Perspectives and Implications for Agricultural Market Development. *Progress in Development Studies, 18*(1), 36–51. https://doi.org/10.1177/1464993417735389.

Patel, R. (2013). The Long Green Revolution. *The Journal of Peasant Studies, 40*(1), 1–63. https://doi.org/10.1080/03066150.2012.719224.

Phillips, T. (2008). Genetically Modified Organisms (GMOs): Transgenic Crops and Recombinant DNA Technology. *Nature Education, 1*(1), 213.

Puplampu, K. P. (2014). The Shifting Boundaries of the African State in Agricultural Institutions and Policies in an Era of Globalization. In E. Shizha & A. A. Abdi (Eds.), *Indigenous Discourses on Knowledge and Development in Africa*. New York: Routledge.

Puplampu, K. P. (2015). Regionalism, Globalization and Economic Integration in Africa. In K. T. Hanson (Ed.), *Contemporary Regional Development in Africa* (pp. 27–45). Surrey: Ashgate Publishing.

Puplampu, K. P., & Essegbey, G. O. (2018). From MDGs to SDGs: The Policy and Institutional Dynamics of African Agriculture. In K. Hanson, K. P. Puplampu, & T. M. Shaw (Eds.), *From Millennium Development Goals to Sustainable Development Goals: Rethinking African Development* (pp. 53–73). Abingdon/New York: Routledge.

Reardon, T., Echeverria, R., Berdegué, J., Minten, B., Liverpool-Tasie, S., Tschirley, D., & Zilberman, D. (2019). Rapid Transformation of Food Systems in Developing Nations: Highlighting the role of Agricultural Research and Innovations. *Agricultural Systems, 172*, 47–59.

Schaffnit-Chatterjee, C. (2014). *Agricultural Value Chains in Sub-Saharan Africa: From a Development Challenge to a Business Opportunity*. Frankfurt: Deutsche Bank Research.

Stür, W., Tan Khanh, T., & Duncan, A. (2013). Transformation of Smallholder Beef Cattle Production in Vietnam. *International Journal of Agricultural Sustainability, 11*(4), 363–381.

Swaans, K., Cullen, B., van Rooyen, A., Adekunle, A., Ngwenya, H., Lema, Z., & Nederlof, S. (2013). Dealing with Critical Challenges in African Innovation Platforms: Lessons for Facilitation. *Knowledge Management for Development Journal, 9*(3), 116–135.

Swaans, K., Boogaard, B., Bendapudi, R., Taye, H., Hendrickx, S., & Klerkx, L. (2014). Operationalizing Inclusive Innovation: Lessons Form Innovation Platforms in Livestock Value Chains in India and Mozambique. *Innovation and Development,   4*(2),   239–257.   https://doi.org/10.1080/21579 30X.2014.925246.

Sylvester, G. (2015). *Success Stories on Information and Communication Technologies for Agriculture and Rural Development*. Bangkok: FAO Regional Office for Asia and the Pacific (RAP Publication 2015/02).

Takeda, S., & Matsuoka, M. (2008). Genetic Approaches to Crop Improvement: Responding to Environmental and Population Changes. *Nature Reviews Genetics, 9*, 444–457. https://doi.org/10.1038/nrg2342.

Thiele, G., Devaux, A., Reinoso, H., Pico, H., Montesdeoca, F., Pumisacho, M., Andrade-Piedra, J., Velasco, C., Flores, P., Esprella, R., Thomann, A., Manrique, K., & Horton, D. (2011). Multi-Stakeholder Platforms for Linking Small Farmers to Value Chains: Evidence from the Andes. *International Journal of Agricultural Sustainability, 9*(3), 423–433.

Toenniesse, G., Adesina, A., & Devries, J. (2008). Building an Alliance for a Green Revolution in Africa. *Annals of the New York Academy of Sciences, 1136*, 233–242.

Tomich, T. P., Lidder, P., Coley, M., Gollin, D., Meinzen-Dick, R., Webb, P., & Carberry, P. (2019). Food and Agricultural Innovation Pathways for Prosperity. *Agricultural Systems, 172*, 1–15.

Trendov, N. M., Varas, S., & Zeng, M. (2019). *Digital Technologies in Agriculture and Rural Areas – Status Report*. Rome. Licence: cc by-nc-sa 3.0 igo.

United Nations Development Program. (2003). *Human Development Report 2003 Millennium Development Goals: A Compact Among Nations to End Human Poverty*. New York: Oxford University Press for United Nations Development Program.

United Nations Development Program (UNDP). (2015). *Sustainable Development Goals*. New York: United Nations Development Program.

Webber, C. M., & Labaste, P. (2010). *Building Competitiveness in Africa's Agriculture: A Guide to Value Chain Concepts and Applications*. Washington, DC: The World Bank.

World Bank. (2012). *Agricultural Innovation Systems: An Investment Sourcebook*. Washington, DC: World Bank.

World Bank. (2013). *Growing Africa: Unlocking the Potential of Agribusiness*. Washington, DC: World Bank.

World Bank. (2019a). *Mainstreaming the Approach to Disruptive and Transformative Technologies at the World Bank Group*. Washington, DC: The World Bank.

World Bank. (2019b). *The Basics of Food Traceability*. Washington, DC: The World Bank.

Yonazi, E., Kelly, T., Halewood, N., & Blackman, C. (Eds.). (2012). *Transformational Use of Information and Communication Technologies in Africa*. Washington, DC: AfDB Temporary Relocation Agency (Tunis): The World Bank and the African Development Bank, with the support of the African Union.

CHAPTER 4

Scientific Innovations and the Environment: Integrated Smart Sensors, Pollution and E-waste in Africa

Samuel M. Mugo and Korbla P. Puplampu

INTRODUCTION

The twin issues of population growth and consumption patterns pose significant problems for the natural environment, specifically the sustainability and stewardship of resources. Underlying the problems are the steady increases in standards of living around the world, even as socioeconomic disparities remain within and among nations in both the global North and global South. The growing urbanization and the increase of the middle-class population in the global South have spurred massive demand for

S. M. Mugo (✉)
Department of Physical Sciences, Grant MacEwan University,
Edmonton, AB, Canada
e-mail: mugos@macewan.ca

K. P. Puplampu
Department of Sociology, Grant MacEwan University,
Edmonton, AB, Canada
e-mail: puplampuk@macewan.ca

© The Author(s) 2020
P. Arthur et al. (eds.), *Disruptive Technologies, Innovation and Development in Africa*, International Political Economy Series,
https://doi.org/10.1007/978-3-030-40647-9_4

food, water and other consumer products. The result is a solid and wastewater management headache, especially in jurisdictions where the infrastructure is poorly designed, and not subject to adequate and frequent maintenance.

Therefore, the lack of awareness on sustainability and stewardship has choked the environment. Some unsustainable economic activities that depress the environment and its inhabitants include deforestation, e-waste and occupation of water catchment and riparian lands. It is anticipated that a 70% growth in global food production is required to feed the growing population, expected to hit 9.8 billion by 2050 (UNFAO 2018). Agriculture currently accounts for 70% of freshwater use, and as such the demand for an already rare commodity like water will become intensified to precarious and risky levels (World Bank Group 2019; UNFAO 2018). Currently, majority of the countries in the world are classified as high water-stressed regions. Given that resource utilization and reuse problems, including e-waste, take on a global dimension, it is useful to address these problems from a global perspective.

The United Nations Sustainable Development Goals (2015–2030) have direct and indirect goals on environmental sustainability and stewardship (UNDP 2015). Global 'land degradation-neutral world' will be the cornerstone to achieving the SDGs. Specifically, SDG 1 is on poverty, SDG 2 is directed at hunger, SDG 3 seeks to attain good health and well-being, SDG 4 is about education, SDG 5 seeks to address gender equality, SDG 8 calls for measures to address clean water and sanitation, SDG 6 clean water and sanitation, SDG 11 sustainable cities and communities, SDG 12 responsible production and consumption, SDG 14 life below water, and SDG 17 calls for global partnerships in development (UNDP 2015). The 17 SDGs are interdependent and inseparably linked and converge on the quality of life and a healthy environment. Attaining the SDGs requires concerted collaborative global efforts, with a focus on protecting the world and its ecosystems for equitable sustenance of all, now and into the future. Progress on SDGs demands a mindset and behavioral change, cross-sector policy formulations and engagement of trusted actors (e.g. local universities, industries and principally the government). The key to making the SDGs successful is the need for adequate tools that measure and quantitatively monitor the indicators to the goals, track and visualize progress.

This chapter, with a focus on Africa, examines the extent to which smart sensors interlinked with cellular phones can provide a global platform for information gathering and sharing the required data to monitor and address problems in the environment, natural resource utilization and e-waste. It is proposed here that one fundamental requirement in understanding the scope and finding the solution to the problem is the availability of tools needed to adequately measure, diagnose and quantify the extent of the problem. We argue, therefore, the development and deployment of smart sensors would be the key disruptive technology that can go a long way to addressing the global environmental burdens and ensuring its effective management. In the first section, we outline the case for smart sensors as disruptive technologies in environmental and natural resource discussions. The second section presents the selected and relevant information on the nature of environmental pollution as well as e-waste. The third section analyzes the relevance of sensors in discussions on pollution and e-waste. The last section presents the way forward, specifically the nature of collaboration, with the help of universities as innovation drivers, to better deal with environmental sustainability and concluding remarks.

Smart Sensors as Disruptive Technologies: A Theoretical Framework

Smart sensors, as part of the broader framework of disruptive technology, can provide some answers to unsustainable resource utilization activities. Specifically, sensors are miniaturized platforms that by design respond to molecular entities in diverse sample specimens in a measurable way. Sensors can be activated on cellular phones, for example, to make the platforms become smart, hence the idea of smart sensors. The connectivity of the sensors to cellular phones and their capacity for wireless connectivity make them sometimes to be referred synonymously as Internet of Things (IoT) (Zhang and Mugo 2019; Dhanjai et al. 2019). Sensors, in the context of disruptive technology, have become significant because of the dramatic improvements in communication and information technologies. According to Mayer and Baeumner (2019), technologies from smartphones to sensors and wearable gadgets make it possible for disruptive changes to occur in various social systems. Chemical analysis technologies developed in the last century are bulky and expensive and require the appropriate laboratory infrastructure and highly trained specialists to operate. In addition, specimens must be brought to the lab for analysis, further demanding adequate infrastructure and access. As such, these instrumentations have been a preserve for well-resourced countries in the global North without any relevance to countries in the global South.

However, with the development of nanotechnology and miniaturized computational platforms, miniaturized sensors can be deployed in the field, at the point of use, precluding the need for established infrastructure. Indeed, some of these sensors can be worn, hence their christening as 'wearable sensors'. The use of wearable sensors for real-time monitoring of chemical entities that index performance and wellness and for medical diagnostics in humans is an especially rapidly growing field. Newer wearable sensors can be placed on livestock and plants to monitor their microcosmic and physiological environments. Some sensors have also been developed to monitor environmental contaminants (Halachmi et al. 2019; Giraldo et al. 2019).

Wireless network technologies create unique possibilities for hyphenating decentralized sensors wirelessly (through various technologies) to cellphone interfaces, embedded with big data analytic algorithms. These networked sensors open tremendous opportunities for decentralized data generation, structured and unstructured data visualization, and transcription of data to information that can be utilized to inform the status of the problem, monitor the effectiveness of mitigation strategies, and inform the decision making by, for example, farmers and the general public. These platforms are lately called 'uber' sensors, for artificial intelligence, or more synonymously called the Internet of Things (IoT) or Internet of Everything (IoE) (Shi et al. 2019b; Yang et al. 2018; Thompson 2016). These devices are drivers in the digital era, the essential features of disruptive technology, which is influencing the massive change in the world while extending the limits of what is technically possible.

When properly harnessed, sensors are tools for social disruption in that they afford an unlimited amount of democratized knowledge to the fingertips of individuals. The result is that technologically advanced platforms have disruptively informed and highlighted the intersectionality of things, people and societies, affording new ways of interaction and communication with each other, and the world, and blurring previous geographical boundaries. These platforms afford the decentralization of innovation and spur the sharing economy, sharing resources including cars, data storage, internet, solar energy and most importantly knowledge. Further, sensors and IoT have made possible the concept of decentralizing innovation, where the public can be involved in the development, data generation and application of smart sensors in their areas of interest. However, like any technological change, risks and uncertainties cannot be ruled out. The optimist's argument is that if properly contextualized, a highly interconnected world and the IoT can offer more rewards that off-set and minimize the risks and uncertainties (Gharakheili et al. 2019; Servida and Casey 2019). Smart sensors can contribute to socially and environmentally conscientious, sustainable technology industries and pre-cipitate a fundamental paradigm shift in human and economic activities.

Pollution and E-waste in Africa: Selected Cases

The deployment of smart sensors for environmental management is one of the best ways to collect the useful data to measure the extent of the problem, which will inform and evaluate the effectiveness of mitigation strategies. The use of smart sensors for environmental monitoring remains a nascent but rapidly developing area. In general, African countries lag in the adoption of smart sensor technologies in environmental management. A vicious cycle, the lack of focus on development and adoption of tools to measure the environmental pollution, underlines the environmental degradation. A case in point is a river in Nairobi, which after years of neglect has been transformed into a toxic soup, heavily contaminated from agricultural and industrial activities to urban settlement (Njuguna et al. 2017). Toxic rivers are common in many other African capital cities and towns.

It can be argued, the African continent has been late in learning from past failures in the global North when environmental management was neglected, and industries ballooned and caused ecosystem damage such as the spectacle of Cuyahoga River in Cleveland, USA, that caught fire in the 1930s (Stradling and Stradling 2008). Another example was the untargeted poisoning of birds due to endocrine-disrupting chemicals such as the PCBs in the 1950s (Danse et al. 1997). These historical disasters necessitated countries such as the USA, Canada and others in the global North to create robust environmental protection agencies, armed with strong legislative and executive authority to regulate chemical use and waste disposal. They invested in resources to equip agencies with analytical instrumentations and scientists to serve as regulatory watchdogs on environment and food quality, on behalf of the public.

One environmental platform required in Africa from an adoption and innovation standpoint is smart tools enabled to monitor and manage the nexus between natural resources and the human environment. This is because of extensive anthropogenic activities, among them fossil and biomass fuel burning and the emission of carbon dioxide. Emerging technologies can capture carbon and store it to prevent carbon dioxide from entering the atmosphere. Hitherto, carbon capture and storage technologies have mainly been used in the global North, but China, in the context of the global South, has become a formidable player in technology innovation with an ambitious goal of a net zero carbon emission by 2050 (Chen et al. 2019).

Miniaturized versions of smart technology could also be used as components in catalytic convertors in cars and other carbon emission sites. Natural sinks of carbon dioxide are lakes and plants, with the latter being ideal, as plants symbiotically utilize carbon dioxide in their photosynthetic reaction to produce food. As such, plants can be effective in regulating carbon dioxide. Hence the need for more government efforts in ensuring land coverage with trees and forests. However, anthropogenic production of carbon dioxide is very high, and with decreasing plant coverage due to desertification, global warming is the outcome. Sensors have been developed and utilized for remote sensing to monitor efficiency of carbon capture technologies and, in general, to monitor levels of carbon dioxide in the environment. Most of the deployed sensors use hyperspectral transduction, measuring carbon dioxide by infrared absorption. There are, however, other emerging carbon dioxide sensors based on electrochemical detection, which are more sensitive (Santonico et al. 2017).

Beyond carbon dioxide, there are plethora of other environmental air pollutants such as ammonia, hydrogen sulfide, particulate matter (aerosols) and other volatile organic matter from various industrial and agricultural activities. In general, these air pollutants can be detected using different transduction systems as each of the chemical species has different spectral and electrochemical signatures. As such, they can be distinguished from each other. The molecular spectral signature is related to the unique character of how different features of light are absorbed, transmitted and scattered when they encounter a chemical species, and each electrochemical signature is based on molecular effects to electric field as a stimulus. There are rapidly growing trends in the development of electrochemical sensors due to their sensitivity, cost-effectiveness and versatility for hyphenation to cellular phones.

Electrochemical sensors are in general more amenable to miniaturization and can be fashioned into wearables and integrated for example on clothing and hats. The idea of developing sensors that demand minimal use of energy to even self-power further makes electrochemical-based platforms desirable. To ensure wearability, there is a growing trend toward fabrication of sensors using flexible materials rather than the use of silicon-based microchips, which have been associated with the electronic waste (e-waste) problem (Akram et al. 2019; Dhanjai et al. 2019). Flexible sensors can be fabricated on fabrics and different consumer-based plastics often used in textiles, a sustainable and an economical approach, favorable for resource-limited countries.

However, a bottleneck in chemical analysis is not only the availability of an appropriate sensor but also sampling, where composition of the sample (e.g. water or air) would geographically differ. The potential to engage the public in sampling using their cellphones, with integrated smart sensors, is an effective approach to empower the end user with the data related to pollution exposure. But it is also a useful approach to gather representative data using minimal costs, which can be used by regulators for policy formulation, regulation and in general environmental management. Maximilian et al. (2019) demonstrated the use of these air quality sensors with cyclists or even on cars as an approach to monitor exposure of urban dwellers on pollutants. This approach effectively utilizes the large number of vehicles that routinely navigate city streets with on-board sensors, transforming them into a dynamic network that monitors the urban environment. The result is a complete data set that show the spatiotemporal variations, thus giving a comprehensive picture of the status of the environment. In Africa, this technique could provide useful data to evaluate exposure in epidemiology and risk studies. For example, urban cities in Africa are flooded with cyclists and motorcyclists, often called 'boda bodas' in Kenya and 'okadas' in Ghana. Such vehicles could be integrated with GPS smart sensors for air quality monitoring, effectively mapping air pollution status. Sensors integrated on robotics and unmanned aerial vehicles (UAVs) such as drones will be another growth area where automation will be used in precise tasks and monitoring in unstructured remote environments (Bacco et al. 2018).

Another significant example of smart sensor application is in the use of waste management, a major air and water pollution contributor in African urban cities. The limitation and inefficient use of resources is a key problem in, for example, garbage collection. To optimize waste collection at minimal cost, a garbage container integrated sensor for measuring maximum limit of waste in the container, temperature and ratio of carbon dioxide inside the container, and the evolution of other hazardous gases such as sulfur dioxide and nitrogen oxides has been demonstrated in Kayseri, Turkey (Misra et al. 2018). Using what is referred to as 'ant colony algorithm' and predictive analytics, the data collected from the sensors are relayed to municipality web servers, and the most efficient waste collection route to collect filling garbage containers is delivered to garbage truck drivers' cellular-enabled smart tablet. This smart waste management system which decreased the fuel cost, carbon emissions, traffic, truck wear, noise pollution and work hours constitutes a classic example of using smart sensors to understand spatiotemporal analysis of garbage produced in certain communities and the types of gases produced to inform community-targeted policy-making (Misra et al. 2018).

Furthermore, smart sensors are valuable in water pollution management. In developing countries, 80% of people are without access to portable water (UNDP 2015). In Africa, 75% of the drinking water comes from underground sources, which makes water monitoring an issue of key concern, as water monitoring can be used to track water quality changes over time, identify existing or emerging problems, and design effective intervention programs to remedy water pollution (WHO 2006). A case in point is the recent water shortage problem in Cape Town, though in general most of the major cities in Africa such as Lagos and Nairobi bear much worse water shortages (Rodina 2019).

The future of the water availability for Africa and across the world is bleak, especially in context of increasing urbanization. Cities such as Nairobi and Accra continue to experience rapid population growth (Tajuri and Naim 2018). With fixed sewage infrastructure and water in short supply, poor design and management of the growth of cities, African cities struggle intensely with wastewater and solid waste management. As such, waterborne diseases remain a significant problem in most of these cities, as well as the rural communities who rely on rivers that orbit through these cities, flowing with it the pathogens and toxins from waste effluents. The plethora of chemical entities can be daunting, from heavy metals to various organic contaminants such as pesticides, herbicides, pharmaceuticals, cosmetic additives, microplastics and carcinogens such as polycyclic aromatic hydrocarbons (PAHs) and polychlorinated biphenyls (PCBs) (Agudelo-Castaneda et al. 2017).

Across the world, in academic labs and even industries, there are numerous effective membrane technologies based on renewable nanotechnology materials such as cellulose, activated carbon and variants of hybrid carbon-based photocatalyst particles. These membranes have the capacity for water reuse and recycling, effectively conserving fresh water (Shi et al. 2019a). While some of the technologies may be deemed expensive, the true cost from loss of productivity and cost related to treatment of diseases are much higher. As such, it can be argued that the technologies for waste-water purification are available and what is needed is investment in these technologies, especially in adapting the technologies with the use of local materials to make the functional nanomaterials (Madivoli et al. 2016). The effectiveness of water purification technologies go hand in hand with smart sensor platforms for assessment. Smart sensor platforms are needed to cope with the daunting task, where hitherto specialized, expensive, laboratory localized separation analytical techniques have been used. With the growth of targeted chemistry, often bioinspired from the behavior of enzymes and antibodies, which are in themselves often used to make sensors, it is possible to develop synthetic intelligent molecular platforms that are responsive to capture chemical entities of interest. There are smart sensor platforms that provide the Affordable, Sensitive, Specific, User-friendly, Rapid and robust, Equipment-free and Deliverable to end-users (ASSURED) with, guidelines focused on low-resource settings for detection of these chemical and pathogen contaminants, impacting global public health, and have implications for the management of e-waste (Dhanjai et al. 2019; Mugo et al. 2019).

The Case of Electronic Waste (E-waste)

The short lifespan of the numerous electronic devices in our explosive digital era and electronics industry poses a headache in dealing with the massive and complex waste composition of devices. The devices range from laptops, hard disk drive, mobile phones, computers, stereos, televisions, lights, lithium-ion battery packs, kitchen appliances, to photovoltaic panels (World Economic Forum 2019). E-waste is now the fastest-growing waste stream in the world, with an estimated waste stream of 48.5 million tonnes in 2018 (Liu et al. 2019). Comprising organic, organometallic and inorganic chemical entities, disposal and recycling strategies are growing global problems (Andrade et al. 2019).

In the global North, environmental policies have evolved with the growth of these devices and their disposal question. As such, recycling strategies have been adopted that have worked with reasonable levels of success and ongoing improvements (Dias et al. 2019). However, the problem is far from being solved. According to the World Economic Forum (2019), only about 20% of global e-waste is formally recycled, and the remaining 80% is often incinerated or dumped in landfills. In the USA, the recycling rate is reported to be ~25%, with much of the e-waste being shipped offshore. Meanwhile, countries in the global South seem to be in the infant stage in terms of developing legislative policies and recycling strategies, and e-waste ends up in storage, landfills and dumpsters, contributing to environmental air and water pollution (Burns et al. 2019; Odeyingbo et al. 2019; Ohajinwa et al. 2019).

Some of the toxic substances from e-waste include lead, mercury, cadmium, chromium and organic compounds such as flame retardants. Flame retardants such as polybrominated diphenyl ethers (PBDEs), polychlorinated dibenzo-p-dioxin and dibenzofurans (PCDD/Fs) and polychlorinated biphenyls (PCBs) are known endocrine-disrupting chemicals and persistent organic pollutants, meaning they do not degrade easily in the environment and bioaccumulate posing even more danger. In a policy vacuum, haphazard recycling in the informal sector constitutes danger to workers when it comes to the handling of hazardous waste with minimal personal protective clothing and equipment (Burns et al. 2019; Odeyingbo et al. 2019; Ohajinwa et al. 2019). Most of these toxicants are known probable carcinogens. Ironically, electronic waste contains deposits of elements such as cobalt, lead, lithium, manganese, nickel, zinc and chromium and precious rare earth elements such as gold and platinum. Recycling of these valuable metals could yield significant economic benefits. The generalized material composition in e-waste comprises approximately 60% metals, 15% plastics, 5% metal-plastic mixture, 2% halogenated flame retardants (Golev et al. 2019; Kitila and Woldemikael 2019; Prata et al. 2019).

In addition to the policy vacuum, there are technical challenges related to isolation due to the complexity of the composition, which have hindered the recycling. However, in the global North, capital-intensive integrated smelters (both pyrometallurgical and hydrometallurgical techniques) are employed in formal industries. Often the viability of these industries is from the support of government policy and incentives. The key priority in the global South is the establishment of e-waste management strategy and legislative framework support for establishing effective facilities for collection, sorting and recycling and the enhancement of pollution control priorities. There is potential in engaging local universities and industries in developing cost-effective and environmentally friendly hydrometallurgical and pyrometallurgical recycling processes, thus formalizing the recycling industry (Yu et al. 2019; Pietrelli et al. 2019; Yong et al. 2019). In addition, the manufacturing of these devices needs to integrate an end-of-life design, rather than the reductive designing approach that is short-term thinking. The isolation of reuse of these valuable metals would afford a closed-loop circular economy, a sustainable approach where rare metals are not mined from the earth, operations that are highly ecosystem disturbing, and where environment is saved from e-waste pollution (Cordova-Pizarro et al. 2019; Isernia et al. 2019).

Embracing the Potential of Smart Sensors and the Need for Collaboration

While the progress of integrating innovative technologies into environmental and agricultural operations is slow, there are commendable initiatives, with African universities demonstrating the role of smart sensors in environmental issues (Amegah 2018). The Meru University of Science and Technology in Meru, Kenya, is developing a foundational project on the use of Raspberry Pi-based moisture sensors for automating irrigation system. They are also attempting to develop an electronic device for real-time monitoring of crop diseases and pests. While the university funding model of such projects may need to be refined to account for the years of trials that are needed before commercialization, some progress is being made (Memeu et al. 2018). Another initiative on the deployment of sensors is by the organization Pan-African Citizen Network Initiative, Code for Africa, dubbed 'sensors.AFRICA project', which uses sensors to collect data on air pollutants such as carbon monoxide, nitrous oxides and particulate matter all linked to acid rain that chronically destroys ecosystems and more acutely cause respiratory illness. According to a 2014 report by the World Health Organization (WHO), premature deaths caused by air pollution every year were a staggering ~ 7 million worldwide and, in many cities in Africa, there is insignificant or no information about air quality (Amegah and Agyei-Mensah 2017; Amegah 2018; Brauer et al. 2012; Naiker et al. 2012).

The sensors.AFRICA project uses digital technology to quantitatively map pollutants, which journalists, citizens and civic watchdogs can then use to advocate for regulatory, preventative and mitigation policies and a better quality of life for citizens (Amegah 2018). This organization has done work deploying air pollution monitoring sensors in Nigeria, Kenya, Tanzania, Uganda and South Africa. Their efforts could be enhanced by the deployment and development of more frugal smart sensors that can be availed by the public for the assessment of the health of their environment. While these smart sensors are in various stages of development, African countries can work with entities like Code for Africa and academics to develop and bring these platforms to bear on environmental stewardship activities, create value and increase productivity in industrial activities such as agriculture and environmental conservation, particularly wildlife monitoring.

Africa is a highly water-stressed continent with most of the land mass falling under arid and semiarid region category (Lickley and Solomon 2018). Investment in technologies for blackish water purification which is otherwise left to flow untreated into rivers and reusing this water conservatively for agriculture is a prudent approach. Also, investment in technologies for desalination of sea water would be a bold approach in reclamation efforts. Unfortunately, most of these technologies are in general more expensive using conventional nanotechnology materials. Through research collaborations within and across developing and developed countries, research on nanomaterials from local biomasses could be a multipronged beneficial approach for adding value to local biomasses, while solving water pollution problems (Madivoli et al. 2016). There are numerous examples of government investment in irrigation schemes that have general low rates of success, partly due to water management issues, among other financial management problems. Examples are irrigation schemes such as Galana Kulalu irrigation scheme in Kenya, which have not met the expectations vis-à-vis the cost of investment. As such, smart technologies for water resource management, conservation and reuse, would help in mitigating the problem. A simple sensor such as soil humidity sensors can precisely monitor crop needs, thus providing plants 'a drink on demand' (Gonzalez-Teruel et al. 2019; Jesus et al. 2013; Khan et al. 2018).

Humidity and leaf wetness sensors, temperature, solar ultraviolet radiation and carbon dioxide sensor probes are useful for effective management of irrigation system for smart and autonomous wireless decision support system (Viani et al. 2017). In addition, the data generated, especially temperature and carbon dioxide, could be very meaningful data over time to monitor climate change. This is especially useful with the heightened issue reported by the Intergovernmental Panel on Climate Change (IPCC) in 2018 of expected 1.5 °C global temperature rise, if the increase in greenhouse gas emissions is not reversed (Hornero et al. 2017; Hamrita and

Hoffacker 2005). Convergent in various fields, molecular entities and sensors can also be applied in monitoring food quality for managing not only crop growth, but also quality control of foods along supply and value chain to the consumers, some across the globe far from the first place of crop production (Chung et al. 2017; Ghasemi-Varnamkhasti et al. 2018; Giraldo et al. 2019).

These sensors could also be very useful in guaranteeing food and beverages quality from adulterations and integrated in the so-called intelligent packaging technologies (Mugo et al. 2019; Yousefi et al. 2019). They have been used, for example, to monitor food spoilage, detecting volatile gases such as ammonia and carbon dioxide, greenhouse gases that contribute to global warming. As such, prevention of global food waste would go a long way to mitigate the effects of greenhouse gases. In addition, these sensors have been used to detect pathogens such as *E. coli*, which causes cholera, which according to the World Health Organization (WHO) is estimated to cause almost two million deaths per year, more than 90% of which occur in the global South (Bergstrom and Dong 2015; Zachary 2015). Innovation is key to the ability of African countries to address environmental challenges and create stability and ensure growth in the coming decade.

Innovation, specifically the widespread use of digital instruments, will be the creative force and the catalyst that will drive the economic growth. From South Africa to Kenya, Tanzania and beyond, cellphones and the mobile money technology have transformed socioeconomic relations and activities. With the explosive growth of smartphones in Africa, expected to reach 700 million across the continent in the next few years, Africa is ripe for a digital revolution. As of 2015, more than 222 million mobile money accounts were registered across Africa. African countries account for more than half of all mobile money services worldwide (Asamoah et al. 2019; Batchelor 2012). These platforms have significantly influenced productivity and public services provision and provided inclusiveness even of the poor to the formal banking sector, such as with the Kilimo Salama and M-Farm initiatives, an agricultural mobile money microinsurance and market access services, respectively. Smart sensors hyphenated to smartphones can be developed and deployed in unlimited applications as part of innovative strategies to solving problems in, for example, environmental monitoring and waste management.

There are many low-cost, local-centric ideas such as grassroots frugal innovations related to valorization of local low-value and waste products. To structurally transform the economy, through regional and international collaborations, the passion for learning on innovation and application of technology in every sector would propel Africa as a player in inventing today's and tomorrow's technologies. Tapping into innovation requires the requisite mindset and focus on training the workforce that can guide the innovation culture and building technological capabilities. Strong investments in human capital, with a broad investment in basic education, and higher education that nurtures creativity and policies that support innovation ecosystems, could be the missing link for economic takeoff in Africa (Puplampu and Mugo in this volume). This is because the development and application of smart sensors have cost implications. If global partnerships are to be of any value in this regard, the need for collaboration cannot be overemphasized.

One form of such a collaboration is tapping into the diaspora and their contributions to sub-Saharan Africa. In some African countries, diaspora remittances have exceeded the inflow of official development aid and other private capital (World Bank Group 2019). Policies should be enacted to tap this inflow as a major government expenditure financing opportunities, offering government investment bonds. Investment in research and innovation has remained anemic in Africa over the years, partly due to systemic inadequate funding which stems from lack of government education policy frameworks that nurture and value innovation mindset. Indeed, beyond financial remittances, the largest untapped potential of knowledge mobilization remains utilization of sub-Saharan African diaspora academics and professionals. For example, on the topic of valorization of local biomass and fabrication of smart sensors, collaborations between global North and South universities can foster the creation of homegrown innovations. A case in point is the work of Madivoli et al. (2016), Mugo et al. (2019) and Dhanjai et al. (2019) in Canada on the use of microstructured polydimethylsiloxane (PDMS) or polymers used in textiles such as polyesters, nanocellulose (obtained from wood), chitosan (obtained from shells of sea foods), fish gelatin and different allotropes (forms) of carbon materials such as carbon nanotubes, graphene, carbon black, carbon fibers, carbon soot and biochar produced from agricultural waste. In some cases, certain metals such as silver are integrated into the nanomaterials to impact desired sensing functionalities in the nanomaterials. The nanomaterials are adequately suited to function as miniaturized flexible electronics.

These nanomaterials have the capacity to soak water and other chemical entities, which change certain inherent measurable properties, such as their size, ability to conduct electricity (resistance, capacitance, impedance, etc.) and even color, which can be correlated to the chemical entity captured (Antonacci et al. 2019; Dhanjai et al. 2019; Tessarolo et al. 2018; Wu et al. 2019; Zhang and Mugo 2019). They are amenable to be made into inks and have the ability to make the sensors using rapid prototyping approaches such as inkjet printing at lower cost. These examples call for a rethink in strategy and policy and policy execution, since the professional and academic diaspora could hold the key to scientific innovation and smart sensors in Africa, with contextualized applications. This is because Africa has increasingly lost its talent, with many professionals immigrating to the global North. According to UNESCO (2015), the share of high-skilled individuals in sub-Saharan Africa is among the lowest in the world. Paradoxically, the same source states that the high-skilled emigration rate from these countries especially to the USA and Europe has also steadily increased since the mid-1990s (from 11% in 1995 to 16% in 2010), representing today the highest high-skilled emigration rate from the global South.

Some countries have outlined and implemented various mobilization to foster engagements. China for instance, facilitates the intermobility of Chinese professionals between their home country and host countries, often the USA and Canada (Tian 2016). This ongoing mobility complements the circulation of knowledge obtained from reverse migration, where 25% of the 1.21 million Chinese scientists were enticed back to China, following their research studies and work abroad (Tian 2016). This phenomenon greatly contributed to the science and technology innovation takeoff in China. African countries can do the same. African academic diaspora can collaborate and even establish research groups in their motherland universities, leveraging bilateral opportunities (Frittelli 2018; Ndofirepi and Cross 2017). The opportunities could include sharing of research infrastructure and innovation ideas across, mobilizing research students between their research groups spread between the two countries, and fostering bilateral research networks, thus creating a knowledge exchange and innovation ecosystem. While the universities in Africa have grown in number, the same cannot be said of the quality of learning at both graduate and undergraduate levels (see Puplampu and Mugo in this volume).

Africa is in dire need for university programs in science and technology. African universities struggling to achieve their core mandate of research, innovation and academic excellence could especially benefit if they adopt an open collaborative approach where African diaspora academics find a sense of acceptance in African universities and are embraced to create research groups and innovation hubs housed in African universities. As such, if African universities open their world to the tremendous untapped potential of the diaspora African academia and possibly international academia, it is unthinkable the far-reaching benefits such an approach could present in promoting economic dynamism through technology innovation and highly qualified personnel training, transforming Africa to a truly knowledge economy. Notably, the African diaspora is often most willing for such opportunities, but the policy frameworks and territorialization attitude in African universities undermine collaboration. Efforts to connect African universities to the diaspora academics have been the focus of the Carnegie African Diaspora Fellowship Program (CADFP) (Ndofirepi and Cross 2017; Kot 2016). In this human capital inflow initiative, Africa remains a spectator, reflecting the donor-driven development paradigm, and as such the lack of the required, sustained, long-term active collaborative engagement dims the optimal innovation outcomes that could otherwise ensue.

CONCLUSION

It is becoming increasingly clear that efforts must be made to inculcate and enforce stewardship of the environment, which will afford the equitable support of present and future generations, with an understanding that we share the environment with numerous fauna and flora species that symbiotically co-depend in a networked ecosystem. The role of education cannot be ignored in such an undertaking. While higher education in general requires significant capital investment, science education, to take advantage of improvements in sensors and disruptive technologies, would also require capital investment. In the twenty-first century, the trend is toward a shared digital economy, demanding partnership and interdisciplinary collaboration of skill sets that integrate science, social sciences and technology innovation. That is the reason why African universities should explore to adopt brain recirculation possibilities to fast-track Africa's science and technology innovation and social development.

Ultimately, African universities need to train students to enhance their creativity and technical skills on technology innovation and mastery of the nuances of human interaction and experience in the digital age. With its enviable youthfulness and energy, the African continent can become a hotbed of innovation, beginning with iterative innovations and deployments. While many challenges remain, and the best time to plant the seed of innovation tree was years ago, African countries are poised in adopting infrastructure-less technologies such as smart sensors and data analytics, which can spur economic growth and well-being for its population.

References

Agudelo-Castaneda, D. M., Teixeira, E. C., Schneider, I. L., Lara, S. R., & Silva, L. F. (2017). Exposure to Polycyclic Aromatic Hydrocarbons in Atmospheric PM1.0 of Urban Environments: Carcinogenic and Mutagenic Respiratory Health Risk by Age Groups. *Environmental Pollution, 224,* 158–170.

Akram, R., Natasha, & Fahad, S. (2019). Trends of Electronic Waste Pollution and Its Impact on the Global Environment and Ecosystem. *Environmental Science and Pollution Research, 26*(17), 16923–16938.

Amegah, A. K. (2018). Proliferation of Low-Cost Sensors. What Prospects for Air Pollution Epidemiologic Research in Sub-Saharan Africa? *Environmental Pollution, 241,* 1132–1137.

Amegah, A. K., & Agyei-Mensah, S. (2017). Urban Air Pollution in Sub-Saharan Africa: Time for Action. *Environmental Pollution, 220*(Pt A), 738–743.

Andrade, D. F., Romanelli, J. P., & Pereira-Filho, E. R. (2019). Past and Emerging Topics Related to Electronic Waste Management: Top Countries, Trends, and Perspectives. *Environmental Science and Pollution Research, 26*(17), 17135–17151.

Antonacci, A., Arduini, F., Moscone, D., Palleschi, G., & Scognamiglio, V. (2019). Nanostructured (Bio)Sensors for Smart Agriculture. *TRAC- Trends in Analytical Chemistry, 98,* 95–103.

Asamoah, D., Takieddine, S., & Amedofu, M. (2019). Examining the Effect of Mobile Money Transfer (MMT) Capabilities on Business Growth and Development Impact. *Information Technology for Development.* https://doi.org/10.1080/02681102.2019.1599798.

Bacco, M., Berton, A., Gotta, A., & Caviglione, L. (2018). IEEE 802.15.4 Air-Ground UAV Communications in Smart Farming Scenarios. *IEEE Communication Letters, 22*(9), 1910–1913.

Batchelor, S. (2012). Changing the Financial Landscape of Africa: An Unusual Story of Evidence-Informed Innovation, Intentional Policy Influence and Private Sector Engagement. *IDS Bulletin-Institute of Development Studies, 43*, 84–90.

Bergstrom, J. P., & Dong, T. (2015). Rapid Detection of E. coli Cells in Urine Samples Using a Self-Capacitance Touchscreen Device. *Proceedings of the Annual International Conference of the IEEE Engineering in Medicine and Biology*, 5545–5548.

Brauer, M., Amann, M., Burnett, R. T., Cohen, A., Dentener, F., Ezzati, M., Henderson, S. B., Krzyzanowski, M., Martin, R. V., Van Dingenen, R., van Donkelaar, A., & Thurston, G. D. (2012). Exposure Assessment for Estimation of the Global Burden of Disease Attributable to Outdoor Air Pollution. *Environmental Science & Technology, 46*, 652–660.

Burns, K. N., Sayler, S. K., & Neitzel, R. L. (2019). Stress, Health, Noise Exposures, and Injuries Among Electronic Waste Recycling Workers in Ghana. *Journal of Occupational Medicine and Toxicology, 14*, 1. https://doi.org/10.1186/s12995-018-0222-9.

Chen, Y., Guerschman, J. P., Cheng, Z., & Guo, L. (2019). Remote Sensing for Vegetation Monitoring in Carbon Capture Storage Regions: A Review. *Applied Energy, 240*, 312–326.

Chung, W. Y., Le, G. T., Tran, T. V., & Nguyen, N. H. (2017). Novel Proximal Fish Freshness Monitoring Using Batteryless Smart Sensor Tag. *Sensors and Actuators B-Chemical, 248*, 910–916.

Cordova-Pizarro, D., Aguilar-Barajas, I., Romero, D., & Rodriguez, C. A. (2019). Circular Economy in the Electronic Products Sector: Material Flow Analysis and Economic Impact of Cellphone E-waste in Mexico. *Sustainability, 11*(5), 1361.

Danse, I. R., Jaeger, R. J., Kava, R., Kroger, M., London, W. M., Lu, F. C., Maickel, R. P., McKetta, J. J., Newell, G. W., & Shindell, S. (1997). Position Paper of the American Council on Science and Health: Public Health Concerns About Environmental Polychlorinated Biphenyls (PCBs). *Ecotoxicology and Environmental Safety, 38*, 71–84.

Dhanjai, Yu, N., & Mugo, S. M. (2019). A Flexible-Imprinted Capacitive Sensor for Rapid Detection of Adrenaline. *Talanta, 204*, 602–606.

Dias, P., Bernardes, A. M., & Huda, N. (2019). Ensuring Best E-waste Recycling Practices in Developed Countries: An Australian Example. *Journal of Cleaner Production, 209*, 846–854.

Frittelli, C. (2018). African Academic Diaspora: Training and Research. *International Higher Education*, (95), 18–19. https://doi.org/10.6017/ihe.2018.95.10724.

Gharakheili, H. H., Sivanathan, A., Hamza, A., & Sivaraman, V. (2019). Network-Level Security for the Internet of Things: Opportunities and Challenges. *Computer, 52*, 58–62.

Ghasemi-Varnamkhasti, M., Apetrei, C., Lozano, J., & Anyogu, A. (2018). Potential Use of Electronic Noses, Electronic Tongues and Biosensors as Multisensor Systems for Spoilage Examination in Foods. *Trends in Food Science and Technology, 80*, 71–92.

Giraldo, J. P., Wu, H., Newkirk, G. M., & Kruss, S. (2019). Nanobiotechnology Approaches for Engineering Smart Plant Sensors. *Nature Nanotechnology, 14*(6), 541–553.

Golev, A., Corder, G. D., & Rhamdhani, M. A. (2019). Estimating Flows and Metal Recovery Values of Waste Printed Circuit Boards in Australian E-waste. *Minerals Engineering, 137*, 171–176.

Gonzalez-Teruel, J. D., Torres-Sanchez, R., Blaya-Ros, P. J., Toledo-Moreo, A. B., Jiménez-Buendía, M., & Soto-Valles, F. (2019). Design and Calibration of a Low-Cost SDI-12 Soil Moisture Sensor. *Sensors, 19*(3), 491.

Halachmi, I., Guarino, M., Bewley, J., & Pastell, M. (2019). Smart Animal Agriculture: Application of Real-Time Sensors to Improve Animal Well-Being and Production. *Annual Review of Animal Biosciences, 7*, 403–425.

Hamrita, T. K., & Hoffacker, E. C. (2005). Development of a "Smart" Wireless Soil Monitoring Sensor Prototype Using RFID Technology. *Applied Engineering in Agriculture, 21*(1), 139–143.

Hornero, G., Gaitan-Pitre, J. E., Serrano-Finetti, E., Casas, O., & Pallas-Areny, R. (2017). A Novel Low-Cost Smart Leaf Wetness Sensor. *Computers and Electronics in Agriculture, 143*, 286–292.

Isernia, R., Passaro, R., Quinto, I., & Thomas, A. (2019). The Reverse Supply Chain of the E-waste Management Processes in a Circular Economy Framework: Evidence from Italy. *Sustainability, 11*, 2430. https://doi.org/10.3390/su11082430.

Jesus, R. M.-A., Irineo, T. P., & Carlos, D.-G. (2013). FPGA-Based Wireless Smart Sensor for Real-Time Photosynthesis Monitoring. *Computers and Electronics in Agriculture, 95*, 58–69.

Khan, S. M., Shaikh, S. F., Qaiser, N., & Hussain, M. M. (2018). Flexible Lightweight CMOS-Enabled Multisensory Platform for Plant Microclimate Monitoring. *IEEE Transaction on Electron Devices, 65*(11), 5038–5044.

Kitila, A. W., & Woldemikael, S. M. (2019). Waste Electrical and Electronic Equipment Management in the Educational Institutions and Governmental Sector Offices of Addis Ababa, Ethiopia. *Waste Management, 85*, 30–41.

Kot, C. F. (2016). The Perceived Benefits of International Partnerships in Africa: A Case Study of Two Public Universities in Tanzania and the Democratic Republic of Congo. *High Education Policy, 29*(1), 41–62. https://doi.org/10.1057/hep.2015.2.

Lickley, M., & Solomon, S. (2018). Drivers, Timing and Some Impacts of Global Aridity Change. *Environmental Research Letters, 13*(10), 104010.

Liu, C., Lin, J., Cao, H., & Sun, Z. (2019). Recycling of Spent Lithium-ion Batteries in View of Lithium Recovery: A Critical Review. *Journal of Cleaner Production, 228*, 801–813.

Madivoli, E. S., Kareru, P. G., Gachanja, A. N., Mugo, S. M., Murigi, M. K., Kairigo, P. K., Cheruiyot, K., Mutembei, J. K., & Njonge, F. K. (2016). Adsorption of Selected Heavy Metals on Modified Nanocellulose. *International Research Journal of Pure & Applied Chemistry, 12*(3), 1–9.

Maximilian, U., Schlink, U., Dijst, M., & Weiland, U. (2019). Cyclists' Multiple Environmental Urban Exposures-Comparing Subjective and Objective Measurements. *Sustainability, 11*(5), 1412.

Mayer, M., & Baeumner, A. J. (2019). A Megatrend Challenging Analytical Chemistry: Biosensor and Chemosensor Concepts Ready for the Internet of Things. *Chemical Reviews, 119*, 7996–8027.

Memeu, D., Sarroney, M., & Maina, C. (2018). Photo-Thermal Induced Optical Scattering Modulation Sensor for Malaria Diagnosis. *Open Journal of Biophysics, 8*, 185–193.

Misra, D., Das, G., Chakrabortty, T., & Das, D. (2018). An IoT-Based Waste Management System Monitored by Cloud. *Journal of Material Cycles and Waste Management, 20*, 1574–1582.

Mugo, S. M., Lu, W., Berg, D., & Mundle, T. (2019). Thin Film Composite Conductive Polymers Chemiresistive Sensor and Sample Holder for Methanol Detection in Adulterated Beverages. *IEEE Sensors*. https://doi.org/10.1109/JSEN.2019.2943088.

Naiker, Y., et al. (2012). Introduction of Local Air Quality Management in South Africa: An Overview and Challenges. *Environmental Science and Policy, 17*, 62–71.

Ndofirepi, A., & Cross, M. (Eds.). (2017). *Knowledge and Change in African Universities*. Rotterdam: Sense Publishers.

Njuguna, S. M., Yan, X., Gituru, R. W., Wang, Q. F., & Wang, J. (2017). Assessment of Macrophyte, Heavy Metal, and Nutrient Concentrations in the Water of the Nairobi River, Kenya. *Environmental Monitoring and Assessment, 189*, 454.

Odeyingbo, A. O., Nnorom, I. C., & Deubzer, O. K. (2019). Used and Waste Electronics Flows into Nigeria: Assessment of the Quantities, Types, Sources, and Functionality Status. *Science of Total Environment, 666*, 103–113.

Ohajinwa, C. M., van Bodegom, P. M., & Osibanjo, O. (2019). Health Risks of Polybrominated Diphenyl Ethers (PBDEs) and Metals at Informal Electronic Waste Recycling Sites. *International Journal of Environmental Research and Public Health, 16*(6), 906.

Pietrelli, L., Ferro, S., & Vocciante, M. (2019). Eco-Friendly and Cost-Effective Strategies for Metals Recovery from Printed Circuit Boards. *Renewable and Sustainable Energy Reviews, 112*, 317–323.

Prata, J. C., Silva, P., Ana, L., & da Costa, L. J. P. (2019). Solutions and Integrated Strategies for the Control and Mitigation of Plastic and Microplastic Pollution. *International Journal of Environmental Research and Public Health*, *16*(13), 2411.

Rodina, L. (2019). Planning for Water Resilience: Competing Agendas among Cape Town's Planners and Water Managers. *Environmental Science & Policy*, *99*, 10–16.

Santonico, M., Pennazza, G., Parente, F. R., Grasso, S., Zompanti, A., Stornelli, V., Ferri, G., Bizzarri, M., & D'Amico, A. (2017). Proceedings a Gas Sensor Device for Oxygen and Carbon Dioxide Detection. *Proceedings, 1*, 447.

Servida, F., & Casey, E. (2019). IoT Forensic Challenges and Opportunities for Digital Traces. *Digital Investigation, 28*, S22–S29.

Shi, Y., Huang, J., Zeng, G., Cheng, W., & Hu, J. (2019a). Photocatalytic Membrane in Water Purification: Is It Stepping Closer to Be Driven by Visible Light? *Journal of Membrane Science, 584*, 364–392.

Shi, X., An, X., Zhao, O., Liu, H., Xia, L., Sun, X., & Guo, Y. (2019b). State-of-the-Art Internet of Things in Protected Agriculture. *Sensors, 19*(8), 1833.

Stradling, D., & Stradling, R. (2008). Perceptions of the Burning River: Deindustrialization and Cleveland's Cuyahoga River. *Environmental History, 13*, 515–535.

Tajuri, A. M., & Naim, H. (2018). Assessing the Impacts of Population Growth and Climate Change on Performance of Water Use Systems and Water Allocation in Kano River Basin, Nigeria. *Water, 10*(12), 1766.

Tessarolo, M., Gualaridi, I., & Fraboni, B. (2018). Recent Progress in Wearable Fully Textile Chemical Sensors. *Advanced Materials Technologies, 3*, 10, Special Issue: 1700310.

Thompson, J. E. (2016). Crowd-Sourced Air Quality Studies: A Review of the Literature & Portable Sensors. *Trends in Environmental Analytical Chemistry, 11*, 23–34.

Tian, F. M. (2016). Brain Circulation, Diaspora and Scientific Progress: A Study of the International Migration of Chinese Scientists, 1998–2006. *Asian and Pacific Migration Journal, 25*(3), 296–319.

United Nations (UN). (2015). *Transforming Our World: The 2030 Agenda for Sustainable Development.* Washington, DC: United Nations A/RES/70/1. sustainabledevelopment.un.org

United Nations Development Program (UNDP). (2015). *Sustainable Development Goals.* New York: United Nations Development Program.

United Nations Educational, Scientific and Cultural Organization (UNESCO). (2015). *Education 2030 Incheon Declaration: Towards Inclusive and Equitable Quality Education and Lifelong Learning for All.* https://unesdoc.unesco.org/ark:/48223/pf0000245656

United Nations Food and Agriculture Organization (UN FAO). (2018). *How to Feed the World in 2020*. http://www.fao.org/3/I8429EN/i8429en.pdf

Viani, F., Bertolli, M., Salucci, M., & Polo, A. (2017). Low-Cost Wireless Monitoring and Decision Support for Water Saving in Agriculture. *IEEE Sensors Journal, 17*(13), 4299–4309.

World Bank Group. (2019). *Record High Remittances Sent Globally in 2018*. https://www.worldbank.org/en/news/press-release/2019/04/08/record-high-remittances-sent-globally-in-2018

World Economic Forum (WEF) Report. (2019). *A New Circular Vision for Electronics. Time for a Global Reboot*. https://www.weforum.org/reports/a-new-circular-vision-for-electronics-time-for-a-global-reboot.

World Health Organization. (2006). *Meeting the MDG Drinking Water and Sanitation Target: The Urban and Rural Challenge of the Decade*. http://www.who.int/water_sanitation_health/monitoring/jmpfinal.pdf

World Health Organization. (2014). *WHO Burden of Disease from Ambient Air Pollution for 2012*. Geneva: WHO.

World Health Organization. (2016). *WHO Global Urban Ambient Air Pollution Database (Update 2016), Urban Ambient Air Pollution Database*. World Health Organization.

Wu, Y., Huang, Q., Nie, J., et al. (2019). All-Carbon Based Flexible Humidity Sensor. *Journal of Nanoscience and Nanotechnology, 19*(8), 5310–5316.

Yang, L., Li, W., Ghandehari, M., & Fortino, G. (2018). People-Centric Cognitive Internet of Things for the Quantitative Analysis of Environmental Exposure. *IEEE Internet of Things Journal, 5*(4), 2353–2366.

Yong, Y. S., Lim, Y. A., & Ilankoon, I. M. S. K. (2019). An Analysis of Electronic Waste Management Strategies and Recycling Operations in Malaysia: Challenges and Future Prospects. *Journal of Cleaner Production, 224*, 151–166.

Yousefi, H., Su, H. M., Imani, S. M., Alkhaldi, K., Filipe, C. D. M., & Didar, T. F. (2019). Intelligent Food Packaging: A Review of Smart Sensing Technologies for Monitoring Food Quality. *ACS Sensors, 4*(4), 808–821.

Yu, M., Zhang, Z., Xue, F., Yang, B., Guo, G., & Qiu, J. (2019). A more Simple and Efficient Process for Recovery of Cobalt and Lithium from Spent Lithium-Ion Batteries with Citric Acid. *Separation and Purification Technology, 215*, 398–402.

Zachary, D. B. (2015). The Unexhausted Potential of E. coli. Blount. *eLife, 4*, e05826.

Zhang, Q., & Mugo, S. M. (2019). Nano-Sized Structured Platforms for Facile Solid-Phase Nanoextraction for Molecular Capture and (Bio) Chemical Analysis. In O. V. Zenkina (Ed.), *Nanomaterials Design for Sensing Applications* (pp. 111–130). Amsterdam: Elsevier.

CHAPTER 5

Disruptive Technologies, Sustainable Energy Generation and Storage as Forms of Green Economy

Benjamin Ofori-Amoah

INTRODUCTION

This chapter is about the role of disruptive technologies in Africa's transition to green economy with reference to sustainable energy generation and storage. Since the introduction of the concept of sustainable development by the World Commission on Environment and Development in 1987, there has been a growing interest in what is now called green economy, an economy that is able to take care of both people and the environment. This interest reached a crescendo just around the time of Rio+20 meeting of 2012, when three consecutive reports released by UNEP (2011), the World Bank (2012), and OECD (2011) emphasized the urgency for a green economy. Since then sustainable energy generation and storage has become front and center in most of the discussion of green economy because of the unsustainable nature of how most of our

B. Ofori-Amoah (✉)
Department of Geography, Western Michigan University, Kalamazoo, MI, USA
e-mail: ben.ofori@wmich.edu

© The Author(s) 2020   85
P. Arthur et al. (eds.), *Disruptive Technologies, Innovation and Development in Africa*, International Political Economy Series,
https://doi.org/10.1007/978-3-030-40647-9_5

current energy is generated. This in turn has galvanized interest in paying more attention to renewable energy sources as well as the technologies for generation and storage of such energy.

Of interest in this regard are disruptive technologies, which are current non-mainstream technologies that have the potential of displacing mainstream technologies in the future (Christensen 1997). In the global North (developed countries), researchers have been talking about disruptive energy innovations and disruptive low-carbon technologies as forms of energy transformation (e.g., Dixon et al. 2018; McDowall 2018; Wilson 2018). In the global South (developing countries) in general, and on the African continent in particular, disruptive technologies may be seen as opportunities to leverage such innovative but non-mainstream technologies for development without building the large-scale energy infrastructure of the type present-day countries in the global North (developed) have spent a lot of money to build over the years. Thus, although the term disruptive technologies has not been explicitly used, it is implied in a number of studies that have promoted decentralized electrification systems using energy sources other than fossil fuels to serve under-grid and off-grid market segments (Lemaire 2011; Azimoh et al. 2014; Lee et al. 2016).

However, both green economy and disruptive technologies are contested concepts with a lot of proponents and critics. For example, proponents of green economy see it as (1) an effective way for African countries to achieve sustainable growth; (2) an opportunity to address poverty, create employment, and improve the overall well-being of the population; (3) a preservation of the natural capital and ecosystem services that support the lives of millions of people and economies in Africa; and (4) an improvement in the overall performance of key sectors in the economy (UNEP 2015). In contrast, critics charge that green economy (1) is based on over-optimistic assumptions, (2) projects the notion of limitless growth, (3) overemphasizes economic aspect of growth at the expense of social aspects, (4) is based on unattainable requirements such as being able to price the environment (Borel-Saladin and Turok 2013), (5) a "re-legitimization for creating strong and authoritative green states in the global south" (Death 2015), and (6) new ways of maintaining neoliberal capitalism (Wanner 2015; Buseth 2017).

Disruptive technologies as a concept have been a subject of vigorous debates especially in developed countries. These debates have produced three main reactions—the first embraces the concept as it was originally formulated and its applicability to energy transformation, the second rejects the concept and its applicability to the energy sector, and the third prefers to see energy transformation in a broader framework (Wilson and Tyfield 2018). In developing countries, The Breakthrough Institute (2016), for example, charges that decentralized off-grid energy technologies can be useful when employed to augment centralized grid system to support targeted activities such as increasing agricultural productivity, but they cannot substitute for energy and other infrastructure needed to support industrial-scale development.

Against these backgrounds, the central question of this chapter is to what extent can disruptive technologies foster Africa's transition to a green economy through sustainable energy generation? The chapter argues that the deployment of disruptive technologies to sustainable energy generation and storage holds potential for Africa's transition to green economy, but only if African countries can rise to the challenge of developing policies and institutional mechanisms with the commitment needed for their execution. The chapter is divided into five sections. The section "Disruptive Technologies, Sustainable Energy Generation and Storage, and Green Economy" provides the theoretical framework for the chapter. It summarizes the debates over the definitions, dimensions, and conceptual validity of disruptive technologies, sustainable energy generation and storage, and green economy and establishes a relationship among them. The section "Energy Sources and the State of Current Energy Generation in Africa" provides an assessment of current energy generation in Africa to make a case for sustainable energy generation in Africa. The section "Disruptive Energy Technologies and Prospects for Sustainable Energy Generation as a Form of Green Economy in Africa" discusses the prospects of sustainable energy generation, through disruptive energy technologies, while the section "Going Forward" outlines some policy recommendations for how African countries can use disruptive energy technologies for sustainable energy generation and transition to green economy.

DISRUPTIVE TECHNOLOGIES, SUSTAINABLE ENERGY GENERATION AND STORAGE, AND GREEN ECONOMY

The concept of green economy has gained prominence over the past few decades. Research work and commentary indicate that the idea of green economy had been implicitly discussed in economics texts since the 1950s, but its current prominence can be traced to the work of the United

Nations World Commission on the Environment and Development
(WCED)'s (1987) publication *Our Common Future* (Mundaca et al.
2016). As it is well known, the publication introduced the term "sustainable development," defined as "development that meets the needs of the
present without compromising the ability of future generations to meet
their own needs" (WCED 1987). Pearce et al. (1989) used the term
"green economy" in the title of their book *Blueprint for a Green Economy*,
a follow-up publication to *Our Common Future* for the UK government.
Although they did not provide an explicit definition of the term, the
authors focused and affirmed that the idea of sustainable development was
feasible from the perspectives of economics, through application of modern technology, efficiency, natural capital, and human development
(Mundaca et al. 2016). However, the concept received a big boost after
the 2008 global financial crisis. In its report *Global Green New Deal*, the
United Nations Environment Programme (UNEP) (2009) tied the global
financial crises and climate change to misallocation of resources that had
ignored environmental and natural resources concerns. The report called
for a new greener economy. From 2011 to 2012, three reports all focusing
on variations of green economy were issued. These were UNEP's (2011)
Towards a Green Economy, OECD's (2011) *Towards Green Growth*, and
the World Bank's (2012) *Inclusive Green Growth*. The UNEP (2011: 16)
report defined green economy as "one which is low carbon, resource efficient and socially inclusive. In a green economy, growth in income and
employment should be driven by public and private investments that
reduce carbon emissions and pollution, enhance energy and resource efficiency, and prevent the loss of biodiversity and ecosystem services."

OECD (2011) defined "green growth" as "involving operational policy agenda that can help achieve concrete measurable progress at the interface of between economy and the environment." On its part, the World
Bank defined its "inclusive green growth" as "economic growth that is
environmentally sustainable." Since then green growth and its variants
including green resilience, green transformation, and green revolution
have been used extensively in international conferences, discussion, and
policy circles (Death 2015).

Theoretically, green economy is rooted in environmental and ecological economics (Loiseau et al. 2016). Environmental economics assumes
that natural and human-made capital are substitutable and that economic
growth and sustainable use of resources can be achieved simultaneously.
Under these assumptions, environmental issues are a result of inefficient

use of natural resources and undervaluation of natural capital. To address this inefficiency, the right prices for natural capital must be set through proper valuation and supported with incentive packages such as taxes, permits, subsidies, and liability payments. The idea is that if society gets the prices right, the substitution between natural and human capital will stop (Loiseau et al. 2016). On its part, ecological economics sees the economy as a subsystem of the ecological or natural system, with the latter setting a limit within which the former can operate. Consequently, societies must adapt their economies to the natural system. Structural changes within the economy and society involving activities and lifestyles that are less destructive on the nature are seen as main solutions to environmental issues and emissions (Loiseau et al. 2016).

From this background, a green economy is a low-carbon resource-efficient economy, in which public and private sectors work in tandem, but the predominant role of setting policies and creating the right environment is reserved for the government. It is an economy that seeks to improve human well-being while minimizing impact of such improvement on the environment. It emphasizes environmentally based strategies, green products that generate less pollution and waste reduction or complete elimination of raw material content optimization of energy use, and minimization of waste (Loiseau et al. 2016). Five main policy areas are emphasized in the green economy discussion (Borel-Saladin and Turok 2013). They include (1) behavior-changing policies through the establishment of appropriate instructions, norms, and regulations; (2) innovation and industrial policies, which encourage the development of new technologies for existing and new industries; (3) education and labor market policies, which include training and retraining in new skills for new technologies and industries; (4) better management of natural capital, agriculture, and ecosystem services through investment improvement and proper maintenance; and (5) infrastructure, building, urbanism, transportation, and energy (Borel-Saladin and Turok 2013).

If the above summarizes the meaning, approaches, and policy areas of green economy, what is sustainable energy generation and how does it fit into the green economy? Following the general acceptable meaning of sustainable development, sustainable energy generation and storage may be defined as the current production of energy that does not jeopardize future generation's ability to meet their energy needs. Implied in the idea of sustainability is the impact of the energy generation on the environment. Thus, sustainable energy generation is low-carbon emission, efficient, and less destructive on the environment. Given that most of the world's energy is currently generated from sources which are nonrenewable and also major contributors to greenhouse gases, the idea of sustainable energy generation quickly points to energy generation from renewable and low-carbon sources such as biomass, water, sun, wind, and geothermal. These sources place sustainable energy generation at the center of green economy and make it one of the two major investment areas of green economy, with the other one being investment in natural capital. Consequently, UNEP (2011: 2) sees the green economy as a "way to substitute renewable energy and low carbon technologies for fossil fuels and to improve resource and energy efficiency." What then are disruptive technologies and how can they foster sustainable energy generation and a green economy?

The concept of disruptive technologies was first introduced by Bower and Christensen (1995) when they defined it as technologies that damage established companies not because they are radically new or difficult technologies but because they often offer a package of different attributes, and because of the rapid speed at which they can invade established markets. In a further elaboration of the term, Christensen (1997) distinguished disruptive technologies from sustaining technologies. Sustaining technologies respond to improvements in established products along the lines of what mainstream customers have historically valued, while disruptive technologies are innovations in existing products but on attributes that are different from what mainstream customers value. Thus, disruptive technologies may not perform well in mainstream markets. Rather they are low-cost, low-end goods and services that appeal to customers marginalized or excluded from the mainstream market. These technologies and their accompanied product innovations become disruptive to established companies most of the time because the established companies fail to pay attention. Since then, the concept has become a subject of numerous discussions and debates regarding its meaning, applicability, and relevance to various sectors of the economy (National Research Council of the National Academies 2010; Arundel et al. 2011; Lucas 2012; Armstrong 2017; Vermeulen 2017).

In the energy sector, these debates have produced three streams of reaction (Wilson and Tyfield 2018). The first embraces the concept as it was originally formulated and its applicability to energy transformation. For example, Sprei (2018) points out that disruptive technologies in the form of novel goods and services do not have to come from below only but can come from the top as well. Similarly, Wilson (2018) argues that a disruptive low-carbon emission innovation must reduce greenhouse emissions considerably for society in general and also for the consumer. Dütschke and Wesche (2018) see disruptive technologies in the form of a system change and that the transition to renewable energy at the community level is disruptive not in the way of product and market changes but in the functionality and organization by which energy is generated.

The second stream rejects the concept and its applicability to the energy sector. Geels (2018) finds that disruptive technologies idea is more interested in disruption by a single product unseating an existing one and less in the social, political, economic, and infrastructural dimensions. Consequently, it ignores changes that can occur when technology aligns with political struggles, societal debates, and strategic games. McDowall (2018) finds three main shortcomings with Christensen's presentation of disruptive technologies. First, low-carbon transitions require a network of actors, clusters of technologies, institutions, and users that go beyond the narrow framework of disruptive technologies. Second, disruptive technologies focus on only niche market as the way for disruption to occur, ignoring other ways such as social movements, landscape developments, and reconfiguration by incumbents. Third, the disruptive technologies concept is particularly limiting in lower-carbon transitions because it does not consider the role of public policy, which will be needed for such transition to occur. Johnstone and Kivimaa (2018) argue that there are different varieties of disruptions—including disruptions of actors and networks, market structures, business models, and institutions. They note that given the sunk cost of energy systems and the central role energy systems play in the overall economy, disruption of the system is not just a matter of new firms disrupting established firms. Instead energy disruption involves the whole structure of the economy, and this can only occur with the help of public policies. Dixon et al. (2018) also argue that disruptive technologies by nature are hard to detect until after the fact, so what is needed is a methodology for detecting them. They also apply the multilevel purpose (MLP) framework to develop a methodology for identifying disruptive energy technologies for urban retrofitting.

The third stream prefers to see disruption and energy transformation in a broader framework. Thus, Kramer (2018) and Winskel (2018) argue that the term disruptive technologies is at best too narrow and at worst meaningless to the energy transformation that society has to go through in the face of the climate change and for that matter transition to green economy. Kramer sees three levels of disruption: light disruption which will occur if climate change is at the low end of predictions; economic disruption, which will be akin to Malthus' preventive checks (abstinence from use of fossil fuels); and environmental disruption, which will be equivalent to Malthus' positive checks (catastrophe, famine, and misery). Tyfield (2018) also argues that understanding disruptive innovations such as low-carbon emission is not just a sociotechnical system process but one of power and knowledge systems and relations. He shows that a combination of digital innovation and disruptive low-carbon innovation might hold promise for the future, but the transition is not going to be easy due to the power and knowledge relations and systems embedded in capitalism in general and with specific reference to social inequities.

From the above, the question of whether the concept of disruptive technologies is applicable to the energy sector depends on how one sees technological innovations in general and one's definition of disruption in particular. This is because the history of technological innovations is replete with disruptions. These disruptions occur during shifts in technological paradigms and trajectories (Dosi 1982) as well as changes in technological regimes and hegemonies. Technological paradigms define models or patterns of solution to a given technological problem based on selected principles, whereas technological trajectory defines clusters of possible directions within a given technological paradigm (Dosi 1982, 1984; Nelson and Winter 1977; Ofori-Amoah 1995). Each technological paradigm and trajectory is also accompanied by changes in technological regimes and hegemonies, during which a dominant technology and its supporting system and structures are replaced by a new one. These processes may disrupt the status quo, established and comfortable ways of life, jobs, and for that matter livelihoods and force us out of our old ways of life while unleashing new jobs and new ways of life. The extent to which all these occur depends on the type of technological, the business, and the geographic as well as cultural contexts.

To this end, this chapter takes the view that the concept of disruptive technologies is applicable to the energy sector. It however adopts a broader view of disruptive technologies and defines disruptive energy technologies as low-carbon innovations that offer more efficient ways of energy generation compared to existing sources of energy generation (Wilson 2018). These innovations are disruptive not in the sense of market competition, but in the sense that they represent a new technological paradigm and trajectories in energy generation that have the potential of transforming the entire socioeconomic, political, and technical systems. In this view, disruptive energy technologies include the renewable or low-carbon sources—solar, wind, water, geothermal, and biomass—the generating devices or plants of photovoltaic (PV) solar panels, wind turbines, mini-hydroelectric plants, and anaerobic digesters, stand-alone and decentralized grid systems which deliver the energy, and the geographic, socioeconomic, and policy environments that make these possible. In the remaining sections of the chapter, we will examine the current state of energy generation and how disruptive energy technologies can be used to enhance the transition into sustainable energy generation and green economy in Africa.

ENERGY SOURCES AND THE STATE OF CURRENT ENERGY GENERATION IN AFRICA

Like elsewhere in the world, energy in Africa may be classified in several ways. One classification is renewable and nonrenewable energy. The former includes solar, wind, water, geothermal, and biomass (wood, municipal solid waste, and animal waste), while the latter includes fossil fuels (coal, petroleum, natural gas) and uranium. However, global energy statistics are usually compiled under primary and secondary energy. Primary energy is energy in the form of natural resources and includes both renewable and nonrenewable sources of fossil fuels, water, wind, solar, geothermal, uranium, and biomass. Secondary energy is energy converted or transformed from primary energy through refineries or electric plants into refined fuels, used to run machines and electricity. Biomass is usually not included in official energy generation statistics, but given its prominent role as a source of energy in Africa, wood is included in this discussion.

Since 1980, Africa has ranked last but one of the seven major regions of the world in primary energy production with very little variation (Fig. 5.1). Thus, in 1980, Africa produced only 6% of the world's primary energy. In 2015, it accounted for just 7% of the world's total production. About 82% of this production came from five countries—Nigeria, Algeria, Angola, Egypt, and South Africa. This low production reflects in part the limited nature of Africa's conventional primary energy sources (coal, crude oil, natural gas, uranium, water) and in part Africa's inability to harness its more abundant but nonconventional energy sources (solar, wind, nonwood biomass, and geothermal). A brief overview of these sources will make this point clearer.

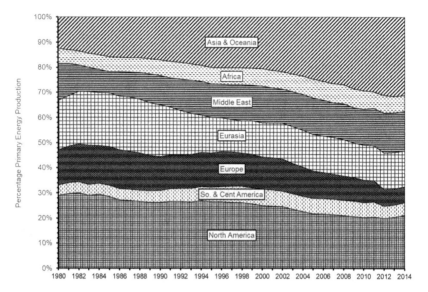

Fig. 5.1   World energy production, 1980–2014. (Ofori-Amoah B. (2019) Figure 13.4 World Primary Energy Production, 1980–2014 *Africa's Geography: Dynamics of Place, Cultures, and Economies.* Hoboken: Wiley p. 475. Copyright (C) 2020 John Wiley & Sons Inc. All rights reserved. Data source: US Energy Information Administration)

Crude oil or petroleum is the single largest source of Africa's primary energy production. In 2015, it accounted for 45.8% of total primary energy production (Ofori-Amoah 2019). However, Africa has only about 8.3% of the world's proven crude oil reserves, of which 37.6% is in Libya, 30.1% in Nigeria, 9.9% in Algeria, and 7.7% in Angola. The remaining deposits were in Egypt, Chad, the Congo Republic, Equatorial Guinea, Benin, and Cameroon. From these reserves, Africa produced about 10% of the world's crude oil production in 2015 (Table 5.1). Recent new oil deposits found in Ghana, Uganda, and Kenya could boost Africa's crude oil production.

Wood is the second largest source of primary energy in Africa after crude oil. In 2015, it accounted for 25% of the total primary energy production of Africa (Ofori-Amoah 2019). Wood provides two sources of primary energy—wood fuel and wood charcoal. In 2015, Africa accounted for about 24% of the world's total wood fuel production. Wood fuel accounts for 90% of Africa's wood energy, while the remaining 10% comes from wood charcoal. Africa's share in the world production of both wood fuel and wood charcoal has been rising to global dominance as the rest of the world has become

Table 5.1 Petroleum production (thousand metric tons) in 2007–2015

Country	2007	2008	2009	2010	2015 Quantity	2015 % of Africa production
Algeria	86,500	85,600	77,800	75,500	68,500	17.3
Angola	82,500	93,100	87,600	90,500	88,700	22.4
Cameroon	4343.4	4300	3700	3200	4860	1.2
Chad	7500.0	6700	6200	6400	4100.0	1.0
Congo	11,091.8	11,558.3	13,335	15,581.9	12,500.0	3.4
Cote d'Ivoire	2423.0	2964	2897	2197	1984	0.5
DRC	1105	995	1100	1050	1132.1	0.3
Egypt	34,100	34,700	35,300	35,000	35,600.0	9.0
Equat. Guinea	17,300	17,200	15,200	13,600	13,500	3.4
Gabon	12,100	12,000	11,829	12,431	11,600.0	3.0
Ghana	301.0	301	301	360	5161.0	1.3
Libya	85,000.0	85,500	77,400	77,700	21,100	5.3
Mauritania	739.5	592.7	550.1	412	260.0	0.1
Morocco	11.1	9.0	9.3	10.4	6.0	0.0
Niger	0.0	0.0	0.0	0.0	995	0.1
Nigeria	114,100	105,300	101,500	117,200	111,300	28.1
Senegal	42.9	13.4	33.6	53.8	22.9	0.0
South Africa	502	403	270	316	71	0.0
South Sudan	0.0	0.0	0.0	0.0	7300	1.8
Sudan	23,100.0	23,700.0	23,400.0	22,800.0	5200	1.3
Tunisia	4546.0	4146.0	3902.0	3731.4	32,800	0.7
Africa	487,305.7	489,082.3	462,327.0	478,043.5	396,410.8	–
World	**3,904,158**	**3,803,437.7**	**3,849,266.2**	**3,932,361.1**	**4,324,722.6**	**–**

Source: Author's compilation based on British Geological Survey (2013) and Brown et al. (2018)

Ofori-Amoah, B. (2019). Table 13.11 Petroleum Production (Thousand Metric Tons) in 2007–2015. *Africa's Geography: Dynamics of Place, Cultures, and Economics*. Hoboken: Wiley p. 477. Copyright (C) 2020 John Wiley & Sons Inc. All rights reserved. Data source: World Mineral Statistics contributed by permission of British Geological Survey.

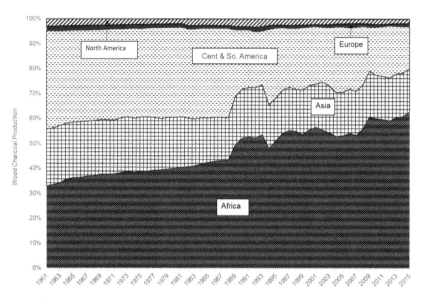

Fig. 5.2   World charcoal production, 1961–2015. (Ofori-Amoah, B. (2019) Figure 13.5 Percentage Wood Charcoal Production of Major World Regions *Africa's Geography: Dynamics of Place, Cultures, and Economies*. Hoboken: Wiley p. 480. Copyright (C) 2020 John Wiley & Sons Inc. All rights reserved. Data source: FAOSTAT)

increasingly dependent on other energy sources. Figure 5.2 shows Africa's share of the world's wood charcoal production. The leading countries include Nigeria, Ethiopia, DRC, Tanzania, Ghana, and Madagascar (Fig. 5.3). For much of rural Africa, wood is the chief source of energy for heating, cooking, and for processing in small-scale and traditional manufacturing.

Coal accounts for about 16% of Africa's primary energy production, but globally Africa produces only about 3.5% of the world's coal output. A starker statistic is that about 94% of this production comes from South Africa (Ofori-Amoah 2019). Other minor coal producers include Zimbabwe, Botswana, Niger, Egypt, Tanzania, and Mozambique (Table 5.2). However, as a result of new coal projects in South Africa, Mozambique, and Botswana, USGS (2012) projected that Africa's coal production will grow by an annual rate of 5% through 2018.

Natural gas accounted for about 6.7% of Africa's primary energy production in 2015. Africa had about 8.7% of the world's proven reserves of natural gas in 2015 out of which it produced 9% of the world's total output. Most of the reserves were in Nigeria (30%), Algeria (26%),

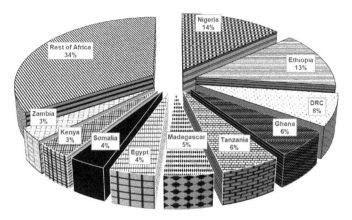

Fig. 5.3 Top wood charcoal producers in Africa, 2015. (Ofori-Amoah, B. (2019) Figure 13.6 Top Producers of Wood Charcoal in Africa, 2015 *Africa's Geography: Dynamics of Place, Cultures, and Economies.* Hoboken: Wiley p. 480. Copyright (C) 2020 John Wiley & Sons Inc. All rights reserved. Data source: FAOSTAT)

Mozambique (16.5%), Egypt (13%), and Libya (9%). However, about 86% of production came from four countries—Algeria (34%), Nigeria (27.5%), Egypt (17.5%), and Tanzania (14.6%) (Table 5.3).

Africa has only 18% of the world's known uranium reserves, distributed among South Africa (6%), Niger (5%), Namibia (5%), and Botswana and Tanzania with 1% each. Out of these reserves, Africa produced about 12.4% of the world's uranium output, about 54% of which came from Niger. The other producers were Namibia (39%) and South Africa (6%). In addition to recent projects in Namibia, uranium has also been found in 16 African countries, including Zambia, Botswana, Malawi, Tanzania, Uganda, DRC, and Burundi. However, they remain unexploited (Ofori-Amoah 2019).

Of the conventional energy sources, water is the one that has the most potential in Africa. However, for a long time, most of this potential remained untapped because only a few large dams were completed in the 1960s and 1970s (Table 5.4). As recent as 2011, it was estimated that 93% of this hydropower, about a tenth of the world's total, was still unexploited (Eberhard et al. 2011). Much of Africa's water energy potential is locked up in the Congo River (Ofori-Amoah 2019). Since the colonial period, it has been known that this is one of the best natural sources of electricity in the world, and when fully tapped (Pearce 2013), it can supply electricity to half of Africa. Over the past several years, this situation appears to be changing due to both completed and proposed projects.

Table 5.2 Coal production (thousand metric tons) in 2007–2015

Country	2007	2008	2009	2010	2015 Quantity	2015 % of Africa production
Botswana	828.2	909.5	737.8	988.2	2065.8	0.8
DRC	126.1	128.8	133.4	133.4	132.50	0.0
Egypt	146.8	0.0	0.0	109.9	650.0	0.2
Ethiopia	0.0	0.0	15.0	20.0	20.0	0.0
Malawi	58.6	57.5	59.2	79.2	71.0	0.0
Mozambique	23.6	37.7	25.9	35.7	8600.0	3.2
Niger	171.3	182.9	225.1	246.6	221.0	0.1
Nigeria	20.0	30.0	40.0	44.1	45.0	0.0
South Africa	247,600.2	252,213.4	250,581.7	257,205.8	252,076.0	93.1
Tanzania	27.2	15.2	16.5	179.5	281.6	0.1
Zambia	14.1	14.0	14.0	0.0	0.0	0.0
Zimbabwe	2080.2	1509.1	1667.3	2668.2	6362.0	2.4
Africa	251096.3	255098.1	253515.9	261710.6	270,686.6	100.0
World	6,585,745.1	6,810,789.4	6,887,823.9	7,250,577.3	7,860,378.1	–

Source: Authors compilation based on British Geological Survey, Brown et al. (2018)

Ofori-Amoah, B. (2019). Table 13.10 Coal Production (Thousand Metric Tons) in 2007–2015. *Africa's Geography: Dynamics of Place, Cultures, and Economies.* Hoboken: Wiley p. 476. Copyright (C) 2020 John Wiley & Sons Inc. All rights reserved. Data source: World Mineral Statistics contributed by permission of British Geological Survey

Table 5.3 Production of natural gas (metric tons) 2007–2015

Country	2007	2008	2009	2010	2015 Quantity	2015 % of Africa production
Algeria	84,800	85,800	79,600	80,400	83,000	39
Angola	830	680	690	733	830	0.4
Congo	283	368	538	934	1750	0.6
Cote d'Ivoire	1574	1300	1300	1352	2200	1.0
Egypt	55,700	59,000	62,700	61,300	45,600	21.4
Equatorial Guinea	2920	6670	5900	6136	6900	3.2
Gabon	167	170	85	85	340	0.0
Libya	15,300	14,300	15,900	16,800	12,800	6.0
Morocco	61	50	41	50	97	0.0
Mozambique	2800	3300	3600	3744	5600	2.6
Nigeria	35,000	35,000	24,800	36,600	50,100	23.5
South Africa	1600	1500	1200	1600	1333	0.6
Tunisia	2285	2596	3056	3402	2500	1.2
Africa	203,320	210,734	199,410	213,136	204,658	100
World	3,062,836	3,159,366	3,095,043	3,299,713	3,162,287	–

Source: British Geological Survey (2013) and Brown et al. (2018)

Ofori-Amoah, B. (2019). Table 13.12 Production of Natural Gas (Metric Tons) 2007–2015. *Africa's Geography: Dynamics of Place, Cultures, and Economies.* Hoboken: Wiley p. 478. Copyright (C) 2020 John Wiley & Sons Inc. All rights reserved. Data source: World Mineral Statistics contributed by permission of British Geological Survey

Table 5.4 Major hydroelectric power projects in Africa

Name	Country	River	Year opened	Capacity (MW)
Inga I	DRC	Congo	1972	351
Inga II	DRC	Congo	1982	1424
Gilgel Gibbe III	Ethiopia	Omo	2015	1870
Aswan	Egypt	Nile	1970	2100
Roseires	Sudan	Blue Nile	2013	1800
Merowe	Sudan	Nile	2009	1250
Akosombo	Ghana	Volta	1965	1020
Kainji	Nigeria	Niger	1968	800
Cahora Bassa	Mozambique-Zambia	Zambezi	1976	2075
Ruacana	Namibia	Cunene	1978	330
Drakensberg Pumped Storage	South Africa	Tugela-Vaal	1981	1000
Kafue Gorge	Zambia	Kafue	1973	990
Kariba	Zimbabwe/Zambia	Zambezi	1977	750
Capanda	Angola	Kwanza	2007	520
Spmg Loulou	Cameroon	Sanaga	1981	384
Gariep	South Africa	Orange	1971	360
Palmiet Pumped Storage	South Africa	Palmiet	1988	400

Compiled from various sources

Ofori-Amoah, B. (2019). Table 13.13 Major Hydroelectric Power Projects in Africa. *Africa's Geography: Dynamics of Place, Cultures, and Economies.* Hoboken: Wiley p. 479. Copyright (C) 2020 John Wiley & Sons Inc. All rights reserved

These include the 250-MW Bujagali Dam project on the Nile in Uganda, the 300-MW Tekeze Canyon project on the Nile in Ethiopia, the 1800-MW Gibe II Dam on the Omo River also in Ethiopia, the 120-MW Djibloho Dam on the Welle River in Equatorial Guinea, and the 1250-MW project on the Nile at Merowe, Sudan (Ofori-Amoah 2019). In addition, there are some large dam projects currently going on including Ethiopia's 6000-MW Grand Renaissance power project on the Blue Nile, the 1600-MW Batoka Gorge project on the Zambezi in Zambia and Zimbabwe, and the 1500-MW Mphanda Nkuwa project also on the Zambezi in Mozambique. The most ambitious of all the projects is the Grand Inga or Inga III power project on the Congo, an estimated $80 billion which when completed might generate 40,000 MW of electricity, twice the amount of electricity generated by the Three Gorges Dam of China, currently the world's largest HEP project (Donaldson 2014).

In contrast, there are no clear datasets on Africa's nonconventional energy sources. However, by their nature we can observe that these nonconventional energy sources are more abundant than the conventional sources. For example, solar and wind are ubiquitous in Africa, although a few hours of cloudiness and nighttime prevent solar energy, for example, to be available for 24 hours. Similarly, wind speed variation may cause differences in wind energy potential across the continent. By comparison, non-wood biomass (municipal and animal waste) is also more abundant and more widely distributed on the continent than any of the conventional energy sources. The only nonconventional energy source that is limited in extent is geothermal because its distribution is determined by geological formations of places. As a result, Africa's greatest geothermal potential is in the Great Rift Valley region (Otieno and Awange 2006; IRENA 2013).

Africa's capacity to convert its primary energy (both conventional and nonconventional) into secondary energy (electricity and refined fuels) is very low. It accounts for only 3% of the global output of secondary energy and only 6% of Africa's total energy use, which is the lowest of all of the major regions of the world. About 80% of this electricity is generated from fossil fuels, 17% from hydroelectricity, and 2% from nuclear energy. The remaining 1% comes from solar, wind, and geothermal. Electricity production is dominated once again by a handful of countries. About 85% of the total electricity production in 2015 was by ten countries. Within this group, South Africa produced 33% and Egypt 23%, while the remaining 44% was due to Algeria, Libya, Nigeria, Morocco, Tunisia, Mozambique, Zambia, and Ghana. In Egypt, Algeria, and Libya, most of the electricity generation was from gas-fired plants; in Nigeria it was from oil, while in South Africa it was from coal (Ofori-Amoah 2019). In contrast, electricity generation from renewable sources on the continent is spotty, isolated, and in most cases anecdotal. For example, only Kenya appears to be tapping into the geothermal resources of the rift valley, which is still very small, less than 10% (Eberhard et al. 2011; Otieno and Awange 2006). Both Uganda and Tanzania have the potential but have not made any concrete efforts to develop them yet. Similarly, the harnessing of solar energy has been a scattered, isolated, individual, or corporate activity. The only countries that have made some efforts at this are Egypt and South Africa. In North Africa, there is the proposed Mediterranean Solar Plan (MSP), which is estimated to generate 20,000 MW of solar capacity by 2020 and its subsequent integration into a new transnational and trans-Mediterranean grid (Ofori-Amoah 2019). For biomass, only South Africa has made some concrete efforts to generate energy from municipal solid waste (Dlamini et al. 2019). With respect to wind energy, only few countries, South Africa, Morocco, Egypt, Ethiopia, Kenya, and Tunisia, have taken concrete actions in establishing wind farms in order to generate electricity (Monforti 2011; Tryou 2016). The result is that hydro and wood continue to be the largest source of renewable energy production in Africa.

This poses several problems for Africa in terms of its transition to green economy and sustainable energy generation and storage. First, the conventional sources from which Africa derives most of its energy are very limited in quantity and are unevenly distributed across the continent, with a vast majority of countries without any of those resources. This creates unequal access among African countries, with the countries that have the resources and financial capabilities able to do better than the countries that do not. Second, they are mostly nonrenewable and for that matter unsustainable in the long term. Third, except for water, all these sources have major environmental issues. Fossil fuels are the leading sources of environmental pollution, including emission of greenhouse gases, and air and water pollution. Wood burning contributes to greenhouse gases, while depletion of woodland also leads to environmental degradation. Even water and nuclear energy that may be renewable have their own environmental problems. For example, large-scale hydroelectric power projects create large bodies of slow-moving water that often destabilize the ecosystem and become breeding grounds for tropical waterborne diseases. Related to this is the concern that too many dams on rivers could turn them into intermittent streams, which has happened in the Lake Chad Basin. Besides, existing hydroelectric power projects have had difficulties operating at full capacity due to water level fluctuations from erratic rainfall patterns due to climate change. Apart from these, there are also cost concerns about such projects, especially the cost of extending and exporting the power across such a vast continent. For example, Warner et al. (2019) report that the Inga III project in DRC has not taken off due to funding constraints. There are also the politics of energy generation. The Inga III project has already raised concerns that the beneficiary of the project will not be the people of DRC but South Africa, which is funding the bulk of the project. Similarly, the construction of dams on the Blue Nile by Ethiopia raised some concerns from Egypt and Sudan. For nuclear energy, the major problems are the disposal of spent fuel and can be catastrophic human and environmental impact in case of an accident.

There are also problems of accessibility, affordability, reliability, and efficiency. Affordable energy in tropical countries is when it does not cost more than 5% of household income and not more than 10% in temperate climates (World Bank 2018). African countries do not only have the least affordable energy, they also have some of the egregious supply of reliable energy (World Bank 2018). Apart from these, Africa's energy production efficiency is yet to reach the minimum benchmark technology (Adom 2018). Similarly, the provision of energy services in Africa is not efficient because there are no economies of scale in providing the service. The result is that energy consumption increases only with income.

As a result of these, many studies have commented that Africa lags behind the rest of the world when it comes to energy use (Karekezi 2002; Bugaje 2006; Razavi et al. 2012; Ahlborg and Hammar 2014; Lee et al. 2016; World Bank 2018). In its recent Energy Tracking Report, the World Bank (2018) indicated that while the whole world is not currently on track in meeting its Sustainable Development Goal 7 (SDG7) which states "access to affordable, reliable, sustainable and modern energy for all by 2030," the largest deficit in these lags with respect to electrification were in sub-Saharan Africa and South Asia. The report shows that sub-Saharan Africa's share in global access deficit more than doubled between 1990 and 2016, with the gap widening between urban and rural areas. Indeed, 16 of the top 20 access-deficit countries were in Africa. With respect to clean cooking, the report indicated that sub-Saharan African countries have performed only marginally, with the population without access to clean cooking technology growing four times faster than the population that had access between 2014 and 2016. In summary, we can characterize the current state of energy generation and provision of energy services in Africa by three market segments: a centralized national grid system, which, in the majority of the countries, depends on fossil fuels and is inefficient, unreliable, and inadequate; an under-grid segment, which consists of consumers in the grid area but has no access to energy for economic and geographic reasons; and the off-grid segment, which consists of people who are completely out of reach of the existing national grid. The task facing African countries is to eliminate these energy market segments. In the ideal world, such a task could be accomplished by infusion of capital, but this is Africa, where capital is scarce. So could disruptive energy technologies help? We answer this question in the next section.

Disruptive Energy Technologies and Prospects for Sustainable Energy Generation as a Form of Green Economy in Africa

In an extensive review of the prospects of renewable energy in Africa, Karekezi (2002) laid a solid foundation that we can build on as a first step toward the use of disruptive energy technologies in Africa. He argued that fossil fuels are unevenly distributed on the continent compared to the almost ubiquitous distribution of most renewable energy resources. Second, the conventional centralized power systems require an enormous capital outlay, which is not the case in decentralized system that can be undertaken with renewable energy sources because of their distribution. Third, the modular nature of renewable energy could allow even the poorest countries to start a phased-out energy program that will be more manageable in relation to their budget. Fourth, the extension of conventional grid to individual homes and dispersed settlements in rural areas will be costly compared to the use of decentralized system for such areas. Clearly, Karekezi was calling for a decentralized system of energy generation from renewable energy sources that could be distributed to unreached areas on the continent.

We have already mentioned the conventional renewable sources that Africa generates energy from, most notably wood and water. However, very little energy is being generated from other renewables. For example, the International Renewable Energy Agency (IRENA) (2013) reported that 21 African countries had completed both solar and wind energy assessments and at least 14 countries had also completed their geothermal assessments, although it did not provide a list of the countries. What is left now is to start developing these resources. A renewable source that has not received much mention in the literature is biomass, especially municipal solid waste. Two recent studies in Nigeria (Ayodele et al. 2017) and South Africa (Dlamini et al. 2019) show that the potential of municipal solid waste as a source of electricity is high. Ayodele et al.'s (2017) study of Nigeria also confirmed that waste-to-energy (WTE) technologies can reduce global warming potential (GWP) by 75–93% compared to current practice of landfill only. Similarly, the city of Johannesburg generated three megawatts of electricity that could supply electricity to more than 5500 homes in 2016 (Dlamini et al. 2019).

With respect to decentralized system of energy generation, two main types are mentioned in the literature—grid-connected (GC) and stand-alone (SA) (Kaundinya et al. 2009). Both systems run on renewable energy, but in the GC system any surplus electricity is fed to the grid so the grid acts as an infinite source of energy supply. This avoids all the cost of additional battery storage. A common form of GC system is the mini-grid, micro-grid, or isolated grid, which is a collection of electricity generators and storage systems that are connected to supply entire electricity to a local group of consumers (Verma and Singh 2013). They can be designed to operate outside the national grid or they can be connected. They do have storage facilities to store electricity generated for use during off-peak times. They can be supplied by different kinds of energy resources.

As already noted, energy-generating devices or plants associated with decentralized grid system include electric diesel generators, photovoltaic systems (PVs), wind turbines, hybrid incinerators, and anaerobic digesters. Diesel-powered electric generators are not ideal for the long term given the environmental impact of fossil fuels and also the cost as well as intermittent shortages in supply. Of the remaining equipment, the most popular is the PV, partly because of its portability and cost of installation. In a review of PV use in East Africa (Kenya, Tanzania, and Uganda), Hansen et al. (2015) show that there are different PV market segments. They include

> (1) the smallest pico-applications for solar lanterns and mobile phone chargers; (2) solar home systems (SHS), which are off-grid electricity supply systems for private homes in scattered villages or at the outskirts of electrified towns and villages but have not been reached by the grid. They are also used in private homes in electrified towns that are concerned with intermittent power supply from the grid or are environmentally conscious; (3) stand-alone institutional PV systems for public or private institutions located in remote areas that are off-grid; (4) telecommunications and tourism-oriented PV systems, which are stand-alone PV systems to support telecommunication base receiver stations and isolated hotels and lodges in tourist destinations; (5) mini-grids consisting of hybrid and PV systems for towns and villages outside the national grid; and (6) large-scale grid-connected PV systems used as extension of existing grid. The most dominant of these is SHS (Hansen et al. 2015).

Unlike PVs, wind turbines, hybrid incinerators, and anaerobic digesters are beyond individual household level but very appropriate at the community level.

Disruptive energy technologies could also be in a form of innovative and creative financing models, which could help with affordability. Lemaire (2011) describes two such models, a fee-for-service and micro-credit, which have been used for large-scale dissemination of SHS in off-grid areas in South Africa. In the fee-for-service scheme, a small private company obtains a long-term concession and may do so with government loans. The company then charges a low monthly fee for installation of the solar home system and delivery of electricity. In the second case, the solar enterprise does the maintenance of the system, but a separate institution provides the financing. The fee-for-service scheme is used when there are no appropriate financial institutions in the area. Another financing scheme is the feed-in tariffs (FiT). In the traditional FiT scheme, electricity generated from renewable energy sources is fed into the grid through fixed electricity payments. Moner-Girona et al. (2016) examine off-grid feed-in tariffs (FiT) for renewable energy for mini-grids and isolated areas in Tanzania. FiT allows renewable energy generators, private companies and individuals, to sell power generated from renewable sources to the national grid at an agreed cost. The tariffs provide three financial incentives, a payment for all the electricity produced even if the producer uses them, a payment for the portion of electricity generated that is sold to the grid, and a reduction in the payment of electricity used by the person who generates it. They conclude that off-grid FiT offers an opportunity to bring electricity to rural areas of Tanzania without harmful environmental impact while contributing to improved living conditions of the people (Moner-Girona et al. 2016). Other funding schemes include direct schemes such as donor funds, government subsidies, and private investments and indirect schemes such as value-added tax (VAT), import duty exemptions, and loan and credit schemes for importers of supplies (Hansen et al. 2015) and the "last-mile," a pay-as-you-go system (Barrie and Cruickshank 2017).

The deployment of disruptive energy technologies in Africa is not extensive, but several problems have been identified with the few that have been implemented. First and foremost is the cost. In recent years, the drop-in prices of PVs have been hailed in many circles as an important driver in the diffusion of PV systems. Yet the initial cost is still very high in places like Africa (Lemaire 2011). The result is that the adoption of PVs in many African countries seems to come from the top, the middle-class households, who are also environmentally conscious (Hansen et al. 2015). For some of the technologies such as waste-to-energy through hybrid incinerators or anaerobic digesters, the full cost of installation, operation, and maintenance is not known (Ayodele et al. 2017; Dlamini et al. 2019). Similarly, in their study of the adoption of the pay-as-you-go system to extend solar energy to rural homes in East-Central Africa, Barrie and

Cruickshank (2017) found that both the technology and business model were more complex and expensive than current alternatives.

Second, the load of PV systems tends to be intermittent and needs to be often supplemented by diesel-powered electric generators, which is not good for the environment. Azimoh et al. (2014) point out that this might be due to less optimal positioning of panels, and several measures taken by users to prevent solar panel thefts, which is a major problem in itself. These measures include positioning security lights around panels, setting panels flat in front of homes and moving them inside at night, and putting panels in iron cages. They suggest that in order to increase power-generating capacities of these systems, they must be at an appropriate angle. They suggest a bench-rack solar mounting system that will allow not only the appropriate tilt but will be easier to move the panel inside at night and out during daytime, to prevent theft.

Third, there is a perception of low profit margin in renewable energy investment. As a result, renewable energy investment is generally considered as public investment rather than a private one. This lack of domestic capital and investment leads to dependency on foreign capital (donor dependency). Dispersed settlement system coupled with rudimentary rural economy leads to low capacity to pay, while traditional houses of mud and grass in many areas of rural Africa are considered not conducive for electricity (Ahlborg and Hammar 2014).

Fourth, Dlamini et al. (2019) identify a very important problem related to WTE that can be extended to the deployment of all disruptive energy technologies, and that there is no large-scale effort to take advantage of the full range of disruptive energy technologies in Africa. As a result, there is no comprehensive regulatory framework, roadmap, or policy on these technologies. This has also led to limited demand for these technologies, difficulty in attracting capital into their development, and inadequate human capacity and know-how in the development, installation, and maintenance of these technologies. This perhaps is the biggest problem facing the use of disruptive energy technologies in Africa.

Going Forward

This chapter set out to examine the role of disruptive energy technologies in Africa's transition to sustainable energy generation and by extension green economy. Adopting a broader definition of disruptive energy technologies, as low-carbon technologies that have the potential to change

Africa's entire socioeconomic and political system, the chapter has shown that disruptive technologies could play a major role in sustainable energy generation and storage in Africa and for that matter in Africa's transition to a green economy. However, at their current state, this role cannot be realized because of barriers and the lack of a conducive policy environment. Previous works have offered several suggestions as to how to remove these barriers and create the right environment. Drawing on these suggestions, it is recommended that African countries should make sustainable energy generation and green economy a national policy. Such a policy should have several components. First, it should include the development of long-term renewable energy program (Karekezi 2002). This component should integrate the current energy generation into the new national energy policy, with a gradual phase-out strategy of reducing the dependence on fossil fuel-generated energy. It should also pave the way for legislation and other regulations that will influence the behavior of people—incentives such as tax breaks and subsidies. Second, the policy should include the development and deployment of carefully selected technological and institutional leapfrogging strategies (Karekezi 2002) or disruptive energy technologies. Given the abundance of sunlight and wind, these two could be the focus of such policies, but it should not be a one-size-fits-all strategy (Kaundinya et al. 2009; Lee et al. 2016). Given the geographic variation and location-specific problems within and among countries, the policy must be flexible enough to allow for local and regional specific assessment of socio-demographic, techno-economic and environmental feasibility of which disruptive energy technologies to adopt (Kaundinya et al. 2009).

Third, there should be a development of long-term renewable energy generation using disruptive energy technologies training and capacity building programs (Karekezi 2002; Aluya 2014). This should include training and capacity building in the knowledge and skills of renewable energy generation; training in the design, installation, and maintenance of disruptive energy technologies; as well as education of private enterprises and consumers of the potential benefits and uses of disruptive energy technologies, respectively. Fourth, the policy should also make provisions for new and flexible financing mechanisms (Karekezi 2002). One of the contributing factors to the success of PVs in East Africa is the long support by international donors (Hansen et al. 2015), but African countries need to wean themselves from this donor dependency that seems to permeate every development effort on the continent.

Fifth, the policy should also have a component on the development of strategies for wider application and dissemination of disruptive energy technologies (Karekezi 2002). Finally, the policy should go beyond the narrow goal of generating energy from sustainable sources using disruptive technologies. It should create and enable opportunities for harnessing the energy to productive activities, which will then ensure Africa's transition to a green economy. The formulation of such a policy should engage all stakeholders, which include local governments, private investors, consumers, as well as international agencies and NGOs. Lemaire's (2011) work in South Africa shows that when public stakeholders focus on creating an enabling environment, a well-articulated public-private partnership could deliver large-scale sustainable rural energy services.

While these challenges might be daunting, there are examples from both developed and developing countries that can provide very useful learning to African countries. Droste et al. (2016) report several case studies from European countries that show energy transitions from government initiative (Germany) and municipalities (Finland). Another example is India where the government's National Solar Mission of 2012 aimed at increasing solar power generation from 0.1 GW to 20 GW by 2022 reached 13 GW by 2017 at a lower cost than a newly built coal-powered plant (Pegels et al. 2018). Similarly, South Africa went from zero capacity of solar power generation in 2011 to more than 3.2 GW in 2017 (Pegels et al. 2018). These should serve as models for learning how to transition from current energy generation technologies to sustainable energy generation and green economy using disruptive energy technologies. Most importantly, this must be a long-term commitment, because Africa's future will depend on it.

REFERENCES

Adom, P. K. (2018). An Evaluation of Energy Efficiency Performances in Africa Under Heterogeneous Technologies. *Journal of Cleaner Production, 209,* 1170–1181.

Ahlborg, H., & Hammar, L. (2014). Drivers and Barriers to Rural Electrification in Tanzania and Mozambique: Grid-Extension, Off-Grid, and Renewable Energy Technologies. *Renewable Energy, 61,* 117–124.

Aluya, J. (2014). Leadership Styles Inextricably Intertwined with the Alternative Energy of Solar, Wind, or Hybrid as Disruptive Technologies, Energy Sources. *Part B: Economics, Planning, and Policy, 9*(3), 276–283.

Armstrong, P. (2017). *Disruptive Technologies: Understand, Evaluate, Respond.* New York: Kogan Page.

Arundel, A., Kanerva, M., & Kemp, R. (2011). *Integrated Innovation Policy for an Integrated Problem.* Europe: INNO-Grips II Report Brussels: European Commission, DG Enterprise and Industry.

Ayodele, T. R., Ogunjuyigbe, A. S. O., & Alao, M. A. (2017). Life Cycle Assessment of Waste-to-Energy (WtE) Technologies for Electricity Generation Using Municipal Solid Waste in Nigeria. *Applied Energy, 201,* 200–218.

Azimoh, C. L., Wallin, F., Klintenberg, P., & Karlsson, B. (2014). An Assessment of Unforeseen Losses Resulting from Inappropriate Use of Solar Home Systems in South Africa. *Applied Energy, 136,* 336–346.

Barrie, J., & Cruickshank, H. J. (2017). Shedding Light on the Last Mile: A Study on the Diffusion of Pay as You Go Solar Home Systems in Central East Africa. *Energy Policy, 107,* 425–436.

Borel-Saladin, J. M., & Turok, I. N. (2013). The Green Economy: Incremental Change or Transformation? *Environmental Policy and Governance, 23,* 209–220.

Bower, B. J. L., & Christensen, C. (1995). Disruptive Technologies: Catching the Wave. *Harvard Business Review, 73*(January-February), 43–53.

British Geological Survey. (2013). *World Mineral Production: 2007–2011.* Nottingham: British Geological Survey.

Brown, T. J., Idione, N. E., Raycraft, E. R., Shaw, R. A., Hobbs, S. F., Everett, P., Deady, E. A., & Bide, T. (2018). *World Mineral Production, 2012–2016.* Nottingham: British Geological Survey.

Bugaje, I. M. (2006). Renewable Energy for Sustainable Development in Africa: A Review. *Renewable and Sustainable Energy Reviews, 10,* 603–612.

Buseth, J. T. (2017). The Green Economy in Tanzania: From Global Discourses to Institutionalization. *Geoforum, 86,* 42–52.

Christensen, C. (1997). *The Innovator's Dilemma: When Technologies Cause Great Firms to Fail.* Boston: Harvard Business School Press.

Death, C. (2015). Four Discourses of the Green Economy in the Global South. *Third World Quarterly, 36*(12), 2207–2224.

Dixon, T., Lannon, S., & Eames, M. (2018). Reflections on Disruptive Energy Innovation in Urban Retrofitting: Methodology, Practice and Policy. *Energy & Social Science, 37,* 255–259.

Dlamini, S., Simatele, M. D., & Kubanza, N. S. (2019). Municipal Solid Waste Management in South Africa: From Waste to Energy Recovery Through Waste-to-Energy Technologies in Johannesburg. *Local Environment, 24*(3), 249–257.

Donaldson, D. B. (2014). *World's Biggest Hydro Power Project—Bigger than China's Three Gorges—in Africa Given Go-ahead by World Bank.* Available at: https://guardianlv.com/2014/04/worlds-biggest-hydro-power-project-bigger-than-chinas-three-gorges-in-africa-given-go-ahead-by-world-bank/. Accessed 1 Aug 2014.

Dosi, G. (1982). Technological Paradigms and Technological Trajectories: A Suggested Interpretation of the Determinants and Directions of Technical Change. *Research Policy, 11*, 147–162.

Dosi, G. (1984). *Technical Change and Industrial Transformation*. London: Macmillan.

Droste, N., Hansjürgens, B., Kuikman, P., Otter, N., Antikainen, R., Leskinen, P., Pitkanen, K., Saikku, L., Loiseau, E., & Thomsen, M. (2016). Steering Innovations Towards a Green Economy: Understanding Government Intervention. *Journal of Cleaner Production, 135*, 426–434.

Dütschke, E., & Wesche, J. P. (2018). The Energy Transformation as a Disruptive Development at Community Level. *Energy Research & Social Science, 37*, 251–254.

Eberhard, A., Rosnes, O., Shikaratan, M., & Vennemo, H. (2011). *Africa's Power Infrastructure: Investment, Integration, Efficiency*. Washington, DC: The World Bank.

Geels, F. W. (2018). Disruption and Low-Carbon System Transformation: Progress and New Challenges in Socio-technical Transitions Research and the Multi-Level Perspective. *Energy Research & Social Science, 37*, 224–231.

Hansen, U. E., Pedersen, M. B., & Nygaard, I. (2015). Review of Solar PV Policies, Interventions and Diffusion in East Africa. *Renewable and Sustainable Energy Reviews, 46*, 236–248.

International Renewable Energy Agency (IRENA). (2013). *Africa's Renewable Future: The Path to Sustainable Growth*. Abu Dhabi: IRENA.

Johnstone, P., & Kivimaa, P. (2018). Multiple Dimensions of Disruption, Energy Transitions and Industrial Policy. *Energy Research & Social Science, 37*, 260–265.

Karekezi, S. (2002). Renewables in Africa—Meeting the Energy Needs of the Poor. *Energy Policy, 30*, 1059–1069.

Kaundinya, D. P., Balachandra, P., & Ravindranath, N. H. (2009). Grid-Connected Versus Stand-Alone Energy Systems for Decentralized Power—A Review of Literature. *Renewable and Sustainable Energy Reviews, 13*, 2041–2050.

Kramer, G. J. (2018). Energy Scenarios—Exploring Disruption and Innovation. *Energy Research & Social Science, 37*, 247–250.

Lee, K., Brewer, E., Christiano, C., Meyo, F., Miguel, E., Podolsky, M., Rosa, J., & Wolfram, C. (2016). Electrification for "Under Grid" Households in Rural Kenya. *Development Engineering, 1*, 26–35.

Lemaire, X. (2011). Off-Grid Electrification with Solar Home Systems: The Experience of a Fee-for-Service Concession in South Africa. *Energy for Sustainable Development, 15*, 277–283.

Loiseau, E., Saikku, L., Antikainen, R., Droste, N., Hansjürgens, B., Pitkanen, K., Leskinen, P., Kuikman, P., & Thomsen, M. (2016). Green Economy and Related Concepts: An Overview. *Journal of Cleaner Production, 139*, 361–371.

Lucas, H. C., Jr. (2012). *The Search for Survival: Lessons from Disruptive Technologies.* Santa Barbara: Praeger.

McDowall, W. (2018). Disruptive Innovation and Energy Transitions: Is Christensen's Theory Helpful? *Energy Research & Social Science, 37,* 243–246.

Moner-Girona, M., Ghanadan, R., Solano-Peralta, M., Kougias, I., Bódis, K., Huld, T., & Szabó, S. (2016). Adaptation of Feed-in Tariff for Remote Mini-grids: Tanzania as an Illustrative Case. *Renewable and Sustainable Energy Reviews, 53,* 308–318.

Monforti, F. (2011). *Renewable Energies in Africa.* Luxembourg: European Union.

Mundaca, L., Neij, L., Markandya, A., Hennicke, P., & Yan, J. (2016). Towards a Green Energy Economy? Assessing Policy Choices, Strategies and Transitional Pathways. *Applied Energy, 179,* 1283–1292.

National Research Council of the National Academies. (2010). *Persistent Forecasting of Disruptive Technologies, Report 2.* Washington, DC: National Academies Press.

Nelson, R. R., & Winter, S. (1977). In Search for a Useful Theory of Innovations. *Research Policy, 6,* 36–76.

OECD. (2011). *Towards Green Growth.* Paris: OECD.

Ofori-Amoah, B. (1995). Regional Impact on Technological Change: The Evolution and Development of the Twin-Wire Paper Machine from 1950 to 1968. *Environment & Planning A, 27,* 1503–1520.

Ofori-Amoah, B. (2019). *Africa's Geography: Dynamics of Place, Cultures, and Economies.* Hoboken: Wiley.

Otieno, H. O., & Awange, J. L. (2006). *Energy Resources in East Africa: Opportunities and Challenges.* Heidelberg: Springer-Verlag.

Pearce, F. (2013). Will Huge New Hydro Projects Bring Power to Africa's People? http://e360.yale.edu/feature/will_huge_new_hydro_projects_bring_power_to_africas_people/2656/. Accessed 1 Aug 2014.

Pearce, D., Markandya, A., & Barbier, E. (1989). *Blueprint for a Green Economy.* London: Earthscan.

Pegels, A., Vidican-Auktor, G., Lutkenhorst, W., & Altenburg, T. (2018). Politics of Green Energy Policy. *Journal of Environment & Development, 27*(1), 26–45.

Razavi, H., Nzabanita, E., & Santi, E. (2012). Energy Sector. In E. Santi, S. B. Romdhane, & W. Shaw (Eds.), *Unlocking North Africa's Potential through Regional Integration: Challenges and Opportunities* (pp. 26–54). Tunis-Belvedere: African Development Bank.

Sprei, F. (2018). Disrupting Mobility. *Energy Research & Social Sciences, 37,* 238–242.

The Breakthrough Institute. (2016). *Energy for Human Development* [Online]. Available at: https://thebreakthrough.org/articles/energy-for-human-development. Accessed 15 Oct 2018.

Tryou, T. (2016). *The Five Biggest Wind Energy Markets in Africa*. Available at: http://www.renewableenergyfocus.com/view/44926/the-five-biggest-wind-energy-markets-in-africa/. Accessed 15 Oct 2018.

Tyfield, D. (2018). Innovating Innovation—Disruptive Innovation in China and the Low-Carbon Transition of Capitalism. *Energy Research & Social Science, 37*, 266–274.

UN WCED. (1987). *Our Common Future—The Brundtland Report*. Report of the World Commission on Environment and Development. Oxford: Oxford University Press.

UNEP. (2011). *Towards a Green Economy: Pathways to Sustainable Development and Poverty Eradication. A Synthesis for Policy Makers*. France: UNEP.

UNEP. (2015). *Building Inclusive Green Economies in Africa Experience and Lessons Learned, 2010–2015*. Nairobi: UNEP.

Verma, R. K., & Singh, S. N. (2013). A Review of Mini-Grid Used for Electrification in Rural Areas. *American International Journal of Research in Science, Technology, Engineering & Mathematics, 3*(2), 140–144.

Vermeulen, N. (2017). Disruptive Technologies. *Magazine of the South African Institution of Civil Engineering*, 25 (8), 43–49.

Wanner, T. (2015). The New 'Passive Revolution' of the Green Economy and Growth Discourse: Maintaining the 'Sustainable Development' of Neoliberal Capitalism. *New Political Economy, 20*(1), 21–41.

Warner, J., Jomantas, S., Jones, E., Ansari, M. S., & de Vries, L. (2019). The Fantasy of the Grand Inga Hydroelectric Project on the River Congo. *Water, 11*(407), 1–14.

Wilson, C. (2018). Disruptive Low-Carbon Innovations. *Energy Research & Social Science, 37*, 216–227.

Wilson, C., & Tyfield, D. (2018). Critical Perspectives on Disruptive Innovation and Energy Transformation. *Energy Research & Social Science, 37*, 211–215.

World Bank. (2012). *Inclusive Green Growth: The Pathway to Sustainable Development*. Washington, DC: World Bank Publications.

World Bank. (2018). *Tracking SDG7: The Energy Progress Report. A Joint Report of the Custodian Agencies*. The World Bank Group: Washington, DC.

PART III

Transformations in the Socioeconomic Sphere

CHAPTER 6

Disruptive Technologies and the African Health-Care Crisis: A Path to Sustainability

Joseph Oppong

Introduction

Despite global efforts to reduce health inequality through the Millennium
Development Goals (MDGs) and the expanded Sustainable Development
Goals (SDGs), Africa's health indicators remain much worse than other
continents. Within the African continent itself, extreme health disparities
exist, and health outcomes and indicators are worst particularly in fragile
countries, rural areas, urban slums, conflict zones, and among poor, dis-
abled, and marginalized populations. In addition, African countries face a
worsening double burden of communicable and noncommunicable diseases. Chronic health conditions such as hypertension, diabetes, and mental health disorders continue to surge in addition to traditional challenges
such as malaria, tuberculosis, and malnutrition. Child and maternal mortality rates remain much higher than in the rest of the world. Shrinking
health budgets, escalating health-care costs, and diminishing skilled health
worker populations, due to an ever-worsening brain drain of trained health

J. Oppong (✉)
Department of Geography and Environment, University of North Texas,
Denton, TX, USA
e-mail: joseph.oppong@unt.edu

© The Author(s) 2020   117
P. Arthur et al. (eds.), *Disruptive Technologies, Innovation and
Development in Africa*, International Political Economy Series,
https://doi.org/10.1007/978-3-030-40647-9_6

workers, exacerbate these problems. These challenges demand urgent and radical solutions, especially the deployment of new health technologies to expand the current reach of health care, but their potential and limitations in the African context remain unclear.

This chapter examines the potential role of disruptive technologies in Africa's health-care crisis. It begins with a brief review of the major health crisis of African countries and demonstrates the exciting potential of new health technologies to make health care more accessible and convenient while outlining the challenges in deploying them in the African context. Citing examples from several countries, it highlights the policy framework needed to facilitate the deployment of such disruptive health technologies. It argues that the huge potential benefit of such technologies is not achievable or sustainable in Africa in the absence of critically important infrastructure, including secure but accessible personal health data systems and supportive legal environment. The chapter concludes by outlining policy options for expanding geographic access to health care through disruptive technologies across Africa.

The African Health-Care Crisis

Africa's health care is in a crisis. In addition to new disease outbreaks such as Ebola and endemic malaria and long-term challenges such as HIV and tuberculosis, the continent faces the most severe health worker shortage worldwide. The World Health Organization (WHO) recommends a threshold of an aggregate density of 4.45 physicians, nurses, and midwives per 1000 population to meet the SDG health-related goals (WHO 2016), but most African countries do not meet this standard. In fact, according to the latest available data for the period 2007–2016, most African countries reported having less than one physician per 1000 population (WHO 2016). For example, between 2014 and 2017, Malawi had 1 physician for 62,500 people, Tanzania had 1:25,000, and Chad, Togo, Burundi, and Niger all exceeded 1:20,000. Ethiopia, Zambia, Zimbabwe, Mozambique, and Uganda had in excess of 10,000 people served by 1 physician (Table 6.1 and Figs. 6.1 and 6.2). Moreover, rural-urban disparities in the distribution of health workers are the norm—most health workers are in the major urban centers leaving rural areas with a severe dearth of health workers.

Table 6.1 and Fig. 6.1 illustrate these issues. Using data extracted from the World Health Organization (WHO) Global Health Observatory, the first two columns of Table 6.1 show the medical doctor density, defined as the number of doctors per 10,000 population, for 2003–2005 and

Table 6.1 Medical doctor density per 10,000 people

Country	Doctor density 2014–2017	Doctor density 2003–2005	Percent change	People per physician 2003–2005	People per physician 2014–2017
Algeria	18.3	10.2	79.4	980	546
Angola	2.2	0.6	247.7	16,129	4651
Benin	1.6	0.4	292.0	25,000	6369
Botswana	3.7	3.9	−5.7	2558	2710
Burkina Faso	0.6	0.5	10.5	18,519	16,667
Burundi	0.5	0.3	79.9	35,714	20,000
Cape Verde	7.7	No data	NA	No data	1300
Côte d'Ivoire	2.3	1.2	101.2	8621	4292
Comoros	No data	1.9	NA	5181	No data
Congo	No data	2.1	NA	4762	No data
Democratic Republic of the Congo	No data	No data	NA	No data	No data
Central African Republic	0.6	0.8	−22.9	12,195	15,873
Chad	0.5	0.4	33.8	27,778	20,833
Djibouti	2.2	1.7	31.6	5988	4545
Egypt	7.9	5.2	51.9	1923	1266
Equatorial Guinea	4.0	2.1	90.7	4762	2500
Eritrea	No data	0.6		17,857	No data
Ethiopia	1.0	0.3	274.5	37,037	10,000
Gabon	3.6	2.9	24.7	3448	2770
Gambia	1.1	1.2	−9.3	8403	9259
Ghana	1.8	1.5	16.6	6494	5556
Guinea	0.8	1.0	−24.2	9615	12,658
Guinea-Bissau	2.0	1.4	43.7	7194	5000
Kenya	2.0	No data	NA	No data	5025
Liberia	0.4	0.3	15.1	31,250	27,027
Lesotho	No data	0.5	NA	21,739	No data
Libya	21.6	12.4	74.1	807	463
Madagascar	1.8	1.6	16.0	6410	5525
Malawi	0.2	0.2	−25.2	47,619	62,500
Mali	1.4	0.9	63.9	11,765	7194
Mauritania	1.8	1.0	74.0	9709	5587
Mauritius	20.3	10.7	88.9	933	494
Morocco	7.3	5.3	37.2	1887	1376
Mozambique	0.7	0.3	190.5	40,000	13,514
Namibia	No data	3.0	NA	3356	No data
Niger	0.5	0.2	122.2	43,478	20,000
Nigeria	No data	2.8	NA	3546	No data

(*continued*)

Table 6.1   (continued)

Country	Doctor density 2014–2017	Doctor density 2003–2005	Percent change	People per physician 2003–2005	People per physician 2014–2017
Rwanda	1.4	No data	NA	No data	7407
São Tomé and Príncipe	3.2	5.3	−40.0	1876	3125
Senegal	0.7	0.5	27.7	18,519	14,493
Sierra Leone	No data	0.3	NA	32,258	No data
Somalia	0.2	No data	NA	No data	43,478
Seychelles	9.5	13.8	−31.6	723	1057
South Africa	9.1	7.2	26.1	1385	1099
Sudan[a]	4.1	2.5	NA	4000	2439
Togo	0.5	0.4	10.4	22,727	20,408
Tunisia	12.7	13.3	−4.4	751	786
Tanzania	0.4	No data	NA	No data	25,000
Uganda	0.9	0.8	13.4	12,500	10,989
Zambia	0.9	1.3	−28.6	7813	10,989
Zimbabwe	0.8	1.6	−53.3	6135	13,158

[a]The most recent data on Sudan is not comparable to the older data because of South Sudan's 2011 independence. There is no data in this dataset on South Sudan

Source: WHO Global Health Observatory Data Repository. http://apps.who.int/gho/data/node.main.HWFGRP_0020?lang=en. Accessed 8/19/19

Column 1: Medical doctors per 10,000 population: 2014–2017. World Health Organization, Global Health Observatory Data Repository

Column 2: Medical doctors per 10,000 population: 2004–2005. World Health Organization, Global Health Observatory Data Repository

Table 6.1 shows the medical doctor density, defined as the number of doctors per 10,000 population, for 2003–2005 and 2014–2017 as reported by the WHO (Global Health Observatory). To facilitate meaningful comparison, I computed the total number of people per physician as well as the percent change, rounding them to one decimal place. For example, for Algeria in 2014–2017, the medical doctor density of 18.3 per 10,000 people translates into each physician serving 546 people. This is a 79.4% improvement over the 2003–2005 period figure of 10.2 doctors per 10,000 people and a physician population ratio 1:980.

2014–2017. To facilitate meaningful comparison, I computed the total number of people per physician and the percent change rounded to one decimal place. For example, for Algeria in 2014–2017, the medical doctor density of 18.3 per 10,000 people translates into each physician serving 546 people. This is a 79.4% improvement over the 2003–2005 period with 10.2 doctors per 10,000 people and a physician population ratio

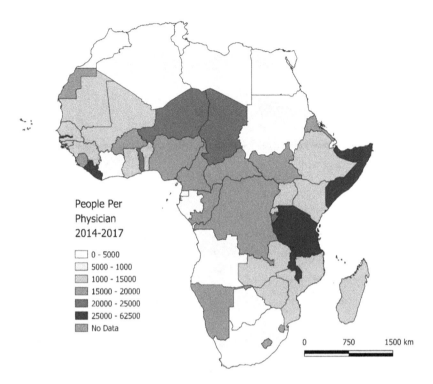

Fig. 6.1 Physician density 2014–2017. (Created using data extracted from WHO Global Health Observatory Data Repository)

1:980. In 2003–2005, only a handful of African countries including Algeria, Botswana, Egypt, Equatorial Guinea, Gabon, Mauritius, São Tomé and Príncipe, Seychelles, South Africa, and Tunisia met the WHO standard of medical doctor density per 10,000 people (Table 6.1). Some of the countries with extremely high physician population ratios included Liberia, Burundi, Chad, Ethiopia, Malawi, Mozambique, and Somalia (Fig. 6.1). For 2014–2017, the situation had improved in most countries but worsened significantly in Central African Republic, Guinea, Malawi, Zambia, and Zimbabwe (Fig. 6.3).

This worsening physician-population ratio has been attributed to the ever-increasing health worker brain drain (Mwang'ombe 2017). While high-ranking politicians and the affluent travel for medical treatment in more developed countries, the poorly paid and overworked health

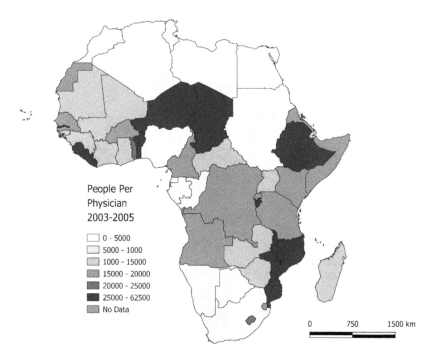

Fig. 6.2 Physician density 2003–2005. (Created using data extracted from WHO Global Health Observatory Data Repository)

workers leave for better working conditions in more economically developed countries, exacerbating the health worker-population ratios.

The case of Malawi is illustrative. From 1 doctor to 47,619 people in 2004, it worsened to 1:62,500 people in 2016, a 25% decline. According to Vidal (2015), Malawi's health-care brain drain was due to several factors including low salaries (a doctor earned $7000 (US) a year in 2012), poor working conditions, overwork, and limited career opportunities, in a climate of political instability, and a high risk of HIV infection at work due to inadequate protection. Overall, about 20% of African-born physicians work in high-income countries such as the United States, United Kingdom, Canada, and Australia (Mullan 2005; Duvivier et al. 2017).

Moreover, health spending is low (Micah et al. 2019) and continues to shrink in a global environment of escalating health-care costs (Table 6.2). Across the continent, per-person government health spending ranged

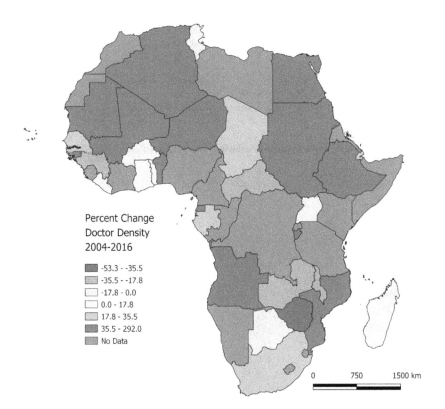

Fig. 6.3 Physician density change (2003–2005 to 2014–2017). (Created using data extracted from WHO Global Health Observatory Data Repository)

from $16.36 (US) in Central African Republic to $553.10 (US) in Mauritius (Table 6.2). For the Democratic Republic of the Congo (DRC), Mozambique, Gambia, Niger, Burundi, Madagascar, Ethiopia, Malawi, Mali, and Eritrea, the annual per capita government health expenditure in 2016 was less than $30 (US). In fact, most African countries spent less than $70.00 per capita (Fig. 6.4). Such low government spending on health reflected high individual out-of-pocket expenditures, a major factor in health inequities. As a percentage of government health expenditure, out-of-pocket expenditure ranged from 2.1, 5.2, and 6.4 in Seychelles, Botswana, and Rwanda, respectively, to 75.2 in Nigeria (Table 6.2).

Table 6.2 Health-care costs and percentage of GDP, health expenditures per capita (US $), out-of-pocket (OOP) costs, and percentage of health expenditures that come from OOP

Countries	Health expenditures as % of GDP	Per capita health expenditures in PPP	Per capita health expenditures in US $	Out-of-pocket health expenditures per capita (US $)	% of health expenditures from OOP
Algeria	6.6	998.15	260.41	80.42	30.9
Angola	2.9	185.82	95.22	33.53	35.2
Benin	3.9	83.48	30.40	13.22	43.5
Botswana	5.5	931.30	379.92	19.94	5.2
Burkina Faso	6.8	115.60	40.94	12.85	31.4
Burundi	7.7	62.41	22.93	5.63	24.6
Republic of Cabo Verde	5.3	349.40	159.88	41.38	25.9
Cameroon	4.7	169.29	64.47	44.81	69.5
Central African Republic	4.3	29.91	16.36	7.05	43.1
Chad	4.5	94.95	31.69	19.38	61.2
Comoros	7.6	115.85	59.00	43.15	73.1
Congo	4.6	263.29	70.38	34.99	49.7
Côte d'Ivoire	4.4	162.64	67.57	27.13	40.1
Democratic Republic of the Congo	3.9	34.49	20.52	7.68	37.4
Djibouti	3.5	122.08	70.19	18.09	25.8
Egypt	4.6	516.34	130.99	81.20	62.0
Equatorial Guinea	3.4	838.74	281.37	204.94	72.8
Eritrea	3.0	55.33	29.89	17.65	59.1
Ethiopia	4.0	69.52	27.52	10.30	37.4
Gabon	3.1	555.63	220.35	49.61	22.5
Gambia	4.4	74.31	20.93	4.94	23.6
Ghana	4.4	189.37	67.51	25.53	37.8
Guinea	5.5	107.72	37.46	18.64	49.8
Guinea-Bissau	6.1	97.97	39.05	13.83	35.4
Kenya	4.5	143.54	66.21	18.35	27.7
Lesotho	8.1	242.73	85.52	16.15	18.9
Liberia	9.6	133.15	68.31	32.29	47.3
Madagascar	6.0	90.43	24.12	5.39	22.4

(*continued*)

Table 6.2 (continued)

Countries	Health expenditures as % of GDP	Per capita health expenditures in PPP	Per capita health expenditures in US $	Out-of-pocket health expenditures per capita (US $)	% of health expenditures from OOP
Malawi	9.8	115.16	29.59	3.37	11.4
Mali	3.8	81.18	29.79	10.51	35.3
Mauritania	4.2	163.92	46.77	23.81	50.9
Mauritius	5.7	1206.74	553.10	266.38	48.2
Mozambique	5.1	61.65	19.21	1.47	7.7
Namibia	9.1	969.26	402.76	31.09	7.7
Niger	6.2	61.43	22.68	13.27	58.5
Nigeria	3.6	213.74	79.34	59.67	75.2
Rwanda	6.8	130.38	48.08	3.07	6.4
São Tomé and Príncipe	6.0	196.90	105.13	15.14	14.4
Senegal	5.6	143.96	53.45	27.23	51.0
Seychelles	3.9	1122.56	596.92	12.44	2.1
Sierra Leone	16.5	244.04	86.31	35.86	41.6
South Africa	8.1	1071.35	428.18	33.19	7.8
South Sudan	3.2	148.30	7.51	3.83	51.1
Sudan	5.7	297.86	152.02	112.34	73.9
Swaziland	7.7	663.25	220.59	21.84	9.9
Togo	6.6	99.90	38.77	19.55	50.4
Tunisia	7.0	806.34	256.50	102.35	39.9
Uganda	6.2	117.11	37.61	15.16	40.3
United Republic of Tanzania	4.1	111.98	35.50	7.77	21.9
Zambia	4.5	175.18	56.54	6.85	12.1
Zimbabwe	9.4	185.05	93.94	19.96	21.2

Source: World Health Organization, Global Health Expenditure Database. http://apps.who.int/nha/database/Select/Indicators/en. Accessed 8/19/19

The African region has a much higher disease burden. With 11% of the world's population, Africa has 60% of the global population with HIV/AIDS, more than 90% of the 300–500 million malaria cases each year, and the highest maternal and child mortality (WHO 2019a, b). In addition to these communicable diseases, noncommunicable diseases such as hypertension, heart disease, and diabetes are surging. In 2016, heart disease was the fourth leading cause of death, surpassing malaria and tuberculosis,

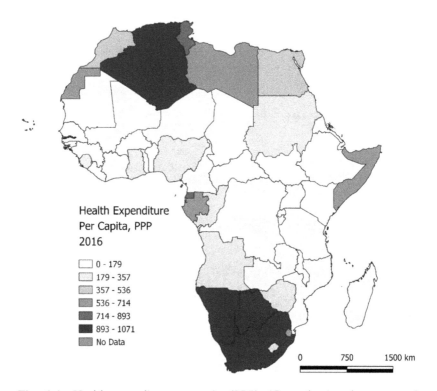

Fig. 6.4 Health expenditure per capita (PPP). (Created using data extracted from World Health Organization, Global Health Expenditure Database. (Table 6.2 in the text). http://apps.who.int/nha/database/Select/Indicators/en. Accessed 8/19/19)

followed by stroke in seventh place (WHO 2018) (Table 6.3). In fact, stroke and heart disease accounted for 10% of all deaths.

Hypertension has emerged as a major health challenge, but most African countries have no national plans to address the problem (Dzudie et al. 2018). In 2014, only about one-quarter of African countries had a national hypertension control policy (Wang et al. 2018). Because the rising prevalence of hypertension coincides with persistently low awareness, treatment, and control rates, stroke has become a leading cause of mortality, disability, and dementia in Africa and has the highest incidence of stroke worldwide, 316 per 100,000 population (Owolabi et al. 2015).

Table 6.3 WHO African region: Top 20 leading causes of death

		2016				2000	
Rank	Cause	% of total deaths	Deaths per 100,000 population	Rank	Cause	% of total deaths	Deaths per 100,000 population
	All causes	100.0	867.2		All causes	100.0	1461.9
1	Lower respiratory infections	10.4	89.9	1	HIV/AIDS	12.2	178.6
2	HIV/AIDS	8.1	70.5	2	Lower respiratory infections	10.6	155.2
3	Diarrheal diseases	7.4	64.0	3	Diarrheal diseases	9.7	142.3
4	Ischemic heart disease	5.8	50.2	4	Malaria	7.3	106.2
5	Malaria	4.6	40.0	5	Measles	4.3	62.3
6	Tuberculosis	4.6	39.8	6	Tuberculosis	4.0	57.8
7	Stroke	4.2	36.6	7	Preterm birth complications	3.9	57.4
8	Preterm birth complications	3.9	33.7	8	Ischemic heart disease	3.8	55.9
9	Birth asphyxia and birth trauma	3.7	31.7	9	Birth asphyxia and birth trauma	3.8	55.6
10	Road injury	3.2	27.8	10	Stroke	3.1	44.7
11	Protein-energy malnutrition	2.4	20.5	11	Meningitis	2.5	36.8
12	Maternal conditions	2.2	19.0	12	Maternal conditions	2.4	35.3
13	Congenital anomalies	2.1	18.6	13	Protein-energy malnutrition	2.3	33.6
14	Meningitis	2.1	18.2	14	Road injury	1.8	27.0
15	Cirrhosis of the liver	2.0	17.1	15	Neonatal sepsis and infections	1.6	23.8
16	Neonatal sepsis and infections	2.0	16.9	16	Congenital anomalies	1.5	22.5
17	Diabetes mellitus	1.9	16.4	17	Cirrhosis of the liver	1.4	21.2

(*continued*)

Table 6.3   (continued)

		2016				2000	
Rank	Cause	% of total deaths	Deaths per 100,000 population	Rank	Cause	% of total deaths	Deaths per 100,000 population
	All causes	100.0	867.2		All causes	100.0	1461.9
18	Chronic obstructive pulmonary disease	1.3	11.5	18	Diabetes mellitus	1.0	14.9
19	Interpersonal violence	1.2	10.4	19	Interpersonal violence	1.0	13.9
20	Alzheimer disease and other dementias	1.0	8.9	20	Chronic obstructive pulmonary disease	0.9	13.2

Data Source: WHO 2000 and 2016 (Global Health Observatory Data Repository)

Unlike other world regions where stroke incidence and mortality are decreasing, Africa has the highest age-standardized stroke incidence, prevalence, and mortality and the rates are increasing (Norrving and Kissela 2013; Owolabi et al. 2015). Because it affects a relatively younger age group, the long-term disability toll of stroke across Africa is a huge problem (Owolabi et al. 2019).

AFRICAN MENTAL HEALTH

Worldwide, 24% of countries that reported to the WHO's 2014 Mental Health Atlas survey lacked stand-alone mental health policies; in Africa, this proportion rose to 46%. The African region had 1.4 mental health workers per 100,000 population, compared with a global average of 9 per 100,000 (van Rensburg and Fourie 2016). It also performs relatively poorly in the number of psychiatrists, the number of hospital beds for patients with mental illness, and the coverage of outpatient facilities. Consequently, the proportion of Africans who receive treatment for mental health problems is extremely low. While the global annual rate of visits to mental health outpatient facilities is 1051 per 100,000 population, in Africa the rate is 14 per 100,000. In Sierra Leone, for example, an estimated 98.8% of those in need of formal mental health services go untreated (Sankoh et al. 2018). Thus, in addition to the dual burden, Africa faces looming mental and behavioral health problems (WHO Mental Health Atlas 2014). To summarize, the resources to address Africa's complex health problems remain severely inadequate. In addition, infrastructure limitations exacerbate the health problems. Water and sanitation are inadequate in many countries and many people in rural areas have no access to electricity.

DEFINING DISRUPTIVE TECHNOLOGIES

First proposed by Clayton Christensen, disruptive innovation explains the process whereby simpler, affordable products and services eventually replace cumbersome, expensive, and inaccessible ones. In the process, new technologies displace existing businesses and technologies and create new markets and business practices, requiring new infrastructure and different labor skills. The result usually lowers costs, increases quality, and expands access (Christensen et al. 2015). For example, as Christensen, Bohmer, and Kenagy (2000:135) and colleagues argue, "health care delivery is convoluted, expensive, and often deeply dissatisfying to consumers." Disruptive health innovation will simplify, reduce cost, and increase access to those currently without access. Consequently, the concept of disruptive technologies is particularly pertinent to African health care; it is extremely expensive, inaccessible to most people, and unsatisfactory to most consumers. High-quality, inexpensive or low-cost, and accessible alternatives are a pressing necessity.

The idea of disruptive innovation is simple enough. New technologies such as internet communication technologies and mobile phones have completely transformed communication. Previously, phone calls required landlines and had fixed origins and destinations, and only the affluent could own a phone. The ubiquity of mobile phones today means that phone calls can originate from and reach almost everywhere, and instant phone communication is accessible to everyone, not only to the wealthy. Even more important, mobile phone technology has spawned new lines of business such as mobile money and telemedicine, expanding banking and health-care access. The previous dependence and restrictions imposed by landlines and telephone poles are history, and previously inaccessible locations and people are now easily accessible.

Likewise, new technologies are disrupting and improving health and health care in developed countries and gradually in Africa. For example, the use of portable monitors in diabetes and hypertension is widespread. Previously, diabetes patients could determine their blood glucose levels only through a hospital visit and trained physicians using an expensive glucometer in a hospital setting. New technologies now allow patients to manage their blood sugar levels using simple, portable blood glucose meters conveniently with no need for physicians. Thus, diabetes patients get better quality care more conveniently. By enabling patients to manage their blood glucose level, portable glucose monitors have expanded the reach of diabetes control and management and improved the quality of their lives (Vashist 2013).

Similarly, portable blood pressure monitors are making a huge difference. In fact, out-of-office blood pressure monitoring may be superior to conventional office blood pressure monitoring in the diagnosis, treatment, evaluation, and prediction of cardiovascular events (Bonafini and Fava 2015). Blood pressure monitoring at home can improve care and control and reduce the hypertension and stroke disease burden. This is essential because optimal blood pressure control and prevention of cardiovascular events require that the blood pressure profile of each hypertensive patient be determined based on 24-hour ambulatory blood pressure monitoring (ABPM) or home blood pressure monitoring (HBPM), and their antihypertensive drug regimen tailored accordingly (Ndip Agbor et al. 2017). Previously this would have required costly hospitalization of such patients.

Indeed, self-monitoring using portable monitors is pivotal and the preferred method for the management of chronic diseases such as diabetes and hypertension. Self-monitoring of blood glucose helps in diagnosing glycemic extremes and facilitates treatment adjustment to achieve long-term goals (Klonoff 2007). In addition, it reduces morbidity and mortality by permitting patients to confirm glycemic extremes quickly, facilitates patient education, and improves glycemic control. The wide use of self-blood glucose monitoring devices can significantly reduce the disease burden and mortality rates associated with diabetes as has happened in more developed countries. Likewise, due to its cost-effectiveness, wide availability, ability to increase patient compliance to treatment, and consequently its potential to achieve optimal blood pressure control, home blood pressure monitoring is preferred (Ndip Agbor et al. 2017).

In the African context, disruptive technologies should enable a larger population of less-skilled health workers to provide in more convenient, proximate, and less expensive settings services previously provided only by physicians and medical specialists in centralized, inconvenient, and distant locations (Christensen et al. 2000). Disruptive innovations could ease the African health-care crisis significantly, cut health-care costs, and improve health-care access to the millions currently without access. New precision diagnostic tests allow less-skilled health workers such as physician assistants and nurses to diagnose simple diseases such as malaria and strep infections or as serious as diabetes.

Disruptive Health Technologies and Africa

Traditionally, medicine has relied on costly specialists whose extensive training and lengthy experience enables them to recognize disease patterns and arrive at reasonable diagnoses. New diagnostic technologies such as imaging and molecular biology now make it possible to pinpoint the causes of a disease, replacing "intuitive medicine" (Christensen, et al 2009). Despite the existence of new equipment that enables high quality and low cost, health care remains costly and inaccessible for many due to obsolete business models. The fee-for-service business model dates from the nineteenth century, long before diagnostic imaging and biochemical testing became matters of routine. Protective regulatory barriers erected since that time have blocked innovation in health-care business models (Hwang and Cristensen 2008). For example, the physicians' trade associations determine who will receive licenses to practice medicine, and then the government reimburses care only when the doctors who dispense it have those licenses. Although using new technology and less expensive technicians to perform work that previously required doctors could cut costs significantly, physicians have little incentive to allow that.

Nevertheless, innovations are creeping into health care with admirable results. Information management and health-care delivery using mobile phones, computers, and iPad have become a routine in developed countries fostering drastic improvements. Automating repetitive manual image analysis tasks using artificial intelligence is reducing radiologist fatigue and improving diagnostic accuracy and patient outcomes. Essentially, by extending the reach of doctors and off-site specialists and improving their ability to diagnose and record patient information accurately and efficiently, portable medical technology is improving health-care access.

Across Africa, glimpses of the use of new health technologies are everywhere. In Uganda, government health workers use mTrac, a portable medical technology based on mobile phones, to report on national medicine stocks (Jimenez 2015). In Kenya and Ghana, respectively, two mobile applications, Miti Health and mPedigree, authenticate the currency of prescription and over-the-counter drugs, thereby significantly reducing the risk of administering expired drugs. In Tanzania, Ifakara Health Institute uses modern ultrasound devices to monitor the welfare of pregnant women in rural areas.

The emergence of smartphones is radically improving health care. For example, smartphone apps facilitate the timely delivery of prescriptions from the pharmacy and scheduling of medical appointments. In addition to global positioning system (GPS) in smartphones facilitating ambulance and emergency service delivery, it provides the geographical location of patients, crucial information for diagnosis. Sonderman et al. (2018) reported on using mobile phones and community health workers to improve follow-up and referral of patients with cesarean-related surgical site infections in rural Rwanda. The app prompted the health worker to evaluate and take a photograph of the wound, which is then sent to a surgeon for assessment.

Remote Imaging, Diagnostics, and Robots

Particularly exciting and rapidly increasing applications of disruptive technology are remote radiology, imaging services, and diagnostics. Facilitated by mobile phone technology, it allows experts to respond with diagnosis and treatment recommendations almost instantly. Teleradiology operates in Ethiopia, Uganda, Zimbabwe, Djibouti, Botswana, Nigeria, Cameroon, Tanzania, and Zambia (Santra et al. 2019). Potentially, this could have a huge side benefit, making health data collection routine.

A similar application of remote technologies is making a huge impact on the diagnosis and treatment of tuberculosis in Ghana. According to the World Health Organization 2015 report, despite an excellent 85% cure rate for known cases, about 67% of all new tuberculosis cases in the country remained undetected due to the slow and expensive diagnostic process. Through the application of Computer-Aided Detection for TB (CAD4TB) and teleradiology technology, Delft Imaging Systems installed permanent and mobile X-ray units across the country. Because the units are connected to a central database and diagnostic viewing station, health providers can benefit from the assistance of remote experts when needed.

Through such technology, remote consultations and regular self-health monitoring can replace routine medical consultations. Quality metrics drawn from a system of interconnected digital health tools can enhance both outpatient and hospital care. Patient care decisions can benefit from the collective wisdom of a huge pool of international experts, allowing health workers to become skilled interpreters of precision diagnostics, tracking, and treatment tools.

In developed countries, robots are invading traditional laboratories and transforming them through automation. Due to their flexibility and ability to work long hours in any environment, robots are now employed to perform repetitive tasks in hazardous environments and to complete toxic medical experiments (Tan et al. 2016). Previously, magnetic microbots have been in various medical surgeries, including kidney and open-heart surgery. Newer robots, advanced machine vision, access to huge volumes of artificial intelligence, and improved sensors have expanded such use (Manyika et al. 2013). Now, robots are used not only for diagnostics and surgery but also to rehabilitate patients and restore lost body parts. In Monrovia, a robot created by Vecna Technologies using a two-way communication system—an iPad on wheels—enabled doctors to assess incoming Ebola patients without physically examining them (West 2015). The approach was effective because it reduced potential infections in health-care workers.

CareAi

Artificial intelligence (AI) may be a game changer for health-care services. One of the technologies, an "AI doctor," an AI-powered computing system anchored on blockchain that can diagnose infectious diseases, such as malaria, typhoid fever, and tuberculosis, within seconds, has great potential for health care in Africa (Ekekwe 2018). CareAi uses a blood sample from a finger prick, deposited onto a chip for analysis (Tsaloglou et al. 2018). After referencing numerous medical and diagnostic libraries and quick statistical analysis, the system provides diagnosis with statistical probabilities. For example, "given your geographic location and demographics, the presence of xx in your blood specimen suggests that there is a 95% probability that you have malaria." The system thus quickly diagnoses a disease where one exists, delivers the results with confidence analysis, and recommends additional actions such as prescriptions at participating pharmacies or referral for further medical treatments (Ekekwe 2018).

CareAi can extend health care to those living in areas with limited health-care facilities, especially if the recommendations are personalized with the patients' medical records. Using AI to treat common diseases such as malaria routinely could free up the limited health-care professionals to focus on the more complicated health issues. Indeed, technology could improve the areal reach of health services while cutting the need for health-care professionals (Ekekwe 2018).

BIMA Doctor Service

BIMA, a provider of mobile-based insurance and health products, provides an excellent illustration of how disruptive technologies can improve access to health care in African countries. BIMA's mobile health service, BIMA Doctor, was launched in 2015 in Ghana to address the scarcity of traditional health-care resources. Since then BIMA Doctor Service has operated in Bangladesh, Pakistan, Paraguay, and Cambodia, reaching 26 million subscribers in 15 markets across Africa, Asia, and Latin America.

For one fee, paid via mobile money, BIMA Doctor offers unlimited mobile phone medical consultation and health programs to subscribers and their families. In addition to preventive care and unlimited consultations through chat or calls, BIMA Doctor provides referrals to a network of laboratories and hospitals when necessary, and patients may receive discounts. Additionally, the BIMA Doctor App allows digital customers to access and manage their medical records, locate the nearest health facility, and talk to the BIMA Doctor medical team by phone or chat.

This provides very good care to those who need it and eliminates the need for traveling long distances and long waiting times in a clinic before seeing a doctor. The flexibility to consult a physician when needed is particularly suited to farmers and those working in the informal sector, who are typically not available during normal health facility operating hours. Typically, the inability to find the time and money to reach a health facility translates into delayed diagnosis, treatment, and poorer health outcomes.

BIMA's technology platforms create a paperless experience and enable scale while distributing health products and providing customer health education. Integrating the mobile insurance platform with the billing infrastructure of mobile phone operators permits customers to register and pay for insurance premiums entirely via their mobile phones. This innovative approach removes the high distribution cost and provides an effective recurring payment channel for those without regular bank accounts. BIMA Doctor provides helpful support, offering customers advice and tips on managing common health conditions such as diabetes and hypertension, weight loss, and women and children's health.

Getting Medical Supplies to Remote Areas: Medical Drones to the Rescue

Severe bleeding during delivery or after childbirth contributes to around 34% of maternal deaths in Africa (African Health Observatory 2014). Because timely access to safe supplies of blood for transfusion is critically important to saving these women's lives, in many countries, family members are often pressured to donate blood or find other donors during emergencies. Besides the emotional and financial stress, the significant delays in obtaining suitable blood put the recipients at risk of blood-borne infections since there is often no time or facilities to screen the donated blood properly (African Health Observatory 2014). In Rwanda and Ghana, drones are making a difference providing timely access to needed blood and medical supplies.

In 2016, Zipline, a San Francisco-based company, began what has become a national on-demand medical drone network in Rwanda, delivering 150 medical products, mostly blood and vaccines, to hard-to-reach places (Medical Futurist 2018a). This service has put every Rwandan within 30 minutes of life-saving medical supplies. After its Rwandan success, Zipline extended the service to Ghana where drones travel to 500 health facilities within an 80 km range drone delivery network and distribute vaccines, blood products, medications, and other products (Asiedu 2019). The service operates from four distribution centers, delivers to 12,000 health-care facilities, and reaches an estimated 12 million people, providing emergency and routine deliveries 24 hours a day, 7 days a week. In addition to the expected decline in maternal mortality through timely delivery of blood products, drone deliveries can enable routine immunization on demand and expand vaccination coverage, especially for children. It can help to contain outbreaks of life-threatening communicable diseases (CNBC 2019).

Despite these benefits, the high cost of the drone program is a source of contentious debate (Sigal 2019). In Ghana, the price tag of $12 million (US) for the four-year contract was a huge point of contention. Critics questioned whether these funds could not be invested in ways that are more beneficial.

E-Health

E-health deals with the internet-based provision of health-care services. It addresses the challenges in health-care information systems and improves information transfer between medical institutions and facilitates communication between consumers (patients and medical personnel) and access to the consumer online system (Eysenbach 2001). The improved communication between physician and patient ensures active patient involvement in treatment decision-making. In the United States, options of different health-care providers through e-health facilitate quality care as competition among providers for patients drives up the quality of health-care services. E-health could make a huge difference in Africa.

One version of e-health, electronic health records (EHR), is defined as real-time, patient-centered records that provide immediate and secure information to authorized users (WHO 2019c). A substitute for the traditional paper charts that collect, store, and display patient information, EHR typically contain a patient's medical history, diagnoses and treatment, medications, allergies, immunizations, as well as radiology images and laboratory results. EHR systems can increase access to reliable patient information to multiple health-care providers and are vital for universal health coverage (Evans et al. 2013).

Tierney (2010) implemented EHR in six HIV clinics in Kenya, Tanzania, and Uganda and reported that successful implementation depended critically on funding. Successful EHR use and sustainability were enhanced by local control of funds, academic partnerships (mainly by leveraging research funds), and in-country technology support. Similarly, West (2015) describes several applications of EHR in Nigeria, Liberia, Sierra Leone, and Morocco. In Nigeria, the system, CliniPAK, enabled midwives with tablets to capture patient medical information, including demographics, and personal and family health history, which were then used in the diagnosis and treatment of clinical conditions associated with infant and maternal mortality. It was also deployed to provide Ebola tutorial content to frontline health workers in Liberia (West 2015).

However, data security is a potential problem. The threat of unauthorized access to individual patient health data remains a huge concern. It may worsen health disparities between the rich and poor as well as urban and rural areas due to differential access to technology such as smartphones. Rural residents typically have poorer access to most advanced technologies (e.g., internet networks).

For e-health to play its full role in helping health systems achieve the targets of universal health care (UHC) and to be truly integrated into daily health-care services, several political and policy changes will have to be made in many health-care systems. For example, a comprehensive legal framework for e-health must address the transfer and use of information between health-care workers and patients. Issues of privacy and confidentiality of patient data, rules on access rights and sharing rights for data, as well as data quality and integrity must be addressed. An excellent appraisal of the inherent challenges of developing appropriate legal frameworks for e-health and telemedicine in developing countries is available in a European Space Agency (ESA) 2013 report.

CHALLENGES OF DISRUPTIVE HEALTH TECHNOLOGIES

While these examples suggest almost limitless improvement to health care in African countries through the employment of such new technologies, significant and formidable challenges remain. Perhaps the most difficult challenge is infrastructure. Telemedicine requires large and dependable information communication networks. Weak communication networks slow information transmission, interrupt video streaming, and undermine the efficiency of telemedicine. Eliminating the "dead zones" requires installing additional cellphone towers but may not always make economic sense to profit-minded businesses. Yet, this infrastructure is key.

Even more fundamental, stable electrical power access remains a serious challenge in many countries. The 20 countries with the lowest electrification rates worldwide are in Africa and include Burundi, Chad, Malawi, the Democratic Republic of the Congo, and Niger, the 5 countries with the lowest electrification rates in 2017 (IEA, IRENA, UNSD, WB, WHO 2019). Most countries simply lack the ability to generate and distribute dependable electrical power. To successfully operate, telemedicine requires costly but critically important maintenance and support. Failing that, equipment failure can shut down the entire system and interrupt service. Remote monitoring tools that permit off-site support can reduce downtime. Locally trained technicians to maintain and service such equipment are vital.

Other challenges include the high illiteracy rate and the gap between the rich and poor that could limit the benefits to only specific portions of the population—the affluent, educated urban residents. The cost of smartphones is prohibitive for many, but even pricier is the cost of data. In addition, expertise to train people to use such technologies is vital. Finally, serious mass education efforts will be necessary to overcome the inertia many people have of using new technology. Some populations prefer to see a doctor in person and consider telemedicine as impersonal and inferior (Santra et al. 2019).

Good, clean health data is an enormous challenge. For example, the effective treatment of a case of malaria requires not just diagnosis but also knowledge of the medical history of the person, their current medications, and other considerations. Feeding that data to AI systems could make it possible for the AI to prescribe medication confidently and connect the specific patient to the right pharmacy, with all processes handled digitally. However, the paucity of reliable digital health data remains a huge challenge across the continent. Good data, with strong privacy and security, is a foundational, core requirement, in a future of digital health care.

Political interference with communication and information networks and disruption by unscrupulous hackers threaten digital health care. It is necessary to invest heavily in the routine collection and protection of health-care data systems from the growing threat of hackers and unscrupulous users. Similarly, political interference with networks must end. The shutting down of networks, or certain sites, during elections or moments of crisis, well documented during the Arab Spring and recently in Tanzania, Uganda, and Chad, must cease. Even more fundamentally, universal home address systems or some other systems to facilitate the collection and use of health data are overdue.

The role of programming and using artificial intelligence cannot be overemphasized. Artificial intelligence is only as good as the humans programming it and the system in which it operates. Improperly used, AI could unintentionally exacerbate many of the worst aspects of our current health-care system. This is because using deep and machine learning, AI systems analyze enormous amounts of data to make predictions and recommend interventions. In the United States, for example, a major concern about all health-care datasets is that they perfectly record a history of unjustified and unjust disparities in access, treatments, and health outcomes (Kocher and Emanuel 2019). Incorporating such patient-generated data from sensors, phones, and social media may simply exacerbate historical inequities and biases (Kocher and Emanuel 2019).

Results from the training datasets could worsen historical disparities because the machines assume that the underlying data accurately reflect optimal health-care treatment and outcomes. Moreover, addressing

AI-generated disparities in health care will be extremely difficult because people rarely question their underlying algorithms. As Kocher and Emmanuel point out, we need to identify and fit biases in our datasets before we entrust our health care to AI systems and "doctor robots" (Kocher and Emanuel 2019).

PROSPECTS: MOVING FORWARD WITH DISRUPTIVE HEALTH TECHNOLOGIES IN AFRICA

Information and communications technology is crucial in overcoming the physical limitations of traditional health care. Unlike the past, when patients could only visit a doctor in person, it is now possible to have remote consultations via voice, video, instant messaging, or email. The ability to deliver health care without the confines of physical space is surely a disruptive technology that increases access to health care by overcoming the obstacles of cost, distance, and availability of experienced health personnel. It can help patients manage chronic diseases through effective self-monitoring, provision of information to influence behavior, leading to better outcomes.

However, since disruptive innovation could jeopardize public safety, we need to proceed with caution. Although current regulations maintain the status quo and perpetuate the costly and cumbersome health-care system, entirely replacing them is not feasible. For example, current regulations requiring only physicians to write prescriptions entrench the need to visit a physician to get a prescription even for health conditions that can easily be diagnosed by an untrained health worker. However, a situation where untrained health workers freely prescribe medications with little regulation or oversight is not the answer. Essentially, the hegemony of established structures and institutions must be dismantled, but slowly and carefully. We need to develop policies that incentivize easy adoption and support new technologies specifically geared toward improving health care. In fact, African governments have a huge role to play in facilitating the adoption and deployment of digital health technologies in African countries. They must carefully weigh the benefits and dis-benefits and share such information where possible.

A policy that neither stifles innovation nor is reckless in its implementation is needed. Despite the risks that every new technology presents, drone technology, for example, can drastically improve health-care service delivery. The African continent is the perfect setting to explore this technology because the rural-urban divide, transportation challenges, and financial constraints make delivering quality health care to the entire population a daunting task. We need to exploit the opportunities that drone technology provides in a creative and responsible manner.

Yet some risk is necessary. The development of innovative technologies should be guided by an appropriate regulatory framework as most people accept novelties if some quality and safety guarantees are in place. Moreover, technology companies can also work more efficiently if they can adjust their operation to a stable policy framework (Medical Futurist 2018b). Thus, the regulation must be transparent enough to encourage innovation while simultaneously providing guidelines in line with international best practices. Governments and regulatory agencies have a huge role in shaping people's attitudes and approach toward technologies and innovation in general. If the adoption of novelties is not hindered but facilitated by institutions, positive change is more likely to happen. We can learn from the experiences of more developed countries.

In 2017, the British National Health Service (NHS) rolled out a program that encourages physicians to prescribe apps for their patients with chronic conditions such as chronic obstructive pulmonary disease (COPD) or gestational diabetes. The apps can transmit patient data from a tablet or smartphone directly to clinicians. A two-year trial at the Royal Berkshire NHS Foundation Trust found that the system reduced the number of patient visits by 25%. We need to remember that technology enables behavior change, but technology alone is insufficient to induce behavior change.

By deploying disruptive technologies, remote consultations and regular self-health monitoring can replace routine medical consultations. Quality metrics drawn from a system of interconnected digital health tools can enhance care. Through AI, patient care decisions can benefit from the collective wisdom of a huge pool of international experts and allow health workers to become skilled interpreters of precision diagnostics, tracking, and treatment tools. However, moving forward requires significant investment in infrastructure, including basic national address systems for electronic health data collection and routine use of such data. The fragmented health-care infrastructure will need to integrate in order to achieve the benefits of disruptive health technologies.

CONCLUSION

Disruptive technologies can potentially improve health-care access in African countries and bring health care to those currently without access. To realize this potential requires effective regulation and policies that facilitate, not obstruct, their deployment. Improved data and data security are essential to avoid misuse. Universal address systems are essential. Improving access to electrical power and internet access to those currently without access is vital. Government policies should aim to eliminate the dead zones, especially in cases where it does not make economic sense for private investors to expand the bandwidth.

Most people have already embraced the digital future. While developed countries have advanced in the use of these disruptive technologies, African countries are slowly crawling into the use of these technologies. There is a need to adapt these technologies for the African continent. Addressing such challenges can provide interventions to tackle Africa's health-care crisis and bring quality health care to the many who currently have no care.

However, we should not overemphasize the role of new technologies in addressing Africa's health-care crisis. The real benefit of technology is physician decision support. Technology cannot be a substitute for trained health-care workers. However, it can expand the reach, efficiency, and access to such workers. Employing disruptive health technologies can provide help for those who currently need it most but have the least access to modern health care, the poor rural residents of African countries. It is about time.

REFERENCES

African Health Observatory. (2014). *Blood Safety and Maternal Mortality in the African Region*. Retrieved from http://www.aho.afro.who.int/en/blog/2014/08/07/blood-safety-and-maternal-mortality-african-region . Accessed 21 Sept 2019.

Asiedu, K. G. (2019, April 25). An Ambitious Drone Delivery Health Service in Ghana is Tackling Key Logistics Challenges. *Quartz Africa*. Retrieved from https://qz.com/africa/1604374/ziplines-drone-delivery-launches-in-ghana-with-vaccines/. Accessed 20 Sept 2019.

Bonafini, S., & Fava, C. (2015). Home Blood Pressure Measurements: Advantages and Disadvantages Compared to Office and Ambulatory Monitoring. *Blood Pressure, 24*(6), 325–332. https://doi.org/10.3109/08037051.2015.1070599.

Christensen, C. M., Bohmer, R. M. J., & Kenagy, J. (2000). Will Disruptive Innovations Cure Health Care? *Harvard Business Review, 78*(5), 102–117.

Christensen, C. M., Grossman, M. D., & Hwang, J. (2009). *The Innovator's Prescription: A Disruptive Solution for Health Care.* McGraw-Hill.

Christensen, C. M., Raynor, M., & McDonald, R. (2015). What Is Disruptive Innovation? *Harvard Business Review, 93*(12), 44–53.

CNBC. (2019). *Zipline Takes Flight in Ghana, Making it the World's Largest Drone-Delivery Network.* Extracted from https://www.cnbc.com/2019/04/24/with-ghana-expansion-ziplines-medical-drones-now-reach-22m-people.html

Duvivier, R. J., Burch, V. C., & Boulet, J. R. (2017). Correction to: A Comparison of Physician Emigration from Africa to the United States of America Between 2005 and 2015. *Human Resources for Health, 15*(1), 76–76. https://doi.org/10.1186/s12960-017-0251-y.

Dzudie, A., Rayner, B., Ojji, D., Schutte, A. E., Twagirumukiza, M., Damasceno, A., & PASCAR Task Force on Hypertension. (2018). Roadmap to Achieve 25% Hypertension Control in Africa by 2025. *Global Heart, 13*(1), 45–59. https://doi.org/10.1016/j.gheart.2017.06.001.

Ekekwe, N. (2018). How New Technologies Could Transform Africa's Health Care System. *Harvard Business Review.* Retrieved from https://hbr.org/2018/08/how-new-technologies-could-transform-africas-health-care-system. Accessed 21 Sept 2019.

European Space Agency. (2013). *Satellite-Enhanced Telemedicine and E-health for Sub-Saharan Africa (eHSA) Programme.* Kimberly: Greenfield Management Solutions. Extracted from: http://www.greenfield.org.za/downloads/eHSA%20Reg%20Study%20Summary%20Report.pdf. Accessed 21 Sept 2019.

Evans, D. B., Hsu, J., & Boerma, T. (2013). Universal Health Coverage and Universal Access. *Bulletin of the World Health Organization, 91,* 546–546A. https://doi.org/10.2471/BLT.13.125450.

Eysenbach, G. (2001). What is e-health? J Med Internet Res 2001;3(2):e20 https://www.jmir.org/2001/2/e20. https://doi.org/10.2196/jmir.3.2.e20. PMID: 11720962. PMCID: PMC1761894.

Hwang, J., & Christensen, C. M. (2008). Disruptive Innovation in Health Care Delivery: A Framework for Business-Model Innovation. *Health Affairs, 27*(5), 1329–1335.

International Energy Agency, International Renewable Energy Agency, United Nations Statistics Division, World Bank, & World Health Organization. (2019). *Tracking SDG 7: The Energy Progress Report 2019.* Washington, DC: World Bank.

Jimenez, J. (2015). *3 Ways to Improve Healthcare in Africa.* World Economic Forum. Extracted from https://www.weforum.org/agenda/2015/01/3-ways-to-improve-healthcare-in-africa/. Accessed 20 Sept 2019.

Klonoff, D. C. (2007). Benefits and Limitations of Self-Monitoring of Blood Glucose. *Journal of Diabetes Science and Technology, 1*(1), 130–132. https://doi.org/10.1177/193229680700100121.

Kocher, B., & Emanuel, Z. (2019). *Will Robots Replace Doctors?* Washington, DC: The Brookings Institution.

Manyika, J., Chui, M., Bughin, J., Dobbs R., Bisson, P., & Marrs, A. (2013). *Disruptive technologies: Advances that will transform life, business, and the global economy.* (May). McKinsey Global Institute Available at: https://www.mckinseypp..com/business-functions/digital-mckinsey/our-insights/disruptive-technologies. Accessed 10 June 2019.

Medical Futurist. (2018a). *Africa is a Hotspot for Digital Health.* Retrieved from https://medicalfuturist.com/africa-hotspot-digital-health/. Accessed 20 Sept 2019.

Medical Futurist. Digital Health Best Practices for Policy Makers: A Free Report. (2018b). Retrieved from https://medicalfuturist.com/digital-health-best-practices-policy-makers-free-report/. Accessed 1 Sept 2019.

Micah, A. E., Chen, C. S., Zlavog, B. S., Hashimi, G., Chapin, A., & Dieleman, J. L. (2019). Trends and Drivers of Government Health Spending in Sub-Saharan Africa, 1995–2015. *BMJ Global Health, 4*(1), e001159–e001159. https://doi.org/10.1136/bmjgh-2018-001159.

Mullan, F. (2005). The Metrics of the Physician Brain Drain. *The New England Journal of Medicine, 353*(17), 1810–1818. https://doi.org/10.1056/NEJMsa050004.

Mwang'ombe, N. J. (2017). The African Health Workforce Brain Drain. The Socioeconomic and Geopolitical Realities. *SciFed Journal of Surgery, 1*(1). https://doi.org/10.23959/sfjos-1000002.

Ndip Agbor, V., Temgoua, M. N., & Noubiap, J. J. N. (2017). Scaling Up the Use of Home Blood Pressure Monitoring in the Management of Hypertension in Low-Income Countries: A Step Towards Curbing the Burden of Hypertension. *Journal of Clinical Hypertension, 19*(8), 786–789. https://doi.org/10.1111/jch.12999.

Norrving, B., & Kissela, B. (2013). The Global Burden of Stroke and Need for a Continuum of Care. *Neurology, 80*(3), S12.

Owolabi, M. O., Akarolo-Anthony, S., Akinyemi, R., Arnett, D., Gebregziabher, M., Jenkins, C., & H3Africa Consortium. (2015). The Burden of Stroke in Africa: A Glance at the Present and a Glimpse into the Future. *Cardiovascular Journal of Africa, 26*(2), S27–S38. https://doi.org/10.5830/CVJA-2015-038.

Owolabi, M., Sarfo, F. S., Akinyemi, R., Gebreyohanns, M., & Ovbiagele, B. (2019). The sub-Saharan Africa Conference on Stroke (SSACS): An Idea Whose Time Has Come. *Journal of the Neurological Sciences, 400*, 194–198. https://doi.org/10.1016/j.jns.2019.03.026.

Sankoh, O., Sevalie, S., & Weston, M. (2018). Mental Health in Africa. *The Lancet Global Health,* 6(9), e954–e955. https://doi.org/10.1016/S2214-109X(18)30303-6.

Santra, S., Santra Mandal, T., & Das, P. (2019). *Leveraging Disruptive Technology Innovations for Healthcare Delivery in Sub-Saharan Africa* (No. Brief 298). Observer Research Foundation.

Sigal, S. (2019). *Ghana's New Lifesaving Drones: Like Uber, but for Blood.* Extracted from https://www.vox.com/future-perfect/2019/6/4/18647685/medical-drones-ghana-africa-zipline-global-health. Accessed 21 Sept 2019.

Sonderman, K. A., Nkurunziza, T., Kateera, F., et al. (2018). Using Mobile Health Technology and Community Health Workers to Identify and Refer Caesarean-Related Surgical Site Infections in Rural Rwanda: A Randomised Controlled Trial Protocol. *BMJ Open, e022214,* 8. https://doi.org/10.1136/bmjopen-2018-022214.

Tan, A., Ashrafian, H., Scott, A. J., Mason, S. E., Harling, L., Athanasiou, T., & Darzi, A. (2016). Robotic Surgery: Disruptive Innovation or Unfulfilled Promise? A Systematic Review and Meta-Analysis of the First 30 Years. *Surgical Endoscopy,* 30(10), 4330–4352. https://doi.org/10.1007/s00464-016-4752-x.

Tierney, W. M. (2010). Experience Implementing Electronic Health Records in Three East African Countries. *Studies in Health Technology and Informatics,* 160(Pt 1), 372–374.

Tsaloglou, M., Nemiroski, A., Camci-Unal, G., Christodouleas, D. C., Murray, L. P., Connelly, J. T., & Whitesides, G. M. (2018). Handheld Isothermal Amplification and Electrochemical Detection of DNA in Resource-Limited Settings. *Analytical Biochemistry, 543,* 116–121. https://doi.org/10.1016/j.ab.2017.11.025.

van Rensburg, A. J., & Fourie, P. (2016). Health Policy and Integrated Mental Health Care in the SADC Region: Strategic Clarification Using the Rainbow Model. *International Journal of Mental Health Systems, 10*(1), 49–49. https://doi.org/10.1186/s13033-016-0081-7.

Vashist, S. K. (2013). Continuous Glucose Monitoring Systems: A Review. *Diagnostics (Basel, Switzerland), 3*(4), 385–412. https://doi.org/10.3390/diagnostics3040385.

Vidal, P (2015). The Migration of Health Workers: Malawi's Recurring Challenges. (Washington, DC: Migration Policy Institute, 2015). https://www.migrationpolicy.org/article/emigration-health-care-workers-malawi%E2%80%99s-recurring-challenges.

West, D. M. (2015). *Using Mobile Technology to Improve Maternal Health and Fight Ebola: A Case Study of Mobile Innovation in Nigeria.* Brookings Institute. Available at: https://www.brookings.edu/wp-content/uploads/2016/06/CTINigeria.pdf. Accessed 20 Sept 2019.

World Health Organization. (2014). *Mental Health Atlas 2014.* Retrieved from http://www.who.int/mental_health/evidence/atlas/executive_summary_ en.pdf?ua=1. Accessed 20 Sept 2019.

World Health Organization. (2016). *Global Strategy on Human Resources for Health: Workforce 2030.* http://www.who.int/hrh/resources/pub_glob-strathrh-2030/en/. Accessed 20 Sept 2019.

World Health Organization. (2018). *Global Health Estimates 2016: Burden of Disease by Cause, Age, Sex, by Country and by Region, 2000–2016.* Retrieved from http://www.who.int/healthinfo/global_burden_disease/estimates/en/ index1.html Accessed 20 Sept 2019.

World Health Organization. (2019a). *Global Health Expenditure Database.* Retrieved from http://apps.who.int/nha/database/Select/Indicators/en Accessed 20 Sept 2019.

World Health Organization. (2019b). *Global Health Observatory Data Repository.* Retrieved from http://apps.who.int/gho/data/node.main.HWFGRP_0020? lang=en. Accessed 20 Sept 2019.

World Health Organization. (2019c). *Global Observatory for e-health.* Retrieved from https://undatacatalog.org/dataset/global-observatory-ehealth-goe. Accessed 25 Apr 2020.

World Health Organization. *Global Health Observatory Data Repository.* Medical Doctors per 10,000 Population 2004–2005. Retrieved from: http://apps. who.int/gho/data/node.main.HWFGRP_0020?lang=en. Accessed 19 Sept 2019.

World Health Organization. *Global Health Observatory Data Repository.* Medical Doctors per 10,000 Population 2014–2017. Retrieved from http://apps.who. int/gho/data/node.main.HWFGRP_0020?lang=en. Accessed 19 Sept 2019.

Wong, N. D., Moran, A., & Narula, J. (2018). Hypertension Control in Africa: A Call to Action. *Global Heart, 13*(1), 1–2. https://doi.org/10.1016/j. gheart.2018.03.002.

CHAPTER 7

Disruptive Technology and Knowledge Development: African Universities, Human Capital and Educating for Global Citizenship

Korbla P. Puplampu and Samuel M. Mugo

INTRODUCTION

The role of higher education or universities has been vital in the global and national development discourse since the post- World War II. In more recent times, higher education featured in both the United Nations-inspired Millennium and Sustainable Development Goals and other global initiatives. While the former set of goals, 2000 to 2015, had a commitment to education (MDG 2), the latter goals, from 2015 to 2030, expanded the interest in education with SDG 4, focusing on quality education and other levels of education (UNDP 2003, 2015). SDG 4 has a 2030 target to ensure equal access to affordable and quality technical,

K. P. Puplampu (✉)
Department of Sociology, Grant MacEwan University, Edmonton, AB, Canada
e-mail: puplampuk@macewan.ca

S. M. Mugo
Department of Physical Sciences, Grant MacEwan University,
Edmonton, AB, Canada
e-mail: mugos@macewan.ca

© The Author(s) 2020
P. Arthur et al. (eds.), *Disruptive Technologies, Innovation and Development in Africa*, International Political Economy Series,
https://doi.org/10.1007/978-3-030-40647-9_7

vocational and tertiary education for all (United Nations 2015:21). The UNESCO Incheon 2015 Declaration within the Education 2030 Framework for Action also reiterated SDG 4 (UNESCO 2015). While SDG 4 is directly on education, SDG 10 (reduced inequalities) and SDG 17 (partnerships for development) are indirectly contingent on education. The importance of university education, the focus in this chapter, is not only based on the university's role as the premier enterprise for educating members of society and contributing to knowledge production and dissemination in the name of social development, but also because when it comes to the rate of return on education, as an investment, the return on universities is much higher than was previously acknowledged (McCowan 2016).

However, universities, their outlook, mandate and overall role in society reflect the nature of the global divide, a product of political and socio-historical factors. For universities in the global South, particularly in the case of the African subregion, interest in their role takes on an added significance in any discourse on knowledge production and utilization in the national development agenda, especially in an era of neoliberal globalization. A key feature of neoliberal globalization is the changing role of the state and the wholesale restructuring of state institutions based on market principles of efficiency in the allocation of resources. With the rise of public demand and quest for a share of state resources, allocations to universities have declined. As such, universities have undertaken and pursued myriad strategies to innovate and respond to neoliberal globalization (Puplampu and Wodinski 2016). The strategies include the amalgamation or closure of departments and learning sites that are not seen as profitable, the recruitment of part-time instructors with full-time instructors taking on additional administrative and service obligations, intense efforts to open overseas satellite campuses, links with for-profit organizations and soliciting funds from wealthy private donors or foundations and alumni, the recruitment of foreign students who are charged a differential tuition and claims as educating for global citizenship.

Globalization and its compression of time and space features, engendered by communication and informational technological changes, precisely the internet have led to transformations in universities and potential disruptive outcomes (Internet Society 2017). Policy makers and analysts therefore cite the internet and disruptive technology as central in how universities can transform learning (Christensen et al. 2011; Christensen et al. 2008). The argument is that technological innovations make it possible to offer online learning opportunities with the necessary changes in curriculum. Online learning and curriculum reforms better the position of universities in their mission to deepen the human capital of learners. Students, the argument also goes, given their knowledgeability in utilizing technology in learning, can become global citizens, since learning in the online environment, by default, makes possible their global awareness and transformative orientations. While the emerging role of technology can be considered as a game changer, it is debatable whether online learning platforms can, without adequate resources, provide the level of deep learning especially in science, engineering and technology programs, where laboratory discovery-based experiential skills are necessary to acquire any level of proficiency, if creativity is also an objective.

African universities, as their counterparts elsewhere, are confronted with several conflicting demands. For public universities in Africa, the situation is more dire since the growing demand for university education with declining resources raises questions about the quality of education and labor market performance for learners. There is growing literature on how African universities have responded to these changes and justify their existence (Swartz et al. 2019; Puplampu 2006; Wangenge-Ouma and Nafukho 2011). Several of these studies have placed the changes in African universities and, rightfully so, in the broader context of globalization. Drawing on these studies, this chapter seeks, first, to survey the contemporary higher educational environment in Africa, identify and analyze the extent to which the disruptive and transformational possibilities of open innovation through online learning and curriculum reforms influence education. Second, the chapter will examine how these opportunities can elevate human capital development and educating for global citizenship. We argue that disruptive technology per se is not the magic bullet to engender human capital development and global citizenship, because technology functions in a social context and, like academic knowledge production and utilization, is not neutral in terms of impact.

In what follows, we first present a conceptual and theoretical overview of innovation, disruptive technology and higher education, human capital and global citizenship. The second section examines notable aspects of higher education in contemporary African universities. The third section will analyze the intricacies in the relationship among disruptive technology, online learning and curriculum reforms for meaningful transformations in human capital and educating for global citizenship. The last section will present the concluding remarks and some thoughts on policy directions for African universities in a milieu of innovation and disruptive technology.

DISRUPTIVE TECHNOLOGY, EDUCATING FOR HUMAN CAPITAL AND GLOBAL CITIZENSHIP

Technology has been part of human systems and institutions of learning since time immemorial. Universities have incorporated technology into learning, beginning with early distance learning and adult education based on postal services to the black or white board, overhead projectors, to contemporary PowerPoint and smartboards based on breakthroughs in communication and information technologies. With these breakthroughs, the nature of instructor learning relations has also undergone significant changes. For example, while earlier forms of learning involved face-to-face interaction between educators and learners in a physical location, changing technology has made learning relationships to defy time and space constrains (Isabirye and Dlodlo 2014).

The paradigm shifts in the relationship between learners and educators as well as the consequent proliferation of different forms of pedagogy can be situated in the Open Educational Resources (OER) movement (Yuan and Powell 2013). UNESCO (cited in Patru and Balaji 2016:20) defines OER as

> teaching, learning and research materials in any medium, digital or otherwise, that reside in the public domain or have been released under an open license that permits no-cost access, use, adaptation and redistribution by others, with no or limited restrictions. Open licensing is built within the existing framework of intellectual property rights as defined by relevant international conventions and respects the authorship of the work.

The digital aspects of OER are best actualized by disruptive technology and learning. Disruptive technology is about changes in the creation and dissemination of products and services, respectively. As an innovative system, disruptive technology seeks to focus on products or services within a market context with respect to market competitors (Christensen 1997). There are several innovative features of disruptive technology. For example, universities can provide products and services based on market principles. Disruptive technology demonstrates the impact that technology can have on learning without the constrains of time and space. In applying disruptive to higher education, Christensen and Eyring (2011) draw attention to how online learning in higher education would make universities, both public (nonprofit) and private (for-profit), to rethink the traditional model for higher education.

The relationship between disruptive technology and higher education requires a focus on the nature of, and the relationship between, the curriculum and online learning. This is because curriculum constitutes the basis of any educational experience (Barrier et al. 2019; Luckett 2016). Curriculum according to Forquin refers to "what is supposed to be taught and learned in a determined order or programming and progression within a given course" (cited in Barrier et al. 2019:34). With the emerging technologies, universities can, through curriculum transformation, keep themselves globally competitive and better able to cater to the learning needs of their digital natives, who are forever wired and live in a wired world (Garrison and Kanuka 2004; Czerniewicz and Brown 2009). However, curriculum, as the basis of what is taught, could contain omissions, hidden or implicit biases and reflect the legitimation of knowledge and power in the society (Puplampu 2008). Thus, the curriculum is an expression of normative values, the subject of contestations and not a neutral document in the education process. Even in the case of universities where the curriculum is organized based on expert knowledge with notions of professional autonomy and academic freedom at stake, the curriculum is still containing omissions and a reflection of knowledge and power (Barrier et al. 2019).

The question becomes how the curriculum can be transformed and the implications of online learning systems for student learning. Online learning or electronic learning is basically "the provision of education or training electronically through the Internet" (Keegan 2003:1). Electronic systems of learning amount to complex relations between hardware and software and other cognitive ways for learning because of the interface and presentation of learning material. When the *New York Times* famously declared 2012 as the Year of the Massive Open Online Course (MOOC), the declaration obscured its historical background (Pappano 2012).

The term MOOCs is the brainchild of Dave Cormier, University of Prince Edward Island in Canada, who used the label in 2008 to describe a course called *Connectivism and Connective Knowledge* that was developed by other Canadian academics, George Siemens and Stephen Downes of Athabasca University and the University of Manitoba, respectively (Flynn 2013). The unique aspect of the course was that it had a small group of fee-paying students and a substantially large number of nonpaying online learners. MOOCs denote what McCowan (2016:516) calls the unbundling of higher education, which is the dramatic shift of the unity of universities, and reveals "not only the extraction of the teaching elements of universities, but a further paring down of the instructional process. MOOCs represent the presentation of knowledge content and learning activities, but in most cases without personal tutoring and without the validation aspect of credit-bearing awards." The online environment is therefore the best illustration of how digital forms of learning and curriculum transformations have revolutionized pedagogy worldwide.

Online education can take on two main forms. First, it can be an initiative within a university and a specific course that learners can enroll in as part of their program requirements. In this case, students are fee paying and would get certification at the end of their program of study. It is important to note that students in different locales can also register for the course. In the second scenario, the online course assumes a global bearing in the sense that it is promoted by a global and often external partner to students the world over, irrespective of location. For example, MOOCs, even though online, can also be differentiated from an online course on several grounds (Patru and Balaji 2016:19). MOOC, in theory, does not have a cap on class size, requires no entry qualifications and may be accessible at no charge or for a fee.

There are four major players at the helm of the global MOOC revolution; these are Coursera, Udacity, edX (all based in the United States) and FutureLearn located in the United Kingdom (UK) (Internet Society 2017). Both Coursera and Udacity have roots in Stanford University and are for-profit organizations, the former associated with Daphne Koller and Andrew Ng who established it in 2012, while the latter was founded by Sebastian Thrun in 2011. edX was created by MIT and Harvard as a nonprofit entity, while FutureLearn is the MOOC platform for UK's Open University. Beyond the four major MOOCs, other countries such as Germany, China and Brazil continue to establish MOOC platforms. MOOCs do not always neatly fit into any program of study or toward certification but cater mostly to professionals looking for professional development opportunities. When such a course is offered by a MOOC giant like Coursera, which is a profit entity, learners must pay for it, the issue is if the credit they receive could count toward any certification, especially when Coursera is not affiliated with a local university. The challenge is that online courses are often designed in distant locales and inherently local in terms of context, but through the magic of communication technologies such courses are distributed across national borders and available to students in locations beyond the site where course was initially created. The fundamental question is the relevance of online courses for the local context when it comes to the acquisition of human capital and educating for global citizenship.

Human capital is a range of individual attributes, including knowledge, skill sets and abilities, which in the collective sense can contribute to both human and social development. Universities constitute an important conduit for acquiring human capital, through their teaching, research and service roles. In each of these roles, there is the transmission of knowledge that is supposedly essential for human and ultimately social development. Herein lays the power of the curriculum and its ability to impact values and knowledge that would be unleashed to support various productive sectors of the society. In other words, the theoretical ambiguities of the curriculum, academic power and knowledge, are magnified as universities are caught up in the business of producing knowledge for social development and educating for global citizenship.

To discuss global citizenship, the initial problem is the relationship between the state and universities, since the state in its historical incarnation catered for internal processes and universities, in the main, were closely tied to the national state (Puplampu 2005). Furthermore, to speak about global citizenship requires some brief remarks on classical citizenship. Following Marshall (1964), citizenship is made up of three main components: civil, political and social. Civic citizenship is about individual liberty and freedom of speech, while a main feature of political citizen is the right to vote and contest for political office. Social citizenship seeks to address economic welfare and security within the context of existing social norms. The duties and rights of citizenship are tied to the state, as the key agent in the redistribution of rights and duties (Gibbins et al. 1996). With the citizenship discourse closely aligned with the state, the idea of global citizenship stems from the changing role of the state in an era of neoliberal globalization.

These led to changing ideas, not only on citizenship but the ascendancy of various forms of citizenship such as global, multicultural and transnational (Falk 1994). Global citizenship "challenges the conventional meaning of citizenship as exclusive membership and participation within a territorially bounded political community" (Gaventa and Tandon 2010:9). Thus, global citizenship is first about an internalized sense of belonging to a global community, the idea of a global polity in charge of enforcing legal and human rights as part of an international law regime (Schattle 2008; Stromquist 2009). Second, global citizenship is dynamic, incorporating both the global and national levels, and impacts people's abilities to address their common interests. As pointed earlier, universities, as part of the broader changes in response to and as a result of neoliberal globalization, have positioned themselves as institutions that can educate learners toward global citizenship (Puplampu and Wodinski 2016). A survey of the higher educational situation in Africa will contextualize how online and curriculum reforms can contribute to human capital and global citizenship in Africa.

African Universities and Disruptive Technology: Emerging Trends

African countries continue to grapple with the changing role of the state in funding its public universities and increasing demands for higher education, a situation that has led to the idea of institutional massification, the increased enrolment at the universities (The Economist 2019; Mohamedbhai 2008). For example, from 1999 to 2012, enrolment has increased by 170%, with the number of students rising from 3.5 million to 9.54 million (Fredua-Kwarteng and Ofosu 2018). According to the World Bank, several African countries have recorded jumps in enrolment; the situation has been particularly acute in Rwanda (55%), Namibia (46%), Uganda (37%), Tanzania (32%), Côte d'Ivoire (28%), Kenya and Chad (27% each) and Botswana and Cameroon (22% each) (cited in Fredua-Kwarteng and Ofosu 2018). Increasing enrolments with dwindling resources and the impact on the quality of student learning have compelled institutional change, specifically the move toward e-learning, m-learning and other forms of online learning, including MOOCs (Rambe and Moeti 2017; Makokha and Mutisya 2016; Oyo and Kalema 2014; Boga and McGreal 2014; Hollow and ICWE 2009; Sanga et al. 2007; Lwoga 2012).

At the continental level, the African Virtual University (AVU) is the premier institution on e-learning (Africa Virtual University 2019). AVU's mandate is to provide quality higher education and increase access through the innovative use of digital and other forms of information and communication technologies. Established by the World Bank in 1997, and later transferred to Kenya in 2002, AVU has become a Pan African Intergovernmental Organization of 19 African governments (Benin, Burkina Faso, Cape Verde, Cote d'Ivoire, Democratic Republic of Congo, Ghana, Guinea, Guinea-Bissau, Kenya, Mali, Mauritania, Mozambique, Niger, Nigeria, Senegal, South Sudan, Sudan, Tanzania, The Gambia). In working across several African countries, the AVU presides over the largest e-learning network in Anglophone, Francophone and Lusophone Africa.

Beyond the AVU, several, if not all, public universities on the continent have unveiled different modalities of digital learning in countries like Uganda, South Africa, Kenya, Ghana, Nigeria, Tanzania and Zimbabwe. Kasse and Balunywa (2013) found several universities in Uganda, for example, Makerere University in Kampala and Islamic University in Uganda, employing e-learning in the delivery of learning material. In Nigeria, a survey of more than a dozen universities showed a high degree of awareness of e-learning, but the uptake is slow (Manir 2009). Universities in Tanzania have also embarked on several e-learning initiatives, with studies showing a low uptake, but institutions like the University of Dar es Salaam and Sokoine University of Agriculture are making the most progress with e-learning platforms (Ndume et al. 2008; Sanga et al. 2007).

In Kenya, both the Kenyatta University and University of Nairobi are pushing to establish open distance and e-learning presence, while the Jomo Kenyatta University of Agriculture and Technology has a low acceptance and usage of e-learning (Nyerere et al. 2012; Odhimbo 2009). According to Tagoe and Abakah (2014), the University of Ghana is trying to leverage mobile learning in its distance education program, since m-learning enhances teaching and learning. The underlying reason is that studies on e-learning programs in other universities in Ghana have been found to be effective in comparison to other methods of learning (Adanu et al. 2010).

The case of MOOCs deserves further comments, since it is the best exemplar of a disruptive technology learning system in African universities. There are two trends about the MOOC environment in African universities. First, as "late adopters of MOOCs, African universities have been trying to catch up … [even though the efforts] on the continent remain emergent and fragmentary" (Rambe and Moeti 2017:642). Asunka's (2008) pioneering study, *Online Learning in Higher Education in Sub-Saharan Africa: Ghanaian University Students' Experiences and Perceptions*, showed the complexities and difficulties of the MOOC environment.

South Africa, in a post-apartheid context, is a useful case study (Czerniewicz et al. 2014; Rambe and Moeti 2017).

The Government of South Africa's White Paper for Post School and Education Training, 2013, set out to address the high attrition rate with a commitment to increasing access to education as well as improving chances of success in the educational system (Czerniewicz et al. 2014:123). The University of South Africa (UNISA), although one of the largest long-distance educational institutions in the world, has "next to no experience of online education" (Czerniewicz et al. 2014:123). However, South African government's White Paper is a good impetus for African university leaders and administrators to come to a better understanding of the potential of MOOCs.

A second trend is the nature of MOOC platforms in African universities. This trend, in part, reflects the donor-driven development paradigm on the continent. The World Bank, under its 2008 New Economy Skills for Africa Program (NESAP)-ICT, partnered with Coursera to develop information technology (IT) courses in Tanzania (Boga and McGreal 2014). An overriding principle in this program was to bring it in line with the local context in order to maximize its relevance, hence the concerted effort to involve various IT lecturers, entrepreneurs and other local businesses in designing the curriculum (Rambe and Moeti 2017).

Coursera and edX are in partnership with the AVU and some French-speaking African institutions to expand their market presence in Africa, even as the AVU is "harnessing its academic and support staff to develop its own online course materials to tackle various challenges ranging from ... network operations, computer repairs, educator support ... [to] network access" (Rambe and Moeti 2017:644). The African Management Initiative (AMI), which focuses on business education, has developed and customized a MOOC, free of charge, for African managers and entrepreneurs and drawing on top academics from leading business schools on the continent to deliver the knowledge (Rambe and Moeti 2017:644). The focus remains the implications of online learning and curriculum reforms, including MOOCs, for human capital development and global citizenship. This focus calls for an analysis of the social context within which disruptive technology functions, the development challenges facing African universities, and the politics of knowledge production and utilization.

DISRUPTIVE TECHNOLOGY AND AFRICAN UNIVERSITIES: HUMAN CAPITAL AND GLOBAL CITIZENSHIP

The idea that disruptive technology would transform the educational landscape of African universities cannot be denied (Lwoga 2012). Yet, there are variations in the extent of the transformation. One underlying reason is "that the significant penetration of mobile phones across the continent has not been tapped into for educational purposes, because of high communication costs, low bandwidth and the absence of locally relevant applications and content for mobile learning" (Internet Society 2017:26). At the core of harnessing the potential of the internet for mobile learning, human capital and global citizenship are several interrelated factors, ranging from the policy and regulatory framework, infrastructure for learners and professional development, to the nature of collaborations among universities, at the national, regional, continental and global levels (Internet Society 2017; Patru and Balaji 2016).

Contrary to the pronouncements by proponents for a minimal role of the state in the political, economic and social spheres, there is growing evidence that the state remains the sole entity in charge of the public good and thus in charge of enacting policies that would maximize the economies of scale for internet providers so as to lower the cost of communication across the region. Lower internet cost would make it possible for universities to better establish and enhance digital networks. The variation in state support to the policy process is reflected in the ranking of countries within the National Research and Education Network (NREN) from Mature to Connecting, Starting and No Activity. According to the Internet Society (2017:46), the Mature NREN countries, for example, Algeria, Egypt, Kenya and South Africa, have secured adequate government commitment, providing support to both public and private universities by way of investments and there is a favorable regulatory regime. Connecting NREN countries, like Ghana and Tanzania, have made links to international networks a priority, while Starting NRENs, for example, Benin and Zimbabwe, have not yet built any physical networks among universities. No Activity NRENs, as the name suggests, have no initiatives on the ground and include countries such as Sierra Leone and South Sudan.

Notwithstanding the significant variations in the policy regime, most, if not all, African universities have stepped up their activities to deepen and benefit from educational technology. Universities in Tanzania, as Lwoga (2012:91) argues, have "taken various initiatives to integrate information and communication technologies (ICTs) to improve curricula," relying on open and distant learning. The South African government, committed to improving access and success, seems poised to harness disruptive technology for equitable educational outcomes and "use of e-learning technologies for teaching and learning is quite high" (Lwoga 2012:96). The challenge is attaining equitable learning outcomes in a context of historical and political forms of inequality and imperialism. It was therefore not surprising that students in the University of Cape Town, South Africa, embarked upon a sustained campaign contesting their educational curriculum, its sins of commission and omission with calls for broad reforms (Luckett 2016). The contestations, taking place in a South African university, even though "South African universities now have enough uncongested bandwidth, with most having the Gigabit speed now typical of European universities" (Czerniewicz et al. 2014:124), are significant. This suggests that having the appropriate infrastructure, though necessary, is not enough to deepen student learning in the age of digital education. Indeed, the challenge may be with the lack of skill sets and fatigue among the aging professoriate in Africa. This implies that even if the learner may be eager to learn, the educator might be ill equipped.

The significance of infrastructure is key in the learning process, particularly for faculty and students. Mbatha (2015) found that faculty at the University of South Africa (UNISA), a leading distance education provider, have been using and are interested to be trained in utilizing technology to improve their pedagogical activities. The faculty have a high level of comfort faculty with smartphones and other educational technology platforms, including Google. This development is an improvement upon an earlier finding by Tettey and Puplampu (2000) that faculty did not show any willingness to take advantage of training opportunities to better interact with online learning platforms in some African universities. For learners, mostly characterized as digital natives, many of them own mobile phones and are keen participants in the online world. However, that does not necessarily mean they are digital literates when it comes to using the online work to augment their learning. For both faculty and learners, especially the latter, the question becomes the availability and cost of laptops and the high cost of internet services on the continent. It is obvious that the laptops are tools and need to be populated with content from skillful educators who are themselves knowledge creators, and not mere users of content. With anemic growth in research capacity, most faculty remain users of content.

Furthermore, access, by itself, does not necessarily equate optimal learning. Tossell et al. (2015) draw attention to the distractive power of smartphones in the learning process. At issue is the decidedly informal character or nature of employing digital devices in the learning process. The argument is that any

> incompatibility between smartphones and higher education may not have to do with the technology per se but might rather be due to the fact that the current model of education does not require this type of informal learning. Smartphones support ubiquitous learning opportunities, but the educational model being used currently provides limited need for this beneficial activity. (Tossell et al. 2015:722)

The fact that learners are in possession of smartphone and other digital devices should not be construed as effective learning.

Another important variable in analyzing digital higher education in Africa is the relationship between collaboration and partnership, the implications for curriculum, knowledge and the educational experience and outcomes. Partnership for global transformation can only be beneficial under certain conditions: the partners possess relatively the same amount of power and respect, perceive each other as equals, and are committed to work toward mutual benefits. These assumptions involve several issues, first, the question of knowledge production and dissemination, via the curriculum of MOOCs. Take the World Bank-led NESAP-ICT pilot program in Tanzania launched in 2008 to deepen IT knowledge. The politics of knowledge was obvious in this project, which involved Coursera, a major global player in the MOOC industry, a for-profit company that by default has copyright provisions on course material. While the explicit aim of the project was to develop new skills in the IT sector for youth, the pilot program begets several questions.

The main one was the perspective of the curriculum and the ability of Coursera to tailor the curriculum to the Tanzanian sociocultural situation. In other words, it is the question of control over the creation and dissemination of knowledge in English language relevant to Tanzania, largely Swahili-speaking learners. The issue, well captured by Boga and McGreal (2014:8), is that if "developing countries allow themselves to be locked in to a certain MOOC platform, they have to adhere to the foreign values put forth by the platform owners.... This exclusivity will prevent true collaboration with other developing countries that may be facing similar issues." With the MOOC platform, dominated by elite United States (US)-based institutions, there is a unidirectional transfer of knowledge, from the US institutions to African universities. As Rambe and Moeti (2017:633) argue, "dominance of MOOC provision by Western institutions ... and [the] visibility of African universities in the exportation of MOOC knowledge to the developed world are all potentially indicative of academic elitism and by extension intellectual neo-imperialism." Contestations about knowledge, by extension, also reveal the problematic aspects of human capital development. Contrary to popular notions, academic knowledge, like other forms of knowledge, is not neutral, more so in the context of the flow of knowledge from the global North to the global South (Collyer 2018).

Perhaps, to assuage the unidirectional flow of knowledge, Coursera has moved from creating all their courses from Stanford to involving local academics. The University of Cape Town, the site of recent intense contestations over curriculum, is the only African university in partnership with Coursera (Coursera 2019). The problem is that with only "one dedicated distance education provider, the South African higher education has limited experience in online education" (Czerniewicz et al. 2014:123). Besides, the extent to which developing the curriculum underpinning global partnerships can contribute to human capital will depend on outcomes like certification and validation of knowledge. However, in view of issues of ownership and control of knowledge, there will be difficulties in ascertaining learning outcomes (Tettey 2006).

Equally problematic is the areas of concentration or study in several MOOC courses. From the AVU to Coursera's courses in both Tanzania and South Africa, the focus has been disproportionally on the physical sciences. The focus raises two questions. First, studies in the sciences would require laboratory platforms and infrastructure that are generally expensive, but necessary for effective learning. Without the required structural prerequisites, including faculty orientation and professional development, digital technology and its related promise or potential will remain simply a mirage. Second, studies in the physical sciences are, no doubt, significant in addressing the development potential of the African condition. Yet, doing so at the expense of the social sciences or humanities is shortsighted. It is the social sciences that will provide the nuanced knowledge required for a better understanding of the environment within which the physical sciences would operate. A sophisticated understanding of the social will help to address the relevance of technical knowledge. It is therefore problematic that the World Bank (2019) initiatives, such as the innovative approaches to higher education, continue to focus on technical and vocational training in the sciences, evidence in regional programs like the African Centers of Excellence and Partnership for Applied Sciences, Engineering and Technology, notwithstanding the attention to educational opportunities for girls. Put differently, with a curriculum infused by external values and a focus on technical issues, the quality of the human capital from MOOC-trained programs would not have the requisite human capital for social development. This shortfall also has consequences toward educating for global citizenship.

Curriculum reforms, online education and human capital do not necessarily account for the development of global citizenship. The inability of universities, even with the help of disruptive technologies to educate for global citizens, stems from several sources. For example, the large enrolment of students from several countries for online education, without a decontextualized curriculum, or face-to-face interaction and separated by different political and sociocultural factors do not bode well for global citizenship. Whatever knowledge students are exposed to must first be decontextualized to enhance its relevance for learning and any aspirations toward educating for global citizenship. As a result, the assumption that students learning in an online environment would necessarily develop notions of global citizenship cannot be sustained (Puplampu and Wodinski 2016). This is because online learning modalities are framed by the structural location of the learners, which, in turn, is the reflection of the global divide. Equally important is that market-based notions of online learning via MOOCs are based on the idea of generating a profit, while notions of global citizenship draw attention to issues of equity. Thus, market-driven educational reforms do not necessarily go hand in hand with equity imperatives of global citizenship (Garson 2016; Stein 2016; Khoo 2011).

Constrains and Policy Options

The success or failure of online learning, e-learning, m-learning and MOOCs is contingent on several conditions. First is the internal dynamics of the African academy and, second, the global context, specifically the case of MOOCs and other disruptive learning practices. The state is the primary site in the fortunes or misfortunes of universities in Africa, providing for or setting up the appropriate framework that will inform outcomes. African governments that have prioritized the establishment of a robust policy and regulatory framework are more likely to optimize outcomes. As the case of Singapore and South Korea clearly shows, government commitment and allocation of resources is vital in any attempt to integrate digital technology into learning systems, given the latter's 2015 drive in which all schools were linked to high-speed wireless and digital textbooks (Internet Society 2017:20). Closer home on the African continent, because of government commitment, sometimes working with foreign donors, universities in countries like Egypt, Kenya, Morocco, Senegal, Tunisia and South Africa have attained acceptable degrees of internet access comparable to their peers in the global South, specifically in the Asia and Latin America subregions, with South African universities mirroring conditions of access in European universities (Internet Society 2017:8; Czerniewicz et al. 2014:124).

Digital learning is meant or assumes some degree of fluidity and persistent change. So, the success of digital learning calls for an appropriate environment. That suggests that digital learning cannot be a substitute for scanning of dated material on online platforms. Such an environment, even though could afford learning, is inconsistent with trends toward human capital development and educating for global citizenship. While access to educational material could be enhanced through subscription of e-books, the cost implications and intellectual property problems cannot be ignored. In effect, digital education might just contribute to or deepen the digital divide if policy makers do not enact bold policy initiatives to address the cost dimensions of technology.

Physical resources or the hard infrastructure constitute the architecture of any disruptive learning. The state of the institutional infrastructure will enable faculty members to better integrate and utilize disruptive technologies into their teaching practices, especially with the emergence of online courses. For public institutions, the changing role of the state has led to the dwindling state support to university and the ascendancy of the market ethos. The result has been dramatic changes in the relationship between educators and learners. That suggests that disruptive technology and higher education reveal tensions in terms of profit and public good concerns like access and equity.

The tension offers opportunities for authentic change. To directly address the politics of knowledge production and dissemination, African universities can pool their resources to produce and disseminate their own MOOCs. African universities can take advantage of the technological innovations and through, for example, the AVU, develop and disseminate knowledge. No region of the world has the monopoly over knowledge. That calls for a new form of collaboration, tapping into the skills of knowledgeable Africans on the continent and in the diaspora to create knowledge that is consistent and relevant to the continent. Indeed, the engagement with the diaspora, under laudable initiatives such as the Carnegie African Diaspora Fellowship Program and other forms of diasporic networks, does not constitute an end in and of themselves (Tettey 2016; Foulds and Zeleza 2014). This is because when it comes to engaging the African academic diaspora, the question, as Ogachi (2015) asks, is "how ready are universities in Africa?" The focus must be a bold effort in mobilizing resources, improvements in institutional capacity with the clear goal to enhance the quality of learning and learners in order to better position "universities as engines of innovation for sustainable development and transformation" (Zeleza 2017:1).

Creating knowledge that speaks to the African reality is necessary in view of the nature of the global MOOC industry. With most of the global players set up for-profit, it is necessary for African universities to rethink the parameters of their partnership with for-profit MOOCs. The need for local institutional autonomy and capacity cannot be overemphasized. To Oyo and Kalema (2014), developing MOOCs for Africa by Africa would involve issues such as the formation of a national MOOC coordination office, program accreditation and content development, online and offline e-learning platform and finally ubiquitous access to computers and the internet. Given that universities are made up of several departments, a holistic approach in terms of technology policy should seek to involve every department, thus incorporating both physical and social sciences. That calls for digital policies linked to the university's overall vision and strategy, investing in communities built around willing and capable digital innovators, specifically senior management, and supported by staff and students of all departments and an approach that focuses on students' learning needs.

Finally, while global partnerships and collaborations are part of the current discourse about the global village, such partnerships cannot replace serious domestic planning and resource allocation in African universities. With the demographic headwinds pointing toward the need for more spaces, innovative planning, including partnership with the private sector, should be part of the policy mix (The Economist 2019). This planning cannot avoid the perennial issue of the funding formula for higher education, given that no country has an unlimited supply of resources and foreign sources of resources are not problem-free. African countries should harness available resources to support their universities, if these institutions are still expected to play a critical role in the national and continental development program.

REFERENCES

Adanu, R., Adu-Sarkodie, Y., Opare-Sem, O., Nkyekyer, K., Donkor, P., Lawson, A., & Engleberg, N. C. (2010). Electronic Learning and Open Educational Resources in the Health Sciences in Ghana. *Ghana Medical Journal, 44*(4), 159–162.

Africa Virtual University. (2019). *AVU at a Glance.* https://avu.org/avuweb/en/avu-at-a-glance/. Retrieved August 30, 2019.

Asunka, S. (2008). Online Learning in Higher Education in Sub-Saharan Africa: Ghanaian University Students' Experiences and Perceptions. *International Review of Research in Open and Distance Learning, 9*, 3. http://www.irrodl.org/index.php/irrodl/article/view/586/1130

Barrier, J., Quéré, O., & Vanneuville, R. (2019). The Making of Curriculum in Higher Education Power, Knowledge, and Teaching Practices. *Revue d'anthropologie des connaissances, 13*(1), 33–60.

Boga, S., & McGreal, R. (2014). *Introducing MOOCs in Africa: New Economy Skills for Africa Program – ICT.* Vancouver: Commonwealth of Learning.

Christensen, C. (1997). *The Innovator's Dilemma: When New Technologies Cause Great Firms to Fail.* Harvard Business Review Press.

Christensen, C. M., & Eyring, H. J. (2011). *The Innovative University: Changing the DNA of Higher Education from the Inside Out.* San Francisco: Jossey-Bass.

Christensen, C., Johnson, C. W., & Horn, M. B. (2008). *Disrupting Class: How Disruptive Innovation Will Change the Way the World Learns.* New York: McGraw Hill.

Christensen, C. M., Horn, M. B., Caldera, L., & Soares, L. (2011). *Disrupting College: How Disruptive Innovation Can Deliver Quality and Affordability in Postsecondary Education.* Center for American Progress and Innosight Institute. https://cdn.americanprogress.org/wpcontent/uploads/issues/2011/02/pdf/disrupting_college.pdf. Retrieved August 30, 2019.

Collyer, F. M. (2018). Global Patterns in the Publishing of Academic Knowledge: Global North, Global South. *Current Sociology, 66*(1), 56–73.

Coursera. (2019). *About.* https://the-courserian-blog.mystagingwebsite.com/about/. Retrieved August 30, 2019.

Czerniewicz, L., & Brown, C. (2009). A Study of the Relationship Between Institutional Policy, Organisational Culture and e-Learning Use in Four South African Universities. *Computers and Education, 53*(1), 121–131.

Czerniewicz, L., Deacon, A., Small, J., & Walji, S. (2014). Developing World MOOCs: A Curriculum View of the MOOC Landscape. *Journal of Global Literacies: Technologies and Emerging Pedagogies, 2*(3), 122–139.

Falk, R. (1994). The Making of Citizenship. In B. Van Steenbergen (Ed.), *The Condition of Citizenship* (pp. 42–61). London: Sage.

Flynn, J. (2013). MOOCS: Disruptive Innovation and the Future of Higher Education. *Christian Education Journal, 10*, 149–162.

Foulds, K., & Zeleza, P. T. (2014). The African Academic Diaspora and African Higher Education. *International Higher Education, 76*(Summer), 16–17.

Fredua-Kwarteng, E., & Ofosu, S. K. (2018, February 16). How Can Universities Address Spiralling Enrolment? *University World News.* https://www.universityworldnews.com/post.php?story=20180214094656754. Retrieved August 30, 2019.

Garrison, D. R., & Kanuka, H. (2004). Blended Learning: Uncovering its Transformative Potential in Higher Education. *Internet and Higher Education, 7*(1), 95–105.

Garson, K. (2016). Reframing Internationalization. *Canadian Journal of Higher Education, 46*(2), 19–39.

Gaventa, J., & Tandon, R. (2010). Citizen Engagements in a Globalizing World. In J. Gaventa & R. Tandon (Eds.), *Globalizing Citizens: New Dynamics of Inclusion and Exclusion* (pp. 3–30). London: Zed Books.

Gibbins, R., Youngman, L., & Stewart-Toth, J. (1996). Ideologies, Identity, and Citizenship. In R. Gibbins & L. Youngman (Eds.), *Mindscapes: Political Ideologies Towards the Twenty-First Century* (pp. 266–292). Toronto: McGraw-Hill Ryerson.

Hollow, D., & ICWE. (2009). *E-Learning in Africa: Challenges, Priorities and Future Direction.* http://www.gg.rhul.ac.uk/ict4d/workingpapers/Hollowelearning.pdf. Retrieved August 30, 2019.

Internet Society. (2017). *Internet for Education in Africa: Helping Policy Makers to Meet the Global Education Agenda Sustainable Development Goal 4.* Geneva: Internet Society. www.internetsociety.org. Retrieved August 30, 2019.

Isabirye, A. K., & Dlodlo, N. (2014). Perceived Inhibitors of Innovative E-Learning Teaching Practice at a South African University of Technology. *Mediterranean Journal of Social Sciences, 5*(4), 390–398. https://doi.org/10.5901/mjss.2014.v5n4p390.

Kasse, J. P., & Balunywa, W. (2013). *An Assessment of E-learning Utilization by a Section of Ugandan Universities: Challenges, Success Factors and Way Forward.* Paper Presented at the International Conference on ICT for Africa 2013, Harare.

Keegan, D. (2003). Introduction. In *The Role of Student Support Services in e-Learning Systems* (Working Paper in ZIFF Papiere 121) (pp. 1–6). Hagen: Fern Universität, University of Hagen.

Khoo, S. (2011). Ethical Globalisation or Privileged Internationalisation? Exploring Global Citizenship and Internationalisation in Irish and Canadian Universities. *Globalisation, Societies and Education, 9*(3–4), 337–353.

Luckett, K. (2016). Curriculum Contestation in a Post-Colonial Context: A View from the South. *Teaching in Higher Education, 21*(4), 415–428. https://doi.org/10.1080/13562517.2016.1155547.

Lwoga, E. (2012). Making Learning and Web 2.0 Technologies Work for Higher Learning Institutions in Africa. *Campus-Wide Information Systems, 29*(2), 90–107. https://doi.org/10.1108/10650741211212359.

Makokha, G. L., & Mutisya, D. N. (2016). Status of E-Learning in Public Universities in Kenya. *The International Review of Research in Open and Distance Learning, 17*(3), 341–359.

Manir, K. M. (2009). Problems, Challenges and Benefits of Implementing E-Learning in Nigerian Universities: An Empirical Study. *International Journal of Emerging Technologies in Learning, 4*(1), 66–69. https://doi.org/10.3991/ijet.v4i1.653.

Marshall, T. M. (1964). *Class, Citizenship and Social Development.* New York: Double Day.

Mbatha, B. (2015). A Paradigm Shift: Adoption of Disruptive Learning Innovations in an ODL Environment: The Case of the University of South Africa. *The International Review of Research in Open and Distance Learning, 16*(3), 218–232.

McCowan, T. (2016). Universities and the Post-2015 Development Agenda: An Analytical Framework. *Higher Education, 72*, 505–523. https://doi.org/10.1007/s10734-016-0035-7.

Mohamedbhai, G. (2008). *The Effects of Massification on Higher Education in Africa.* Accra: Association of African Universities.

Ndume, V., Tilya, F. N., & Twaakyondo, H. (2008). Challenges of Adaptive e-Learning at Higher Learning Institutions: A Case Study in Tanzania. *International Journal of Computing and ICT Research, 2*(1), 47–59.

Nyerere, J. K. A., Gravenir, F. Q., & Mse, G. S. (2012). Delivery of Open, Distance and e-Learning in Kenya. *The International Review of Research in Open and Distance Learning, 13*(3), 185–205. Retrieved from http://www.irrodl.org/index.php/irrodl/article/view/1120.

Odhimbo, O. O. (2009). *Comparative Study of the E-learning Platforms Used in Kenyan Universities: Case Study of Jomo Kenyatta University of Agriculture and Technology and United States International University.* https://su-plus.strathmore.edu/bitstream/handle/11071/3261/Comparative

Ogachi, I. O. (2015). Engaging the African Academic Diaspora: How Ready Are Universities in Africa? *International Journal of African Higher Education, 2*, 1. https://doi.org/10.6017/ijahe.v2i1.9263.

Oyo, B., & Kalema, B. M. (2014). Massive Open Online Courses for Africa by Africa. *International Review of Research in Open and Distance Learning, 15*(6), 1–13.

Pappano, L. (2012, November 2). The Year of the MOOC. *New York Times.* https://www.nytimes.com/2012/11/04/education/edlife/massive-open-online-courses-are-multiplying-at-a-rapid-pace.html?searchResultPosition=1. Retrieved August 30, 2019.

Patru, M., & Balaji, V. (2016). *Making Sense of MOOCs: A Guide for Policy-Makers in Developing Countries.* Paris/Burnaby: United Nations Educational, Scientific and Cultural Organization (UNESCO) and Commonwealth of Learning (COL).

Puplampu, K. P. (2005). National 'Development' and African Universities: A Theoretical and Socio-Political Analysis. In A. Abdi & A. Cleghorn (Eds.), *Issues in African Education: Sociological Perspectives* (pp. 43–62). New York: Palgrave Macmillan.

Puplampu, K. P. (2006). Critical Perspectives on Higher Education and Globalization in Africa. In A. Abdi, K. P. Puplampu, & S. Dei (Eds.), *African Education and Globalization: Critical Perspectives* (pp. 34–52). Lanham: Lexington Books.

Puplampu, K. P. (2008). Knowledge, Power and Social Policy: John M. MacEachran and Alberta's 1928 Sexual Sterilization Act. *Alberta Journal of Educational Research, 54*(2), 129–146.

Puplampu, K. P., & Wodinski, L. (2016). Study Abroad Programs, International Students, and Global Citizenship: Colonial-Colonizer Relations in Global Higher Education. In R. C. Mizzi, T. S. Rocco, & S. Shore (Eds.), *Disrupting Adult and Community Education: Teaching, Learning, and Working in the Periphery* (pp. 293–306). Albany: State University of New York Press.

Rambe, P., & Moeti, M. (2017). Disrupting and Democratising Higher Education Provision or Entrenching Academic Elitism: Towards a Model of MOOCs Adoption at African Universities. *Education Technology Research Development, 65,* 631–651. https://doi.org/10.1007/s11423-016-9500-3.

Sanga, C., Sife, A. S., & Lwoga, E. T. (2007). New Technologies for Teaching and Learning: Challenges for Higher Learning Institutions in Developing Countries. *International Journal of Education and Development using Information and Communication Technology, 3*(2), 57–67.

Schattle, H. (2008). *The Practices of Global Citizenship.* Lanham: Rowman and Littlefield.

Stein, S. (2016). Rethinking the Ethics of Internationalization: Five Challenges for Higher Education. *InterActions: UCLA Journal of Education and Information Studies, 12*(2). https://escholarship.org/uc/item/2nb2b9b4

Stromquist, N. P. (2009). Theorizing Global Citizenship: Discourses, Challenges and Implications for Education. *Inter-American Journal of Education for Democracy, 2*(1), 6–29.

Swartz, R., Ivancheva, M., Czerniewicz, L., & Morris, N. P. (2019). Between a Rock and a Hard Place: Dilemmas Regarding the Purpose of Public Universities in South Africa. *Higher Education, 77*, 567–583. https://doi.org/10.1007/s10734-018-0291-9.

Tagoe, M., & Abakah, E. (2014). Determining Distance Education Students' Readiness for Mobile Learning at University of Ghana Using the Theory of Planned Behavior. *International Journal of Education and Development using Information and Communication Technology, 10*(1), 91–106.

Tettey, W. J. (2006). Globalization, Information Technologies, and Higher Education in Africa: Implications of the Market Agenda. In A. Abdi, K. P. Puplampu, & S. Dei (Eds.), *African Education and Globalization: Critical Perspectives* (pp. 93–115). Lanham: Lexington Books.

Tettey, W. J. (2016). Regenerating Scholarly Capacity Through Diaspora Engagement: The Case of a Ghana Diaspora Knowledge Network. In A. Chikanda, J. Crush, & M. Walton-Roberts (Eds.), *Diasporas, Development and Governance. Global Migration Issues* (Vol. 5, pp. 171–186). Cham: Springer.

Tettey, W. J., & Puplampu, K. P. (2000). Social Science Research and the Africanist: The Need for Intellectual and Attitudinal Reconfiguration. *African Studies Review, 43*(3), 81–102.

The Economist. (2019). A Booming Population is Putting Strain on Africa's Universities. August 10th https://www.economist.com/middle-east-and-africa/2019/08/10/a-booming-population-is-putting-strain-on-africas-universities. Retrieved August 30, 2019.

Tossell, C. C., Kortum, P., Shepard, C., Rahmati, A., & Zhong, L. (2015). You Can Lead a Horse to Water but You Cannot Make Him Learn: Smartphone Use in Higher Education. *British Journal of Educational Technology, 46*(4), 713–724. https://doi.org/10.1111/bjet.12176.

United Nations (UN). (2015). *Transforming our World: The 2030 Agenda for Sustainable Development.* Washington, DC: United Nations A/RES/70/1, sustainabledevelopment.un.org

United Nations Development Programme (UNDP). (2003). *Human Development Report 2003 Millennium Development Goals: A Compact Among Nations to End Human Poverty.* New York: Oxford University Press.

United Nations Development Program (UNDP). (2015). *Sustainable Development Goals.* New York: United Nations Development Program.

United Nations Educational, Scientific and Cultural Organization (UNESCO). (2015). *Education 2030 Incheon Declaration: Towards Inclusive and Equitable Quality Education and Lifelong Learning for All.* https://unesdoc.unesco.org/ark:/48223/pf0000245656

Wangenge-Ouma, G., & Nafukho, F. M. (2011). Responses to Conditions of Decline: The Case of Kenya's Public Universities. *Africa Education Review, 8*(1), 169–188. https://doi.org/10.1080/18146627.2011.586163.

World Bank. (2019). *Mainstreaming the Approach to Disruptive and Transformative Technologies at the World Bank Group.* Washington, DC: World Bank.

Yuan, L., & Powell, S. (2013). *MOOCs and Open Education: Implications for Higher Education.* A White Paper, JISC and Centre for Educational Technology and Interoperability Standards. http://publications.cetis.ac.uk/2013/667

Zeleza, P. T. (2017). Positioning Universities as Engines of Innovation for Sustainable Development and Transformation. *Journal of Higher Education in Africa, 15*(2), 1–22. https://www.jstor.org/stable/10.2307/26640368.

Disruptive Financial Technology (FinTech) and Entrepreneurship in Burkina Faso

Euphrasie Kouame and Abbi M. Kedir

INTRODUCTION

This chapter explores how access to finance (formal finance, informal finance and mobile money) impacts private sector development via entrepreneurship in Burkina Faso. Specifically, disaggregating our analysis by gender using evidence from Burkina Faso FinScope Consumer Survey, 2016, of 5066 individuals drawn both from rural and urban Burkina Faso, one of the countries in Africa with a fast growth of mobile money transaction adoption.[1] The study seeks to understand the demand side of financial

---

[1] This is part of a larger study on the role of financial technology on financial inclusion by the United Nations Capital Development Fund (UNCDF). A future work will involve exploring similar issues in Benin, Cameroon and Togo which have also completed FinScope Consumer Survey data.

E. Kouame
United Nations Capital Development Fund (UNCDF), Dakar, Senegal

A. M. Kedir (✉)
Sheffield University Management School, University of Sheffield, Sheffield, UK
e-mail: a.m.kedir@sheffield.ac.uk

© The Author(s) 2020   171
P. Arthur et al. (eds.), *Disruptive Technologies, Innovation and Development in Africa*, International Political Economy Series,
https://doi.org/10.1007/978-3-030-40647-9_8

inclusion in Burkina Faso. We investigate the role of disruptive FinTech (financial technology) in the process by focusing on mobile money transactions and the use of this ICT-enabled payment and deposit system, which took off in Burkina Faso in 2012. Looking at the role of digital money on entrepreneurship matters greatly because self-employment is a sustainable route out of poverty.

Access to and use of finance facilitate the transition to secure livelihoods via the establishment of entrepreneurial ventures that might help job creation (Parker 2005). Beyond the role of traditional, formal and informal finance access and usage indicators, we will also investigate whether the latest rapid expansion in financial technology has a role in increasing the probability of entrepreneurship. Regardless of its scale, running enterprises makes an important contribution for households with limited means of livelihood. This study is part of a bigger cross-country study with United Nations Capital Development Fund (UNCDF) with the aim to study financial inclusion in West Africa using FinScope survey which covered over 30 countries so far. In April 2019, the World Bank approved an IDA credit to the tune of 87.6 million euros to help the country's effort in the provision of increased digital financing services and provide loans to the financially excluded such as women, farmers, youth and SMEs (World Bank 2019). The Bank's support is aligned with Burkina Faso's development vision (i.e. National Economic and Social Development Plan—PNDES) which constitutes entrepreneurship and private sector development with the eventual goal of eliminating extreme poverty as set out in the globally agreed Sustainable Development Goals (SDGs).

It is obvious that for African youth (both women and men), it is important that they play a role in development so that the demographic explosion that the continent is experiencing becomes a demographic dividend. With conditions laid out for a transition to self-employment and enterprising culture, the youth will be a driving force transforming their respective economies. Even if our study covers all demographic groups, part of our analysis focuses on the youth, a demographic group that is embracing FinTech more enthusiastically than the rest of the population. The aim of inclusive finance is poverty reduction. Hence, it is pertinent to ask: Does greater access to finance increase the likelihood of self-employment? If yes, it means that one possible channel through which Burkina Faso can reduce poverty is via bank branch expansion and provision of a variety of financial services such as insurance. Recent choice experiment and pilot insurance evidence from Burkina Faso shows a strong willingness to pay (WTP) for weather-indexed insurance by farmers (Fonta et al. 2018, 2019).

Theory

The introduction of a new or disruptive technology (here a financial technology) is a recurring theme in an era of technological changes, and new forms of technology might pose a threat to or destroy existing firms (e.g. formal financial institutions). However, the idea of destruction or creative destruction due to technological innovation is not a novel idea. As a conceptual framework for our study, it is relevant to refer to the work of Joseph Schumpeter who is the originator of disruptive innovation theory and who identified innovation as the critical dimension of economic development, including entrepreneurship (Schumpeter 1937, 1939, 1942). Departing from the static view of Walras (1874) and Marshall (1890) and highlighting the importance of technological dynamic, Schumpeter acknowledged how technological innovations (e.g. the invention of railways) change 'ways of doing things' over time. In the same vein, we argue that the current wave of financial technologies (FinTech) often popularized via entrepreneurial start-ups will be a creative destructive force that can change the financial landscape and force conventional banks to do things differently. This is because households and individuals can access not only traditional formal and informal finance, but mobile money without the need to travel to a bank branch or being a member of a traditional rotating savings and credit association (ROSCA). However, conventional formal and informal finance will play an important role in the livelihood of many individuals in developing countries for many years to come. The innovation theory of Schumpeter was popularized by growth theorists and the new growth theorists who explored the relationship between innovation and economic growth, albeit without a focus on the role of an entrepreneurial firm, such as a FinTech start-up (Romer 1990, 1994, 1996; Solow 1956, 1957). Spencer and Kirchhoff (2006), based on a careful discussion of the role of technology in economic growth, address how New Technology-Based Firms (NTBFs) such as FinTech start-ups constitute a source of disruption and serve as key drivers of Schumpeterian creative destruction.

Apart from the extensive discussion in economics of technology in growth theories, we can also learn a lot from the management literature, which discusses the effect of disruptive innovative technology on existing and new firms (e.g. in financial activities). The Schumpeterian view that disruptive innovation originates as a series of incremental innovations by new entrants (often innovative small technology firms) to an industry often leads to disruption to the activities of larger firms (e.g. banks) and the disruptive technology might precipitate their fall. Therefore, there is always a tension between innovating small- or medium-sized firms and established large firms. In addition to financing their daily operations, incumbent large firms can be threatened by what is happening externally and resource constraints might impede their ability to adapt to techno-logical changes (Henderson 1993). Disruptive technologies lead to recon-figuration of the way firms organize their activities in the future and contest the competitive advantage of rivals (Eisenhardt and Martin 2000). Hence, there is a constant balancing act between resource constraints and development of dynamic capabilities as firms attempt to establish dynamic mechanisms to make use of the disruptive technology for various growth enhancing purposes (e.g. financial inclusion). That is what is happening in the FinTech space and banking in many African countries today.

FinTech in Burkina Faso and Financial Inclusion

There is a growing enthusiasm behind FinTech, specifically its potential as a pathway for escaping poverty via self-employment with the potential to benefit women and the unbanked (Bateman et al. 2019; Beck and Frame 2018). One of the ways to explore the potential development impact of mobile finance is its role in entrepreneurship, the foundation of sustain-able development, hence the significance of FinTech as a tool to achieve SDGs. The mobile money transaction and other technology-inspired financial products are not the outcome of a FinTech start-up but a provi-sion by the telecom of Burkina Faso (ONATEL). In the mobile money arena, Orange is a major strategic player in West Africa, and it acquired Airtel Money of Burkina Faso in 2016. Orange Money provides mobile financial services and the other payment service is Mobicash by Telmob. For our analytical work for this paper, we will concentrate on both Orange/Airtel Money and Mobicash.

The digital connectivity of regions and distant locations in Burkina Faso has been made possible by global companies such as Huawei which is at the centre of building key mobile infrastructure and supplying equip-ment. Huawei, working in partnership with a French company (Burkina Faso was a former French colony), since 2018, has laid thousands of miles of optical fibre, with 60% of the financing provided by the Bank of China and 40% by BNP Paribas, a French company. Huawei manages the Orange Group's network in West Africa and is a key supplier of equipment and

Table 8.1 Access to finance

Access variable	All	Female	Male
Banked	781 (15.4)	302 (12.4)	479 (18.2)
Other formal (non-bank)	1120 (22.1)	445 (18.3)	675 (25.7)
Informal only	1169 (23.1)	591 (24.3)	578 (22.0)
Excluded	1996 (39.4)	1098 (45.1)	898 (34.1)

Source: FinScope Consumer Survey, Burkina Faso 2016

services. The result is that the mobile infrastructure in Burkina Faso is progressively developing with more than 80 mobile subscriptions per 100 inhabitants among the 19.7 million population in 2017.

With the sole aim of providing financial inclusion, the question of who are financially excluded is an important one. According to Table 8.1, a non-negligible proportion of individuals are excluded from financial services. From the total sample of 5066 individuals, 39.4% are excluded from accessing finance. However, we would like to highlight the gender dimension of exclusion which stands 45.1% for females and 34.1% for males.

The digital divide is gendered as much as it is regional. According to survey data, about 26% of the general population use mobile money compared to 30.8% of males and 21.1% of females. Women are yet to derive the benefits of technology and disproportionately represent the relatively larger group of financial excluded population. Since 2010, the UNCDF has been actively working to address the challenges of financial inclusion of women and youth and their transition to economic independence via sustainable livelihood systems such as entrepreneurship.

Burkina Faso has the second largest mobile money market in West African Economic and Monetary Union (WAEMU) after Cote d'Ivoire. The mobile money market started in 2012 which makes it a late comer into the scene compared to countries like Kenya which started the mobile money revolution in 2007 and Ghana which started in 2009 (Sakyi-Nyarko 2018; Yenkey et al. 2015). In recent years, there are encouraging developments in mobile money transactions. According to the World Bank (2019), the percentage of adults with transaction account grew to 43% in 2017 compared to 2014 when only 13.4% of them had a transaction account. However, the depressing development is the widening of the gender gap. In 2014, there was no gender gap in mobile transaction account ownership but, in 2017, the gender gap in mobile transaction ownership grew to 17% and this trend should be reversed with aggressive and fair financial inclusion initiatives that target and benefit women. The underlying reason for the widening gap is unclear, but most likely it might be related to ownership of mobile phone itself, awareness and familiarity with the mobile money transaction facility.

According to FinMark (2017), 40% of the respondents in Burkina Faso were aware or use mobile money agents. This does not mean the remaining 60% are not aware or financially illiterate. With more operators coming into the picture in the future, a larger number of individuals will be using mobile money. Currently, mobile money transactions are allowed in a limited number of networks. The licensed e-money issuers in the country are the two subsidiaries of telecom operators (i.e. Orange and Telmob). Hence, mobile money transactions are not the outcome of FinTech start-ups. The customer base of Orange and Telmob is close to 7 million which is almost 37% of the total population of the country.

A good deal of mobile money transaction users might be financial literate but might be prevented by infrastructural bottlenecks (e.g. remote rural locations). However, when one looks at the national reporting average number of minutes that individuals spend to get to a mobile money agent, it is only 20 minutes. Hence, we cannot rule out the presence of a fair degree of ignorance or there are other complex factors at work that need to be explored. Part of the recent support from the World Bank is aimed at funding nationwide financial education campaigns via mobile phones for a six-year period (2019–2025) to reach 200,000 by the end of the funding cycle. If only 40% of the population is using a mobile phone, the education campaign is set to benefit a great proportion of the adult population. Alternative ways of delivering the education campaign need to be devised to reach the digitally excluded for reasons other than awareness (infrastructure barriers).

Most financial inclusion interventions from donors and national governments require users to have an account or evidence of use of formal financial service products. For instance, the recent World Bank (2019) support for increasing the country's digital financial services targets beneficiaries using transaction accounts (e.g. banks, Microfinance Institutions (MFIs) or mobile money accounts such as 'wallet-to-account'). This perpetuates the financial exclusion of marginalized groups and the ultra-poor. Against this backdrop, the education campaign plays a critical role in encouraging informal finance to move to mobile phone-based transaction accounts since most individuals have mobile phones. The way forward to benefit from FinTech is to nudge and encourage them to have mobile money accounts by raising their financial awareness with transparent information about all the potential benefits and associated risks. Alternatively, as MFIs are progressively serving large section of the population, most will come to appreciate the potential benefits this may have for their livelihoods. This is because MFIs are making loan disbursements and repayments using mobile accounts that are linked with MFI accounts.

Financial literacy and education are specific and different initiatives underway to increase financial awareness in Burkina Faso. For instance, recently the Ministry of Economy, Finance and Development[2] organized what they call the Global Money Week 2019, a week-long financial education and financial inclusion awareness-building sessions in different schools in some cities (e.g. Bobo-Dioulasso). In this initiative, the Ministry of Economy, Finance and Development plays an active role in coordinating and supervising all activities. It is not only the government which is providing the financial awareness training sessions, but we observe also the role of financial institutions, non-governmental organizations and international organizations (e.g. the UN). For instance, the Reseau des Caisses Populaires of Burkina Faso (RCPB), the largest credit and savings co-operative network in Burkina Faso (established in 1972), carried out several training activities, including financial education training sessions in schools and training centres and the opening of accounts for young people. RCPB organized guided visits of credit unions for young people.

Another NGO, the Association Internationale des Etudiants en Sciences Economiques et Commerciales (AIESEC), established in 1948 after World War II, in consultative status with the United Nations Economic and Social Council (ECOSOC), is mainly a global network of people who believe in youth leadership. One of the tasks that it undertook in Burkina Faso is to organize a guided visit for young people to the Regional Stock Exchange in the capital city—Ouagadougou. In addition, the United Nations Capital Development Fund (UNCDF) recently launched the 'Bank the Youth' advocacy campaign in the capital city again targeting young people. This campaign was aimed at improving the financial inclusion of young people and including the awareness covered critical policy issues in the legal and regulatory framework. In fact, the training focus was

[2] https://www.globalmoneyweek.org/countries/167-burkina-faso.html. Accessed on 19 September 2019.

mainly on the development of financial services adapted to the needs of young people, and the development of financial skills through financial education. To date, financial awareness activities (e.g. guided tours and intensive training sessions) are encouraging and will be beneficial if the training includes a wider group of the population such as women and economically active adults regardless of their age. Furthermore, the coverage needs to incorporate both rural and urban areas. In fact, scale can be an issue and such training activities should be given not in a week-long campaign but via multi-sector commitment to provide sustained regular awareness training for a broader section of the population.

Entrepreneurship

Burkina Faso performs poorly in terms of entrepreneurship. According to the latest available information in Global Entrepreneurship Index, the country ranked 129 out of 137 countries (Ács et al. 2018). Therefore, identifying the enablers of entrepreneurship is a paramount policy initiative. In addition to access and use of existing formal and informal finance, it is good news that the unbanked can make use of mobile money transactions. If the use of digital money is geared towards savings and investment, it promotes the creation of microenterprises and improves the entrepreneurship trajectory of the country. Our research is aimed at finding the significant factors that enhance the likelihood of self-employment using a recent survey evidence of more than 5000 individuals both from rural and urban areas covering all age ranges.

Here we proxy entrepreneurship by the reported self-employment which can take the form of either registered or unregistered own business. Most of the entrepreneurship is own-account worker type or self-employment in the informal sector running small and micro businesses. About 63% of individuals perceive that entrepreneurship as a good career choice. But very few are employers running small businesses and the ownership rate of established businesses is about 7.5% (GEM 2016). The majority live on the margins (IMF 2018; Dolan and Rajak 2016). Despite the strong propensity to be business owners, entrepreneurial drive of individuals is hampered by the lack of access to financial services. Wage employment is not the default but a rare opportunity in countries such as Burkina Faso. The default is that most opt to be entrepreneurs or self-employed out of necessity. Economies such as that in Burkina Faso suffer from long years of structural problems with volatile macroeconomic conditions and prolonged recessions. These macro-level realities and business-cycle conditions (e.g. austerity during downturns) drive the proliferation of necessity-driven entrepreneurship, which is a countercyclical response of economic agents to macroeconomic shocks. This mirrors the spike in entrepreneurship and self-employment rates in recessions in advanced countries, reinforcing the argument of a positive correlation between necessity entrepreneurship and economic downturns (Fairlie and Fossen 2018). However, the economic downturns and volatility characterize poorer countries and hence the necessity of entrepreneurship persists and is a widespread phenomenon.

There is a growing body of work that focus on the effect of finance on development outcomes such as household consumption, education and self-employment or business start-ups (Menon and Rodgers 2011). However, few studies show empirically the importance of FinTech revolution on access and use of financial products by households in Africa. With the advent of consumer survey data that capture FinTech indicators, such an analysis is possible in poor countries such as Burkina Faso, given the intensification in financial transaction.

Data and Methodology

To show the significance of disruptive technologies such as FinTech for entrepreneurship, we use the recent data collected via FinScope Consumer Survey of Burkina Faso in 2016. The survey was designed to understand the livelihood, source of income, financial needs and demands of those who are 15 and older. In addition to information on demographic and geographic distribution of the population, data was collected on a range of indicators such as financial perceptions, attitudes and behaviours; current levels of access to, and utilization of, financial services and products; and drivers and barriers to the utilization of, and access to, financial products and services (FinMark 2017).

The data collection methodology is applied to nationally representative individual-based sample of the adult population (15 years and older) at regional, urban and rural levels. The sampling frame (i.e. the total sample of individuals covered in the survey) and data weighting was conducted by the National Institute of Statistics and Demography (INSD), and the weights were consistent with projected population based on the latest available census data. Data was collected from 5066 individuals through face-to-face interviews conducted from May to September 2016.

We use F to represent a range of variables that capture access to finance and use of technology-driven financial products (e.g. using mobile phone for financial transactions) by an individual i in region j is given by:

$$F_{ij} = \alpha^F X_{ij} + \beta Z_{ij} + \lambda_j^F + \varepsilon_{ij}^F \qquad (8.1)$$

where X_{ij} represents a vector containing variables that capture individual and household socioeconomic characteristics, Z_{ij} is a vector of different set of determinants of access and use of finance that are not directly affecting self-employment decisions of individuals (e.g. property title), and the parameters to be estimated are represented by α^F and β. Equation (8.1) constitutes the first stage regression similar to the specification used by Menon and Rodgers (2011) and Pitt and Khandker (1998). The parameter λ_j^F represents an unobserved region-specific and time-invariant determinant of access to and use of finance and ε_{ij}^F captures unobserved factors affecting access and use of finance that vary by individual and is normally distributed with zero mean and constant variance.

The probability of self-employment S_{ij} of individual i in region j conditional on individual and household characteristics X_{ij} and access and use of finance is given as:

$$S_{ij} = \alpha^S X_{ij} + \phi F_{ij} + \lambda_j^S + \varepsilon_{ij}^S \qquad (8.2)$$

where α^S and ϕ are parameters to be estimated, λ_{ij} is an unobserved region-specific and time-invariant factor affecting self-employment and ε_{ij}^S is the unobserved error term that is normally distributed with zero mean and constant variance. Since F_{ij} is endogeneous, there are non-zero correlations among the region-specific unobservables and the error terms of the two equations, that is, $\text{cov}\left(\lambda_j^F, \lambda_j^S\right) \neq 0 \ and \ \text{cov}\left(\varepsilon_{ij}^F, \varepsilon_{ij}^S\right) \neq 0$. Therefore, we need to account for this endogeneity while estimating Eq. (8.2). Model estimation without controls for these correlations leads to biased estimates of the parameters of Eq. (8.2) due to the endogeneity of participation in using financial products.

Two empirical problems that make endogeneity an issue in our study are as follows: the use of financial products is a choice variable but it is on the right-hand side of our equation so it makes our estimates biased; simultaneity between self-employment and use of loans or other financial products. For instance, self-employment affects the use of different financial products because liquidity problems increase demand for finance. Getting access to varied financial products increases the likelihood of self-employment. Hence, loan=f(self-employment) and self-employment, f(financial access). In estimation, we used a system estimation using a seemingly unrelated bivariate probit model allowing for potential dependence between Eqs. (8.1) and (8.2).

FinTech's Benefits Are Yet to Arrive

Our study confirms that financial exclusion is detrimental to entrepreneurship. Access to informal finance is still the most important positive force that promotes entrepreneurship via self-employment. This is particularly true for women who rely on informal finance schemes better than men (e.g. rotating savings and credit associations (ROSCAs)). Our findings suggest that the use of mobile money technology is not necessarily for investment purposes but to make livelihood changes by investing in the creation of new enterprises or self-employment ventures. Most of the current use of mobile money is for transaction payments (e.g. utility bills) and/or payment of fees (e.g. tuition fees) (Table 8.2).

Table 8.2 Seemingly unrelated bivariate probit model of self-employment

Variable	Model 1 All	Model 2 Females	Model 3 Males
Formal finance	0.148*(0.085)	0.200(0.132)	0.144(0.114)
Informal finance	0.182***(0.075)	0.315**(0.125)	0.118(0.098)
Mobile money	0.087(0.668)	0.062(0.103)	0.104(0.091)
Age	0.053***(0.007)	0.036***(0.010)	0.064***(0.010)
Age squared	−0.001***(0.000)	−0.000***(0.000)	−0.001***(0.000)
Married	0.320***(0.049)	0.304***(0.070)	0.368***(0.073)
Female	−0.075*(0.041)	–	–
Primary education	0.275***(0.058)	0.262***(0.093)	0.286***(0.075)
Secondary	−0.268***(0.069)	−0.192*(0.103)	−0.032***(0.093)
University	−1.109***(0.152)	−1.350***(0.342)	−1.070***(0.176)
Urban	0.622***(0.055)	0.643***(0.080)	0.587***(0.078)
Constant	−1.996***(0.140)	−1.878***(0.187)	−2.143***(0.201)
Rho	0.263***(0.054)	0.240***(0.080)	0.234***(0.067)
LR test for rho=0 (p-value)	24.41***(0.000)	8.040***(0.000)	10.96***(0.000)
N	5066	2436	2630

Source: FinScope Consumer Survey, Burkina Faso 2016

* = significant at 1% level; ** = significant at 5% level; and *** = significant at 10%

Informal finance has stronger effect for women's entrepreneurship than in the significant coefficient for the whole sample and underscores its importance. FinTech is yet to deliver for expansion of entrepreneurship in Burkina Faso despite encouraging speed of access and use by a large section of the rural and urban population. Relative to no schooling which is the reference category, those who completed primary education are more likely to be self-employed. In contrast, completing secondary schooling and university education are negatively and significantly associated with self-employment. When we investigate the nature of self-employment, our data indicate that there are two categories, that is, registered self-employment and unregistered self-employment, and the latter represents the largest proportion of individuals engaged in own-account work often in the informal sector. Thus, the results suggest self-employment is a low skilled and low return economic activity which is not appealing for those above primary schooling. Unsurprisingly, being in an urban area is linked with higher likelihood of self-employment. This is mainly attributed to better infrastructure (e.g. internet) and availability of diverse livelihood activities as opposed to very limited off-farm employment in much of the rural Burkina Faso.

CONCLUSIONS AND POLICY IMPLICATIONS

The cost of services can be a factor for individuals to limit their use of mobile money transactions. However, there are encouraging Africa-wide and specific subregion developments that facilitate such transactions by a wider population, especially those who are at the lower end of the income distribution. Macro policy changes are making it cheaper to use mobile financial services such as the abolishing of roaming charges since 31 March 2017 among five West African nations: Burkina Faso, Cote d'Ivoire, Guinea, Mali and Senegal. This policy initiative is part of a wider plan to create an integrated African continent through organizations such as the Economic Community of West African States (ECOWAS). The trends in West Africa mirror the 'One Network Area' scheme involving East African nations of Kenya, Rwanda and South Sudan (launched in October 2014).

FinTech diffusion is low in many parts of Africa and the reasons are multiple: low level of financial development, lack of knowledge of financial products, lack of trust and scepticism in financial services provided by formal institutions and taxation of mobile and internet users (Kedir et al. 2011). Governments, in their zeal to expand fiscal space to finance development, often adopt aggressive tax measures including mobile and internet users (Kedir et al. 2017). An aggressive tax regime could easily perpetuate the existing digital divide and financial exclusion of the marginalized. Thus, one important latest development that might jeopardize financial inclusion is the worrying trend in taxation of mobile money transactions and introduction of social media tax in several African countries (Ndung'u 2019a, b).

In the wake of declining ODA and other forms of foreign capital for the development of most African countries, most have resorted to taxing upcoming and innovative sectors and users of FinTech. Experts on mobile money transaction facility, for example, M-Pesa, are warning against taxing the mobile phone industry and treating it as a golden goose tax (Ndung'u 2019a, b). The taxes target the transactions and devices used by consumers and this is on top of a very good tax collection from the phone companies and operators. Regulators of East African countries such as Uganda and Kenya must proceed with caution with the introduction of social media tax and fees on mobile money transactions or FinTech activities. This is because such a taxation may not have the intended outcome of increasing government revenues. Rather, the tax could serve as a disincentive for FinTech users, driving them to lesser use of the available technology and revert to conventional transactions and use of cash. This is already having a negative impact on internet and mobile money users, with a significant drop in Uganda (Nanfuka 2019; Pollicy 2018).

According to Dahir (2019), three months after the introduction of mobile transaction fees in July 2018, the Uganda Communications Commission internet subscription declined by more than 2.5 million users. During the same period, the sum of taxpayers from over-the-top (OTT) media services decreased by more than 1.2 million users, while the value of mobile money transactions fell by 4.5 trillion Ugandan shillings (approximately $1.2 million). In sum, regulators have to realize that taxation of the fast-growing sector and imposing mobile money usage taxes will put a brake to an encouraging trend in FinTech innovation and its diffusion in Burkina Faso and across the African continent.

REFERENCES

Ács, Z. J., Szerb, L., & Lloyd, A. (2018). *Global Entrepreneurship Index.* Washington, DC: The Global Entrepreneurship and Development Institute.

Bateman, M., Duvendack, M. & Loubere, N. (2019). Is fin-tech the new panacea for poverty alleviation and local development? Contesting Suri and Jack's M-Pesa findings published in Science, *Review of African Political Economy,* 46(161), 480–495.

Beck, T., & Frame, W. S. (2018). Technological Change, Financial Innovation, and Economic Development, In T. Beck & R. Levine (Eds.). *Handbook of Finance and Development*. Cheltenham.

Dahir, A. (2019). *Uganda's Social Media Tax Has Led to a Drop in Internet and Mobile Money Users, Quartz*. https://qz.com/africa/1553468/uganda-social-media-tax-decrease-internet-users-revenues/?utm_source=email&utm_medium=africa-weekly-brief. Accessed 11 Aug 2019.

Dolan, C., & Rajak, D. (2016). Remaking Africa's Informal Economies: Youth, Entrepreneurship and the Promise of Inclusion at the Bottom of the Pyramid. *The Journal of Development Studies, 52*(4), 514–529.

Eisenhardt, M., & Martin, J. (2000). Dynamic Capabilities: What Are they. *Strategic Management Journal, 21*, 1105–1121.

Fairlie, R., & Fossen, F. (2018). *Opportunity Versus Necessity Entrepreneurship: Two Components of Business Creation*. IZA Discussion Paper, DP No. 11258, Bonn, Germany.

FinMark Trust. (2017). *FinScope Consumer Survey Highlights Burkina Faso 2016*.

Fonta, W., Sanfo, S., Kedir, A., & Thiam, D. (2018). Estimating Farmers' Willingness to Pay for Weather Index-Based Crop Insurance Uptake in West Africa: Insight from a Pilot Initiative in Southern Burkina Faso. *Agricultural and Food Economics, 6*, 1–20.

Fonta, W., Thiam, D., Houessionon, P., Yameogo, Thomas B., & Kedir, A. (2019). *Smallholder Farmers' Preferences for Weather-Indexed Crop Insurance in Africa: Evidence from a Choice Experiment in Burkina Faso*. Mimeo.

GEM. (2016). *Burkina Faso: Global Entrepreneurship Monitor Report*.

Henderson, R. (1993). Under-Investment and Incompetence as Responses to Radical Innovation: Evidence from the Photolithographic Alignment Equipment Industry. *RAND Journal of Economics, 24*, 248–270.

IMF. (2018). *Burkina Faso: Economic Development Report*. Country Report No. 18/85. Washington, DC

Kedir, A., Disney, R., & Dasgupta, I. (2011). *Why Use ROSCAs When You Can Use Banks? Theory and Evidence from Ethiopia?* IZA Discussion Paper No. 5767, Bonn, Germany.

Kedir, A., Elhiraika, A., Chinzara, Z., & Sandjong, D. (2017). Growth and Development Finance Required for Achieving Sustainable Development Goals (SDGs) in Africa. *African Development Review, 29*(1), 15–26.

Marshall, A. (1890). *Principles of Economics*. London/New York: Macmillan. Menon.

Menon, N., & Rodgers, Y. (2011). How Access to Credit Affects Self-employment: Differences by Gender during India's Rural Banking Reform. *The Journal of Development Studies, 47*(1), 48–69.

Nanfuka, J. (2019). *Social Media Tax Cuts Ugandan Internet Users by Five Million, Penetration Down from 47% to 35%*. Collaboration on International ICT Policy in East and Southern Africa (CIPESA), Kenya.

Ndung'u, N. (2019a). *Taxing Mobile Phone Transactions in Africa: Lessons from Africa, Policy Brief, Africa Growth Initiative at Brookings*. Washington, DC

Ndung'u, N. (2019b). Could Taxation of Mobile Banking in Africa Stall Financial Inclusion? In B. S. Coulibaly & J. Miller (Eds.), *Foresight Africa: Top Priorities for the Continent in 2019*. Washington, DC: Africa Growth Initiative, Brookings Institution.

Parker, S. (2005). *The Economics of Entrepreneurship: What We Know and What We Don't*. Hanover: Now Publishers.

Pitt, M., & Khandker, S. (1998). The Impact of Group-Based Credit Programs on Poor Households in Bangladesh, *Journal of Political Economy, 106*(5), 958–996.

Pollicy. (2018). *Offline and Out of Pocket: The Impact of the Social Media Tax in Uganda on Access, Usage, Income and Productivity*. Uganda.

Romer, P. M. (1990). Endogenous Technological Change. *Journal of Political Economy, 98*(October, Part 2), 1002–1037.

Romer, P. M. (1994). The Origins of Endogenous Growth. *Journal of Economic Perspectives, 8*(1), 3–22.

Romer, D. (1996). *Advanced Macroeconomics*. New York: McGraw-Hill Companies.

Sakyi-Nyarko, C. (2018). *Financial Inclusion and Human Development in Sub-Saharan Africa, Middle East and North Africa with a Special Focus on Ghana*. Unpublished PhD thesis, Loughborough University.

Schumpeter, J. A. (1937). Preface to Japanese Translation of Theorie der Wirtschaftcilhen Entwicklung. In R. V. Clemence (Ed.), *Essays: On Entrepreneurs, Innovations, Business Cycles, and the Evolution of Capitalism*. New Brunswick: Transaction Publishers.

Schumpeter, J. A. (1939). *Business Cycles: A Theoretical, Historical, and Statistical Analysis of the Capitalist Process*. New York: McGraw-Hill Book Company Inc.

Schumpeter, J. A. (1942). *Capitalism, Socialism, and Democracy* (3rd ed.). New York: Harper & Row.

Solow, R. M. (1956). A Contribution to the Theory of Economic Growth. *Quarterly Journal of Economics, 70*(February), 65–94.

Solow, R. M. (1957). Technical Change and the Aggregate Production Function. *Review of Economics & Statistics, 39*(3), 312–320.

Spencer, A., & Kirchhoff, B. A. (2006). Schumpeter and New Technology Based Firms: Towards a Framework for how NTBFs Cause Creative Destruction. *International Entrepreneurship Management Journal, 2*, 145–156.

186   E. KOUAME AND A. M. KEDIR

Walras, L. (1874). *Elements of Pure Economics; or, The Theory of Social Wealth* (W. Jaffe, Trans.). Homewood: American Economic Association and The Royal Economic Society.
World Bank. (2019). *Financing Agreement for Financial Inclusion Support Project in Burkina Faso*. Washington, DC.
Yenkey, C, Doering, L, & Aleves, P. (2015). *Multiple Uses of Mobile Money, Implications for Financial Inclusion*. Working Paper.

CHAPTER 9

Disruptive Technology, Mobile Money, and Financial Mobilization in Africa: M-Pesa as Kenya's Solution to Global Financial Exclusion?

Nafisa A. Abdulhamid

INTRODUCTION

The current global financial markets are failing to include and meet the needs of many sub-Saharan African societies, particularly those who work and reside in rural areas. While bank account ownership may be almost universal among people in developed economies, only 54 percent of adults in developing countries own a bank account (Demirgüç-Kunt et al. 2015:3). Today, approximately 1.7 billion adults remain unbanked, or excluded from formal financial institutions, with a majority of these residing in the developing world (The World Bank 2018). Generally, the term "financial inclusion" refers to the process that allows for "the ease of access, availability and usage of the formal financial system for all members of an economy" (Samra and Pais 2011:63). An inclusive financial system

N. A. Abdulhamid (✉)
Department of Political Science, Dalhousie University, Halifax, NS, Canada
e-mail: N.Abdulhamid@dal.ca

© The Author(s) 2020
P. Arthur et al. (eds.), *Disruptive Technologies, Innovation and Development in Africa*, International Political Economy Series,
https://doi.org/10.1007/978-3-030-40647-9_9

enables "the efficient allocation of productive resources" and reduces the cost of capital, improves the daily management of finances, and can reduce the growth and dependence of informal, and often exploitative, sources of credit, such as shark loans (ibid.). Inclusive financial systems therefore enhance "efficiency and welfare by providing avenues for secure and safe practices" through the provision of various financial services (ibid.). Access to financial services is important because it makes it easier for populations to invest in businesses, health, and education. Conversely, financial exclusion refers to "those processes that serve to prevent poor and disadvantaged social groups from gaining access to the financial system" (Leyshon and Thrift 1995:312). Financially excluded individuals lack access to "appropriate, low-cost and safe financial products and services from mainstream providers" (Mohan 2006:5).

To reduce the gap between those who are included and excluded from the global financial system, coupled with the deep penetration of mobile phones in the sub-Saharan African region, Safaricom, Kenya's largest mobile network operator (MNO), established M-Pesa, a mobile money transfer (MMT) service, in March 2007, as an innovative form of branchless banking and a good example of a disruptive technology. Disruptive technologies "are those that cause an upheaval in the existing structure and dominant firms by being cheaper, simpler, and more convenient than the dominant technology" (Schuelke-Leech 2018:261). Initially, these technologies function at the margins, but ultimately, and especially because they are often cheaper, simpler, and more convenient, end up displacing the dominant technologies (Bower and Christensen 1995).

This chapter examines Kenya's experimentation with M-Pesa and its role in fostering financial inclusion. I argue that, albeit relatively successful in allowing for extensive and easily accessible financial services, like the ability to send, receive, and borrow money and manage financial risk, M-Pesa and MMT services in general fall short in promoting widespread financial literacy, with specific reference to issues pertaining to credit and savings, among populations in developing economies. My argument is structured in three parts. First, I will give a brief overview of disruptive technology as the conceptual and theoretical framework underpinning MMT technology as a means of financial inclusion. Second, I will examine the rise and impact of M-Pesa within the social, political, and economic contexts in which it evolved, as well as analyze its impact on financial literacy focusing specifically on the issues of credit and saving. Third, I will evaluate the extent to which M-Pesa impacted the East African Community (EAC), questioning whether the M-Pesa model can be replicated to other contexts.

DISRUPTIVE TECHNOLOGY AND MOBILE MONEY

Christensen's definition and popularization of the term "disruptive technologies" has contributed to our understanding of not only how technological innovations impact firms and industries, but also how these impact consumer behaviors (Bower and Christensen 1995). A disruptive technology is that which "changes the bases of competition by changing the performance metrics along which firms compete" (Danneels 2004:249). Initially, disruptive innovations "do not satisfy the minimum requirement along the performance metric most valued by customers in the mainstream segment" and are therefore considered an inappropriate addition to the mainstream market in terms of satisfying the needs of existing customers (ibid.:247).

The "disruptive" product initially serves the needs of a niche market; however, over time, research and development investments and improvements are made to the product and it matures. This means that the "disruptive technology improves to the point where it also can satisfy the requirements of the mainstream market," thereby displacing incumbent firms (ibid.). Bower and Christensen (1995) argued that technological innovations that displace existing companies are not necessarily radically different from a technological perspective. Disruptive technologies have two significant characteristics: first, they "present a different package of performance attributes," which are not typically valued by existing customers (ibid.:44). Second, the "performance attributes that existing customers do value improve at such a rapid rate that the new technology can later invade those established markets" (ibid.).

Disruptive products do not appeal to many customers in the incumbent market; however, they are often cheaper, simpler, and more convenient, thereby allowing a new segment of customers who were previously excluded from the market to participate (Hwang and Christensen 2008). Disruptive innovations specifically target customers who appear to be least attractive to dominant firms; "successful incumbent firms will almost always choose instead to focus on offering sustaining products to their higher-paying, performance-hungry tiers of customers" (ibid.:1330). However, once the disruptive technology establishes itself in the market and improves itself over time, "customers of the sustaining company find that their needs can be met by the disruptive innovation" (ibid.). Hwang and Christensen cite Canon's slower but more affordable tabletop photocopiers as an example of a disruptive innovation that eventually displaced Xerox as the dominant firm in the market (2008). Similarly, the introduction of mobile money transfer (MMT) technology, including M-Pesa services, into the market has since displaced established formal banking and money transfer technologies (Lashitew et al. 2019:1202).

The term "mobile money" is a "mobile-based money transfer service that uses information and communication technology tools and non-banking channels to offer and extend financial services to subscribers who are not profitable to be reached by formal and traditional service providers" (Bongomin et al. 2018:363). MMT provides low-income earners with basic, yet important, financial services including deposit and withdrawal of funds, remittance delivery, and bill payments. Mobile network operators (MNOs) are leading actors in narrowing the gap between the banked and unbanked people who leverage the fact that mobile phones have become a ubiquitous phenomenon, especially in sub-Saharan Africa. The use of mobile phones has a particularly profound impact on populations with lower levels of literacy and income in rural communities because they are portable, relatively inexpensive, and easy to use.

In 2017, the GSMA estimated that over 5 billion people were connected to mobile phone services; in 2016, 227 million people had mobile phone accounts in sub-Saharan Africa (GSMA 2018). The widespread use of mobile phones, extensive mobile network coverage, and vast retail infrastructure led MNOs to "offer customers more secure and convenient ways to access, send, receive, and store funds, contributing to greater financial access and economic empowerment" (Almazan 2016:68). MMT enables MNOs to service "clients at lower cost-per-transaction, and with a reduced investment in physical infrastructure" (Kendall et al. 2012:50). It has also benefited clients by providing them with multiple transaction outlets where they live and work, even in rural and remote areas, thereby reducing the costs associated with accessing formal financial services.

MMT services are an important means of financial inclusion, which is also essential for sustainable development in the developing world. According to the Global Findex database, the global unbanked are often women from poor households. In Kenya, for example, a fifth of adults remain unbanked with two-thirds of them being women (Demirgüç-Kunt et al. 2018:35). The unbanked are also disproportionately young adults between 15 and 24 years old, who only have primary education or less, and are either employed or seeking work (ibid.:36–38). The Global Findex database also notes that 26 percent of the adults they interviewed claimed that they did not have a bank account because one of their family members already owned one (ibid.:40). Women were more likely than men to cite this as a reason for not having a bank account; in Turkey, for instance, 72 percent of the women interviewed cited this reason (ibid.). The discrepancy in financial inclusion between developed and developing economies can be attributed to several factors, including the fact that most people in developing economies have little or no money to use formal financial institutions. This reason is coupled with the high costs attributed to opening and maintaining a bank account. Formal financial institutions are also unlikely to extend their services to rural populations because the revenue rural clients generate might not be sufficient to justify those investments (Kendall et al. 2012:50). Even in cases where rural clients might not need complex bank deposit services, including those who may receive military pensions or direct government money transfers, these clientele are "rarely seen as profitable customers by banks [or other formal financial institutions] given the low balances they hold and the high transaction costs of traditional banking infrastructure" (ibid.). MMT services therefore seek to narrow the gap between the unbanked and the banked people of the developing world by embodying an innovative form of branchless banking.

SAFARICOM AND M-PESA

In March 2007, Safaricom, Kenya's largest MNO and part of the larger Vodafone Group, established M-Pesa ("M" for "mobile" and "Pesa" being Swahili for "money"), the first MMT technology of its kind in East Africa. Within the first month of operation, 20,000 Kenyans had registered with M-Pesa (Hughes and Lonie 2007:63). The M-Pesa statistics are truly remarkable, because by November 2007, Safaricom managed to register 1.1 million customers, allowing for the transfer of approximately USD 87 million (Mbiti and Weil 2016:247). By September 2009, 8.5 million Kenyans had registered for M-Pesa, and USD 3.7 billion had been transferred over the system, an amount equivalent to Kenya's gross domestic product (GDP) at the time (ibid.). By the end of the 2017 fiscal year, M-Pesa had a total of 27 million subscribers, generating a revenue of USD 535 million (Lashitew et al. 2019:1207).

Initially, the founders of the MMT service designed it in a way that would foster "sustainable development… [and] provide microfinance institutions (MFIs) with an efficient mechanism for the collection of customer loans" (Morawczynski 2009:510). Before its launch, Safaricom ran a pilot program with Faulu Kenya, a local MFI, with the intention of observing and assessing customer transaction needs. During the pilot, it was discovered that urban customers were purchasing mobile phone airtime using M-Pesa and sending it to their relatives in rural Kenya. A deeper investigation uncovered that "most [urban] Kenyans made similar transfers, not only with mobile phone credit, but also with cash" (ibid.).

Informal remittance transfers were often costly and risky and included sending money through family and friends, bus and *matatu* (minibus) services, and the Kenyan postal service. Safaricom identified a major gap in the domestic remittance system, where Kenyans working in the urban centers were always needing and wanting to "send money back home." Nick Hughes, a former Vodafone executive who worked on the M-Pesa project in 2003, notes that the MMT service faced "formidable financial, social, cultural, political, technological, and regulatory hurdles" (Hughes and Lonie 2007:63). The biggest challenge, according to Hughes, was the need to "marry the incredible divergent cultures of global communication companies, banks, and microfinance institutions – and cope with their massive and often contradictory regulatory requirements" (ibid.). The M-Pesa project also needed to accommodate the needs of unconnected, unbanked, and semiliterate clients who were often excluded from formal financial institutions and services.

At its most basic form, M-Pesa allows customers to carry out three simple mobile money transfers. First, a customer can deposit cash into one of the 156,000 M-Pesa outlets in return for e-float (Safaricom 2018). This is also called a "cash-in" transaction. The customer needs to have a valid government-issued identification document (ID); the ID, as well as the amount of money being deposited, are logged into a logbook kept at the outlet. The M-Pesa agent inserts the customer's mobile phone number and deposits the appropriate amount of money into his/her mobile phone. The customer waits at the outlet until he/she receives a confirmation message saying that the transaction has been completed. The entire "cash-in" transaction takes about a minute. Second, a customer can exchange his/her e-float for cash at any M-Pesa outlet. This is called a "cash-out" transaction. The customer must show the M-Pesa agent valid ID, and the agent logs the transaction. The customer notifies the agent of how much cash he/she wants to withdraw, selects the "withdraw cash" option on the M-Pesa application on his/her mobile phone, enters the amount, and inserts the agent's number. The customer is charged a withdrawal fee, which is based on the amount being withdrawn. When the agent receives a text message confirming the completion of the transaction, he/she proceeds to give the customer the appropriate amount of cash.

Third, a customer can transfer e-float from his/her mobile phone to another mobile phone. The customer inserts the recipient's phone number and the transfer amount, and the sender and recipient both receive text messages indicating the completion of the transaction (Mbiti and Weil 2016:248–249). Any customer wanting to use M-Pesa must first register their Safaricom phone number at an agent location using a valid government-issued ID. It is important to note that recipients of M-Pesa need not be registered; however, there are higher transaction fees associated with transferring money to non-registered individuals. For example, it costs KSH 28 (USD 0.27) to withdraw between KSH 1001 (USD 9.65) and KSH 1500 (USD 14.46) from an M-Pesa agent; it costs KSH 59 (USD 0.57) to transfer between KSH 1001 (USD 9.65) and KSH 1500 (USD 14.46) to unregistered customers; and it costs KSH 26 (USD 0.25) to transfer between KSH 1001 (USD 9.65) and KSH 1500 (USD 14.46) to registered M-Pesa customers (Safaricom 2018). In creating such a competitive money transfer price structure, M-Pesa lowered the cost of financial transaction in Kenya, particularly those associated with banks, thereby allowing for the previously unbanked to access financial services.

In its 12 years of operation, Safaricom has managed to expand its M-Pesa services beyond remittance transfers. Customers can use their accounts to purchase goods through the pay bill system; local vendors have a unique pay bill number that customers can use to pay for goods and services through their M-Pesa account. Safaricom also has the Fuliza overdraft service, which allows customers to complete their M-Pesa transactions despite having insufficient funds in their M-Pesa account (ibid.). The availability of Fuliza is contingent upon a customer's credit viability as well as how long they have been using M-Pesa. Customers can repay their Fuliza by depositing cash to their M-Pesa or receiving M-Pesa from someone else, and the overdraft balance will be deducted from the M-Pesa account automatically. Not only has M-Pesa contributed to international money transfers through PayPal, Early Express, WorldRemit, and Western

Union, it has also triggered aggregators like Pesapal, which allows customers to receive and make payments through mobile money, Mastercard and Visa.

Furthermore, in 2012 Safaricom launched M-Shwari, a mobile savings platform that gives previously unbanked Kenyans access to micro-savings and micro-credit directly from their mobile phones. Generally, formal financial institutions, including banks, tend to hinder the poor's ability to access credit, particularly those without collateral. This is based on the assumption that "lending to poor households will fail as the cost of doing so is too high and the risks are great," especially with a lower saving tendency (Bongomin et al. 2018:365). This meant that the poor could only access credit through informal means, including oppressive shark loans. However, M-Shwari, in partnership with the Commercial Bank of Africa (CBA), gives customers access to micro-loans at a "facilitation rate" of 7.5 percent per month, as well as a Lock Savings Account that can earn an interest of up to 70 percent based on the CBA rate (Safaricom 2019). Digital credit has three primary advantages.

First, it has significantly lower transaction costs associated with borrowing because the loans are distributed through mobile money and are later converted into cash through agent networks. Second, loans are disbursed quickly since there is no need for in-person vetting, like there would be with formal financial institutions. Third, because "digital providers use non-traditional data (in particular, mobile money and airtime usage) to develop alternative credit scores," it gives groups without collateral the ability to access credit and loans (Francis et al. 2017:2). As a result, these alternative digital credit programs have become very popular. However, it should be noted that high-interest loans, either in the form of microcredit or digital credit, are harmful to borrowers and can cause overindebtedness, bankruptcy, and the inability to repay their loans. For example, an estimated 2 million people reported to the Kenyan credit bureau for M-Shwari loan defaults (ibid.).

Despite its rapid growth, there have been some barriers to the adoption of the M-Pesa technology in Kenya. In their study of mobile financial services in East Africa, Aker and Mbiti (2010) uncovered that adoption of MMT services positively correlated with bank account possession, urbanity, wealth, and education. In addition, the knowledge gap on mobile financial services widened with the introduction of newer MMT products, including M-Shwari and Fuliza. In their study of mobile money and financial inclusion, Dubus and van Hove (2017) found that "those who do not benefit from the positive effects of M-Pesa (such as the ability to receive more frequent and faster remittances and, ultimately, the ability to save on a formal account) are disproportionally non-educated, poor, and female" (p. 18). Safaricom has tried to overcome this by ensuring that M-Pesa comes inbuilt in the SIM toolkit where the base application has remained the same since the technology's inception in 2007, thereby not requiring the use of smartphones. The M-Pesa user interface is also relatively easy to use with the menu giving customers the option to send money, withdraw cash, buy airtime, save, access micro-loans, and pay with M-Pesa. Moreover, customers are not required to have access to wireless or data internet to access all of these mobile financial services.

The Impact of M-Pesa on Financial Inclusion and Financial Literacy

The logic behind connecting financial inclusion and development strategies is simple: a formal financial system connects savers and investors. A robust financial sector "allows savings to be pooled and invested in assets that can generate much higher rates of return, because of economies of scale and/or the use of better technology" (Kasekende 2014:482). In addition, a competitive financial system means that savings are allocated to assets that have the potential of generating high returns. This will lead to an increase in the marginal return to capital, thereby also increasing the economic growth rate of a country. A financial sector that excludes more than 70 percent of its population, which is the case in sub-Saharan Africa, stifles inclusive growth, especially "if that growth depends on household enterprises to provide incomes for the majority of the workforce" (ibid.:484). The evolution of information technology has therefore become a crucial component of "banking the unbanked" and integrating previously unbanked populations into development and governance programs (Roy 2017:20). The widespread use of mobile phones as well as mobile phone ownership, high rates of mobile phone network adoption, the lack of affordable alternatives, and lower service fees relative to formal banking institutions have led to the swift use of MMT in developing economies (Bongomin et al. 2018:362). This means that MMT has allowed for previously unbanked peoples to have access to financial services and choose which of these services best fulfills their specific needs. In turn, this "low[ers] transaction costs and reliev[es] the stress of meeting everyday needs" (Taylor and Horst 2017:23).

In their qualitative study on M-Pesa, Morawczynski and Pickens (2009) argued that MMT services continue to be used as an alternative to the formal banking system. They especially note that, prior to its establishment, most Kenyans were excluded from the formal financial services provided by banks. M-Pesa represents, or has the potential to serve as, a means for widening the reach of financial services and delivering those to the poorest members of Kenyan society. Indeed, M-Pesa's primary business model was grounded on the idea of "sending money back home." However, remittance transfer is an unsustainable means of income and often leaves recipients in dependent positions. The ability to save in a secure way is therefore a necessity for financial inclusion because it increases the poor's resilience to income shocks and allows them to invest in small-scale business enterprises (Dubus and van Hove 2017:2). M-Pesa has enabled customers to use the application as a rudimentary savings account, although the system does not provide interest on the money being stored. Despite this, M-Pesa provides "a foundation for economic development, and, in particular, allow the poor to climb the 'banking ladder' by facilitating access to the formal economy" (Morawczynski 2009:510). Within eight years of its operation, M-Pesa, and access to mobile financial services, has increased per capital consumption levels, lifting about 194,000 households out of poverty (ibid.). This impact "derive[s] from a more efficient allocation of labor, savings, and risk" (Suri and Jack 2016:1292). Smallholder farmers in rural Kenya have used M-Pesa to manage risk and liquidity restraints, leading to "increased application of farm inputs, increases in marketed products and greater profitability" (Johnson and Krijtenburg 2018:571). These impacts are also more pronounced in female-headed households where the spread of MMT pushed women to switch from agricultural production to business or retail as their primary occupation (Suri and Jack 2016:1292). Women living in patriarchal households in particular are able to increase their savings, especially because M-Pesa gives them privacy so they can manage their households without control and pressure from the patriarch (Suri and Jack 2016).

Morawczynski (2009) also suggests that M-Pesa "was used for the cultivation of livelihood strategies... [which] helped poor Kenyans to cope with, and recover from, stresses and shocks" (p. 518). These strategies have further enabled the poor to acquire positive livelihood out-comes, leading to the "reduction in vulnerability achieved through the solicitation and accumulation of financial capital and the maintenance of social networks" (ibid.). For instance, because M-Pesa allows for the reliable and safe storage and transfer of money, "rural Kenyans no longer need to make lengthy trips to urban areas to make monthly payments for basic services, such as light or heat," thereby saving on the cost of transportation (Buku and Meredith 2013:393). However, despite giving average Kenyans the ability to access financial services, it is equally important to educate them about financial literacy, especially when it comes to fees associated with credit, and the importance of savings. Being financially literate is the capacity and confidence a decision-maker possesses to make responsible and productive financial decisions. Concerns of financial illiteracy are increasing especially since MMT and digital credit services are becoming more complex. Customers need to learn how to use M-Pesa beyond its basic remittance and bill-paying services; they need financial literacy in order to know how to use M-Pesa's other complex services for their own long-term advantages, including saving for retirement, investing in education, and buffers against financial shocks.

Ultimately, the ability to save for future investments is a necessity for financial inclusion; this ability can be primarily achieved through financial literacy. In an effort to address concerns regarding the lack of financial inclusion, M-Pesa has partnered up with banks to provide financial management systems through MMT. As mentioned before, M-Pesa works with CBA to offer M-Shwari services to customers. In addition, M-Pesa has also partnered up with Equity Bank to develop M-Kesho, a mobile financial service that offers insurance and interest-paying bank accounts, ranging from 0.5 percent to 3 percent on the amount saved, to customers (Mbiti and Weil 2016:4). Safaricom has also developed fraud prevention mechanisms into the MMT application; M-Pesa allows customers to request for money transfer reversals if the amount was transferred to the wrong phone number or pay bill number. Once an M-Pesa transfer has been made, the application prompts the customer to reverse it, if the money was sent to a wrong number. Moreover, M-Pesa allows you to check the account balance free of charge and gives customers the ability to request monthly M-Pesa statements to be sent directly to their email.

M-PESA, MMT TECHNOLOGY, AND THE EAST AFRICAN COMMUNITY

The East African Community (EAC) is the regional intergovernmental organization of the Republic of Uganda, Republic of Kenya, Republic of Rwanda, Republic of Burundi, and the United Republic of Tanzania. The primary goals of the EAC "include the widening and deepening cooperation among member states in (among others) the political, economic, and social fields for their mutual benefits" (Nyaga 2014:271). All the states in the EAC have active MMT services and mobile payment services, albeit having different starting points and facing diverse technological and adaption issues. This has been facilitated by two undersea fiber optic cable systems, the first implemented in July 2009 and the other in 2010, which connected the region to faster and cheaper internet and telecommunications networks (ibid.:273). Indeed, M-Pesa in Kenya has been prominent in the region "not only in terms of number of subscribers, cash flow volumes, and agents, but also through its *influence on the regulatory landscape* and the shape of subsequent platforms across the EAC [my emphasis added]" (ibid.:275). For instance, all central banks in the EAC use the Central Bank of Kenya (CBK) as a point of reference for how to regulate mobile money in their countries. Most MNOs in the region, mandated by their central banks, have emulated M-Pesa's thresholds of what and how much, including transaction fees, customers can send and receive through their mobile money applications. Despite this, M-Pesa has still proven to be more successful in Kenya than its counterparts in other parts of the EAC. Nyaga (2014) attributes this to "the cellular market landscape" in Kenya, determined by the penetration of mobile phones among the people, the concentration of the market, the price structure, and the ability of customers to use the application (p. 276).

When Safaricom introduced M-Pesa to the Kenyan market in 2007, 30 percent of the population owned mobile phones; alternatively, when mobile money was launched in Tanzania, only 20 percent of the population had mobile phones (ibid.). In addition, Safaricom in Kenya dominated the market with 80 percent of market shares, while Vodacom in Tanzania had only 45 percent of subscriber market share (Camner et al. 2010:6). M-Pesa was also the only MMT service in Kenya between 2007 and 2009, whereas in Rwanda, MTN launched its MMT services in

February 2010 and Tigo followed a year later, in May 2011. Likewise, Uganda's MTN and Airtel both launched their MMT programs in February and March 2009.

Despite the difference in successes, MMT services across the EAC continue to offer previously unbanked and financially excluded people access to important financial services, thereby bringing them closer to the formal financial systems. For instance, in Rwanda, financial inclusion increased from 21 percent in 2006 to 68 percent in 2016, with 26 percent of the population using commercial banks and 60 percent of the population using mobile financial services (EADB 2019). Similarly, in Uganda, formal financial inclusion increased from 21 percent in 2006 to 58 percent in 2018, where only 11 percent of the population use commercial banks and 56 percent use mobile financial services (ibid.). The East African Development Bank also notes that mobile financial services have moved beyond simple financial transactions within the region to include complex services such as savings, insurance, loans, and investments (ibid.). One of the most impressive financial technological innovations in Uganda, SchoolPay, allows parents and relatives to pay school tuition using a variety of mobile money platforms, including Airtel Money, MTN Mobile Money, and CenteMobile. Currently, about 8542 schools have registered with SchoolPay, giving parents and relatives the option to pay the tuition in installments and "reducing the risk of error and the cost of transport and numerous bank transactions" (ibid.).

MMT services in the EAC also offer online retail services; Jumia has become the most popular online retail store for customers living within the EAC. In addition, Mergims in Rwanda allows customers outside the country to pay electricity, television, and water bills for those living in Rwanda (ibid.). However, at present, there lacks a regional legislative mobile money framework that can regulate the operation of MNOs across the EAC. The regulation of MMT operation and services is left to the discretion of respective member states. Greater regional regulation and cooperation between the EAC member states on issues pertaining to MMT could work toward further reducing transaction costs to customers beyond state borders and also giving customers access to a wider range of private and public sector financial services.

CONCLUSION

Mobile money transfer (MMT) technology, as an example of a disruptive technology, continues to contribute to sustainable and inclusive development in the East African Community (EAC). M-Pesa, the pioneer of MMT technology in the EAC, initially targeted and served the needs of the previously unbanked members of Kenyan society, proving to be a fast, secure, and convenient way to transfer money across the country. Over time, and as the technology became more complex, M-Pesa became the dominant MMT service not only in Kenya but across the EAC, influencing MNOs across the region to emulate its information communication technology and competitive price structure. MMT services in the EAC have been successful, albeit to relative degrees, due to the high rates of mobile phone penetration, mobile network adoption, the lack of affordable and safe alternatives, and the lower transaction fees associated with formal financial institutions.

M-Pesa and other MMT services in the EAC serve as a means for extending the reach of important financial services and delivering these services to the poorest members of their societies. However, as the technology becomes more complex, especially in offering high-interest microloans to customers, it is important for MNOs to educate their customers on issues pertaining to loan defaults and over-indebtedness. Indeed, as I have argued in this chapter, financial inclusion is an important foundation for sustainable development in developing economies. However, financial inclusion must be coupled with financial literacy in order to empower previously unbanked populations to use mobile financial services to foster long-term financial stability.

REFERENCES

Aker, J. C., & Mbiti, I. M. (2010). Mobile Phones and Economic Development in Africa. *Journal of Economic Perspectives, 4*, 7–232.

Almazan, M. (2016). Mobile Money Brings Financial Inclusion. *African Banker, 37*, 68–69.

Bongomin, G. O. C., Ntayi, J. M., Munene, J. C., & Malinga, C. A. (2018). Mobile Money and Financial Inclusion in Sub-Saharan Africa: The Moderating Role of Social Networks. *Journal of African Business, 19*(3), 361–384.

Bower, J., & Christensen, C. (1995). Disruptive Technologies: Catching the Wave. *Harvard Business Review, 73*(1), 43–53.

Buku, M. W., & Meredith, M. W. (2013). Safaricom and M-PESA in Kenya: Financial Inclusion and Financial Integrity. *Washington Journal of Law, Technology & Arts, 8*(3), 375–400.

Camner, G., Pulver, C., & Sjoblom, E. (2010). *What Makes a Successful Mobile Money Implementation? M-PESA in Kenya and Tanzania.* Nairobi: FSD Kenya.

Danneels, E. (2004). Disruptive Technology Reconsidered: A Critique and Research Agenda. *Journal of Product Innovation Management, 21*(4), 246–258.

Demirgüç-Kunt, A., Klapper L. F., Singer, D., & Van Oudheusden, P. (2015). *The Global Findex Database 2014: Measuring Financial Inclusion Around the World.* World Bank Policy Research Working Paper (7255).

Demirgüç-Kunt, A., Klapper, L. F., Singer, D., Ansar, S., & Hess, J. (2018). *The Global Findex Database 2017: Measuring Financial Inclusion and the Fintech Revolution Overview.* World Bank Group.

Dubus, A., & van Hove, L. (2017). *M-PESA and Financial Inclusion in Kenya: Of Paying Comes Saving?* Working Papers hal-01591200, HAL, 1–37.

East African Development Bank. (2019). *Financial Technology in East Africa.* [Online] Available at: https://eadb.org/financial-technology-in-east-africa/. Accessed 30 July 2019.

Francis, E., Blumenstock, J., & Robinson, J. (2017). *Digital Credit: A Snapshot of the Current Landscape and Open Research Questions.* CEGA White Paper, 1–19.

GSMA. (2018). *The Mobile Economy 2018.* [online] Available at: https://www.gsmaintelligence.com/research/?file=061ad2d2417d6ed1ab002da0dbc9ce22&download. Accessed 30 May 2019.

Hughes, N., & Lonie, S. (2007). M-PESA: Mobile Money for the "Unbanked": Turning Cellphones into 24-Hour Tellers in Kenya. *Innovations,* (Winter & Spring), 63–85.

Hwang, J., & Christensen, C. M. (2008). Disruptive Innovation in Health Care Delivery: A Framework for Business-Model Innovation. *Health Affairs, 27*(5).

Johnson, S., & Krijtenburg, F. (2018). 'Upliftment,' Friends and Finance: Everyday Exchange Repertoires and Mobile Money Transfer in Kenya. *The Journal of Modern African Studies, 56*(4), 569–594.

Kasekende, L. (2014). What Role Does Financial Inclusion Play in the Policy Agenda for Inclusive Growth in Sub-Saharan Africa. *Development, 57*(3–4), 481–487.

Kendall, J., Maurer, B., Machoka, P., & Veniard, C. (2012). An Emerging Platform: From Mobile Transfer System to Mobile Money Ecosystem. *Innovations, 6*(2), 49–64.

Lashitew, A. A., van Tudler, R., & Liasse, Y. (2019). Mobile Phones for Financial Inclusion: What Explains the Diffusion of Mobile Money Innovations? *Research Policy, 48*(5), 1201–1215.

Leyshon, A., & Thrift, N. (1995). Geographies of Financial Exclusion: Financial Abandonment in Britain and the United States. *Transactions of the Institute of British Geographers, 20*(3), 312–341.

Mbiti, I., & Weil, D. N. (2016). Mobile Banking: The Impact of M-Pesa in Kenya. In S. Edwards, S. Johnson, & D. N. Weil (Eds.), *African Successes, Volume III: Modernization and Development*. Chicago: University of Chicago Press.

Mohan, R. (2006). Economic Growth, Financial Deepening and Financial Inclusion. *BIS Review, 1*(13), 1–18.

Morawczynski, O. (2009). Exploring the Usage and Impact of 'Transformational' Mobile Financial Services: The Case of M-PESA in Kenya. *Journal of Eastern African Studies, 3*(3), 509–525.

Morawczynski, O., & Pickens, M. (2009). *Poor People Using Mobile Financial Services: Observations on Customer Usage and Impact from M-PESA* (CGAP Brief). Washington, DC: World Bank Group.

Nyaga, J. K. (2014). Mobile Banking Services in the East African Community (EAC): Challenges to the Existing Legislative and Regulatory Frameworks. *Journal of Information Policy, 14*, 270–290.

Roy, A. (2017). The Question of Inclusion. In B. Maurer, S. Musaraj, & I. Small (Eds.), *Money at the Margins: Global Perspectives on Technology, Financial Inclusion and Design*. New York/Oxford: Berghahn.

Safaricom. (2018). *Safaricom Annual Report and Financial Statements 2018*. [Online] Available at: https://www.safaricom.co.ke/images/Downloads/Safaricom_annual_report_070818.pdf. Accessed 30 May 2019.

Safaricom. (2019). *M-Shwari & KCB M-PESA*. [Online] Available at: https://www.safaricom.co.ke/personal/m-pesa/do-more-with-m-pesa/loans-and-savings. Accessed 30 July 2019.

Samra, M., & Pais, J. (2011). Financial Inclusion and Development. *Journal of International Development, 23*(5), 613–628.

Schuelke-Leech, B. A. (2018). A Model for Understanding the Orders of Magnitude of Disruptive Technologies. *Technological Forecasting and Social Change, 129*, 261–274.

Suri, T., & Jack, W. (2016). The Long-Run Poverty and Gender Impacts of Mobile Money. *Science, 354*(6317), 1288–1292.

Taylor, E., & Horst, H. A. (2017). A Living Fence: Financial Inclusion on the Haitian-Dominican Republic Border. In B. Maurer, S. Musaraj, & I. Small (Eds.), *Money at the Margins: Global Perspectives on Technology, Financial Inclusion and Design*. New York/Oxford: Berghahn.

The World Bank. (2018). *Gains in Financial Inclusion, Gains for a Sustainable World*. [Online] Available at: http://www.worldbank.org/en/news/immersive-story/2018/05/18/gains-in-financial-inclusion-gains-for-a-sustainable-world?cid=ECR_TT_worldbank_EN_EXT. Accessed 30 May 2019.

PART IV

The Changing Nature of Wealth Creation

SMEs, Industrialization and Disruptive Technologies in Africa: Enabling or Constraining?

Peter Arthur

INTRODUCTION

The last two decades have seen tremendous growth in information and communication technologies (ICTs) in the global North and global South. It is seen by Seyal, Rahim and Rahman (2000) as a set of well-organized data resources and communication network that aid firms in the collection, transformation and dissemination of related and useful information inside and across other firms to improve performance. The rise in ICTs, which include the Internet, wireless networks and cell phones, has drastically transformed the world by providing a means by which information can easily and readily be passed on (Cant et al. 2015). The increasing availability and improvement in ICT in the developing world have in many ways changed how people operate, especially as they pertain to business practices. Consequently, African policymakers and regulators are beginning

P. Arthur (✉)
Department of Political Science, Dalhousie University,
Halifax, NS, Canada
e-mail: peter.arthur@dal.ca

© The Author(s) 2020   205
P. Arthur et al. (eds.), *Disruptive Technologies, Innovation and Development in Africa*, International Political Economy Series,
https://doi.org/10.1007/978-3-030-40647-9_10

to realize that ICTs can assist with their socioeconomic development efforts, especially in the case of small- and medium-scale enterprises (SMEs), which are the engine that drives world economies and the stepping stone to industrialization.

Even though a number of studies and research work have been done on rethinking the industrialization and development process in Africa through the promotion of SMEs, much of what has been written has been largely focused on the role of micro-credit schemes, SMEs as a means of economic survival, as well as the difficulties and challenges they encounter in their daily activities (Arthur 2012). Similarly, while technology is playing an undeniable role in driving business opportunities and growth in developing countries, and Africa is emerging at the forefront in contemporary debates about the adoption and adaptation of new and old technologies, there is limited research on how emerging technologies have influenced contemporary challenges and opportunities with respect to businesses in Africa (Amankwah-Amoah et al. 2018).

Given that less attention has been paid to how new and emerging ICTs can impact the performance of SMEs, this chapter fills the gap by systematically examining and organizing the current body of empirical and theoretical literature that has explored the role and impact of ICTs on SMEs among African countries. Using a multiperspective framework that involves an examination of the context, as well as technological and organizational factors affecting SMEs, and drawing from several African countries, the chapter reviews the extant research work and theoretical discussions that provide insights into how ICT adoption is shaping the activities of SMEs. Particularly, this chapter examines how ICTs can be used as a tool by SMEs to improve their business operations and drive socioeconomic development and industrialization process. Additionally, it interrogates the impact and extent to which government policies on technology enable or constrain the activities of SMEs. It also sketches out appropriate technology policy measures, strategies, initiatives and practical framework to ensure that SMEs contribute to the overall development and industrialization efforts in African countries. Thus, this chapter contributes to the debate and emerging literature on the effectiveness of using ICT innovations, mobile telephones and social media platforms to improve the performance of SMEs. The contribution to knowledge concerning best practices will be available for other African countries to access as they attempt to ensure that the SMEs help with the industrialization and development process through the activities of digital technologies, mobile telephony and social media.

The chapter has four sections. The section "SMEs: Theoretical Discussions and Literature Review" undertakes a theoretical discussion on SMEs, with a focus on their definition and characteristics. It also reviews the literature on the role and contribution of SMEs in the development and industrialization efforts of various countries. The section "Technological Impact on SMEs" examines the role that ICT plays in the operations of SMEs in African countries. The section "SMEs and ICTs: Challenges and Constraints" discusses the challenges and constraints that SMEs in Africa face in their efforts to employ ICT in their businesses. The last section offers suggestions regarding how to overcome the constraints and ensure that African SMEs' use of ICTs can help their business operations.

SMEs: Theoretical Discussions and Literature Review

Countries throughout the world are very often focused on improving their overall development and providing for the needs of their citizens. The debate though has often centred on the best approach to go about it. Two of the dominant paradigms in the development debate are the state-led and/or structuralist model and the neoliberal perspective. With its reservations about building and having an excessive reliance on the activities and decisions of foreign businesses, Payne and Phillips (2010) point out that governments were natural bases from which to industrialize. In this vein, structuralists urged the pursuit of industrialization based on the substitution of current imports by domestic production, encouraged, at least initially, by protection from foreign competition (Payne and Phillips 2010). In other words, under the state-led approach, governments of developing countries were expected to deepen their process of industrialization and produce their own manufactured goods. This therefore explains the adoption of import substitution industries, which entailed the provision of subsidies, industry protection, high tariffs, restricting foreign investment and the promotion of exports through cheap credits.

Although widely in vogue in the 1950s and 1960s, from the early 1980s, the structuralist approach came under attack from the neoliberal perspective for downplaying the importance of markets in industrial and capitalist development. According to Payne and Phillips (2010), the discrediting of structuralism and rejection of Keynesian growth theory provided ample ammunition for neoliberal theory, which saw state-led approach as creating a wide range of short-term costs and for hindering the long-term development of the industrial sectors of many countries (Weiss 1988). Thus, the prescriptive emphasis of neoliberalism involved freeing markets, creating competitive markets integrated into the international economy, and positioning the private sector as the engine of accumulation and growth (Payne and Phillips 2010). With the focus on a market-based approach to economic and industrial growth, the main aspects of neoliberal policies include rolling back of the state in the economic sphere, the adoption of policies such as privatization, trade liberalization and the retrenchment of government workers. As pointed out by Arthur (2012), with the massive layoff of public sector employees that accompanied the implementation of neoliberal policies, coupled with the inability of the private sector and formal economy to absorb the excess labour force, many individuals sought employment in the SME sector, which was also consistent with the neoliberal perspective that sees the private sector as the engine of socioeconomic growth and development in society. It is under these circumstances that, as discussed in detail below, the SME sector became the largest and fastest growing in many developing countries.

The definition of SMEs has been the subject of contentious debate and discussion. The boundaries of the definitions generally vary in line with the size of the economic activities within the country and the level of development (Maduku et al. 2016; Mbuyisa and Leonard 2017; Ongori and Migiro 2010). With countries defining SMEs to suit their economic or development needs, UNIDO, for example, identified 50 different definitions of SMEs in 75 countries (Onyiriuba 2016). While in the United States, a business with 499 employees is considered medium sized (Muriithi 2017), Onyiriuba (2016) points out that in defining the basic criteria of SMEs, the European Union (EU), for example, relates the number of employees with sales turnover and/or balance sheet size. Apart from defining SMEs as enterprises that employ not more than 250 persons and whose annual turnover is less than €50 million, and/or a maximum annual balance sheet footing of €43 million, the EU unbundles SMEs into three distinct economic units—medium-sized, small and micro-enterprises—that are subsumed in its definition. Similarly, while the African Development Bank defines SMEs as companies with less than 50 employees (Esselaar et al. 2006), in Nigeria, businesses having between 1 and 300 employees are referred to as SMEs. Also, in South Africa, SMEs are businesses having between 1 and 200 employees (Akinyemi and Adejumo 2017). The situation is similar in Senegal where SMEs are typically considered to have between 1 and 250 employees (including micro-enterprises), while in Kenya, SMEs are defined as having fewer than 100 employees (Crick et al. 2018).

Also, involved in all sectors of industrial development, from mining, manufacturing, service industry to agriculture and fishing (Muriithi 2017), Duncombe and Heeks (2002) add that SMEs can be grouped into two broad categories: livelihood and growth enterprises. While livelihood enterprises are generally made up of micro-enterprises, which are established by the poor for economic survival and generate some income, growth enterprises consist of SMEs that have an objective of attaining the long-term benefits of competitiveness and innovation. In sum, SMEs range from very small micro-firms run by one or two persons and very slow growth or no growth to fast-growing medium businesses earning millions of dollars and majority employing as many as 250 employees. The businesses' definitions also vary from those requiring little money to start to others demanding substantial amounts to start (Muriithi 2017).

Whatever their definitions, size, characteristics and sectors in which they are involved, SMEs have grown in importance in the global economy as data from both the developed and developing countries has revealed that the SME sector is an active and vibrant force for economic growth, innovation, job creation, entrepreneurship and increased public revenue (Ngek 2014; Muriithi 2017). In India, for example, Sharma and Bhagwat (2006) indicated that SMEs have generally outperformed large organizations in the areas of employment growth and employment. Particularly, SMEs account for 40% of industrial production, 35% of total exports and 80% of employment in the industrial sector. According to Mah (2018), in South Korea, the ratio of SME employees to those in all industries increased from 75% in 1995 to 88% in 2005, having stabilized at around that level since then. Moreover, the share of SMEs in value added in the manufacturing sector increased from 35% in 1980 to 50% in 2013, while SME exports increased from US$76.8 billion in 2009 to US$100.4 billion in 2015. For Latin America, Urmeneta (2018) indicates that an externality of improving productivity, particularly of SMEs, is their contribution to reducing poverty and income inequality in the region, and a significant share of employment.

In the African context, Muriithi (2017) has pointed out that SMEs account for more than 95% of all firms in the sub-Saharan Africa region. It is notable that SMEs are even more significant given their role to reduce poverty, boost countries' gross domestic product (GDP) and provide employment for majority of the population. The sector is particularly important due to their simple approach in offering affordable goods and services at reasonable terms and prices besides being a source of income and employment. Unsurprisingly, Quartey, Turkson, Abor and Iddrisu (2017) have indicated that the SME sector in West Africa has been exploding over the past three decades mainly as a result of the few formal avenues for pursuing interest-bearing investment options. Most countries within the subregion have shallow stock markets, while at the same time interest rates have not been able to catch up with rising inflation. Under these circumstances, entrepreneurship has been the attraction for investing excess money holdings.

In Nigeria, for example, a report estimated that about 70% of the industrial employment is held by SMEs and more than 50% of the GDP is SME generated (Taiwo et al. 2016). Similarly, in Kenya, SMEs (including micro-enterprises) employ around 80% of the workforce and contribute 20% to GDP (Crick et al. 2018). Also, SMEs contribute 28.5% of the total economy and resulted in a situation where the Kenya Industrial Estates has continued to play a key role in promoting local entrepreneurship through the financing and development of SMEs in the country (Ndiege 2019). Finally, in South Africa, SMEs contribute approximately 57% to GDP and provide about 61% of all the country's employment (Mavimbela and Dube 2016).

Additionally, Duncombe and Heeks (2002) have indicated that SMEs make social contributions to development, through self-development, enabling individuals, often poor women, to gain experience and confidence and to enhance skills, as well as providing for collective development through community-based organizations such as co-operatives. Also, SMEs contribute significantly to economic development by being associated with discovering of new markets and exploiting them to their advantage. Moreover, SMEs are central to wealth creation by stimulating demand for goods, investment and trade (Von Broembsen et al. 2005, cited in Muriithi 2017). Without SMEs, many African governments will experience financial and developmental constraints, all which would only worsen living standards of low-income persons often served by the sector (Muriithi 2017). Besides these, for Muriithi (2017), another important role played by SMEs is that they are the heart of founding new ventures and inventing new ideas and technology. The businesses provide room for pre-incubating, incubating, and introducing and commercializing new products. In many countries, SMEs pioneer new knowledge and test it before it disseminates to large industries. Through their entrepreneurial spirit and central locus, the business founders take the risk to identify and seize opportunities and turn them into workable and market-driven products (Muriithi 2017).

Although facilitating the emergence of a vibrant SME sector is promoted as the new development prescription for low-income countries (Poole 2018), the popular view that SMEs are engines of growth is, however, called into question by critics. Ngek (2014) and Poole (2018) contend that as opposed to being growth-oriented, SMEs never expand or grow beyond their start-up point and generally have much lower productivity than larger firms. Their relatively small size means that they do not reap economies of scale or access new technologies that will enable them to be competitive when compared to their larger counterparts. In fact, all across the world, SME survival and growth rate are low, which goes to show that the numbers of anticipated high-quality SMEs are very small (Ngek 2014). For example, in Latin America, Urmeneta (2018) notes that SMEs struggle to access loans due to the banks' difficulty in assessing risks associated with lending to them. These challenges combined with low productivity levels explain why there is little internationalization and a high rate of turnover of Latin American SMEs. Furthermore, critics argue that because of existing structural and administrative constraints and challenges, small-scale enterprises are often hindered in their efforts to make a positive contribution to socioeconomic development and alleviate poverty in African countries (Arthur 2012). For instance, in Uganda, one-third of new business start-ups don't go beyond one year of operation, while in South Africa, the failure is between 50% and 95% depending on the industry (Muriithi 2017). Cant and Wiid's (2013) work showed that many South African SMEs fail because of macro-environmental factors, such as inflation, interest rates, management skills, lack of a market and crime.

Moreover, because of the prevalence of their widespread informality, SMEs are often associated with low productivity, reduced competitiveness and a lack of innovation capabilities, not forgetting that they also focus mainly on survival, and thereby provide a relatively large number of employees with a subsistence income (Crick et al. 2018). Similarly, problems with exports, technology, competitiveness and interfirm linkages as well as barriers in the institutional and policy environments are obstacles that prevent African SMEs from participating successfully in the global economy (Mutalemwa 2015).

Finally, Poole (2018) asserts that academic analysis of entrepreneurs, entrepreneurship and SME sector development is characterized by a lack of precision and consistency over the core terms employed. This is highly problematic because it allows obfuscation to trump insight and thus makes it extremely difficult to judge the veracity of the development prescription, that is advocated or to undertake any objective assessment of the effectiveness of strategies that have been implemented. He goes on to argue that policymakers are consequently faced with having to initiate measures that constitute little more than leaps of faith based on unproven claims and an inconsistent discourse and are therefore exposed to being influenced by a broad array of vested interests, be they vendors of micro-credit, management consultants, NGOs or economists of various persuasions.

TECHNOLOGICAL IMPACT ON SMEs

Many African countries have moved away from SMEs as the strategy that would increase employment opportunities and spur economic growth and industrialization (Arthur 2012). However, the explosive growth of ICTs, especially the Internet and mobile telephony, has raised corresponding interest in understanding the role of ICTs in enhancing the socioeconomic and industrialization potential of SMEs. ICTs are offering a number of opportunities for SMEs by making knowledge and information available, improving business-related communication, reducing costs, improving decision-making, responsiveness and efficiency, as well as improving overall flexibility (Mbuyisa and Leonard 2017). Ismail, Jeffrey and Van Belle (2011) have pointed out that the benefits for a business that adopts the Internet technologies include improved productivity through process automation, creation and easy access to markets giving rise to innovation and reduction in input costs which can strengthen the competitiveness of an enterprise, leading to competitive advantage. Furthermore, the adopting business can build collaborations, improve processes and is able to store and retrieve information efficiently. In addition, the use of ICTs by SMEs to participate in the knowledge economy offers opportunities to narrow social and economic inequalities and thus help achieve broader development goals (Mbuyisa and Leonard 2017). Song, Park and Park (2017) note that technological improvements often help SMEs with positive effects on their value, business performance and strengthened competitiveness.

Nowhere is the significance of ICT in the activities of SMEs more evident than in the rise of social media, one of the most pervasive ICTs around, and which is shaping various business practices around the world. Social media, as various writers (Trottier and Fuchs 2015; Ateş 2013) have noted, is a collection of online social platforms (chat rooms, discussion forums, location services, social networking, social guides, social bookmarking, social status networks, weblogs, blogs, podcasts, video casts and wikis), which enable users to share information, ideas and interests and to interact via the Internet or mobile systems such as smartphones. It is also defined by Trottier and Fuchs (2015) as a form of electronic communication and networking sites that allows users to follow and share content (text, pictures, videos, etc.) and ideas within an online community. Generally referred to as applications such as Facebook, WhatsApp, Twitter, YouTube, LinkedIn, Pinterest and Instagram, Kapoor et al. (2018) have pointed out that these social media applications are driven by user-generated content and are highly influential in a myriad of settings, from purchasing/selling behaviours, entrepreneurship, political issues to venture capitalism. Moreover, Källander et al. (2013) have argued that mobile phone and other social media platforms have the potential to reach a wide range of populations, where geographical distances can restrict access to in-person services and limit participation.

As Cheng and Shiu (2019) have pointed out, customer involvement using social media should be useful to help firms utilize customer knowledge because, first, the nature of customer knowledge can influence the innovation development. Second, customer involvement using social media enables firms to engage consumers in a timely and direct manner at relatively higher level of efficiency than more traditional communication tools. Third, employing customer involvement using social media should inform an understanding of customer needs, detect defects earlier, attain preliminary feedback regarding possible market reactions and, thus, produce more creative product/service ideas more highly valued by customers.

According to Odoom et al. (2017), Internet-enabled communication media has supported many organizations to conduct their businesses from anywhere across the globe. In Ghana, for instance, Odoom et al. (2017) found that there is a shift in media consumption among Ghanaian consumers such that social media is becoming a key strategic communication platform for both informative and interactive actions for several firms, including SMEs. As a result, social media adoption and usage offer an interesting route for SME competitiveness, especially with its ability to offer affordable segmentation and targeting purposes for communicating product and service brands to consumers. Hence, an advantage social media gives SMEs is that they do not need a physical location before they can make their products visible, and that while not having shops to display their products, social media gives them a virtual shop to do so. Thus, despite the bottlenecks, the use of social media as a strategic tool in optimizing firm performance seems prevalent among SMEs in Ghana.

Additionally, social media technology enables customers and businesses to interact and engage in two-way communication in which both the customer and the business are active participants in the generation and dissemination of the content (Ndiege 2019). Ndiege's (2019) research in Kenya suggests that social media technology appears to be particularly beneficial for supporting SMEs to position themselves better strategically. Also, in their research that explored how social media shapes Nigerian entrepreneurs' motivation to start a business and how they market their businesses via social media, Olanrewaju, Whiteside, Hossain and Mercieca (2018) contend that SMEs are employing social media marketing approaches across different platforms to reach their customers and audiences. Equally, as Amankwah-Amoah et al. (2018) have argued, many small-scale entrepreneurs in African countries have turned to using WhatsApp and Skype to manage their businesses while concurrently reducing the cost of doing business. In addition, some entrepreneurs have taken to social media platforms such as WeChat, LinkedIn, Facebook and Twitter to advertise their businesses and also gain publicity for their businesses. Also, mobile money, where individuals use mobile phones for financial transactions including money transfer, has also gathered momentum.

Finally, recent developments in ICTs, particularly the use of mobile technologies in marketing (also known as mobile marketing), offer great opportunities for businesses to improve on their marketing capabilities (Maduku et al. 2016). Cant, Wiid and Hung's (2015) research study in South Africa showed that business owners were of the view that ICT-enhanced access to market information and knowledge facilitated new ways of managing and organizing business knowledge, increased the speed and reliability of business communication and better communication tools with customers. Other benefits included building of closer relationships, reduction of inefficiencies within the value chain and the resulting lower correspondence costs. In their information playing role, ICTs provide access to valuable, timely and accurate information to buyers and sellers (Mbuyisa and Leonard 2017).

With online marketing becoming very common because of technological advancement and the emergence of the Internet, not only has there been improvement of the communications link between businesses and individuals (Shemi and Procter 2013), but also online marketing helps with businesses' attempt at informing, promoting and selling their products over the Internet (Burgess and Bothma 2007). For example, exploring the role of mobile technology and related service platforms in supporting informal micro-entrepreneurships in rural Ghana, Asiedu et al. (2018) found that mobile technology engendered pride and emotional connectedness and, being easy to use, helped to increase business confidence. Adoption advantages included improved communications with customers and business partners, and effective stock control, providing competitive advantage. Also, Molony's (2007) study (cited in Deen-Swarray et al. 2013), which investigated how the mobile phone was being integrated into Tanzania's business culture, noted that trust, a variable associated with social capital, is a hugely important issue in the use of ICT among African micro- and small enterprises. Particularly, mobile phones were seen as a facilitating technology for existing, trust-based relationships (Molony 2007). Thus, among the transformational benefits of improved technologies for SMEs include the ease of communication, the concomitant cut in business costs and efficiency in operations, improvements in the marketing of products, business expansion, profitability and growth (Arthur and Arthur 2017).

SMEs and ICTs: Challenges and Constraints

The foregoing has shown that various technologies are used by SMEs to interface with their customers, thereby reducing the distance between their businesses and customers, as well lower overheads and overcome inefficiencies. Despite the myriad of opportunities to society and to enterprises particularly through access to information that ICTs such as the Internet, mobile phones and social media present to SMEs (Mureithi 2017), many in developing countries operate in distinctively hostile institutional environments (Abubakar et al. 2019) and thus face a number of challenges and constraints in their use of various technologies.

One of the main challenges facing SMEs in Africa in their efforts to employ technology in their businesses has centred on the digital divide. As Bertot et al. (2010: 268) have observed, there are multiple divides that exist, of which access to the ICTs is but one. Embedded within the divide are such issues as technology literacy (the ability to understand and use technologies); usability (the design of technologies in such ways that are intuitive and allow users to engage in the content embedded within the technology); accessibility (the ability of persons with disabilities to be able to access the content through adaptive technologies—in fact, some mobile technologies such as iPhone are completely inaccessible to persons with visual impairments due to the touchscreen design which lacks a tactile keyboard); and functionality (the design of the technologies to include features, e.g., search, e-government service tracking, accountability measures, that users desire). In fact, while the use of new digital technologies provides essential services to assist SMEs in African countries, sub-Saharan Africa still lags in terms of Internet penetration. In Africa, it is estimated that 412,150,114 people use the Internet as of December 2017, with a penetration rate of 32% (Dzisah 2018). For example, for most Ghanaians, Sey (2014) notes that active Internet use and penetration is constrained by the expense of smartphones and mobile data, availability of relevant content, and awareness of just how Internet services might be used. Barely 20% of mobile phone users have smartphones, 19% of mobile phone owners access social media from their phone and the reach of Facebook, the most popular social networking site in the country, stands at about 7%.

Thus, notwithstanding the benefits that come with the adoption of technology, and the fact that the Internet offers value-added tools to any business (Mavimbela and Dube 2016), Irefin, Abdul-Azeez and Tijani (2012) have stated that poor telecommunications infrastructure, limited ICT literacy, inability to integrate ICT into business processes, high costs of equipment and connectivity, government policy, poor telecommunications infrastructure and poor understanding of the dynamics of the knowledge economy are factors that hinder the adoption of Internet technologies. More significantly, although SMEs in developing countries are beginning to embrace the use of information technology (IT), the majority still struggle with their IT adoption initiatives (Ndiege 2019). This is corroborated by Mbuyisa and Leonard (2017) who have argued that SMEs in developing countries have not been able to realize some of the benefits associated with ICT owing to constraints such as lack of financial resources, poor infrastructure, lack of business and ICT skills, unfavourable policies and legal frameworks, challenges posed by rapid globalization in the form of international competition and limited access to new markets. For example, exploring insight on Kenyan SMEs' experiences on having online marketing use, Wilson and Makau (2017) found that although online marketing use is popularly known, majority of SMEs do not fully take potential advantage of these platforms because most have insufficient budget for IT investment, cannot accommodate IT personnel, lack access to IT-constructed infrastructures and are unaware whether or not there are customers online.

Similarly, Ndiege (2019) found that many SMEs in Kenya struggle to adopt IT because of the scarcity of capital to invest in IT solutions and a lack of adequate knowledge for carrying out the IT adoption process successfully. Furthermore, connectivity, accessibility and digital literacy remain major challenges on the continent, and neither governments nor the industry generally seem particularly eager when it comes to making investments in new knowledge and technologies for further technology development and integration (Onyeji-Nwogu et al. 2017). Coupled with that, while an effective mechanism of communication in reaching the many young people who spend significant amounts of time on their mobile phones, surf the Internet on these devices, and are the most inclined to use social media networks, majority of citizens are not getting their information through platforms made possible by smartphones, simply because they do not have the means and/or the ability to take advantage of all its innovative capabilities (Tettey 2017: 690).

Aside from these, technologies such as social media also open up the possibility for hackers to commit fraud and launch spam and virus attacks; increase the risk of people falling prey to online scams that seem genuine, resulting in data or identity theft; and potentially undermine productivity, especially if the citizenry or employees are always busy updating profiles and fidgeting with their social media devices (Gyampo 2017; Tettey 2017). This is exacerbated by the fact that in countries like Ghana, there are few regulations related to protecting users from online scams. The absence of current laws on emerging issues contributes to social vices such as online scams (Atiso and Kammer 2018). Finally, these challenges and constraints are worsened by the fact that while SMEs using social media can obtain large amounts of new information, most have limited capabilities to develop social networks and convert this information into innovation knowledge (Cheng and Shiu 2019).

Promoting Technological Use in SMEs: The Path Forward

The preceding discussions have shown that inadequate infrastructure and the digital divide, among others, have combined to limit the ability of SMEs to significantly contribute to the development and industrialization process among African countries. Moreover, according to Shemi and Procter (2013), some of the reasons put forward from the literature regarding why SMEs in Africa have not capitalized on the power of technologies like the Internet to extend their business beyond traditional border include cost of acquiring and operating ICTs, lack of IT and e-commerce knowledge, owner/manager low literacy levels, inability to perceive e-commerce benefits, unfriendly regulatory policy and requirements, cultural issues, and dependence on customer or supplier preferences. Particularly, SMEs are substantially behind in competitiveness since they lack resources such as funding, technology, manpower and information.

Despite a current lack of expertise to make use of these recent trends, technology should be considered a part of an SME strategy, as it provides means for connecting with partners, achieving autonomous processes, synchronizing flows and customizing products (Moeuf et al. 2018). It is in this vein that it is important that SMEs are provided with the necessary support by governments and other stakeholders in order for them to achieve their goal of contributing fully to the industrialization and development process among African countries. To increase performance, SMEs should strengthen the relationship between technological strategy and market environment. As noted by Song, Park and Park (2017: 46), SMEs should mobilize outside resources and/or government policy to overcome in-house limitation based on a correct understanding and analysis of the resources acquired. Technology acquisition from government as well as private research institutes is a good way for SMEs to avoid the risk inherent in early stages of R&D and give them opportunities to find new markets.

Also, SMEs cannot achieve competitiveness and remain profitable without the proper adoption of technology at the right market levels (Maduku et al. 2016). However, SMEs face challenges of understanding what ICT or Internet applications to adopt to enhance the competitiveness, productivity or innovativeness of their businesses, and they could benefit from some form of guidance of cost-effective accessibility (Mavimbela and

Dube 2016). With access to computing resources as well as strong and stable IT infrastructure often cited as common challenges to SMEs in sub-Saharan Africa, it is imperative that appropriate structures are put in place to ensure that SMEs in developing countries are able to position themselves strategically to secure their survival (Ndiege 2019). Hence, governments need to lead facilitators to advance ICT adoption, with focus not only on ICT sector and SME sector growth independently but look at strategies that will integrate the two areas for implementation of a broad-based policy (Mavimbela and Dube 2016). Considerable government involvement is required to enhance technology adoption, among other things, by promoting national identification and societal involvement and improving educational infrastructures (Amankwah-Amoah et al. 2018).

Furthermore, SMEs' capacity to respond to their clients' expectations while maintaining a competitive advantage on their market and contributing to the industrialization process calls for constantly improving their industrial management processes, that is, planning, using resources, controlling production, and measuring and evaluating operational performance (Moeuf et al. 2018). The importance of ICT for SMEs means that African governments need to put in place measures to ensure that the necessary infrastructure are readily available and in constant supply since without them, it becomes difficult for SMEs to exploit the benefits that come with IT adoption. In other words, given that ICTs can provide SMEs with competitive advantage, effective management and improved business performance (Enagi and Van Belle 2019), realizing the goals of industrialization and development calls for a policy approach that involves the ability of African governments to develop their technological infrastructure base since without that, SMEs will continue to lag behind their competitors.

In this regard, building and strengthening research and development institutions, providing access to new technologies, skills and training opportunities that can be easily accessible to SMEs will be a step in the right direction. SMEs in Africa will need training in the area of, for example, digital marketing and other digital skills training in order to enable them to fully take advantage of the opportunities that come with various technologies. For instance, while Adeniran and Johnson's (2016) research of South African SMEs found that ICT utilization had positive impacts on competitive advantage, they noted that the ability of ICT to provide SMEs with competitive advantage lies in its usage, and not just merely by possessing ICT tools, applications or functions. Similarly, in Kenya, Ndiege's

(2019) work on SME owners showed that although social media technology appears to be particularly beneficial for supporting SMEs to position themselves better strategically, not only are most of the SMEs yet to fully exploit the capabilities of social media technology, but also they did not have a clear, well-thought-out plan in place prior to making the decision to use this technology in their businesses. It is in this vein that SMEs need to proactively develop a clear social media strategy that is attuned to their business goals and the needs of their customers. Thus, the need for digital marketing training and other capacity-building measures is important because in their absence, not only will SMEs be in danger of losing out of customers, but also only training programmes among others will enable SMEs to be able to derive the full benefit of their social media technology investments.

African countries can learn from, for example, South Korea, where Herreros, Inoue and Mulder (2018) have pointed out that in order to improve the skill level of employees from exporting SMEs, several public institutions offer training grants and funds that support training initiatives. The most successful training support programmes are based on a full diagnosis of exporting SMEs, identifying their stage of development and associated challenges. Moreover, the government collaborates with the private sector to strengthen the SMEs' technological capabilities by providing human capital resources. For instance, at Gumi Industrial Cluster, resident enterprises, universities and Korea Industrial Complex Corporation (KICOX) jointly set up the human resources plan customized for businesses and financed the programme. KICOX identifies the human resources needs of firms in industrial complexes (Mah 2018). Finally, in addition to engaging the broader society in candid discussions regarding both the potential benefits and dangers of disruptive technologies, increasing individuals' digital engagements warrants improving the technological infrastructure, telecommunications policies, and other necessary resources that will increase access to disruptive technologies, and Internet penetration. In sum, the benefits of ICT use can only be realized when institutional foundations such as affordable telecommunications infrastructure, efficient transport systems, legal and regulatory policies and local credit management infrastructure are in place (Mbuyisa and Leonard 2017).

CONCLUSION

One of the most significant developments of the last two decades has been the rapid technological changes that are affecting various facets of life of people and governments. Given that ICTs have become one of the most dynamic segments in the economic sector, many African policymakers and regulators are beginning to realize that ICTs and mobile telephony can assist with their socioeconomic development and industrialization efforts. It is therefore unsurprising that one area that has recently been the focus of discussion has been on the impact of technology on the operations and activities of SMEs, which have become key elements of the industrialization and development efforts of African countries. Despite their potential in helping African countries to realize their objective of industrialization and socioeconomic growth, and the role ICTs can play in the process, this chapter noted that the operations of SMEs in their efforts to adopt ICTs are constrained by and affected by factors such as lack of financial resources, poor infrastructure, lack of business and ICT skills, and unfavourable policies and legal frameworks. It is in this vein that the efforts and policy initiatives by African governments to address these constraints become even more crucial. The benefits of ICT use for SMEs can only be realized when institutional foundations such as affordable telecommunications infrastructure, efficient transport systems, legal and regulatory policies and local credit management infrastructure are in place. Aside from helping with infrastructure development and helping to bridge the digital divide, the provision of capacity building and other training programmes in the area of ICT use by SMEs will also be worthwhile endeavour.

REFERENCES

Abubakar, Y. A., Hand, C., Smallbone, D., & Saridakism, G. (2019). What Specific Modes of Internationalization Influence SME Innovation in Sub-Saharan least Developed Countries (LDCs)? *Technovation, 79*, 56–70.

Adeniran, T. V., & Johnson, K. A. (2016). The Impacts of ICT Utilisation and Dynamic Capabilities on the Competitive Advantage of South African SMEs. *International Journal of Information Technology and Management, 15*(1), 59–89.

Akinyemi, F., & Adejumo, O. (2017). Entrepreneurial Motives and Challenges of SMEs Owners in Emerging Economies: Nigeria & South Africa. *Advances in Economics and Business, 5*(11), 624–633.

Amankwah-Amoah, J., Osabutey, E., & Egbetokun, A. (2018). Contemporary Challenges and Opportunities of Doing Business in Africa: The Emerging Roles and Effects of Technologies. *Technological Forecasting and Social Change, 131*, 171–174.

Arthur, P. (2012). Rethinking Development in Africa Through Small and Medium-Scale Enterprises (SMEs). In T. Shaw, K. Hanson, & G. Kararach (Eds.), *Rethinking Development Challenges for Public Policy* (pp. 234–259). London: Palgrave Macmillan.

Arthur, P., & Arthur, E. (2017). Advent of Mobile Telecommunications in Ghana: Their Role and Contribution to the Business Activities of Small and Medium-Scale Enterprises (SMEs). *Journal of African Political Economy and Development, 2*, 26–51.

Asiedu, E. M., Shortland, S., Nawar, Y., Jackson, P., & Baker, L. (2018). Supporting Ghanaian Micro-Entrepreneurships: The Role of Mobile Technology. *Journal of Entrepreneurship in Emerging Economies*. https://doi.org/10.1108/JEEE-05-2018-0046.

Ateş B. H. (2013). A Study on the Effects of Social Media on Young Consumers' Buying Behaviours. *European Journal of Research on Education*, 65–74.

Atiso, K., & Kammer, J. (2018). *User Beware: Determining Vulnerability in Social Media Platforms for Users in Ghana*. Library Philosophy and Practice (e-journal). 1798. Available at https://digitalcommons.unl.edu/cgi/viewcontent.cgi?article=5057&context=libphilprac. Accessed 2 May 2019.

Bertot, J. C., Jaeger, P. T., & Grimes, J. M. (2010). Using ICTs to Create a Culture of Transparency: E-government and Social Media as Openness and Anti-corruption Tools for Societies. *Government Information Quarterly, 27*, 264–271.

Burgess, S. M., & Bothma, C. H. (2007). *International Marketing*. Cape Town: Oxford University Press.

Cant, M., & Wiid, J. (2013). Establishing the Challenges Affecting South African SMEs. *International Business & Economics Research Journal, 12*(6), 1–10.

Cant, M., Wiid, J., & Hung, Y. (2015). Internet-Based ICT Usage by South African SMEs: Are the Benefits within Their Reach? *Problems and Perspectives in Management, 13*(2-Si), 444–451.

Cheng, C., & Shiu, E. (2019). How to Enhance SMEs Customer Involvement Using Social Media: The Role of Social CRM. *International Small Business Journal: Researching Entrepreneurship, 37*(1), 22–42.

Crick, F., Eskander, S. M. S. U., Fankhauser, S., & Diop, M. (2018). How Do African SMEs Respond to Climate Risks? Evidence from Kenya and Senegal. *World Development, 108*, 157–168.

Deen-Swarray, M., Moyo, M., & Stork, C. (2013). ICT Access and Usage Among Informal Businesses in Africa. *Info: The Journal of Policy, Regulation and Strategy for Telecommunications, Information and Media, 15*(5), 52–68.

Duncombe, R., & Heeks, R. (2002). Enterprise Across the Digital Divide: Information Systems and Rural Microenterprise in Botswana. *Journal of International Development, 14*(1), 61–74.

Dzisah, W. (2018). Social Media and Elections in Ghana: Enhancing Democratic Participation. *African Journalism Studies, 39*(1), 27–47.

Enagi, M. A., & Van Belle, J.-P. (2019). Information Searching and Satisficing Process for IT Decision Making Process of SMEs. *The African Journal of Information Systems, 11*(2), 99–116.

Esselaar, S., Stork, C., Ndiwalana, A., & Deen-Swarray, M. (2006). *ICT Usage and Its Impact on Profitability of SMEs in 13 African Countries.* 2006 International Conference on Information and Communication Technology and Development, ICTD 2006, 40–47.

Gyampo, R. E. V. (2017). Social Media, Traditional Media and Party Politics in Ghana. *Africa Review.* https://doi.org/10.1080/09744053.2017.1329806.

Herreros, S., Inoue, K., & Mulder, N. (2018). Introduction. In S. Herreros, K. Inoue, & N. Mulder (Eds.), *Innovation and SME Internationalization in Korea and Latin America and the Caribbean: Policy Experiences and Areas for Cooperation* (pp. 9–17). Santiago: Economic Affairs Officers of the Division of International Trade and Integration of the Economic Commission for Latin America and the Caribbean (ECLAC), United Nations.

Irefin, I. A., Abdul-Azeez, I. A., & Tijani, A. A. (2012). An Investigative Study of the Factors Affecting the Adoption of Information and Communication Technology in Small and Medium Scale Enterprises in Nigeria. *Australian Journal of Business Management and Research, 2*(02), 1–9.

Ismail, R., Jeffrey, R., & Van Belle J. P. (2011). Using ICT as a Value Adding Tool in South African SMEs. *Journal of African Research in Business Technology,* 1–12. IBIMA Publishing.

Källander, K., Tibenderana, J., Akpogheneta, O., Strachan, D., Hill, Z., Ten, A., et al. (2013). Mobile Health (mHealth) Approaches and Lessons for Increased Performance and Retention of Community Health Workers in low- and Middle-Income Countries: A Review. *Journal of Medical Internet Research, 15*(1), e17.

Kapoor, K., Tamilmani, K., Rana, N. P., Patil, P., Dwivedi, Y. K., & Nerur, S. (2018). Advances in Social Media Research: Past, Present and Future. *Information System Frontiers, 20*, 531–558.

Maduku, D., Mpinganjira, M., & Duh, H. (2016). Understanding Mobile Marketing Adoption Intention by South African SMEs: A Multi-Perspective Framework. *International Journal of Information Management, 36*(5), 711–723.

Mah, J. S. (2018). Korean Policies for SMEs Development and Internationalization. In S. Herreros, K. Inoue, & N. Mulder (Eds.), *Innovation and SME Internationalization in Korea and Latin America and the Caribbean: Policy*

Experiences and Areas for Cooperation (pp. 97–119). Santiago: Economic Affairs Officers of the Division of International Trade and Integration of the Economic Commission for Latin America and the Caribbean (ECLAC), United Nations.

Mavimbela, R., & Dube, E. (2016). Can an Internet Adoption Framework Be Developed for SMEs in South Africa. *Journal of Entrepreneurship and Innovation in Emerging Economies, 2*(2), 120–135.

Mbuyisa, B., & Leonard, A. (2017). The Role of ICT Use in SMEs Towards Poverty Reduction: A Systematic Literature Review. *Journal of International Development, 29*(2), 159–197.

Moeuf, A., Pellerin, R., Lamouri, S., Tamayo-Giraldo, S., & Barbaray, R. (2018). The Industrial Management of SMEs in the Era of Industry 4.0. *International Journal of Production Research, 56*(3), 1118–1136.

Molony, T. (2007). 'I Do Not Trust the Phone; It Always Lies': Trust and Information and Communication Technologies in Tanzanian Micro and Small Enterprises. *Information Technologies and International Development, 3*(4), 67–83.

Mureithi M. (2017). The Internet Journey for Kenya: The Interplay of Disruptive Innovation and Entrepreneurship in Fueling Rapid Growth. In B. Ndemo & T. Weiss (Eds.), *Digital Kenya. Palgrave Studies of Entrepreneurship in Africa*. London: Palgrave Macmillan. https://link.springer.com/chapter/10.1057/978-1-137-57878-5_2

Muriithi, S. (2017). African Small and Medium Enterprises Contributions, Challenges and Solutions. *European Journal of Research and Reflection, 5*(1), 1–13.

Mutalemwa, D. K. (2015). Does Globalization Impact SME Development in Africa? *African Journal of Economic and Management Studies, 6*(2), 164–182.

Ndiege, J. R. A. (2019). Social Media Technology for the Strategic Positioning of Small and Medium-Sized Enterprises: Empirical Evidence from Kenya. *Electronic Journal of Information Systems in Developing Countries, 85*(2), 1–12.

Ngek, N. B. (2014). Determining High Quality SMEs that Significantly Contribute to SME Growth: Regional Evidence from South Africa. *Problems and Perspectives in Management, 12*(4-Si), 253–264.

Odoom, R., Anning-Dorson, T., & Acheampong, G. (2017). Antecedents of Social Media Usage and Performance Benefits in Small- and Medium-Sized Enterprises (SMEs). *Journal of Enterprise Information Management, 30*(3), 383–399.

Olanrewaju, A. S. T., Whiteside, N., Hossain, M. A., & Mercieca, P. (2018). The Influence of Social Media on Entrepreneur Motivation and Marketing Strategies in a Developing Country. In S. Al-Sharhan et al. (Ed.), *Challenges and Opportunities in the Digital Era*, I3E 2018. Lecture Notes in Computer Science (Vol. 11195). Cham: Springer.

Ongori, H., & Migiro, S. O. (2010). Information and Communication Technologies Adoption in SMEs: Literature Review. *Journal Chinese Entrepreneurship, 2*(1), 93–104.

Onyeji-Nwogu, I., Bazilian, M., & Moss, T. (2017). *Challenges and Solutions for the Electricity Sector in African Markets, CGD Policy Paper.* Washington, DC: Center for Global Development. Available at https://scholarship.rice.edu/bit-stream/handle/1911/97770/challenges-and-solutions-electricity-sector-afri-can-markets-final.pdf?sequence=1. Accessed 3 June 2019.

Onyiriuba, L. (2016). *Emerging Market Bank Lending and Credit Risk Control, Evolving Strategies to Mitigate Credit Risk, Optimize Lending Portfolios, and Check Delinquent Loans.* London: Elsevier.

Payne, A., & Phillips, N. (2010). *Development.* Cambridge: Polity Press.

Poole, D. (2018). Entrepreneurs, Entrepreneurship and SMEs in Developing Economies: How Subverting Terminology Sustains Flawed Policy. *World Development Perspectives, 9,* 35–42.

Quartey, P., Turkson, E., Abor, J., & Iddrisu, A. M. (2017). Financing the Growth of SMEs in Africa: What Are the Constraints to SME Financing within ECOWAS. *Review of Development Finance, 7*(1), 18–28.

Sey, A. (2014). *Ghana: Online Class.* Available at https://repositorio.uc.cl/bit-stream/handle/11534/14385/The%20Big%20Question%20Have%20social%20media%20andor%20smartphones%20disrupted%20life%20in%20your%20part%20of%20the%20world.pdf?sequence=1. Accessed 31 May 2019.

Seyal, A. H., Rahim, M. M., & Rahman, M. N. (2000). An Empirical Investigation of Use of Information Technology among Small and Medium Business Organizations: A Bruneian Scenario. *The Electronic Journal of Information Systems in Developing Countries, 2*(7), 1–17.

Sharma, M. K., & Bhagwat, R. (2006). Practice of Information Systems, an Evidence from Select Indian SMEs. *Journal of Manufacturing Technology, 17*(2), 199–223.

Shemi, A. P., & Procter, C. T. (2013). Explaining Contextual Factors Affecting e-Commerce Adoption Progression in Selected SMEs: Evidence from Botswana. *International Journal of Management Practice, 6*(1), 94–109.

Song, M., Park, J.-O., & Park, B. S. (2017). Determinants of R&D Commercialization by SMEs after Technology Transfer. *Asian Journal of Innovation and Policy, 6*(1), 045–057.

Taiwo, J. N., Falohun, T. O., & Agwu, E. (2016). SMEs Financing and Its Effects on Nigerian Economic Growth. *European Journal of Business, Economics and Accountancy, 4*(4), 37–54.

Tettey, W. J. (2017). Mobile Telephony and Democracy in Ghana: Interrogating the Changing Ecology of Citizen Engagement and Political Communication. *Telecommunications Policy, 41*(7–8), 685–694.

Trottier, D., & Fuchs, C. (2015). Theorising Social Media, Politics and the State. In D. Trottier & C. Fuchs (Eds.), *Social Media, Politics and the State. Protests, Revolutions, Riots, Crime and Policing in the Age of Facebook, Twitter and YouTube* (pp. 3–38). London, UK: Routledge.

Urmeneta, R. (2018). Policies, Institutions and Instruments Supporting the Internationalisation of SMEs in Latin America. In S. Herreros, K. Inoue, & N. Mulder (Eds.), *Innovation and SME Internationalization in Korea and Latin America and the Caribbean: Policy Experiences and Areas for Cooperation* (pp. 81–96). Santiago: Economic Affairs Officers of the Division of International Trade and Integration of the Economic Commission for Latin America and the Caribbean (ECLAC), United Nations.

Von Broembsen, M., Wood, E., & Herrington, M. (2005). *Global Entrepreneurship Monitor*. The South African Report. UCT Centre for Innovation and Entrepreneurship.

Weiss, J. (1988). *Industry in Developing Countries: Theory, Policy and Evidence*. London: Croom Helm.

Wilson, V., & Makau, C. (2017). Online Marketing Use: Small and Medium Enterprises (SMEs) Experience in Kenya. *The Operations Research Society of East Africa Journal, 7*(2), 63–77.

CHAPTER 11

Disruptive Technology, Foreign Direct Investment and Private Sector Development Polices in Africa

Joseph Baricako and Abbi M. Kedir

INTRODUCTION

The main objective of this chapter is to give a detailed account of enablers of technology transfer (including disruptive technologies such as financial technology—FinTech) via foreign direct investment (FDI) and private sector development policies of Africa. We also refer to the challenges that hamper technology transfer. Many African countries have been opening their economies and reducing the role of the state to various degrees since the late 1980s. Privatization is not new in Africa and countries such as Cote d'Ivoire embarked on the process as early as the 1960s. However, more privatization efforts were exerted with pressure from Bretton Woods

J. Baricako
Regional Integration and Trade Division, United Nations Economic
Commission for Africa, Addis Ababa, Ethiopia

A. M. Kedir (✉)
Sheffield University Management School, University of Sheffield, Sheffield, UK
e-mail: a.m.kedir@sheffield.ac.uk

© The Author(s) 2020   227
P. Arthur et al. (eds.), *Disruptive Technologies, Innovation and
Development in Africa*, International Political Economy Series,
https://doi.org/10.1007/978-3-030-40647-9_11

institutions in the 1990s on the back of the Structural Adjustment Programmes (SAPs). Currently, despite its slow pace and sporadic nature, there is an increasing trend in privatizing state-owned enterprises in developing countries and encouraging investment policies which are leading to a rapid rise in inward FDI from emerging economies such as China, India and Turkey as well as from traditional development partners of the Organisation for Economic Co-operation and Development (OECD). African countries such as Kenya, Senegal, Ghana and Ethiopia are attracting investment from a diverse set of countries. In 2014 and 2015, Angola, because of the country's oil and gas sectors, became the top recipient of foreign direct investment (FDI) in Africa, but in 2017 and 2018, Egypt become the top destination of FDI while Angola dropped from the top ten destinations (UNCTAD 2019).

Equally, regional developments continue to open economies further. For instance, major continental initiatives such as the Continental Free Trade Area (CFTA) and local policy reforms such as privatization in Ethiopia are expected to strengthen trade and investment links of African nations amongst themselves and with the rest of the world. Countries are keen to mobilize development finance for transforming their economies and embark on industrialization. The purpose of privatization in advanced countries tends to be more focused on efficiency and reduction of production costs, while it is mainly a revenue raising instrument in developing countries via the sale of assets. In addition, regardless of the level of development of the economies in question, divestiture is implemented with a better service delivery to consumers at competitive prices.

Before continuing to discuss substantive parts of the chapter, we make a conceptual distinction between disruptive innovation and technology transfer. Companies (e.g. global players who were to break into protective markets) use technology transfer as a long-term strategy to build and boost R&D capabilities. Current technology either developed locally or acquired via foreign investment is often improved via two possible disruptive innovation routes. Hence, innovations embodied in existing products, services and processes can take place either incrementally (slowly) or in a radical fashion (e.g. as in the case of mobile/digital money transactions). Therefore, the concepts of technology transfer and disruptive innovations are intrinsically linked (Machado and Hatakeyama 2018).

FDI Inflows Trends in Africa

We begin by highlighting key facts about the investment landscape in Africa and trends in FDI inflows using data for the last 30 years (1990–2018). FDI and its contribution to growth have been extensively documented. A strand of literature confirms the positive contribution of FDI to growth on a wide sample of countries. FDI can have positive spillovers on growth through job creation, technology transfer/diffusion, backward and forward linkages with domestic enterprises and capital accumulation (Crespo and Fantoura 2007; Borensztein et al. 1998; Soltani and Ochi 2012). But all these benefits are not automatically granted. There are different variables at play in a strategy, not only to attract FDI but also to retain and optimize their contribution to the economic development of the destination economy (Echandi and Scronce 2016). A different strand of the literature has highlighted a bi-directional linkage between FDI and economic growth. FDI is a vehicle of economic growth, which in turn becomes a critical attraction of FDI (Nguyen and Nguyen 2007). Contrary to the two views above, others find a non-significant or negative effect of FDI to economic growth (Akinlo 2004; Ayanwale 2007; Hermes and Lensink 2003). Even if FDI is unequivocally accepted as a potential source of financing for development, one of the underlying explanations is that an economy controlled by foreigners might derail the direction of development, particularly in Africa where the FDI are mainly channelled in the natural resources sectors (Pigato 2000).

In this section, we look at investment inflows and investment policies in Africa, linking them to the dynamics of regional integration patterns across the continent. It goes beyond the traditional debate of FDI inflows and its contribution to the economic development and reduction of poverty, as well as the country case studies. What matters is not only the size of inflows, but also the way they are managed and channelled in a way to optimize their positive effects such as technology transfer that sustainably support sectoral or nationwide economic development objectives. If they are not properly managed, they will not provide the expected results, especially in Africa where recent experience shows that FDI are targeted to natural resources sector where rent-seeking behaviour and other distorted incentives prevail.

Even if the main beneficiaries have unstable inflows of FDI, the general trend is a fall in 2017 in contradiction to the increase of growth and trade, followed by an expansion of 11 per cent to $46 billion in 2018. This figure stands below the annual average of the last ten years, which was about $50 billion. The main reasons underpinning the rise in 2018 are the continuation of resource-seeking investments, the efforts to diversify investments in a few economies, as well as a quantum leap of FDI flows to South Africa (from $2 billion to $5.3 billion) which were more than doubled. The change of political power in the country signalled confidence in the investors which was subsequently followed by quick investment inflows. However, on the global level, FDI decreased again in 2018 at $1.3 trillion from a revised $1.5 trillion in 2017 (see Fig. 11.1). This was the third

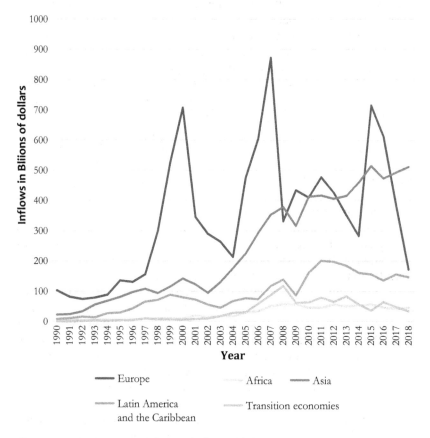

Fig. 11.1 Average FDI inflows in Africa and the world (1990–2018). (Source: Authors with UNCTAD database, 2019)

consecutive year, which registered a fall in FDI on the back of a combination of factors. The gradual and protracted global growth recovery and policy changes in major global economies dictate the trends in FDI and trade. For instance, following tax reforms in the USA in 2017, multinational enterprises engaged in a major repatriation of their foreign earnings. Given the size of this effect, the large cross-border merger and acquisitions (18 per cent), mounting at $694 billion and $816 billion, respectively, in 2017 and 2018, could not be offset. Similarly, the 41 per cent increase of promising greenfield investment (from $698 billion to $981 billion) could not change the general trend. For the sample period of 1990–2018, Europe is the main beneficiary of FDI; hence the fluctuation has been pronounced. Africa, the last beneficiary of the world, recorded a moderate fluctuation across time.

Drivers of FDI and Top FDI Destinations in Africa

As the experiences of Chinese investment in Ethiopia in recent years showed, there are additional constraints that hamper investment. China is becoming one of the largest investment and trade partners of Africa. Some of the bottlenecks we discuss below relate to the importance of having a well-educated manpower as in Mauritius with affordable labour costs. First is the importance of trade logistics. In Ethiopia, Chinese investment is negatively affected by the web of trade regulation and customs clearance inefficiencies. The underdevelopment of trade logistics in many other countries is a major deterrent of many potential other investors. However, the prevalent long-standing institutional weaknesses in many African countries lead to the design of regulations that fail to facilitate imports but rather delay customs clearance of imported materials. Second, risks associated with exchange rates constitute restrictions on the level of foreign currency transactions in places such as Ethiopia. In addition, the relatively common haphazard monetary policy decisions in Africa introduce sudden foreign exchange shocks in the form of devaluation. Such shocks damage the assets valuations of existing firms and lead to hikes in local labour costs and imports since markets do not provide the critical inputs required for production locally. Third, clear tax laws are fundamental but, in many countries, there are far too many tax law changes and investors are faced with unclear and confusing interpretations of the law. Fourth, investors end up having larger training costs instead of saving on labour costs. They must work with existing stock of human capital and skills in Africa, which is much lower than the average skills at home. Fifth, there is no access to loans from local banks (e.g. export finance) and, with excessive delays in applications, SMEs are confronted with complex set of regulations (Geiger and Goh 2012).

The sudden increased inflows in South Africa is mainly attributed to the confidence of investors stemming from change of power in 2018. Nigeria and Ethiopia have been impacted by political turbulence and uncertainty. On an optimistic note, Morocco sustained a slight increase in investment for two consecutive years, thanks to active campaign as well as mergers and acquisitions (M&A). Morocco's recent return to the African Union brought hope of improved business climate in the country and a signal of political commitment and institutional improvement. Since the African continent is big and with heterogeneous institutions and economic conditions and diverse degree of ease of doing business environment, we show a breakdown of FDI inflows by subregion (Fig. 11.2).

At a subregional level, disaggregated data shows strong performance of the North Africa, followed by West Africa and Southern subregion. The Eastern and Central Africa subregions are the least performing. FDI

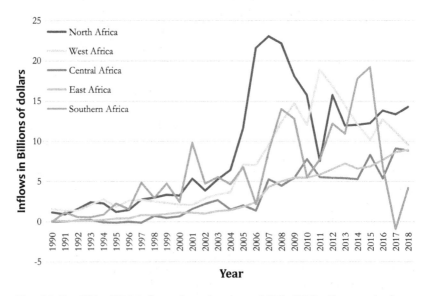

Fig. 11.2 Africa FDI inflows, by subregions, 1990–2018. (Source: Authors, using UNCTAD database, 2019)

inflows to North Africa increased by 7 per cent to $14 billion, due to an overall increase in investments in most countries of the subregion. Egypt remained the largest FDI recipient not only in the Northern subregion but also in Africa in 2018, despite the inflows decrease of 8 per cent to $6.8 billion. The UK plays an important role in trading and investment links with Egypt. From a policy perspective, Egypt is embarking on a few reforms with an ambitious repositioning initiative to be a global destination for investment. FDI flows to Morocco increased by 36 per cent to $3.6 billion, due to a stable economic performance and diversified economy. In Sudan and Tunisia, FDI increased by 7 per cent to $1.1 billion and 18 per cent to $1 billion in 2018, respectively, a bit lower than the 22 per cent registered by Algeria to $1.5 billion. However, the sound performance has been hampered by sharp decline during the economic and financial crises as well as the Arab revolution. The recent political volatility in Sudan dents investor confidence ushering a less optimistic investment outlook for the country. On an opposite side, FDI in Central Africa remained stagnant. FDI flows to East Africa have remained unchanged in 2018 at $9 billion. Inflows in the biggest recipient of the subregion, Ethiopia, decreased by 18 per cent to $3.3 billion. Since April 2018, the new government has been pursuing privatization policies, but recent regional political tensions might lead to a reduction of inflows. Kenya has been the exception of the subregion with a noticeable FDI increase of 27 per cent at $1.6 billion.

Unsurprisingly, looking at the main destination of FDI across the world, any African country is part of the top beneficiaries. Within the continent, Egypt, Nigeria and South Africa remain the top three main destinations of investments inflows from 1990 up to 2018. Nigeria was leading in the 1990s and then Egypt took over and stands at the top position, followed by Nigeria and South Africa. Mozambique and Ghana joined the leading champions in the 2010s and even overtook the long-standing Morocco's position. It is worth to note a dynamism in the 2010s, whereby new comers such as Ethiopia with its vibrant investments in infrastructure, DRC and Congo with dominant investments in primary commodities sector and Sudan complete now the top ten list. In Congo, for instance, more than 90 per cent of FDI are directed to petroleum sector. Additional main destinations data disaggregated by country, year and three recent decades are in Annexes 1 and 2 (Table 11.1).

In terms of FDI outflows, out of the top 20 home economies, no one single African country is amongst the investors in 2017 and 2018. Africa

Table 11.1   Level of FDI inflows (in billions of USD) and change (in %), top five host economies, 2017 and 2018 (%)

	2017			*2018*		
Rank	*Country*	*Inflows*	Δ	*Country*	*Inflows*	Δ
1	Egypt	7.4	−8.8	Egypt	6.8	−8.2
2	Ethiopia	3.6	−10.1	South Africa	5.3	+165.8
3	Nigeria	3.5	−21.3	Congo	4.3	−2.1
4	Ghana	3.3	−6.6	Morocco	3.6	35.5
5	Morocco	2.7	22.9	Ethiopia	3.3	−17.6

Source: Authors with UNCTAD database, 2019

is traditionally recipient of FDI inflows than a potential investor abroad, with some rare exceptions. In 2018, FDI outflows from Africa decreased by 26 per cent to almost $10 billion, following a sharp drop of South Africa outflows by 40 per cent ($4.6 billion) and a complete drying up of outflows in Angola, compared with $1.4 billion in 2017.

POLICY ISSUES

In this section, we cover both national and international initiative designed for promoting FDI. The investment promotion agencies have shown case with substantial results in boosting FDI, particularly in developing countries (Harding and Javorcik 2011a, b, 2013; Gómez-Mera et al. 2015). In 2017, 65 countries adopted at least 126 investment policy measures covering a range of sectors, including infrastructure, manufacturing, energy, and transport. In a bid to attract outside investment, nearly all of them (84 per cent) were favourable to investors. In 2018, 55 economies introduced more than 112 measures affecting foreign investment levels. More than 22 mergers and acquisition deals were withdrawn or blocked for different reasons stemming from regulatory or political motivations. Similarly, cases of screening mechanisms have increased over time since 2011. In Africa, given the FDI's induced benefits and their implication to growth, attracting investments remains a priority. Countries such as Ethiopia are aggressively pursuing privatization policies with selling of varying level of stakes and assets in different state-owned or state-operated enterprises including telecoms and transport.

Accordingly, numerous countries have devised investment reforms and other relevant policies such as liberalization, promotion mainly via provision of tax breaks, facilitation and removal of investment barriers. Investment promotion agencies have been revamped, empowered and created in countries where they did not exist before. In the recent years, entry restrictions of foreign direct investments have been lowered or simply removed in many countries; fiscal incentives and the conditions for start-ups and new firms have been eased.

However, policy makers should not welcome investors with reckless open-door policy due to the pressure they face to raise finance for development purposes. This is because tax incentives to investors in the form of corporate income tax holidays (e.g. for businesses in export processing zones and industrial parks) and reductions of import duties and value-added tax (VAT) have detrimental effect on public finance. The trade-offs should be carefully examined in the interests of sustainable and long-term economic development instead of being victims of open-door policies that lead to a race to the bottom as all countries engage in harmful tax competition to attract the attention of potential investors. Not only government revenue but environmental standards might be compromised as rules and regulations are relaxed to accommodate investors. There is international assistance focused on investment attraction through good summaries of the investment climate countries via the publication of iGuides.

Initially designed by United Nations Conference on Trade and Development (UNCTAD) and the International Chamber of Commerce, the iGuides is an online platform developed jointly by UNCTAD and United Nations Economic Commission for Africa (UNECA) through their respective investment teams. The iGuides provides investors up-to-date online information on business costs, opportunities and conditions in developing countries. The ultimate objective of the electronic investment platform consists of promoting productive investments catalysing the structural transformation process in developing countries. They are developed in partnership with governments, and at their request. UNCTAD and ECA provided technical assistance and capacity-building services to professionals of national investment agencies to develop the necessary skills to manage the platform, identify further areas for reform, understand investor needs and keep it up to date. Likewise, the World Bank Group contributes to the establishment of a competitive investment climate in numerous countries. The initiative is tailored to the needs of the beneficiary countries and is helpful for attracting, retaining and promoting investment. Beyond the international efforts, it has been observed that in many African countries, host economies offer investors infrastructure support and fiscal and regulatory support in special economic zones. The initiative is widely used across the world, both in developing and developed countries. Potential international investors would like to carefully gather information on regulations for starting a business; direct and indirect costs; the availability and price of productive factors such as land, labour and capital; the tax systems; the investor rights; or the potential feasible investment sectors and opportunities (OECD 2015). In Africa as well as elsewhere in the world, governments have established national investment agencies to overcome this information gap and make their country attractive to foreign investment.

In Rwanda, the one-stop shop of Rwanda Development Board allows an investor to start a business within a day. The experience exists in Congo, Ethiopia and Madagascar with different speed and ease of setting up a business. The Government of Rwanda has improved the investment law and defined the priority sectors with a package of incentives to make the country more attractive for investors. In Ethiopia, the national legislation which prohibits a foreigner to own land, a house or related asset has been softened. Industrial parks are decreasing drastically the cost of initial investment and improving the business environment for potential investors. Most of them are operating in the textile industry. From the Ethiopian Investment Commission (EIC), a potential investor has the full free assistance in all the required administrative steps for starting a business. In Madagascar, the investment promotion agency, the Economic Development Board of Madagascar (EDBM) is the entry point for an investor and supports in all the steps required to start and operate a business. It is a one-stop shop providing free tailored advice on regulations and incentives to a business, information on exploration of promising opportunities, planning, opening and operating a business. In Congo, numerous initiatives have been launched to attract FDI with an objective to boost the economy and make Congo an emergent country by 2025. In this context, FDI regulation, starting a business, land access and infrastructure, and taxation systems have been substantially simplified even if challenges and areas of improvement remain. Kenya developed a draft national investment policy with the objective of investment promotion, facilitation and retention. The Kenya Vision 2030 targets a 10 per cent annual growth rate and a transition to a middle-income industrialized country. To achieve these objectives, a strategy is in place to attract, retain and promote foreign direct investment to reach private investment of 24 per cent of GDP by 2030. Accordingly, the investment policy needs to implement and coordinate investment oversight, investment promotion, retention and facilitation, amongst other critical measures.

REGIONAL INTEGRATION AND FDI INFLOWS

The African regional integration effort is gathering pace, moving from its fragmented regional integration blocks to a continent-wide bloc. On March 21, 2018, representatives of over 44 countries launched the African Continental Free Trade Area (AfCFTA) agreement in an extraordinary summit held in Kigali. Five more countries signed the agreement towards the end of the year 2018. The agreement is expected to be extended to the full continent with its 55 countries, covering a combined GDP of US$2.5 trillion, and a population of 1.3 billion, with the majority (60 per cent) being young, below 25 years old. Besides this trade agreement, Africa has been recognized as a land of opportunities which just need to be unleashed (McKinsey 2018). The AfCFTA builds on the long economic integration agenda in the continent. To achieve the African Union Commission (AUC) planned to move with the eight building blocs,[1] the integration process evolved through tripartite arrangements composed of the Southern African Development Community (SADC), the Common Market for Eastern and Southern Africa (COMESA) and the East African Community (EAC).

Moving forward, the critical question we should pose is to know whether the regional integration effort is conducive to the investment flows and the proliferation of investment opportunities. With the removal of import duties in Africa, the AfCFTA is expected to increase intra-African trade by 52.3 per cent. In case non-tariff barriers are reduced or removed, trade may double (Karingi and Mevel 2012). This will open the door for market-seeking FDI. Investors often target relatively big African economies (for market size), countries with the growing middle class (for purchasing power and seizing local demand) and countries with large population. The first phase of the AfCFTA became effective on May 30, 2019, when the 22nd ratification instrument was deposited with the Chairman of the African Union Commission. It concentrated on impor-

---

[1] The eight building blocs are ECOWAS, EAC, ECCAS, SADC, AMU, IGAD, COMESA and CEN-SAD. Other regional initiatives such as CEPGL and CEMAC, among others, exist but are not recognized by the AUC.

tant and contentious areas such as tariff concessions and the rules of origin for trade in goods and services. The negotiations of the 2nd phase are planned to be completed by 2020 concentrating on competition policy, investment and intellectual property rights (IPRs). Therefore, the achievement of this phase should provide the blueprint for more investment promotion across the continent and a relatively clearer direction volume and composition of FDI inflows to the continent.

However, in the meantime, the prospects for 2019 are mixed despite the promising AfCFTA, with a projected modest global increase of FDI. The reasons underpinning this prospect are the slowing down of African growth and uncertainty surrounding macroeconomic policy and the overall business environment as well as the looming recession threats across the world. In terms of policy, the opening up of emerging markets that boosted FDI in the 2000s is losing its momentum (e.g. the economic challenges of Brazil), hampered by restrictions based on national security considerations or strategic technologies. Furthermore, the rate of return on investments continues to decline over time. In Africa, return on investment dropped from 11.9 per cent in 2010 to 6.5 per cent in 2018.

Finally, the fast growth in digital technologies is changing the international production pattern, and economies that are not nearer the technological frontier might be having limited options to attract FDI and improve their chances of promoting production and trade to be part of the global value chain (GVC). At regional level, there are ongoing initiatives spearheaded by the Regional Economic Communities (RECs) which pursue their respective integration agendas. Despite the bright promises of AfCFTA and young generation potential ('the demographic dividend'), the macroeconomic management, the overwhelming conflicts, weak institutions and governance remain as perennial challenges despite the mushrooming of economic policies, reforms and incentives to attract investments. Furthermore, the share of FDI-related R&D in Africa remains low and that limits the technology transfer that can accompany FDI.

FDI AND TECHNOLOGY TRANSFER

Standard growth theory states that frontier advanced countries have a steady-state growth at the rate of technological progress, while other countries play catch-up and attempt to fill the technology gap via diverse set of initiatives aimed at technological convergence. In addition, Romer (1990) reiterates the importance of investment in research and development. Note that not all technology is beneficial. For a conducive develop-ment process to unfold, there is a need for direct linkages between domestic and foreign firms for technology transfer as underscored by Arrow (1969). However, current evidence by Newman et al. (2018) shows the limited link between multinational corporations and domestic firms in Africa. This is a challenge to technology transfer and develop-ment. The study also showed that MNEs that interact with domestic firms transfer technology directly in different industries such as chemicals, phar-maceuticals, textiles, footwear and automobiles. However, two-thirds of the MNEs used technological adaptation in the knowledge transfer pro-cess to be able to use local inputs, which are familiar to domestic firm employees and more suited to their skills.

Many African countries aim to attract foreign direct investment (FDI) with attractive tax breaks. FDI can be a conduit for a technology transfer, which is either damaging or beneficial to the environment (Kedir 2014). This depends on the complex interaction between the behaviour of firms in home as well as host countries in addition to the prevailing respective institutional factors. Institutional weaknesses and absence of conducive infrastructure hamper FDI-driven technological absorption and adoption. For instance, foreign investors who would like to enter a market for export purposes are required to maintain production standards of their home country government. A typical scenario is a transfer of technology from an advanced economy (home/source country) to developing countries (host economy). However, destination countries' institutional contexts (e.g. in regulating and respecting environmental standards) might deter them from entering certain markets with a view to maintaining quality produc-tion systems. Therefore, even if FDI can be a conduit for technology transfer and spread of innovations, the actual process is thwarted due to inherent and long-standing dysfunctional institutions. Hence, opportuni-ties for technology transfer as well as sharing management practices can be lost.

On the other hand, FDI can be a forceful positive agent for inducing firms to adopt environmentally friendly management practices. This is par-ticularly important in developing countries where the context is often saturated with firms with specific environmental impacts such as tannery and textile dyeing factories. For some investors, the destination/host country might be a viable option that enhances exporting. Therefore, market-seeking FDI with a keen interest to expand exporting is most likely to be influenced by the environmental awareness of source/home country citizens which drives the careful choice of destinations. For instance, a German firm investing in an African country is likely to improve environmental standards in host country production systems with a view to sell to environmentally conscious German consumers or consumers in other countries with similar expectations on environmental standards. Here, the external stakeholder pressure (i.e. from the buyer/supply chain perspective) is important in determining the destination of both FDI and the possible technology transfer that might take place (de Oliveira and Jabbour 2017). Equally not all FDI is compatible with ethical and desirable technology transfer. Some foreign firms might flee 'over-regulated' or optimally regulated regions/markets and invest in institutionally weak environments characterized by 'under-regulation' or lax regulation and relational (non-rule-based) work practices (Du 2015; Blackman and Kildegaard 2010).

Technology Transfer Enablers and Barriers

Technology capabilities are fundamental for economic growth and competitiveness, but the process is fundamentally dependent on the absorptive capacity of recipient countries such as the initial level of skills. In addition, there are some exogenous factors such as location and intellectual property (IP) rights, which can determine the success or failure of FDI-induced technology transfer. Africa has ambitious industrialization policies to structurally transform economies. In our subsequent discussion, we take the Mauritius case to show how it makes the most of FDI for technology transfer to benefit its industrialization process with innovative institutional interaction between the public and the private sector.

(i) *Skills*

Clearly, there is a positive correlation between skills and absorptive capacity of available technologies. Excitement about the potential technology is not enough. In the context of Sustainable Development Goals (SDGs) and the future of production in cleaner and climate-conscious systems, the level of skills required is not only to adopt conventional production technologies but also of green production technologies. Therefore, the continent has an insurmountable challenge when it comes to building human capital to be able to benefit from technology transfer that are enabled via private investment from abroad. The set of skills required for future economic development is daunting even for advanced economies where there is already a short of 'green' engineers.

Bowen (2012) maintains that there are at least three ways through which the demand for skills and human capital are affected. First, there is a structural change across industries (e.g. moving energy generation and mining from coal to nuclear or hydro). In this structural change, consideration of employment is important. Given the demographic dividend and growing unemployment challenge, African countries should strategically opt for labour-intensive renewable energy sector relative to a fossil fuel energy, which requires higher skills (Pollin et al. 2009). Second, technology transitions under green growth principles might lead to creation of inclusive green jobs in different sectors (both formal and informal) of the economy and contribute to the reduction of unemployment. These jobs can be in waste management, recycling, carbon footprint assessment, biofuel crop farming and environmentally friendly commercial plantations (Nhamo 2017). Third, the nature of existing jobs changes as they reflect energy efficiency and lower levels of application of potentially harmful technologies which were by far less costly than cleaner technologies. However, the cost of cleaner and eco-friendly technologies is coming down. Regardless, African countries should invest in human capital, which is fit-for-purpose in the changing production landscape so that their required skills are there to benefit from FDI-driven technology spillovers. Existing human capital stock in Africa is one of the lowest relative to all global regions. The future of technology transfer improves if there is a radical and strategic investment in R&D and overhaul of school and university curriculum with sustained financing of the overall education system focusing on quality.

(ii) *Intellectual Property Rights*

We highlighted the importance of institutions for technology above. Weak institutions in Africa, corruption and lack of investment in R&D are at the heart of the current state of poor technological progression at national and regional levels across all economic sectors. Unfortunately, the state of international property rights laws contributes to Africa's technological backwardness. Economic history tells us that many of the advanced countries now (e.g. USA and UK) took advantage of the lack of IPR laws at the beginning of their economic development (Chang 2002). Hence, the current state of technological progress in Africa is partly self-inflicted and partly exogenous. The effectiveness of the domestic privatization policies and reforms depends on addressing the inherent in-country institutional weaknesses. A privatization policy alone with the ambition to attract foreign investors without addressing them does not help to secure diverse benefits of inward FDI including possibilities of appropriate technology transfer. The most common forms of intellectual property are trade secrets, copyrights and patents. There are royalty payments and licensing fees related to patents, which are important for technology transfer. Advanced countries can allow some technologies to be adopted by developing countries without breaking IPR laws. From a policy perspective, a careful consideration of costs and implementation of IPR laws are warranted. African countries should benefit from a number of support initiatives in their bid to step up their effort to improve their technological landscape. As a specialized agency of the UN, the World Intellectual Property Organization (WIPO) is mandated to enable member countries to use the intellectual property (IP) system to drive technology adoption and innovation with the aim to help them achieve the ambitious SDGs.

WHY DOES ATTRACTING FDI MATTER?

To answer this question, we first provide econometric evidence using a firm-level data from the World Bank Enterprise Survey (WBES) on 40 African countries followed by a country case study from Mauritius. Most of the uneasiness as well as the high expectations with regard to foreign ownership of companies in Africa is intrinsically associated with its impact on relieving the prevalent unemployment problem and providing development finance. One of the key policy objectives of African governments in attracting FDI is to boost the employment and this will be our focus here. Therefore, we attempt to show whether foreign ownership has a positive impact on employment growth on the sampled firms from Africa. In cross-country data, we have variables capturing technological innovations used by firms. Hence, we also see their role in employment growth.

Our enterprise data is based on 40 African countries. To empirically examine the relationship between foreign ownership, levels of technological innovations and firm performance (here employment growth), WBES data is analysed using a harmonized questionnaire and common methodology across all surveyed countries. This assures the cross-national and temporal comparability of the data. The data was collected from 40 African countries in 2006, 2007, 2009, 2010, 2011 and 2013. In each country, data was collected from a stratified random sample of formal private sector businesses with five or more employees, stratified by business sector, ownership (foreign and domestic), firm size and geographic region, covering 1200–1800 business owners and top managers in larger countries, 360 in medium-sized countries and 150 in smaller countries. In our sample we have 7520 enterprises/firms.

Our dependent variable is annual employment growth (%) which is a derived variable in the WBES, measuring the annualized growth of permanent full-time workers expressed as a percentage. Annual employment growth is the change in full-time employment reported in the current fiscal year from a previous period. We have controlled for a range of independent variables in our specification. These include foreign ownership, technological innovations, corruption, registration status of firms, firm age, firm size, legal ownership structure (i.e. whether a firm is state- or privately owned, foreign- or domestic-owned and an open- or closed-shareholding, partnership or sole proprietorship) (Barbera and Moores 2013), economic sector, access to finance, human capital factors (e.g. educational level, the skills and experience of the owners, managers and the workforce, the level of professionalism and whether there is numerical flexibility in the workforce) and wider business environment. To evaluate the impact of starting-foreign ownership on firm performance, we apply a pooled OLS regression technique (without controlling for endogeneity) and two-stage least squares (2SLS) (with controlling for endogeneity). In the data, we have a trust variable that can serve as an instrument in our 2SLS estimation. One is a variable which captures the state of trust by asking the firms whether they perceive the court system to be fair, impartial and uncorrupted. We argue that the trust that firms have about the quality of institutions in each economy affects their behaviour and propensity to engage in corrupt practices, and this is not necessarily and directly associated with firm performance such as annual employment growth.

According to both models, the association between foreign ownership and annual employment growth is negative but it is not statistically significant. From this firm-level evidence, the suggestion is that foreign ownership does not lead to an improvement in the employment prospects of individuals in Africa. This might be due to the fact that most FDI in Africa is not of the market-seeking type (e.g. manufacturing where employment generation is a realistic possibility) but rather in the resource sector where employment is restricted to highly skilled individuals in the oil sector or in the mineral sector who are at times employees that come into the continent with the foreign capital. Therefore, countries need to be selective which type of FDI to encourage and which type of FDI to discourage. We found that technology has a positive impact on annual employment growth. However, the only positive and significant technology and innovation indicator is the use of website by firms. Hence, digitally connected firms are more likely to be the ones employing more.

Lessons on Technology-Assisted Industrialization: FinTech in Mauritius

We discuss digital technology and FDI for industrialization in Mauritius. Current disruptive technologies such as mobile money transactions promote financial inclusion. FinTech is changing the payment landscape and a key driver of mobile money transactions across the globe. Africa is benefitting from this disruptive but positive technological development and is heading towards better financial inclusion for the unbanked. Mauritius has an ambition to lead the continent in finance and technology. FinTechs are being provided by start-ups in Mauritius, and banks are embracing the changes, albeit cautiously, particularly in the domain of digital/mobile banking. For instance, mobile apps such as Juice and SMB launched by Mauritius Commercial Bank and the State Bank of Mauritius, respectively (Narraidoo 2018).

In fact, embracing FinTech and making Mauritius a hub for Africa is one of the government's national priorities for 2019. This is in line with the fast developments in the mobile money area in Africa, which started in Kenya in 2007, and the continent is attracting a lot of investment in FinTech (Yenkey et al. 2015). Combining expertise and relatively advanced financial services sector, Mauritius has a unique position to transform its economy further and achieve financial inclusion for all. The country is moving faster than the rest of Africa, and in 2018 it moved towards artificial intelligence and recognition of cryptocurrencies as an asset group for investment. This is along with strengthening its regulatory framework (e.g. licensing of digital assets) for better service delivery and consumer protection due to enhanced exposure to cyberattacks. In Africa the development of FinTech via FinTech start-ups is at its infancy. However, in December 2018 the country established Mauritius Africa FinTech Hub, with the aim of developing FinTech in Africa and laying the foundation for a Pan-African regulatory environment (World Bank 2017).

FDI-Assisted Industrialization

Structural transformation anchored on industrialization improves welfare and lead to long-term economic growth. This belief led to the resurgence of interest in industrial policy that helps to develop robust manufacturing base, increase productivity, promote innovation, diversify economies and create employment. We provide detailed discussion of the various industrial policy schemes and initiatives put in place by Mauritius. What is notable is the continued commitment of the government to its industrialization vision with close cooperation with the private sector. The country created conductive policy for private sector development and FDI from multinational companies (MNCs). Without repeating the mistakes of the 1970s industrialization, the country developed an inclusive industrial policy that stands out as good practice in the African continent.

Mauritius is now one of the most successful countries in Africa with a relatively well-developed industrial policy pursued over the last four decades. Its smart public sector policies that are favourable for private investment showed the importance of good institutions and the merits of technology adoption from abroad for transforming its economy. Mauritius provides a good example of well-timed economic diversification strategies for aspiring developing counties and shows how economies can make a transition from agriculture to industries and services. This is not possible without technology and foreign investors that contributed a lot to its development. The country achieved employment of its cheap but relatively better educated labour force particularly women through its aggressive expansion and investment of the clothing and textile industry (Joomun 2006; Cling et al. 2007; Zafar 2011).

As in Mauritius, countries with educated manpower (e.g. Zimbabwe) can use such human resource as a key strategy to enhance their international business engagement by creating the business environment for foreign companies to invest and provide jobs. This is critical for most African countries where the youth unemployment and general meaningful employment is very limited. Exporting processing zones (EPZs) were established with good infrastructure, skilled work force and appropriate technologies and were based on manufacturing that is geared to international markets (Stein 2008; Robecka et al. 2012).

Mauritius is a good example of how a developmental state can use both fundamental and selective policies to promote industrialization and diversification of an economy with the aim of structural transformation (Wade

2015; Chang 2003). The country pursued a progressive institutional change approach that facilitated a healthy growth of the industrial sector supported by technology transfer via FDI inflows. Hence, institutions matter and there is a widespread lack of it in much of Africa. Industrial policy has been developed carefully and used to diversify the structure of the country's economy unlike other countries that did not acknowledge the transformative potential of such a policy (Stiglitz et al. 2013).

Despite being a small island with a relatively limited endowment of productive resources, Mauritius has been able to transform itself from a low-income monocrop economy to a middle-income country. Without effective adoption of the innovative practices on offer and technologies through FDI flows, value addition and participation in global value chains (GVCs) is virtually impossible. Mauritius has done that better than the rest of the African continent (Kedir 2015).

CONCLUSION

The fact that FDI is still flowing to the continent is encouraging, but the absorptive capacity is hampered by the limited average schooling of the African population coupled with the lack of production of sufficient skilled manpower. This calls for sustained investment in good quality education and R&D to benefit from the ongoing technological revolution. This requires commitment from all African countries which so far have neglected the higher education sector. In addition, even if policy makers hope to generate employment by promoting private investment by increasing the stake and ownership share foreign owners have in African companies, there is no discernible employment-generating impact of FDI in Africa as shown by our econometric analysis of the 2006–2013 World Bank Survey data. This has important policy implications for governments. It is important to put development objectives that deliver for the African economies such as employment growth in the design of investment promotion policies.

Most FDI top recipients are not the best industrialization examples. A case study of Mauritius shows that it is not the amount of FDI inflows that matters but the effective use of FDI inflows for transforming the local economy and generating employment. Mauritius is not one of the top recipients of FDI in Africa, but it is one of its progressive, institutionally astute and relatively technologically advanced industrializing states. There are important lessons that other African countries can derive from its seamless coordination of public sector policies and private investment activities, investment in human capital and skills to make the most of the technology transfer possibilities attached with FDI to promote its industrialization and overall economic development. In an era of declining global FDI from major investors such as the USA due to repatriation of foreign earnings coupled with slow recovery of the major economies from the global financial crisis of a decade ago, Africa has to step up to the challenge of producing skilled manpower and improving institutional quality, addressing the lingering political instability problems, and encouraging intra-Africa trade and investment (UNCTAD 2019).

ANNEX 1: MAIN FDI DESTINATIONS (IN BILLIONS OF DOLLARS)

Destination	2012	Destination	2013	Destination	2014	Destination	2015	Destination	2016	Destination	2017	Destination	2018
Nigeria	7127.39	South Africa	8300.10	South Africa	5770.66	Angola	10028.22	Angola	−179.52	Egypt	7408.70	Egypt	6797.60
Egypt	6031.00	Mozambique	6175.12	Egypt	4901.79	Egypt	6925.20	Togo	−46.28	Congo	4406.04	South Africa	5334.00
Mozambique	5629.41	Nigeria	5608.45	Mozambique	4693.83	Gambia	3866.83	Gambia	−27.70	Ethiopia	4017.10	Congo	4313.14
South Africa	4558.85	Egypt	4256.00	Congo	4612.00	South Sudan	3803.30	South Sudan	−17.00	Nigeria	3503.00	Morocco	3640.38
Congo, DRC	3312.14	Angola	3298.10	Morocco	3657.51	Libya	3254.80	Libya	0.00	Ghana	3255.00	Ethiopia	3310.30
Ghana	3293.43	Morocco	3226.33	Angola	3561.24	Mayotte	3192.30	Mayotte	0.00	Morocco	2686.03	Ghana	2989.00
Morocco	2728.36	Ghana	2099.80	Ghana	3356.99	Reunion	3064.17	Reunion	0.00	Mozambique	2293.10	Mozambique	2711.13
Sudan	2311.00	Congo, DRC	2098.25	Ethiopia	1855.05	Saint Helena	2626.52	Saint Helena	0.00	South Africa	2006.86	Nigeria	1997.49
Tanzania	1799.60	Tanzania	2087.30	South Africa	1843.17	Burundi	1729.38	Burundi	0.06	Gabon	1498.04	Kenya	1625.92
Zambia	1731.50	Algeria	1696.87	Congo, DRC	1659.45	Comoros	1728.37	Comoros	3.57	Congo, DRC	1340.20	Algeria	1506.32

Source: Authors from UNCTAD, 2019, and FDI Markets, 2019

ANNEX 2: MAIN FDI DESTINATIONS, TEN YEARS AVERAGE (IN BILLIONS OF DOLLARS)

Destination	1990–1999	Destination	2000–2009	Destination	2010–2018
Tanzania	1.21	Congo	6.61	Sudan	14.04
Zambia	1.41	Angola	12.19	Congo	17.23
Algeria	1.58	Sudan	12.88	Congo, DR	17.59
Côte d'Ivoire	2.32	Tunisia	13.46	Ethiopia	18.34
Tunisia	4.20	Libya	14.10	Morocco	25.47
Morocco	5.59	Algeria	14.14	Ghana	28.56
Angola	5.74	Morocco	18.27	Mozambique	34.76
Egypt	8.05	South Africa	40.98	South Africa	37.81
South Africa	8.50	Nigeria	41.79	Nigeria	45.46
Nigeria	14.94	Egypt	47.99	Egypt	50.04

Source: Authors from UNCTAD, 2019, and FDI Markets, 2019

ANNEX 3: TOP TEN FDI RECEIVING AFRICAN COUNTRIES, FROM THE 1990S TO THE 2010S (IN BILLIONS OF DOLLARS)

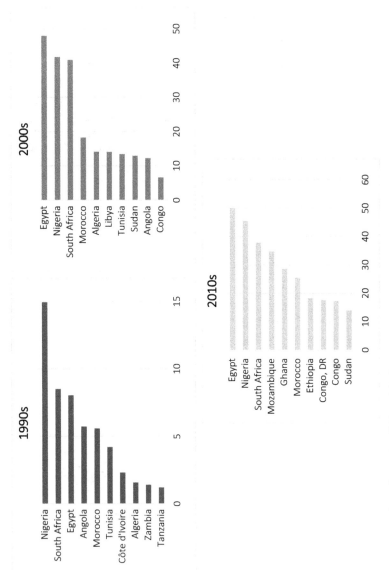

Source: Authors from UNCTAD, 2019

REFERENCES

Akinlo, A. (2004). Foreign Direct Investment and Growth in Nigeria: An Empirical Investigation. *Journal of Policy Modelling, 26*, 627–639.

Arrow, K. (1969). Classificatory Notes on the Production and Transmission of Technological Knowledge. *American Economic Review, 59*(2), 29–35.

Ayanwale, A. B. (2007). *FDI and Economic Growth: Evidence from Nigeria.* African Economic Research Consortium Paper 165. Nairobi.

Barbera, F., & Moores, K. (2013). Firm Ownership and Productivity: A Study of Family and Non-family SMEs. *Small Business Economics, 40*, 953–976.

Blackman, A., & Kildegaard, A. (2010). Clean Technological Change in Developing-Country Industrial Clusters: Mexican Leather Tanning. *Environmental Economics and Policy Studies, 12*(3), 115–132.

Borensztein, J., DeGregorio, J., & Lee, J. W. (1998). How Does Foreign Direct Investment Affect Economic Growth? *Journal of International Economics, 45*, 115–135.

Bowen, A. (2012). *Green Growth, Green Jobs and Labour Markets.* Policy Research Working Paper 5990. Washington, DC: World Bank.

Chang, H. J. (2002). Source Kicking Away the Ladder: An Unofficial History of Capitalism, Especially in Britain and the United States. *Challenge, 45*(5), 63–97.

Chang, H. J. (2003). *Globalization, Economic Development and the Role of the State.* London: Zed Books.

Cling, J.-P., Razafindindirakoto, M., & Roubaud, F. (2007). *Export Processing Zones in Madagascar: The Impact of the Dismantling of Clothing Quotas on Employment and Labour Standards.* IRD Working Document DT/2007–06.

Crespo, N., & Fontoura, M. (2007). Determinant Factors of FDI Spillovers—What Do We Really Know? *World Development, 35*(3), 410–425.

de Oliveira, J. A. P., & Jabbour, C. J. C. (2017). Environmental Management, Climate Change, CSR, and Governance in Clusters of Small Firms in Developing Countries Toward an Integrated Analytical Framework. *Business and Society, 56*(1), 130–151.

Du, X. (2015). Is Corporate Philanthropy Used as Environmental Misconduct Dressing? Evidence from Chinese Family-Owned Firms. *Journal of Business Ethics, 129*(2), 341–361.

Echandi, R., & Scronce, E. (2016). *Three Key Ideas for Creating Effective Investment Policies.* World Bank Blog.

FDI Markets. (2019). The FDI Report 2019, Global Greenfield Investment Trends, FDI Intelligence, UK.

Geiger, M., & Goh, C. (2012). *Chinese FDI in Ethiopia: A World Bank Survey.* Washington, DC: World Bank.

Gómez-Mera, L., Kenyon, T., Margalit, Y., Reis, J. G., & Varela, G. (2015). *New Voices in Investment.* Washington, DC: World Bank.

Harding, T., & Javorcik, B. S. (2011a). Roll Out the Red Carpet and They Will Come: Investment Promotion and FDI Inflows. *Economic Journal, 121*(557), 1445–1476.

Harding, Torfinn, & Beata S. Javorcik. (2011b). *FDI and Export Upgrading.* Economics Series Working Papers 526. University of Oxford, Department of Economics.

Harding, T., & Javorcik, B. S. (2013). Investment Promotion and FDI Inflows: Quality Matters. *CESifo Economic Studies, CESifo, 59,* 337–359.

Hermes, N., & Lensink, R. (2003). Foreign direct investment, financial development and economic growth. *The Journal of Development Studies, 40*(1), 142–163.

Joomun, G. (2006). *The Textile and Clothing Industry in Mauritius in the Future of the Textile and Clothing Industry in Sub-Saharan Africa.* Cape Town.

Kedir, A. (2014). Debating Critical Issues of Green Growth and Energy in Africa: Thinking beyond our lifetimes. In K. T. Hanson et al. (Eds.), *Managing Africa's Natural Resources: Capacities for Development* (International Political Economy Series). New York: Palgrave Macmillan.

Kedir, A. (2015). Enhancing Regionalism for Intra-African and African Inward Foreign Direct Investment. In K. Hanson (Ed.), *Contemporary Regional Development in Africa*, The International Political Economy of New Regionalisms Series. Ashgate Publishers.

Machado, M., & K. Hatakeyama (2018). *From Technology Transfer to Disruptive Innovation: The Case of EMBRAER.* Proceedings of PICMET '18: Technology Management for Interconnected World.

McKinsey, (2018). *Delivering with Diversity.* McKinsey & Company.

Narraidoo, K. (2018). *FinTech in Mauritius – A 'Disruptive' Innovation,* DLA Piper.

Newman, C., Page, J., Rand, J., Shimeles, A., Söderbom, M., & Tarp, F. (2018). *Linked in by Foreign Direct Investment: The Role of Firm-Level Relationships in Knowledge Transfers in Africa and Asia.* WIDER Working Paper 2018/161, Helsinki, Finland.

Nguyen, A. N., & Nguyen, T. (2007). *Foreign Direct Investment in Vietnam: An Overview and Analysis of the Determination of Spatial Distribution.* Working Paper, Development and Polices Research Center, Hanoi, Vietnam.

Nhamo, G. (2017). New Global Sustainable Development Agenda: A Focus on Africa. *Sustainable Development, 25,* 227–241.

OECD. (2015). *Strengthening Chile's Investment Promotion Strategy.* Available at: http://www.oecd.org/investment/investment-policy/chile-investment-promotion-strategy.htm

Pigato, M. A. (2000). *Foreign Direct Investment in Africa: Old Tales and New Evidence.* World BankAfrica Region Working Paper Series No. 8.

Pollin, R., Heintz, J., & Garrett-Peltier, H. (2009). *The Economic Benefits of Investing in Clean Technology*. Department of Economic and Political Economy Research Institute (PERI), University of Massachusetts, Amherst.

Robecka, J., Rosuneeb, S., & Pattison, J. (2012). The Mauritius Apparel Manufacturing Industry: Explorations of the Past to the Present. *International Journal of Trade and Commerce-IIARTC, 1*(2), 163–174.

Romer, P. (1990). Endogenous Technological Change. *The Journal of Political Economy, 98*(5), Part 2: The Problem of Development: A Conference of the Institute for the Study of Free Enterprise Systems, pp. S71–S102.

Soltani, H., & Ochi, A. (2012). Foreign Direct Investment (FDI) and Economic Growth: An Approach in Terms of Cointegration for the Case of Tunisia. *Journal of Applied Finance & Banking, 2*, 193–207. Tang, S., Selvanathan, E., Selvanathan.

Stein, H. (2008). *Africa, Industrial Policy and Export Processing Zones: Lessons from Asia, Center for Afro-American and African Studies (CAAS)*. University of Michigan, USA.

Stiglitz, J., Lin, J., & Monga, C. (2013). *The Rejuvenation of Industrial Policy*. SSRN Scholarly Paper No ID 2333944, Social Science Research Network, Rochester.

UNCTAD (2019). *Special Economic Zones, World Investment Report*. Geneva: Switzerland.

Wade, R. H. (2015). The Role of Industrial Policy in Developing Countries. In A. Calcagno, S. Dullien, A. Marquez-Valazquez, & N. M. J. Priewe (Eds.), *Rethinking Development Policies After the Financial Crisis, Vol. 1, Making the Case for Policy Space*. Geneva: UNCTAD.

World Bank, (2017). *Good Practices for Financial Consumer Protection*. Washington, D.C.

Yenkey, C, Doering, L., & Aleves, P. (2015). *Multiple Uses of Mobile Money, Implications for Financial Inclusion*. Working Paper.

Zafar, A. (2011). *Mauritius: An Economic Success Story*. Washington, DC: World Bank.

CHAPTER 12

Perspectives on Disruptive Innovations and Africa's Services Sector

Kobena T. Hanson and Vanessa T. Tang

Introduction

The advent of the fourth industrial revolution (4IR), and the consequent growth in digital technologies, characterized by technological inventions and applications, and disruptive innovations are radically transforming existing economic sectors, enabling new modes of work, production and consumption which are triggering broader societal changes. According to Schwab (2016), the 4IR has been progressing since the start of the twenty-first century, characterized by the ubiquitous and mobile telephony; Internet of Things (IoT); cheaper, smaller and stronger sensors; and artificial and machine learning. Many have argued that the 4IR and the associated rise in digitization and disruptive innovations are like a double-edged sword, with immense opportunities and challenges (Lee et al. 2018;

K. T. Hanson (✉)
African Development Bank, Abidjan, Côte D'Ivoire
e-mail: k.hanson@afdb.org

V. T. Tang
School of Accounting, Economics and Finance, University of KwaZulu-Natal, Durban, South Africa

© The Author(s) 2020   255
P. Arthur et al. (eds.), *Disruptive Technologies, Innovation and Development in Africa*, International Political Economy Series, https://doi.org/10.1007/978-3-030-40647-9_12

Deloitte 2018; Onyeji-Nwogu et al. 2017; Schwab 2016). The opportunities relate to the possibility of gains in efficiency and productivity that will open new markets and drive economic growth. At the same time, the revolution poses challenges that are related to the possibility of greater inequality, particularly in its potential to disrupt labor markets. The emerging landscape has heralded an introduction of new production processes in manufacturing and services, a predominance of digital products over physical products (e.g., media), and an evolution of a sharing economy (Lee et al. 2018; see also Christensen et al. 2019; Hanson and Puplampu 2018; Onyeji-Nwogu et al. 2017).

The greater spatio-temporal flexibility brought about by the 4IR, digitization and rise in disruptive innovations is not only bringing locations of production and sale closer together but more importantly driving major changes in the design of future value and supply chains (WEF 2017). Digitization is also reinforcing a trend of 'servicification' (increased trade in services), whereby there is an increase in the use, production and sale of services. Across Africa, the growth in Nollywood movies and music is a good example. Relatedly, international production, trade and investments are increasingly becoming organized within global value chains (GVCs), where different production stages are located across different countries.

For African countries, these developments are expected to provide a fresh creative approach in their efforts to drive macro-economic transformation and sustainable development (Shaw and Hanson 2019; Christensen et al. 2019). Cautions of potential threats, the need for legislation and the possibilities of the 4IR to upend the socio-economic status quo also abound (Lee et al. 2018; Deloitte 2018; Ebersold and Glass 2015). Indeed, the potential impact of digitization and disruptive innovation (e.g., AI, augmented and virtual reality and blockchain technology, to mention a few) has far-reaching implications for governance and the law, highlighting not only the possibilities and opportunities but also the scale and scope of the emerging landscape that Africa has to confront with and actively thrive in.

This chapter highlights the impact of the 4IR, digitization and disruptive innovation on the services sector in Africa. In examining the dynamic relationships, the chapter draws on the extant literature on disruptive technologies and innovation (Christensen 1997, 2001; Christensen and Raynor 2003) and that on the services sector (Castro and McQuinn 2015; Manyika et al. 2016; Lanz and Maurer 2015; Shaw and Fanta 2013; Tang 2018) to validate the developments taking place in the African context.

Following the introduction, the chapter discusses the 4IR, digitization and the growth in disruptive innovations. Next, we look at how these innovations are influencing the services sector and the resultant 'servicification'. Here, the chapter highlights ongoing developments in Africa and their implications for the continent's transformation aspirations. The chapter concludes that if Africa seeks to leverage the 4IR, then the continent will need to advance its own variety of 'servicification' in which its IoT innovations and related services, such as design, drones, fashion, film, music, foods, mobile finance and crowdsourcing, diversify the region's global role beyond commodities. Decision and policy makers in Africa also will need to pay special attention to the 4IR developments and, particularly, the potential disruptive effects of technological innovations on future employment growth.

FOURTH INDUSTRIAL REVOLUTION AND RISE IN DISRUPTIVE INNOVATIONS

The 4IR, a transformational change, is characterized by the rise in ubiquitous and mobile technology; cheaper, smaller and stronger sensors; and artificial and machine learning (Deloitte 2018; Onyeji-Nwogu et al. 2017; Schwab 2016). The 4IR is not just about innovative technologies, but also the dynamic entanglements between these technologies with an unprecedented level of data gathering and of communication of physical systems both with humans and with each other in real time, thus the limitless possibilities and opportunities for placing countries onto a much speedier and sustainable path of development (Onyeji-Nwogu et al. 2017). While no single definition for the 4IR exists, the change it portends at its core is the marriage of physical and digital technologies such as analytics, artificial intelligence, cognitive technologies and IoT. This merging of the physical and digital realms has had a phenomenal impact on society in myriad ways, rapidly redefining the provisioning of services, wealth generation and models of decision making (Deloitte 2018; Schwab 2016).

Although the 4IR holds vast opportunities and possibilities, it can also upend the status quo and create nearly as much uncertainty (Hanson and Puplampu 2018; Deloitte 2018). This is because the fusion of breakthrough technologies blurs the lines between the physical, digital and biological and neuro-technological spheres (e.g., advanced robotics, artificial intelligence, IoT, virtual and augmented reality, wearables and additive manufacturing) and is revolutionizing production processes and business practices across different industries (WEF 2017; Cronjé 2016). The resultant disruptive innovation accelerators are shaping the development and the lived experiences of society in many ways (Shaw and Hanson 2019; Hanson and Puplampu 2018; Cronjé 2016). As Cronjé (2016) argues, the exponential and unprecedented speed at which the 4IR is taking place is having a disruptive effect on entire systems including the production, services, management and governance of every industry. Disruptive innovations in this sense are transforming all end-to-end steps in production and business models in most sectors of the economy (WEF 2017). The products that consumers demand, factory processes and footprints and the management of global supply chains are being reshaped to an unprecedented degree and at unprecedented pace. A newcomer's idea can disrupt an established industry, or a broad set of digital data augmented by artificial intelligence and sophisticated models can rival expertise gathered over many years of hands-on experience. This ability to change the game, so to speak, has led to terms such as disruptive technologies and disruptive innovations. Viewed from this perspective, disruptive innovations/technologies are integral to the 4IR.

In fact, the term disruptive innovation is widely used today in the sense introduced originally as disruptive technology by Christensen (1997), and the underlying rationale and analysis can be, mostly, extended to non-technological fields of innovation. In fact, in later work, Christensen and Raynor (2003) replaced disruptive technology with the term 'disruptive innovation'. As Christensen (1997) defines, disruptive innovations are technological advancements that are offered at relatively much lower cost to traditional users of rather similar technology, thus opening the door to new (often low-end) markets. However, disruptive innovations, though initially providing services that are of low functionality or quality to traditional offerings, over time, improve in many dimensions while maintaining low cost or other competitive advantages. In the ideal disruptive innovation situation, a firm introduces a product (or service) with features that appeal to a niche market and sells for a lower price than existing established products.

Disruptive innovations, as Christensen, Raynor and McDonald (2015) further articulate, start from one of two footholds (i.e., two types of markets) that established services/products overlook, low-end footholds and new-market footholds. Given the tendency of established services/products to go after their most lucrative markets with ever-improving products and services, they often tend to neglect the less profitable markets. This creates an opportunity for a disrupter focused (at first) on providing those low-end customers with a 'good enough' product to get their foot in the door and to carve a niche space for themselves (Christensen et al. 2015). In the case of new-market footholds, disrupters create a market where none existed. Thus, simply disrupting and finding a 'new' way to turn current and potential consumers into future profitable consumers is not it. As the new product develops, it becomes more competitive in the established market and is in demand, eventually rendering the established product obsolete. So, while most customers may initially not be attracted to the disruptive innovation, over time, they come to recognize that an equal or better product is available at a lower cost, resulting in a switch to the disruptive innovation (Christensen 1997, 2001).

While the growth and spread of disruptive innovations have been more widespread and driven by companies in the global North and China, including, but not limited to, the FAANGs (Facebook, Apple, Amazon, Netflix and Google) and the BATs (Baidu, Alibaba and Tencent), developments in the global South, particularly in Africa, cannot be ignored. Here, as elsewhere, the projected economic effect of disruptive innovations is vast (Shaw and Hanson 2019; Hanson and Puplampu 2018; Deloitte 2018; Manyika et al. 2013), and it holds the potential to drive growth and socio-economic development by creating new markets and products. Indeed, across Africa, organizations are digitalizing, although the level of digital maturity is not the same across all countries. The potential of the 4IR, rapid digitization and growth in disruptive innovations is increasingly acknowledged (cf. Shaw and Hanson 2019; Hanson and Puplampu 2018; Siemens 2017; EU 2017; ITU and Cisco 2016). In their recent publication, *The Prosperity Paradox: How Innovation Can Lift Nations Out of Poverty*, Christensen et al. (2019: 8) note that "investing in innovations, and more specifically market-creating innovations, has proven a reliable path to prosperity for countries". This view is also echoed in Siemens' *African Digitalization Maturity Report 2017*, which notes that the "digital maturity in Africa is extremely diverse... disruptive technology can be seen as an opportunity to leapfrog".

The aforementioned positives notwithstanding, issues and challenges exist. For one, the rise in the 4IR and allied disruptive innovations calls for a "rethink or revamp of the regulatory structure ... consumer protection, labor regulation, property rights, taxation and discriminatory practices" (Hanson and Puplampu 2018: 139), as extant legal frameworks no longer suffice (Ranchordás 2015). Similarly, negative aspects of the revised landscape such as labor retrenchments, increase in structural unemployment and sunsets for traditional industries (Lee et al. 2018; Deloitte 2018; Onyeji-Nwogu et al. 2017; Grossman 2016) have to be dealt with. The introduction of drone-based delivery systems (e.g., Zipline in Rwanda and recently Ghana for medical drops), for example, while an efficient way to get supplies into rural/remote locations, has changed the platform of medical transportation and delivery services, in the process jeopardizing livelihoods (see Manyika et al. 2017).

Disruptive Innovation, Services Sector, 'Servicification' and Global Value Chains

One area witnessing impactful changes resulting from the rise in disruptive innovation is the increased trade in services. International production, trade and investments are also increasingly becoming organized within global value chains (GVCs), where different production stages are located across different countries. In the evolving landscape, triggered by digital innovation, the relationship between trade in goods and trade in services has become more complex, with limitless threats, possibilities and opportunities to expand and deepen trade, investment and innovation.

Historically, services were generally perceived of as non-tradable, as it is the nature of many services that their provision coincides with their consumption and requires the physical proximity and interaction of the producer and the consumer (EU 2017: 11). Digitization and the rise in disruptive innovations have changed this. Many services, such as in the legal, engineering, computer-related and financial realms, are today offered online in part or in whole, depending on the nature of the service and the extent to which the domestic regulatory framework permits for it. As a result, it is estimated that 50% of global traded services are already digitized and this opens entirely new opportunities for global trade in services (Castro and McQuinn 2015; Manyika et al. 2016).

Overall, the relationship between trade in goods and trade in services has become more complicated in the digital space; previous distinctions between goods and services are no longer valid. Also, the growth in disruptive innovation is reinforcing a trend of 'servicification' (increased trade in services), whereby there is an upsurge in the use, produce and sale of services (Tang 2018; Lanz and Maurer 2015). In fact, the African service industry is gradually growing and becoming more productive and tradable. This is notably reflected in the growth and success of Nigerian Nollywood films and Ivorian *Coupé-Décalé* music (Shaw and Fanta 2013) as well as Kenya's call centres (Tang 2018). Elsewhere, digitization has enabled the instantaneous exchange of virtual goods. E-books, apps, online games, music and streaming services, software and cloud computing services can all be transmitted to connected customers over space and time (EU 2017). Similarly, 'on-demand' services (e.g., delivery, picking up and shipping parcels, food preparation and delivery, and laundry services) have witnessed a boom in activities.

Africa's rapid embrace of mobile telephony is redefining services that revolve around the spread of mobile telecommunications. Undoubtedly, sub-Saharan Africa today leads the world in the adoption of mobile money services. At the end of 2014, over a fifth of mobile connections in the region were linked to a mobile money account, with more registered mobile money accounts than bank accounts in several countries. Improvements in ICTs and mobile telephony are rapidly changing the development landscape and creating opportunities for many who otherwise could not compete. Disruptive innovations such as M-Pesa (mobile money), Ushahidi (crowdsourcing), M-Kopa (off-grid solar services) and more, have opened myriad opportunities, created new jobs and transformed the lives of many (Hanson and Puplampu 2018). Mauritius, for instance, has leveraged WiMAX (Worldwide Interoperability for Microwave Access) to not only make the remote, mountainous island the first 'unwired' nation in the world, but also reduced the costs of broadband access while ensuring affordability.

Across sub-Saharan Africa, creative utilization of disruptive innovations made possible by mobile technology include, but are not limited to, *mPedigree*, a service that verifies whether drugs are genuine by simply sending a text message query—a critical initiative in the fight against the proliferation of counterfeit drugs on the continent. Ghana and Kenya are pioneering this initiative, with Nigeria and others slated to join soon. In Niger, *Tech-Innov*, a tele-irrigation system for fields controlled by mobile telephony, is transforming lives and communities. Yet another app, *M-Farm*, is transforming the agricultural landscape by providing farmers real-time access to information about the weather, current retail prices for their products, potential buyers as well as places where they can buy seeds (Hanson and Puplampu 2018).

Another effect of digitization on the relationship between products and services is the ability of the technology component of some goods to fundamentally affect the value of the good (EU 2017). These so-called digital wrappers, as digital add-ons, can enable or raise the value of other activities: logistics companies use, for instance, sensors to track physical shipments, reducing losses in transit and enabling more valuable merchandise to be shipped and insured. A case in point is Kenya, where the Nairobi County Council and IBM (International Business Machines) installed sensor-based devices on council garbage trucks to effectively monitor them for efficient use (Hanson and Puplampu 2018). Likewise, in Nigeria, the National Agency for Food and Drug Administration and Control (NAFDAC), in an effort to combat counterfeiting, uses tags equipped with RFID (radio-frequency identification) to secure the integrity of the drugs throughout the supply chain from manufacturers, distributors, wholesalers, retailers and to consumers (Hanson and Puplampu 2018). Elsewhere, sensors have also been used to monitor soil conditions and moisture levels, RFID tags for personalized care for livestock, mobile phones for monitoring elections and enhancing governance, and off-grid solar systems to provide affordable electricity to lower-income families (see GSMA 2015; ITU and Cisco 2016).

To build trust in this virtual marketplace, online user-generated reviews and ratings are often relied on to demonstrate legitimacy and boost customer confidence—making it less risky when engaging in cross-border transactions—be it buying a book on Amazon, booking a hotel (Manyika et al. 2016) or choosing an Airbnb property (Hanson and Puplampu 2018). Today, services in both the shared and gig economy have gained prominence across Africa, as attractive opportunities to redistribute goods, services or experiences (Agyeman et al. 2013), and transform complex and expensive products and services into simple and more affordable products (Christensen et al. 2019: 9), while making them accessible to a whole new segment of the populace.

TRENDS IN SERVICES INNOVATIONS IN THE DIGITAL ERA

Technology is permeating our everyday lives in unprecedented ways and driving widespread changes within industries, organizations as well as markets. Economists generally consider innovations in technology as a source of competitive advantage, which leads to efficiency gains, achieving greater economies of scale, an increasing market access, promoting exports and the possibility of diversifying into new or more sophisticated products, making it possible for nations to accelerate their economic growth and development more rapidly. However, while technology is indeed a driving force for growth, for a sizeable number of developing countries, gross domestic product (GDP) is closely dependent on the extent of openness to trade or trade liberalization and the exports of goods and services (Tang 2018; Tang et al. 2019). The emphasis on trade liberalization in the past four decades has led to a remarkable growth in the value of goods and services traded. That said, it is worth noting that relative to goods traded, international trade in services, although rapidly increasing, accounts for a much lower share. In 2017, world trade in goods was valued at around 17 trillion US dollars, while trade in services accounted for only just above 5 trillion US dollars (UNCTAD 2019). Although global trade in services is largely led by developed countries, contributing around two thirds of services traded internationally, the export market is gradually shifting to the advantage of developing economies, particularly China and India. In 2017, even though Africa's contribution by value and share in the world's service exports was anaemic, developing economies in Africa (as well as transition economies) managed to achieve double-digit growth rates in service exports as illustrated in Fig. 12.1. Africa's service exports also grew around 13.7% in 2017, surpassing the growth rates of the mighty developed economies, as can be observed overleaf.

Hence, considering African developing economies' major growth achievements in the service export sector, it is therefore not unreasonable to infer that developing countries in Africa are becoming important suppliers to international markets in services. Presently, the top five leading exporters in services trade in Africa are Egypt, Morocco, South Africa, Ghana and Nigeria. It is worth stressing that although by value and share Egypt, Morocco and South Africa are the leading exporters, Egypt and Nigeria, enjoy the highest growth rates as illustrated in Fig. 12.2. Despite this progress, there still is a need for African countries to increase their service diversification, in order to buffer their economies against trade volatilities. A case in point is Egypt, despite the relatively large importance of services trade; Egypt's service export earnings remain volatile and is still highly concentrated in its traditional sources of service exports, namely, tourism and Suez Canal.

Against this background, the question that arises is how can policy makers in Africa leverage the growing importance of service exports and the associated emerging disruptive innovations (innovation-driven

Fig. 12.1 Leading exporters in services trade (2017). Source: Authors' compilation based on *UNCTAD Handbook of Statistics* data (UNCTAD 2019)

growth) to enhance the sector. One mechanism is by way of global value chains (GVCs). The onset of the African Continental Free Trade Area (AfCFTA) provides added impetus for the development of regional and global value chains in Africa, providing opportunities to leverage the agricultural, manufacturing and service industry potential of the region (see Prakash et al. 2018).

Also, with the fourth industrial revolution in full swing, there are likely several channels that are responsible for Africa's growing contributions in their services trade, including disruptive effects. In that regard, the internet and digitalization are examples that characterize technology that blurs the lines between the physical, digital and biological spheres potentially disrupting industries worldwide (Majumdar et al. 2018: 1248). Notwithstanding, the internet, mobile technologies and many other disruptive technological phenomena are potentially causing profound changes in organizations and society (Brem and Voigt 2009). The internet and mobile technologies have revolutionized the music industry, tourism, trade and services—new services that have emerged include e-tourism, e-heath, e-marketing and digital learning amongst others. With this fourth

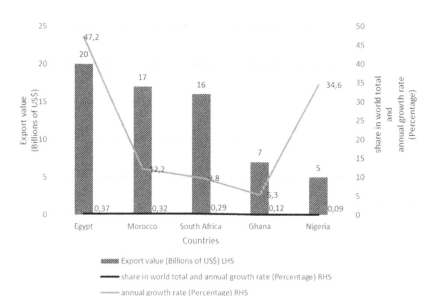

Fig. 12.2 Leading African exporters in services trade (2017). Source: Authors' compilation based on *UNCTAD Handbook of Statistics* data (UNCTAD 2019)

revolution and these advanced technologies, African countries can climb up the ladder and prosper if they diversify their economies and use these technological changes in innovative ways.

There generally is a wide digital divide between the developed and developing economies. However, over the last few years, developing economies (Africa included) are steadily catching up and transforming into digital hotbeds as illustrated in Fig. 12.3. The digital export flow contribution from Africa although on the rise from 17.5% in 2005 to 22.7% in 2017 is, however, much slower than we expected—this trend may in part be attributed to the fact that internet access is low in Africa generally and that the cost of penetration is high where internet access is available.

Internet penetration nowadays plays a significant role in economic growth which can ultimately improve productivity, accelerate innovation and be responsible for the opportunity for new products and services (Stork et al. 2014). Also, in the context of developing Africa, the internet

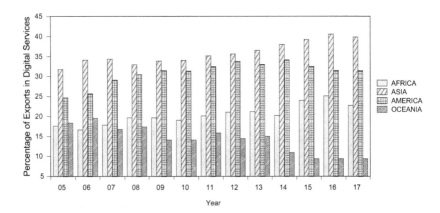

Fig. 12.3 Developing economies' exports in digital services (2005–2017). Source: Authors' compilation based on *UNCTAD Handbook of Statistics* data (UNCTAD 2019)

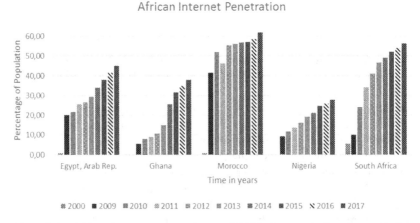

Fig. 12.4 African internet penetration until 2017. Source: Authors' compilation based on World Bank World Development Indicators data (WDI 2019)

penetration, although transforming and rising, is not evenly distributed around the continent (low penetration rate) as illustrated in Fig. 12.4. The internet penetration rate is rather low and slow if one considers using the example of the status quo of the top five leaders in digital services.

Tomer (2019) highlights the importance and need for businesses to be able to develop products that leverage the capabilities of the newest technological platforms. He further notes that getting it right will require public infrastructure networks to promote efficient and equitable movement of goods, data and people; education and workforce systems that support a pipeline of talent, including the promotion of non-routine skills that can help manage the boom in disruptive innovations; and a legal/regulatory system that promotes free-flowing data while protecting consumer privacy.

However, in advancing Africa's digital transformation, policy makers should consider that Africa's educational system needs to be concurrently revised towards the importance of focusing on STEM subjects: science, technology, engineering and mathematics. Again, tertiary education practices need to promote research skills, in particular, the STEM type of research skills that are needed in today's workplace. There is also a serious need to aim at empowering the youth and the current labour force to minimize job losses (Frey and Osborne 2016).

Conclusion

Digital technology and disruptive innovations have begun to alter irrevocably the nature of our collective life (Kissinger 2018). The dynamic possibilities inherent in the leapfrogging potential in disruptive innovations provide the basis for a new kind of twenty-first-century development process in Africa (Besada et al. 2016). Leveraging the full transformational potential of the 4IR and associated disruptive innovations, however, calls for countries to take a broader perspective about how to use smart, connected technologies.

While challenges undoubtedly are ahead, digitization and automation offer unlimited opportunities and possibilities for African countries to leapfrog the technological divide. For example, the boom in mobile telephony and associated electronic applications (e.g., M-Pesa, M-Kopa, eBird, mPedigree, use of RFID) across sub-Saharan Africa is just the tip of the iceberg (Hanson and Puplampu 2018). Recent developments such as Google's AI hubs in Ghana and Rwanda further demonstrate how African nations are embracing their revised 'disrupted' landscape. That said, if Africa seeks to leverage the fourth industrial revolution, then the continent itself needs to become a disrupter (Puplampu, Hanson and Arthur— this volume), advancing its own variety of 'servicification' in which its IoT innovations and related services—such as design, drones, fashion, film, foods, mobile finance and crowdsourcing (IDS 2016) and music—facilitate its global role beyond commodities (Shaw and Hanson 2019). Being able to strategically scan the environment and grasp the signals of disruption is critical. To do so, African 'techpreneurs', thought leaders and decision makers will need to be mindful of the changes happening that stand to shape and impact society and the economy, but also discern which emerging technologies are hype and which are truly transformational. Clearly, the impact of new technology will differ widely across the specific country contexts in which they are introduced. Thus, the appropriate response in terms of regulatory action, government policy and institutional support will also need to be nuanced and fit for purpose.

In closing, with a concern towards the fast growth of digitalization and internet technologies disrupting labour markets, policy makers in Africa should pay close attention to the 4IR developments and, particularly, the potential disruptive effects of this fourth revolution on current and future employment growth and cyber terrorism on the rise, which cannot be ignored.

References

Agyeman, J., Mclaren, D., & Schaefer- Borrego, A. (2013). *Briefing: Sharing Cities* (pp. 1–32). London: Friends of the Earth.

Besada, H., Xue, J., Mathers, A., & Carey, R. (2016). Advancing African Agency in the New 2030 Transformative Development Agenda. *African Geographical Review*, 1–26. https://doi.org/10.1080/19376812.2016.1138232.

Brem, A., & Voigt, K. (2009). Integration of Market-Pull and Technology –Push in the Corporate Front End and Innovation Management – Insights from the German Software Industry. *Technovation, 29*, 351–367.

Castro, D., & McQuinn, A. (2015). *Cross-Border Data Flows Enable Growth in All Industries.* Washington, DC: Information Technology and Innovation Foundation.

Christensen, C. M. (1997). *The innovator's Dilemma – When New Technologies Cause Great Firms to Fail.* Cambridge: Harvard University Press.

Christensen, C. M. (2001). Assessing Your Organization's Innovation Capabilities. *Executive Forum, 81*(2), 27–37.

Christensen, C. M., & Raynor, M. E. (2003). *The Innovator's Solution: Creating and Sustaining Successful Growth.* Boston: Harvard Business School Press.

Christensen, C.M., Raynor, M.E., & McDonald, R. (2015, December). What Is Disruptive Innovation?. *Harvard Business Review,* 44–53. Available at: https://hbr.org/2015/12/what-is-disruptive-innovation. Accessed 17 June 2019.

Christensen, C. M., Ojomo, E., & Dillon, K. (2019). *The Prosperity Paradox: How Innovation Can Lift Nations Out of Poverty*. New York: Harper Collins.

Cronjé, J. (2016). *The Digital Economy and Policy Implications for Trade*. Stellenbosch: TRALAC.

Deloitte Development LLC. (2018). *The Fourth Industrial Revolution Is Here—Are You Ready?* Available at: https://www2.deloitte.com/content/dam/Deloitte/tr/Documents/manufacturing/Industry4-0_Are-you-ready_Report.pdf. Accessed 10 June 2019.

Ebersold, K., & Glass, R. (2015). The Impact of Disruptive Technology: The Internet of Things. *Issues in Information Systems, 16*(IV), 194–201.

European Union. (2017). *Current and Emerging Trends in Disruptive Technologies: Implications for the Present and Future of EU's Trade Policy*. (September 2017 – PE 603 845).

Frey, C. B., & Osborne, M. A. (2016). The Future of Employment: How Susceptible Are Jobs to Computerization? *Technological Forecasting and Social Change, 114*, 1–27.

Grossman, R. (2016, March 21). The Industries That Are Being Disrupted the Most by Digital. *Harvard Business Review*. Available at: https://hbr.org/2016/03/the-industries-that-are-being-disrupted-themost-by-digital. Accessed 21 Mar 2019.

GSMA. (2015). *The Mobile Economy: Sub- Saharan Africa 2015*. London: GSMA.

Hanson, K. T., & Puplampu, K. P. (2018). The Internet of Things and the Sharing Economy: Harnessing the Possibilities for Africa's Sustainable Development Goals. In K. T. Hanson, K. P. Puplampu, & T. M. Shaw (Eds.), *From Millennium Development Goals to Sustainable Development Goals: Rethinking African Development* (pp. 133–151). New York: Routledge.

IDS. (2016). Ten Frontier Technologies for International Development. University of Sussex, November. Available at: www.ids.ac.uk. Accessed 10 June 2019.

ITU (International Telecommunication Union) & Cisco. (2016, June). *Harnessing the Internet of Things for Global Development*. Geneva: ITU. Available at: www.itu.int/en/action/broadband/Documents/Harnessing-IoT-Global-Development.pdf. Accessed 10 June 2019.

Kissinger, H. (2018, June). How the Enlightenment Ends: Philosophically, Intellectually—In Every Way—Human Society Is Unprepared for the Rise of Artificial Intelligence. *The Atlantic*. Available at: https://www.theatlantic.com/magazine/archive/2018/06/henry-kissinger-ai-could-mean-the-end-of-human-history/559124/. Accessed 28 July 2019.

Lanz, R., & Maurer, A. (2015). *Services and Global Value Chains – Some Evidence on Servicification of Manufacturing and Services Networks*. WTO Working Paper ERSD 3. Geneva: WTO.

Lee, M. H., Yun, J. J. H., Pyka, A., Won, D. K., Kodama, F., Schiuma, G., Park, H. S., Jeon, J., Park, K. B., Jung, K. H., Yan, M., Lee, S. Y., & Zhao, X. (2018).

How to Respond to the Fourth Industrial Revolution, or the Second Information Technology Revolution? Dynamic New Combinations Between Technology, Market, and Society Through Open Innovation. *Journal of Open Innovation: Technology, Market and Complexity,* 4(21), 1–24. https://doi. org/10.3390/joitmc4030021.

Majumdar, D., Banerji, P. K., & Chakrabarti, S. (2018). Disruptive Technology and Disruptive Innovation: Ignore at Your Peril! *Technology Analysis and Strategic Management, 30*(11), 1247–1255.

Manyika, J., Chui, M., Bughin, J., Dobbs R., Bisson, P., & Marrs, A. (2013, May). *Disruptive Technologies: Advances that Will Transform Life, Business, and the Global Economy.* McKinsey Global Institute. Available at: https://www.mckinsey.com/business-functions/digital-mckinsey/our-insights/disruptive-technologies. Accessed 10 June 2019.

Manyika, J., Lund, S., Bughin, J., Woetzel, J., Stamenov, K., & Dhingra, D. (2016). *Digital Globalization: The New Era of Global Flows.* Washington, DC: McKinsey Global Institute.

Onyeji-Nwogu, I., Bazilian, M., & Moss, T. (2017, May). *Challenges and Solutions for the Electricity Sector in African Markets.* CGD Policy Paper – 105. Washington, DC: Center for Global Development. Available at: https://www.cgdev.org/publication/challenges-and-solutions-electricity-sector-africanmarkets. Accessed 10 June 2019.

Prakash, A., Patel, A., Coulibaly, B., Gatune, J., Amoako, K. Y., Senbet, L. W., Mouelhi, R. B. A., Altenburg, T., Simbanegavi, W., & Mutanga, S. S. (2018, July 23). *World of Work in the 4th Industrial Revolution: Inclusive and Structural Transformation for a Better Africa.* G20 INSIGHTS.

Ranchordás, S. (2015). Does Sharing Mean Caring? Regulating Innovation in the Sharing Economy. *Minnesota Journal of Law, Science & Technology, 16*(1), 414–475.

Schwab, K. (2016). *The Fourth Industrial Revolution.* New York: Crown (for World Economic Forum).

Shaw, T. M., & Fanta, E. (2013). Introduction: Comparative Regionalisms for Development in the 21st Century: Insights from the Global South. In E. Fanta, T. M. Shaw, & V. T. Tang (Eds.), *Comparative Regionalisms for Development in the 21st Century: Insights from the Global South* (pp. 1–17). Farnham: Ashgate.

Shaw, T. M., & Hanson, K. T. (2019, April). *Artificial Intelligence & International Relations in Africa: Drivers of Sustainable Development?* Paper presented at the Shanghai Conference on AI, China.

Siemens. (2017). *African Digitalization Maturity Report 2017.* Available Online at: https://www.siemens.co.za/pool/about_us/Digitalization_Maturity_Report_2017.pdf. Accessed 20 July 2019.

Stork, C., Calandro, E., & Gamage, R. (2014). *The Future of Broadband in Africa.* [Internet]. Available from: https://www.researchictafrica.net/docs/The_Future_of_Broadband_in_Africa_webversion.pdf. Accessed 20 July 2019.

Tang, V. T. (2018). Does the Sophistication of Exports Matter in Sustaining Growth in Middle- Income African Countries? In K. T. Hanson, K. P. Puplampu, & T. M. Shaw (Eds.), *From Millennium Development Goals to Sustainable Development Goals: Rethinking African Development* (pp. 113–132). New York: Routledge.

Tang, V. T., Shaw, T. M., & Holden, M. (Eds.). (2019). *Development & Sustainable Growth of Mauritius*. New York: Palgrave Macmillan.

Tomer, A. (2019, July 30). Artificial Intelligence in America's Digital City. *Brookings Series – Blueprint for the Future of AI*. Available at: https://www.brookings.edu/research/artificial-intelligence-in-americas-digital-city/. Accessed 1 Aug 2019.

UNCTAD. (2019). *UNCTAD Handbook of Statistics Database*. [Internet]. Available from: https://unctad.org/en/Pages/statistics.aspx#. Accessed 20 July 2019.

WDI. (2019). *WDI Handbook of Statistics Database*. [Internet]. Available from: https://unctad.org/en/Pages/statistics.aspx#. Accessed 20 July 2019.

WEF. (2017, October). *Impact of the Fourth Industrial Revolution on Supply Chains*. Geneva: World Economic Forum. Available at: http://www3.weforum.org/docs/WEF_Impact_of_the_Fourth_Industrial_Revolution_on_Supply_Chains_.pdf. Accessed 18 Aug 2019.

CHAPTER 13

Automation of Knowledge Work and Africa's Transformation Agenda: Threats, Opportunities, and Possibilities

Kobena T. Hanson

INTRODUCTION

In today's rapidly changing digital economy, driven by disruptive technologies and innovation, the means of automation have grown, so too have the number of applications and markets that demand these technologies. Indeed, the growth in AI (artificial intelligence), coupled with machine learning, while transforming the workplace, also free up the need for human labor. The resulting new landscape is impacting labor force patterns, employment, and inequality by creating new markets and business practices, new product infrastructure, and different labor skills. Historical technological forms of digital evolution relied on human beings to create the software and analyze the data that affected our lives. Recent advances have recast this process.

Specifically, AI has made it possible to automate an extraordinary range of tasks by enabling machines to play a role, an increasing and decisive role

K. T. Hanson (✉)
African Development Bank, Abidjan, Côte D'Ivoire
e-mail: k.hanson@afdb.org

© The Author(s) 2020
P. Arthur et al. (eds.), *Disruptive Technologies, Innovation and Development in Africa*, International Political Economy Series,
https://doi.org/10.1007/978-3-030-40647-9_13

273

in drawing conclusions from data and then acting. AI draws lessons from its own experience, unlike traditional software, which can only support human reasoning. The growing transfer of judgment from human beings to machines denotes the revolutionary aspect of AI (Kissinger 2018). Consequently, digital technology and disruptive innovations are irrevocably altering the nature of our collective life.

Disruptive innovations, characterized by a fusion of breakthrough technologies that blur the lines between the physical, digital, and biological and neurotechnological spheres (e.g., advanced robotics, artificial intelligence, the Internet of Things (IoT), virtual and augmented reality, wearables, and additive manufacturing), are revolutionizing production processes and business practices across different industries (WEF 2017). The afore mentioned developments are redefining development, specifically employment in many ways (Shaw and Hanson 2019; Hanson and Puplampu 2018). Indeed, as Kissinger (2018) submits, the exponential and unprecedented speed at which digital innovation is occurring is having a disruptive effect on entire systems including the production, management, and governance of every industry. Relatedly, innovations resulting from the rise of digitization and widespread penetration of mobile technologies are changing the nature of jobs and affecting the labor market prospects of workers. Digital technologies are creating newer opportunities, but also at the same time making certain skills obsolete more quickly, as established jobs give way to newer jobs (Manyika et al. 2017; Choi et al. 2019).

Undoubtedly, the impact of new technology differs widely across the specific country contexts in which they are introduced. Similarly, the impact of automation on jobs depends on the types of jobs. In turn, the types of jobs that are available in an economy depend on the nature of economic activity and the relative importance of different sectors that make up such economy. Manyika et al. (2017) point out the potential impact of automation on employment varies both by occupation and sector. Labor-intensive jobs in predictable environments, such as operating machinery, preparing fast food, or collecting and processing data, are more susceptible to automation. For Africa, the projected economic effect of disruptive innovations is vast and offers the potential to drive growth and socioeconomic development by creating new jobs, markets, and products (Manyika et al. 2013).

African countries, however, are at different levels of development and subsequently feature varied socio-economic trajectories, which will react to digital automation in very different ways. A country's ability to embrace and leverage the new technology will vary depending on sociodemographic, educational, and economic factors, including level of development (i.e., fragile/post-conflict, emerging, developed), natural resource endowments, and human capacity. As each economy has its own strengths and constraints, each also faces different challenges and limitations. Hjort and Poulsen (2019) note that the demand for high-skilled workers as well as those with technological skills has increased across African countries with access to undersea high-speed internet cables. While the exact impact on the labor force is unclear, there have been winners and losers in terms of jobs in the new and emerging industries (Choi et al. 2019; AfDB et al. 2018; Manyika et al. 2017).

A recent World Bank publication—*The Future of Work in Africa Harnessing the Potential of Digital Technologies for All*—notes that African "countries have the potential for positive net job effects from digital technology adoption if they quickly close the gaps in digital infrastructure and digital skills" (Choi et al. 2019:30). With the roll-out of the African Continental Free Trade Agreement (AfCFTA) rapidly taking shape, technological innovation could further help the continent to benefit more from regional trade and manufacturing services linkages (Luke and MacLeod 2019; Choi et al. 2019; Hanson and Tang, Chap. 12, this volume).

Without doubt, the scale and impact of digitization and disruptive innovation in the global North by far outstrips that in the global South in general and Africa in particular. While incomparable in terms of reducing the economic costs associated with search, replication, transportation, tracking, verification (Goldfarb and Tucker 2019), and innovation (Deichmann et al. 2016), one cannot dismiss the emerging technology-driven landscape sweeping across the continent (AfDB et al. 2018; Acemoglu and Restrepo 2017). So, following the abovementioned introduction, the next section briefly conceptualizes disruptive innovations, then turns to examine how disruptive innovations are shaping work and employment in Africa, with a focus on emerging developments such as the shared and gig economies. The analysis highlights how these are shaping the job market and the potential impact on the agricultural, health, banking, and finance sectors. The chapter also addresses the challenges of disruptive innovations and efforts to mitigate the negative impacts. The chapter concludes by mapping out what countries can do to ride the wave of disruptive innovations, drawing on innovative developments already happening across the continent.

Disruptive Innovations and the Automation of Knowledge Work

Christensen (1997) initially used the term "disruptive technology" to address changes in innovation. In a subsequent work, Christensen and Raynor (2003) replaced disruptive technology with the term "disruptive innovation", technological advancements that are offered at relatively much lower cost to traditional users of rather similar technology, thus opening the door to new, often low-end, markets. Disruptive innovation, as Hwang and Christensen (2007) further point out, explains how upstart companies deliver more affordable and accessible solutions and can sweep away once-dominant firms with alarming regularity, often before the incumbents and their leaders realize that their days are numbered. Christensen, Ojomo, and Dillon (2019), WEF (2017), and Manyika et al. (2013, 2017) have suggested that investing in innovations, more specifically market-creating innovations, holds potential to beat a reliable path to prosperity for countries. For example, in the health sector, Christensen et al. (2017) argue that the health industry needs to have the courage to innovate their business models, breaking away from traditional sustaining innovation models to a more value-based model, accepting short-term financial risk in exchange for long-term success. To this end, the concept of disruptive innovation is particularly insightful for the process of automation of knowledge work by making flexible a hitherto inflexible system, easier and more accessible to potentially many more people by providing those low-end customers with a "good enough" product to get their foot in the door (Christensen et al. 2015).

Disruptive innovations that have changed the system of resource allocation and the nature of jobs in many sectors globally and increasingly across Africa include, but are not limited to, artificial intelligence, drones, radio frequency identification (RFID), blockchain, IoT, 5G technology, and digitization. These innovations have triggered a boom in the shared and gig economies.

The shared economy broadly refers to the phenomenon of using the plethora of mobile technologies to turn unused or underutilized assets, skills, or services owned by individuals into productive resources (Hanson and Puplampu 2018). Its ingenuity lies in its uncanny ability to harness new technologies such as smartphones, GPS, payment systems, identification, and feedback mechanisms to reduce transaction cost and connect people offering assets or services to consumers. In so doing, the shared economy generates value by matching these assets with consumers in need of, and willing to pay for, the services those assets could provide (Wosskow 2014). The gig economy, on the other hand, is an all-encompassing term increasingly used to describe people that are not salaried employees, but work independently and get paid for each transaction or "gig" that they complete, in brief, a labor market characterized by freelance and flexible work rather than the traditional nine-to-five working model.

Uber, which is available in over 630 cities worldwide, is today the posterchild of both the shared economy and the gig economy—two disruptive phenomena that have changed the system of resource allocation and the nature of jobs in many sectors. Uber, since 2013, has been operating across much of Africa, primarily Anglophone Africa, notably in Kenya, Tanzania, Uganda, South Africa, Egypt, Morocco, as well as Nigeria and Ghana (Mourdoukoutas 2017). Today, Uber alone employs over 59,000 drivers across Africa, most of whom are part-time or "gig" workers who use their own cars and drive for Uber to supplement their other sources of income (African Business 2019). This number excludes UberBoda, a product allowing riders to hail motorcycle taxis, or UberPoa, which serves tuk-tuk (auto rickshaw) market, as well as other similar car-share platforms such as Yango (Ghana), Taxi-Ivoire and AfriCAB (Côte d'Ivoire), Mondo Ride (Kenya), WhereIsMyTransport (South Africa), and YoTaxi (South Africa), to name a few.

Uber's growth, as well as that of similar ride-hailing apps, undoubtedly highlights how the combination of disruptive innovations can impact jobs, markets, and daily life. This is not to say that it has not been without problems. Uber and other ride-hailing apps have met resistance from traditional taxi drivers who fear they are losing their jobs or incomes to the tech-assisted ride-sharing movement (Mourdoukoutas 2017). Rideshares have been attacked in Nigeria as destroying taxi services with cheaper fares and in Kenya their cars were set on fire. In South Africa, taxi drivers similarly expressed unhappiness with what they perceived to be anticompetitive behavior of ride-share initiatives, leading to taxi drivers protesting against Uber and blocking the main airport roads (Mourdoukoutas 2017). Specifically in Durban, 12 metered-taxi associations banded together to launch their own e-hailing service YoTaxi, following which drivers of Uber and Bolt services were called upon to join them or face violence (Mavundza 2019). Tensions have also been recorded in Ghana and elsewhere. The question that comes up is: is this a glimpse of a new reality?

AFRICA'S REALITY AND THE EMERGING LANDSCAPE

Disruptive innovations in Africa are creating an environment where everyday citizens are being able to access information, healthcare, data, and services in more convenient, affordable, and proximate situations (Hanson and Puplampu 2018; Christensen et al. 2000). Already, capitalizing on the widespread growth of mobile technologies in the 2000s, many African entrepreneurs are embracing disruptive innovations and transforming their lives and communities in radical ways. These technologies, as Choi et al. (2019) state, are also generating new tasks that provide new job opportunities for millions, boosting the creation of direct and indirect jobs, and facilitating information and knowledge transfer between African businesses and workers, thereby enabling them to realign markets by minimizing information asymmetries, which has multidimensional benefits, including making formalization easier. The boom in shared- and gig-economy platforms has intensified the debate about the demise of the traditional employment contract and the persistence of widespread informal employment in Africa. However, unlike Uber or Airbnb, which generally disrupted largely formal sectors, transport services and hotel industry, respectively, many of Africa's new gig economy firms are writing the rules for whole new industries in local markets especially in the informal sector.

Over the past decade and a half, Africa has grown to become the world's second-largest mobile phone market, offering millions access to financial services, public health information, and more (AfDB et al. 2018). With almost one out of every four people currently using the internet, the continent is growing more connected than ever before and digital development in the region is accelerating (Choi et al. 2019). Africa's demographic dividend, the youth, are pacesetters in harnessing the possibilities of disruptive technologies to unleash their entrepreneurial potential. Consequently, there has been an emergence of a growing pool of mostly young, successful entrepreneurs, from Kenya, Rwanda, Uganda in the East, to Nigeria and Ghana in the West, to South Africa, Mozambique, and Mauritius in the South. The proliferation of ICT development clusters, such as iHub and NaiLab (Kenya), Hive CoLab and AppLab (Uganda), ActivSpaces (Cameroon), BantaLabs (Senegal), or infoDev's mLabs in Kenya and South Africa, is a proof of the new environment of collaboration, training, application and content development, and preincubation of firms taking place (World Bank/AFDB/AUC 2012). The result is the growing number of African technology hubs, which rose from 314 in 2016 to 442 in 2018 (Choi et al. 2019:91).

To shed further insight on the scale and impact of the emerging landscape, the following sections focus on how disruptive innovations are revising the work landscape in Africa, drawing on examples from the agricultural, health, and banking/finance industries—three sectors that expand our state of well-being, notably what we eat, how we finance our needs and wants, and what is central to employment generation in Africa.

Agriculture

Across Africa, digitization and disruptive innovations are transforming agricultural and agroforestry sectors. In 2018, an estimated 82 agritech start-ups were operating across Africa with over half launching in the previous two years (Disrupt Africa 2018). Innovations range from micro-weather stations to improve localized weather data and provision of crops in Kenya, to utilizing soil-monitoring sensors to improve tea plantation production in Rwanda, to employing radio frequency identification (RFID)-based livestock programs for tracking, theft prevention, and vaccination records in Botswana, Senegal, and Namibia. Elsewhere in Ghana as well as across the subregion, *Farmerline* is leveraging digital technologies to boost the productivity of farmers, transforming small-scale farmers into successful entrepreneurs by increasing their access to information, inputs and resources, by providing an online platform that connects and communicates with these farmers in their local dialects (Choi et al. 2019:87–88). Approximately 200,000 farmers across 11 countries have had their capacities developed and/or received knowledge on agricultural best practices, weather, market prices, and inputs via the platform (Choi et al. 2019). In Kenya, *DigiCow*, a digital technology from Kenyan Farmingtech Solutions Ltd., offers a mobile-based service delivery platform that links small livestock owners to veterinary and artificial insemination services, feed suppliers, and business enterprises. Yet another enterprise that offers technology services to farmers is *Agri-Wallet* also in Kenya, which avails a mobile financial platform to link farmers and buyers and input suppliers to buy inputs, with payments made through mobile money. *Agri-Wallet* also serves as a digital wallet for savings or to obtain loans. Similarly, across Burkina Faso, Ghana, Liberia, Tanzania, and Malawi, *Esoko* (https://www.esoko.com/) has made it possible for farmers to connect to markets. Here, blockchain technology is being utilized to guarantee food safety standards that are key to participating in lucrative international food markets. Started in 2008, *Esoko* today connects over one million farmers to essential services—weather forecasts, agronomic advice, market linkages, and insurance coverage.

In Côte d'Ivoire, Ghana, Guinea, Lesotho, Tanzania, and Zimbabwe, *EMA-i*, an early warning app developed by FAO, is facilitating quality and real-time livestock disease reporting captured by animal health workers in the field. The system is integrated into FAO's Global Animal Disease Information System (EMPRES-i) where data are safely stored and used by countries. The *EMA-i* system is easily adaptable to countries' existing livestock disease reporting systems (FAO 2019:11).

Other disrupters in this sector are *Hello Tractor*, which offers "Uber-like" tractor services to over 250,000 farmers, and *Farmers Pride Africa*, a one-stop "digishop" supporting 10,000 farmers to access inputs, livestock services, and agricultural insurance from reliable input providers and connecting them with buyers. Put otherwise, the greater spatial and temporal flexibility brought about by technology is bringing locations of production and sale closer together and driving major changes in the design of institutions, future value, and supply chains (WEF 2017; see also Puplampu and Essegbey, Chap. 3, this volume).

Across the continent innovations such as *Digital Green*, *Precision Agriculture for Development*, and *SunCulture* are offering smallholder farmers invaluable advisory services (Choi et al. 2019). Furthermore, digital technologies such as *M-Shamba*, *TruTrade Africa*, *Tulaa*, *ACRE Africa*, *Agri-Wallet*, and *Arifu* are supporting farmers, linking them with markets and fair prices for their produce, loans/finance, and so on (Choi et al. 2019:88). The above reflect some of the tech-savvy initiatives disrupting the agricultural sector by leveraging digitization and mobile technology to provide streamlined, affordable, and reliable services to farmers and agribusinesses, whether large or small. So many new technologies, products, and services are appearing that the entire sector will soon be unrecognizable to participants of a generation ago (Nijhuis and Herrmann 2019). Disruptive innovation tools are also empowering farmers to unlock new plant-based innovations and increasing their resilience to extreme weather events and climate change (Nijhuis and Herrmann 2019). New technologies not only are diffusing more rapidly than old ones, but also are having transformative spillover effects.

Health

Disruptive innovations are equally revolutionizing the healthcare sector in Africa, offering opportunities and opening possibilities to many countries facing shortages in health sector human capital, yet coupled with a high disease burden, and in urgent need of low-cost, efficient, and sustainable healthcare solutions that are easily accessible to the broader society. Across many African countries, GSM-connected refrigeration for vaccine delivery in the "cold chain" is taking place. Technology again played a key role during the 2014–2016 Ebola outbreak in West Africa. Sensor-enabled "band aids" were employed to monitor Ebola patients' ECG, heart rate, oxygen saturation, body temperature, respiratory rate, and position, all remotely, minimizing risk of infection while saving lives. Then there is *CareAi*, an AI-powered computing system anchored on blockchain that can diagnose infectious diseases, such as malaria, typhoid fever, and tuberculosis within seconds (HBR 2018; see also Oppong, Chap. 6, this volume).

Global positioning system (GPS) technology has also been leveraged to facilitate the prompt and precise delivery of medical supplies (e.g., blood, rabies vaccines, and antivenom) to remote and hard-to-reach health clinics in Rwanda and Ghana, through the activities of Zipline, a California-based robotics company. Zipline operates the medical drone delivery service with support from Gavi, Vaccine Alliance, Bill & Melinda Gates Foundation, UPS Foundation, Pfizer, and other partners (Bright 2019). Africa is becoming a testbed for commercial drone delivery and regulatory structures. In the past two years, South Africa passed commercial drone legislation to train and license pilots, Malawi opened a Drone Test Corridor to African and global partners, while Kenya, Ghana, and Tanzania have issued or updated drone regulatory guidelines and announced future unmanned aerial vehicle (UAV) initiatives (Bright 2019; Bright and Stein 2018).

Using mobile technologies, *mPedigree* and *Miti Health*, respectively, are transforming efforts to monitor and tackle the proliferation of fake and expired drugs in Ghana and Kenya. Other players from beyond the continent, notably India, are leveraging technology to address the shortages of health sector workers, in areas with a high disease burden. The situation, according to Santra, Mandal, and Das (2019), is fueling the need for teleradiology services in Africa. One such initiative is *RadSpa* by a Bengaluru-based company named Teleradiology Solutions which enables doctors to receive radiology images from hospitals in areas with low internet bandwidth and revert with diagnostic options. *RadSpa* also provides Continuing Medical Education (CME) programs for radiologists and doctors, to improve their knowledge of the latest advances in the medical field in Africa. The CME initiative is currently servicing populations in nine African countries (i.e., Ethiopia, Uganda, Zimbabwe, Djibouti, Botswana, Nigeria, Cameroon, Tanzania, and Zambia).

Yet another disruptive innovation in the healthcare sector is blockchain technology (Siyal et al. 2019; Gordon and Catalinide 2018). As cities are becoming "smarter", it makes for the utilization of massive amounts of data collected through IoT devices scattered throughout the built environment. Analyzing the data, mapping out patterns and trends, will go a long way to support the development of systems to solve problems, such as shortening emergency response times.

Banking and Finance

The growth of digital platforms in Africa is further offering new opportunities to bridge the current gap between often-insecure informal and formal employment and crucial mechanism for engaging with both existing and potential customers. Bridge companies such as M-Pesa, Jumia, and Car45 are pioneering new ways of injecting efficiency and higher productivity into traditional informal markets. These platforms are also helping to facilitate the operations of banks and financial institutions via cutting-edge software and automation systems. Today, there are an estimated 300 active digital platforms across Africa, employing close to five million workers. Jumia, which started in Nigeria, now operates in 14 countries on the continent. There is also M-Pesa with tentacles spanning the entire East African Community. Since its launch in 2007, M-Pesa, a mobile payment system, has enabled millions of informal sector workers to move money at lower cost, which has provided a significant boost to the Kenyan and Tanzanian economies (see Abdulhamid, Chap. 9, this volume). Another more recent example is Nigeria's Cars45, operated by Frontier Car Group. Nigeria's $12 billion used car industry is largely informal and characterized by distrust, a lack of standardization, and the absence of a structured dealer network. Cars45 facilitates the buying and selling of used cars by pricing and rating their condition in a transparent manner and conducting online auctions (Hruby 2019).

Across the continent, financial technology (FinTech) services, such as *PayStack* from Nigeria, an online payment company powering digital transfers, and *PayLock* from Ghana, a secure escrow platform that enables freelancers and clients to earn each other's trust by holding the payment for a job until it is completed, are transforming financial transactions and client experiences (Udoagwu 2019). *Paga*, another Nigerian digital payment platform, established less than seven years ago, has morphed into a multichannel network and platform to transfer money, pay bills, and buy things digitally. *Paga* currently serves over 13 million customers in Nigeria, along with a nationwide network of more than 21,500 mobile payment agents (Choi et al. 2019). Like M-Pesa in East Africa, the operations of *Paga* in Nigeria have resulted in the creation of "additional low-skill jobs at mom and pop stores, pharmacies, and grocery stores where people can get access to additional financial services" (Choi et al. 2019:9). Yet another FinTech company *Cellulant*, based in Kenya, is estimated to have raised $47 million in 2019 on its business of processing $350 million in payment transactions across 33 African countries (Nsehe 2018; Bright 2018). *Cellulant*, however, unlike M-Pesa, focuses more on people-to-business linkages as opposed to the people-to-people linkages.

In fragile and conflict-affected states, FinTechs are invaluable. For instance, during the West African Ebola crisis, the government of Sierra Leone relied on mobile wallets to help fight the Ebola virus outbreak. The UN also resorted to mobile payments for emergency workers to not only dramatically shorten payment times, but also to minimize fraud during the outbreak (IMF 2019). FinTechs are again being utilized to enhance and advance revenue collection, thereby contributing to domestic resource mobilization, a key objective of many African countries. FinTechs are therefore not only increasingly easing the process via which payments for goods and services are carried out, ensuring citizens have access to credit and capital using platforms that are fit-for-purpose and context specific, they also are driving evolution in financial services as they set new standards and change customer expectations (see Kouame and Kedir, Chap. 8, this volume).

The disruptions are forcing established banks and financial institutions to rapidly adopt new models as FinTechs bring broader financing access to customers through new products and frictionless digital processes. Ecobank, the continent's leading pan-African bank, recognizing the impact of FinTechs, set up its own mobile banking app, which, in just a few years following launch, has processed nine million transactions worth

US$1 billion. In a similar move, Africa's biggest bank in terms of assets, South Africa's Standard Bank, recently purchased a stake in local FinTech firm Nomanini to offer credit to potentially millions of small shop owners and other informal retailers across Africa. The Standard Bank invested US$4 million in Nomanini and aims to roll the service out across 14 African countries including, but not limited to, South Africa, Zambia, Mozambique, Malawi, Angola, Zimbabwe, Namibia, Ghana, Nigeria, Kenya, Tanzania, eSwatini, and Lesotho by early 2021 (Reuters 2019). As FinTechs proliferate, and pan-African banks expand, Hope (2018) cautions that it will be worthwhile for African Continental Free Trade Agreement (AfCFTA) to consider how the AfCFTA can support these developments. This is because the continent's GDP of US$2.6 trillion and a growing middle-class population of some 400 million are not a negligible market and present significant economies of scale and scope possibilities.

CHALLENGES

There are concerns about the negative impacts of automation on employment, labor, and the very nature of work (Acemoglu and Restrepo 2017; Manyika et al. 2017). For instance, the 2017 study by Manyika et al. (2017) suggests that approximately 50 percent of the "activities people are paid to do globally could theoretically be automated using currently demonstrated technologies." Manyika et al. (2017), further note that digital automation will trigger a fundamental restructuring of work, from the foundational structure of companies to the new roles of managers and employees alongside their robot colleagues. Similarly, Choi et al. (2019) argue that the 4IR and associated boom in automation technologies, including artificial intelligence, machine learning, and 5G, will be particularly disruptive to the workforce.

While the global estimates put forth by Manyika et al. (2017) may not necessarily hold true for African continent, given its current level of technological sophistication, there is no doubt that the increasing growth in mobile technology and the rise in disruptive innovations on the continent have implications for labor employment (Hanson and Puplampu 2018). The technological transformations in the agriculture, health, and banking sectors while creating novel employment possibilities, simultaneously raise concerns about the adequacy of existing legal and regulatory labor frameworks (Hanson and Puplampu 2018; Hagemann et al. 2018; McKinsey & Company 2018). Disruptive innovation and its associated shared and gig economies often cross traditional industry boundaries, with evolving products and services, shifting from one regulatory category to another. As Hagemann et al. (2018) point out, if a ride-hailing company begins delivering food, it can fall under the jurisdiction of health regulators. If it expands into helicopter service, it will fall under the purview of aviation regulators. If it uses autonomous vehicles for passengers, it may come under the jurisdiction of telecommunications regulators.

The result is an emerging complex relation between capital and labor, and the perennial question of winners and losers. For instance, according to Bloomberg (2018 cited in Choi et al. 2019), between 2016 and 2018, approximately 39 bank branch closures in Kenya were a direct result of the rapid adoption of mobile payment platforms. While the development is estimated to have resulted in job losses of roughly 6000 bank staff, the same period witnessed a boom in mobile financial services agents in excess of 69,000. Therefore, while the skills mix may be different, the net effect on labor employment can be said to be positive. Potential losers are however pushing back, be they taxi unions contesting Uber and other ride-share disruptors or the South African Commercial, Catering and Allied Workers Union (SACCAWU) fighting against retail chain Pick n Pay's attempts to introduce self-service tills at one of its Cape Town outlets.

In the absence of a strong social safety net in many African countries, there are worrying implications for the future of work and workers in a digital era. Many of the new jobs in the shared and gig economies are fluid and do not adhere to traditional labor regulations, social security, benefits, leave, and compensation. However, Choi et al. (2019) argue otherwise, noting that given Africa's widespread informality and smaller manufacturing base compared to other regions, automation is not likely to displace many workers in the coming years.

Yet another worry is the recent interest and investment by Google, Microsoft, Huawei, and other technology giants in Africa. The past year has witnessed Google's artificial intelligence (AI) center in Ghana, and its Africa Development Centre (ADC) with two initial sites in Kenya, and Nigeria. Microsoft, on the other hand, set up a shop in Nigeria and Kenya. As was expected, Chinese telecom giant Huawei joined the scramble too, announcing the launch of two data centers in South Africa. One hopes these developments, rather than becoming geopolitical flashpoints, will develop into models for innovation-driven development on the continent. However, if the ongoing struggle between the United States and China on 5G technology is anything to judge by, Africa could find itself caught between two technology powerhouses. African countries are already struggling to cope with the nature and speed of technological change. Many governments have only recently started reacting to the speed with which disruptive innovations are transforming their local economies and labor markets, by rushing to enact regulatory policies (Hanson and Puplampu 2018). For example, Ghana in 2016 became the first country in Africa to have a Standard of Understanding (SOU) signed between its Ministry of Transport and Uber. The SOU provides holistic guidelines for taxi operations and encourages the use of technology but regulates it for riders, drivers, and companies (Mourdoukoutas 2017). In South Africa, regulators have since 2013 been closely monitoring FinTechs and digital innovations following the establishment of an intergovernmental working group on FinTech between National Treasury, the South African Reserve Bank (SARB), the Financial Intelligence Centre (FIC), and the Financial Services Board (FSB) (CEFS 2019). South Africa is also using its Protection of Personal Information Act (POPIA) to ensure the safeguarding of personal information collected, processed, stored, and shared.

Mindful of the potential drawbacks, policy and decision makers, together with private sector actors, and tech enthusiasts across Africa at the 2019 World Economic Forum on Africa, themed "Shaping Inclusive Growth and Shared Futures in the Fourth Industrial Revolution", deliberated extensively on the pros and cons of the 4IR and disruptive innovation for Africa (WEF 2019). Likewise, key actors in the African finance arena are taking notice of the disruptive potential to the sector and planning for it. The 2019 Banking Innovation Africa Forum (#BIAF2019) themed "Transforming the African Banking Landscape Through Disruptive Innovations", held in Cape Town, South Africa, from 6–7 November, hosted over 50 plus attendees and experts from the African banking industry to discuss the impact of disruptive innovation on the future of Africa's financial and banking sector (PCM 2019).

Africans undoubtedly recognize the potential dislocation of its workforce as a result of automation, and the urgent need to nurture talent to realize the many opportunities of automation. This, however, will require skills training, enhanced education, capacity development, leadership, and a revisit of existing legal and regulatory frameworks, combined with forward-looking policy planning (WEF 2019; Shaw and Hanson 2019; Hjort and Poulsen 2019; Hanson and Puplampu 2018; Manyika et al. 2017).

CONCLUSION

Disruptive innovations are transforming and disrupting the way work is done today and will be approached in the future. Bridge companies, such as M-Pesa, Jumia, and Car45, are pioneering new ways of injecting efficiency and higher productivity into traditional informal markets. Investing in this trend is critical to solving Africa's pressing job creation need. The growth of digital platforms in Africa is not only offering new opportunities to bridge the current gap between often-insecure informal work and formal employment but is also changing how work and employment are perceived and approached in many sectors across the continent.

However, managing the new workplace and associated workforce transitions with foresight is not just a question of smart policy. Ensuring positive employment outcomes will require a focus on retooling the workforce, stepping up support for workers in transition, and improving how local and national labor markets function (Manyika et al. 2017). The dynamic possibilities inherent in the leapfrogging potential in mobile technologies (WEF 2019; Besada et al. 2016; GSMA 2015) provide the basis for a new kind of twenty-first-century development process in Africa. However, as illustrations highlighted above demonstrate, the impact of disruptive innovations will differ widely across the specific contexts in which they are introduced. The dynamics of South Africa, Kenya, Nigeria, and Rwanda differ markedly from that in Liberia, Sierra Leone, or South Sudan. Thus, leveraging the promise and inherent possibilities of digital technology depends on creating an enabling environment with fit-for-purpose, nuanced, and context-specific supportive policies in place, what Choi et al. (2019:8) refer to as "analog complements", comprising competition, capital, and capacity. Again, innovative ideas and digital technologies will not scale and reach success without a robust education sector policy, strategy, and plan (Hanson and Léautier 2011; AfDB et al. 2018; Hjort and Poulsen 2019). Accordingly, if Africa is to ride the wave of disruptive innovations and the automation of knowledge in a meaningful way, decision/policy makers, champions of industry, and leaders in institutions of higher education will need to embrace automation's benefits (WEF 2019) while addressing the worker transitions brought about by these technologies (Manyika et al. 2017).

References

Acemoglu, D., & Restrepo, P. (2017, March). *Robots and Jobs: Evidence from US Labor Markets* (NBER Working Paper No. 23285). National Bureau of Economic Research, Cambridge, MA.

AfDB, ADB, EBRD & IADB (African Development Bank, Asian Development Bank, European Bank for Reconstruction and Development, and Inter-American Development Bank). (2018). *The Future of Work: Regional Perspectives.* Washington, DC: Inter-American Development Bank.

Besada, H., Xue, J., Mathers, A., & Carey, R. (2016). Advancing African Agency in the New 2030 Transformative Development Agenda. *African Geographical Review,* 1–26. https://doi.org/10.1080/19376812.2016.1138232.

Bloomberg. (2018, March 6). National Bank Kenya Considering Branch Closures to Cut Costs. Available at: https://www.bloomberg.com/news/articles/2018-03-06/national-bank-kenya-considering-branch-closures-to-cut-costs. Accessed 25 Sept 2019.

Bright, J. (2018, September 6). With a $10 Million Round, Nigeria's Paga Plans Global Expansion. *TechCrunch.* Online. Available at: https://techcrunch.com/2018/09/06/paga/. Accessed 29 Oct 2019.

Bright, J. (2019, April 24). Drone Delivery Startup Zipline Launches UAV Medical Program in Ghana. *TechCrunch.* Available at: https://techcrunch.com/2019/04/24/drone-delivery-startup-zipline-launches-uav-medical-program-in-ghana/. Accessed 29 Oct 2019.

Bright, J., & Stein, S. (2018, September 16). African Experiments with Drone Technologies Could Leapfrog Decades of Infrastructure Neglect. *TechCrunch.* Online. Available at: https://techcrunch.com/2018/09/16/african-experiments-with-drone-technologies-could-leapfrog-decades-of-infrastructure-neglect/. Accessed 29 Oct 2019.

CEFS (Centre of Excellence in Financial Services). (2019). The Impact of the 4th Industrial Revolution on the South African Financial Services Market. *Genesis Analytics Online.* Available at: https://www.genesis-analytics.com/uploads/downloads/COEFS-TheimpactofthefourthindustrialrevolutiononfinancialservicesinSouthAfrica-final-1-FR.pdf. Accessed 6 Nov 2019.

Choi, J., Dutz, M., & Usman, Z. (2019). *The Future of Work in Africa Harnessing the Potential of Digital Technologies for All: A Companion to the World Development Report 2019 on the Changing Nature of Work.* Washington, DC: World Bank Group.

Christensen, C. M. (1997). *The Innovator's Dilemma – When New Technologies Cause Great Firms to Fail.* Cambridge: Harvard University Press.

Christensen, C. M., & Raynor, M. E. (2003). *The Innovator's Solution: Creating and Sustaining Successful Growth.* Boston: Harvard Business School Press.

Christensen, C. M., Bohmer, R. M. J., & Kenagy, J. (2000). Will Disruptive Innovations Cure Health Care? *Harvard Business Review, 78*(5), 102–117.

Christensen, C. M., Raynor, M. E., & McDonald, R. (2015, December). What Is Disruptive Innovation? *Harvard Business Review*, 44–53.

Christensen, C. M., Ojomo, E., & Dillon, K. (2019). *The Prosperity Paradox: How Innovation Can Lift Nations out of Poverty*. New York: Harper Collins.

Christensen, C., Waldeck, A., & Fogg, R. (2017). 'How Disruptive Innovation Can Finally Revolutionize Healthcare A Plan for Incumbents and Startups to Build a Future of Better Health and Lower Costs.' INDUSTRY HORIZONS // SPRING 2017 (Christensen Institute). Available at: https://www.christenseninstitute.org/wp-content/uploads/2017/06/How-Disruption-Can-Finally-Revolutionize-Healthcare.pdf. Accessed 29 Oct 2019

Deichmann, U. K., Goyal, A, & Mishra, D. K. (2016). Will Digital Technologies Transform Agriculture in Developing Countries? *Policy Research Working Paper*, no. WPS 7669. Washington, DC: World Bank.

Disrupt Africa. (2018). *African Tech Startups Funding Report 2018*. Available at: http://disrupt-africa.com/funding-report/#. Accessed 10 Sept 2019.

FAO. (2019). *Digital Technologies in Agriculture and Rural Areas - Briefing Paper*. Rome: FAO.

Goldfarb, A., & Tucker, C. (2019, March). Digital Economics, *Journal of Economic Literature, 57*(1), 3–43.

Gordon, W. J., & Catalinide, C. (2018). Blockchain Technology for Healthcare: Facilitating the Transition to Patient-Driven Interoperability. *Computational and Structural Biotechnology Journal, 16*, 224–230.

GSMA. (2015). *The Mobile Economy: Sub- Saharan Africa 2015*. London: GSMA.

Hagemann, R., Huddleston, J., & Thierer, A. D. (2018, February 5). Soft Law for Hard Problems: The Governance of Emerging Technologies in an Uncertain Future. *Colorado Technology Law Journal*. Available at SSRN: https://ssrn.com/abstract=3118539

Hanson, K. T., & Léautier, F. A. (2011). Enhancing Institutional Leadership in African Universities: Lessons from ACBF's Interventions. *World Journal of Entrepreneurship, Management & Sustainable Devt, 7*(2/3/4), 386–417.

Hanson, K. T., & Puplampu, K. P. (2018). The Internet of Things and the Sharing Economy: Harnessing the Possibilities for Africa's Sustainable Development Goals. In K. T. Hanson, K. P. Puplampu, & T. M. Shaw (Eds.), *From Millennium Development Goals to Sustainable Development Goals: Rethinking African Development* (pp. 133–151). New York: Routledge.

Harvard Business Review (HBR). (2018, August). *How New Technologies Could Transform Africa's Health Care System*. Available at: https://hbr.org/2018/08/how-new-technologies-could-transform-africas-health-care-system. Accessed 20 Sept 2019.

Hjort, J., & Poulsen, J. (2019). The Arrival of Fast Internet and Employment in Africa. *American Economic Review, 109*(3), 1032–1079.

Hope, A. (2018). The Right Kind of Disruption... New Banks in South Africa. *TRALAC Blog*. [Online]. Available at: https://www.tralac.org/blog/article/13636-the-right-kind-of-disruption-new-banks-in-south-africa.html. Accessed 30 Sept 2019.

Hruby, A. (2019). A New Kind of Company Is Revolutionising Africa's Gig Economy. *World Economic Forum*. Available at: https://www.weforum.org/agenda/2019/05/new-kind-of-company-revolutionising-africa-gig-economy/. Accessed 29 Oct 2019.

Hwang, J., & Christensen, C. M. (2007). Perspective – Disruptive Innovation in Health Care Delivery: A Framework for Business-Model Innovation. *Health Affairs, 27*(5), 1329–1335.

IMF (International Monetary Fund). (2019). *FinTech in Sub-Saharan African Countries A Game Changer?* (Africa Department No. 19/04). Washington, DC: IMF.

Kissinger, H. (2018, June). How the Enlightenment Ends: Philosophically, Intellectually—in Every Way—Human Society Is Unprepared for the Rise of Artificial Intelligence. *The Atlantic*. Available at: https://www.theatlantic.com/magazine/archive/2018/06/henry-kissinger-ai-could-mean-the-end-of-human-history/559124/. Accessed 28 July 2019.

Luke, D., & MacLeod, J. (2019). Bringing About Inclusive Trade in Africa with the African Continental Free Trade Area. In D. Luke & J. MacLeod (Eds.), *Inclusive Trade in Africa: The African Continental Free Trade Area in Comparative Perspective* (pp. 1–4). London: Routledge.

Manyika, J., Chui, M., Bughin, J., Dobbs R., Bisson, P., & Marrs, A. (2013, May). *Disruptive Technologies: Advances that Will Transform Life, Business, and the Global Economy*. McKinsey Global Institute Available at: https://www.mckinseypp.com/business-functions/digital-mckinsey/our-insights/disruptive-technologies. Accessed 10 June 2019.

Manyika, J., Lund, S., Chui, M., Bughin, J., Woetzel, J., Batra, P., Ko, R., & Sanghvi, S. (2017, November). *Jobs Lost, Jobs Gained: What the Future of Work Will Mean for Jobs, Skills, and Wages*. McKinsey Global Institute. [Online] Available at: https://www.mckinsey.com/featured-insights/future-of-work/jobs-lost-jobs-gained-what-the-future-of-work-will-mean-for-jobs-skills-and-wages. Accessed 20 June 2019.

Mavundza, B. (2019, October 22). Metered Taxis in Durban Want to Take on Uber with Their Own App – and a Bit of Intimidation. *Business Insider – South Africa*. Available at: https://www.businessinsider.co.za/yotaxi-launches-in-durban-to-compete-uber-and-taxify-2019-10. Accessed 29 Oct 2019.

McKinsey & Company (2018, February). *Roaring to Life: Growth and Innovation in African Retail Banking*. https://www.mckinsey.com/~/media/McKinsey/Industries/Financial%20Services/Our%20Insights/African%20retail%20bankings%20next%20growth%20frontier/Roaring-to-life-growth-and-innovation-in-African-retail-banking-web-final.ashx. Accessed 29 Oct 2019.

Mourdoukoutas, E. (2017, August – November). Africa's App-Based Taxis Battle Uber over Market Share: Local Techies Are Tailoring Products and Services to Suit Customers in Cities. *Africa Renewal*. Available at: https://www.un.org/africarenewal/magazine/august-november-2017/africa's-app-based-taxis-battle-uber-over-market-share. Accessed 20 June 2019.

Nijhuis, S., & Herrmann, I. (2019, October 10). The Fourth Industrial Revolution in Agriculture. *Strategy+Business* (Tech and Innovation). Available at: https://www.strategy-business.com/article/The-fourth-industrial-revolution-in-agriculture?gko=75733. Accessed 11 Oct 2019.

Nsehe, M. (2018, May 14). African FinTech Company Cellulant Raises $47.5 Million. *Forbes Online*. Available at: https://www.forbes.com/sites/mfonobongnsehe/2018/05/14/african-fintech-company-cellulant-raises-47-5-million/#5b1f8bbe7efb. Accessed 29 October 2019.

PCM (Payments and Cards Network). (2019). *Banking Innovation Africa Forum*. Online. Available at: https://www.teampcn.com/events/2019/11/06/default-calendar/banking-innovation-africa-forum. Accessed 29 Oct 2019.

Reuters. (2019, August 27). Africa's Biggest Bank Targets Its Smallest Shops in Fintech Deal. *Credit RSS*. Available at: https://www.reuters.com/article/standard-bank-nomanini/africas-biggest-bank-targets-its-smallest-shops-in-fintech-deal-idUSL5N25J30Z. Accessed 3 Nov 2019.

Santra, S., Mandal, T. S., & Das, P. (2019, June). *Leveraging Disruptive Technology Innovations for Healthcare Delivery in Sub-Saharan Africa* (ORF Issue Brief No. 298). Observer Research Foundation.

Shaw, T. M., & Hanson, K. T. (2019, April). *Artificial Intelligence & International Relations in Africa: Drivers of Sustainable Development?* Paper presented at the Shanghai, China.

Siyal, A. A., Junejo, A. Z., Zawish, M., Ahmed, K., Khalil, A., & Soursou, G. (2019). Applications of Blockchain Technology in Medicine and Healthcare: Challenges and Future Perspectives. *Cryptography, 3*(3), 1–16. https://doi.org/10.3390/cryptography3010003.

Thomas, D. (2019, October 29). Africa Can Be a Huge Growth Engine for Uber. *African Business Magazine*. Available at: https://africanbusinessmagazine.com/sectors/technology/africa-can-be-a-huge-growth-engine-for-uber/. Accessed 29 Oct 2019.

Udoagwu, K. (2019, September 27). *How FinTech Helps Power the Gig Economy in Africa*. Online. Available at: https://www.ask.degree/how-fintech-helps-power-the-gig-economy-in-africa/. Accessed 29 Oct 2019.

World Bank, African Development Bank, and African Union. (2012). *The Transformational Use of Information and Communication Technologies in Africa*. [Online]. Available at: http://siteresources.worldbank.org/ EXTINFORMATIONANDCOMMUNICATIONANDTECHNOLOGIES/ Resources/282822-1346223280837/MainReport.pdf. Accessed 10 May 10 2019).

World Economic Forum. (WEF). (2017, October). *Impact of the Fourth Industrial Revolution on Supply Chains*. Geneva: World Economic Forum. Available at: http://www3.weforum.org/docs/WEF_Impact_of_the_Fourth_Industrial_ Revolution_on_Supply_Chains_.pdf. Accessed 18 Aug 2019

World Economic Forum. (WEF). (2019, September 4–6). *World Economic Forum on Africa – 'Shaping Inclusive Growth and Shared Futures in the Fourth Industrial Revolution'*. Cape Town: WEF. Available at: http://www3.weforum.org/docs/WEF_AF19_Report.pdf

Wosskow, D. (2014, November). *Unlocking the Sharing Economy: An Independent Review*. Available at: https://assets.publishing.service.gov.uk/government/ uploads/system/uploads/attachment_data/file/378291/bis-14-1227-unlocking-the-sharing-economy-an-independent-review.pdf. Accessed 15 Aug 2019.

PART V

Emerging Issues, Challenges and the Way Forward

CHAPTER 14

Digital Transformation: A Connected and "Disrupted" Africa

Kobena T. Hanson, Timothy M. Shaw,
Korbla P. Puplampu, and Peter Arthur

INTRODUCTION

Across Africa, glimpses of the development and use of new and disruptive innovations are everywhere. Starting with mobile money platforms, today the continent lists a plethora of such innovations in almost every sector imaginable. Shaw and Hanson (2019) contend that Africa today has

K. T. Hanson (✉)
African Development Bank, Abidjan, Côte D'Ivoire
e-mail: k.hanson@afdb.org

T. M. Shaw
McCormack Graduate School, University of Massachusetts Boston, Boston, MA, USA

K. P. Puplampu
Department of Sociology, Grant MacEwan University, Edmonton, AB, Canada
e-mail: puplampuk@macewan.ca

P. Arthur
Department of Political Science, Dalhousie University, Halifax, NS, Canada
e-mail: peter.arthur@dal.ca

© The Author(s) 2020   295
P. Arthur et al. (eds.), *Disruptive Technologies, Innovation and Development in Africa*, International Political Economy Series,
https://doi.org/10.1007/978-3-030-40647-9_14

advanced as well as benefitted from mobile technologies, extending its own IoT, from cell phones to mobile finance such as M-Pesa, developed in Nairobi (iHub 2019). Such local initiatives have not gone unnoticed by the giants of industry in the technological sector. IBM opened a research lab in Nairobi a few years ago, and now Kenya's major universities are building laptop computers for school children, and other universities are offering MSc degrees in mobile finance supported by M-Pesa and Safaricom (Shaw and Hanson 2019). iHub partners with several local and global IT companies such as Chase Bank, Google, Hivos, Intel, IBM, Microsoft, Omidyar, Oracle, Nation Media Group (connected to the Aga Khan Foundation (AKF), hence the AK University), Safaricom, Samsung and more (iHub 2019). Elsewhere, in October 2016 at the Huawei Southern Africa Partner Summit held at the Huawei Innovation and Experience Center in Johannesburg, Huawei signed music cooperation contracts with global and local music vendors (IT News Africa 2019). Google opened an artificial intelligence (AI) center in Accra and its Africa Development Centre (ADC) with two initial sites in Nairobi and Lagos while Microsoft has set up a shop in Nigeria and Kenya (Hanson, Chap. 13, this volume). Although these developments portend positive possibilities, significant questions remain. One such question is the terms of the engagement between the technological giants and their local counterparts on issues such as intellectual property right, patent protection and knowledge co-creation.

Indeed, as contributors to this volume clearly demonstrate, the assumption often made in the extant literature that Africa's contribution to the digitization, AI and the IoT is minimal, is flawed (Brass and Hornsby 2019; Srinivasan 2019; Schwab 2016). As Shaw and Hanson (2019) suggest, and contributors to this volume validate, this assumption is far from reality. African states, companies, communities (including those in the diaspora), consumers, think-tanks and techpreneurs have been very active in using disruptive technology to address issues in several key sectors, from film and mobile finance to apps and drones (Shaw and Hanson 2019; Srinivasan 2019; Choi et al. 2019; Disrupt Africa 2018). Srinivasan (2019) argues that the dominant and majority users of social media platforms like Facebook are based in the global South. As such, when it comes to technology and innovation, it is important to have systems developed in a context that speaks to the reality of the users. This is the backdrop of the significance of the Nairobi-based innovation companies such as Africa Born 3D or AB3D and BRCK (Srinivasan 2019). While AB3D produces high-quality 3D printers by harnessing and using salvaged electronic waste, and the printers are affordable for the local population, BRCK designs Wi-Fi routers with the expressed aim of providing affordable if not free and accessible internet across Kenya. The work of these two companies are tangible demonstrations of local initiatives and using contextual knowledge to create products that will benefit the community.

Africa has undoubtedly grasped the promise of the 4IR (Liu 2019). The continent currently is home to over 400 tech hubs, with South Africa and Nigeria leading the charge with over 50 hubs each. Other countries like Egypt, Kenya, Morocco and Ghana are also making good strides. Together these countries host thousands of start-ups, along with the incubators, accelerators, innovation hubs, makerspaces, technology parks and co-working spaces that support them (Liu 2019). Several other developments such as the World Economic Forum's Africa Growth Platform, South Africa's new Centre for the Fourth Industrial Revolution (C4IR) and the African Union's African Continental Free Trade Area (AfCFTA) will individually and collectively help spur the connected and disrupted Africa we seek. Together, the growth in tech hubs coupled with the above developments is critical to enhancing and advancing a strong economic future (Liu 2019) while bringing governments, investors and businesses on the same page, safeguarding start-ups to thrive and become sustainable.

Many of the disruptions are happening locally as the unique challenges faced on the continent continue to give rise to new and innovative ideas. More importantly, Africa's policy and decision makers as well as the global community are taking notice (WEF 2019; PCM 2019; Disrupt Africa 2018). Increasingly, investors realizing the potential and possibilities around African technology start-ups are willing to finance these innovations. In 2018, funding raised by African tech start-ups totaled US$1.163 billion, compared to US$560 million in 2017, a +108% growth (Partech 2019). The incoming investments, and evolving enabling environment, at all levels (i.e., local, regional and continental), while promising, could benefit from the continent tapping into the promise of SDG 17 to court new partnerships and ensure effective coordination of its burgeoning innovation landscape (UNFPA 2019).

The contributing authors to this volume, drawing on their nuanced understanding of the continent and the extant literature, have attempted to tease out how digitization and the boom in disruptive technologies and innovation are giving rise to a new development space in Africa. This is one where: a) technology is helping to overcome the traditional barriers of distance and limited access to healthcare; b) products and services are being extended to new customers; and c) access to information, markets, finance and education for many citizens who previously were marginalized, is no longer defined by physical distance (PwC 2016). In this fast-evolving environment, even the very way that governance is undertaken has been fundamentally altered (Arthur, Chap. 2, this volume; see also Humphreys 2016; Gyampo 2017). So without a doubt, digitization and the associated boom in disruptive innovations are shaping both the lives and livelihoods of many across the continent (Manyika et al. 2017; Choi et al. 2019). This volume also acknowledges that the evolving landscape needs structure and capacity, both at the individual and institutional levels, meaningful policy and regulatory frameworks, as well as transformative leadership if Africa is to ride the wave of disruption. In the following sections, we attempt to answer the question: What capacity, policy and leadership imperatives does Africa need?

REALIZING A CONNECTED AND DISRUPTED AFRICA

According to WEF (2018) *Readiness for the Future of Production Report 2018*, notwithstanding the growth in tech hubs and innovation capacity or potential, other factors are essential to realizing the connected and disrupted African vision—notably getting institutional structures right, enhancing capacity and skills development, ensuring competitive trade and investment incentives and sustainable demand (see also Kararach et al. 2016; Besada et al. 2016). Also, of critical importance is having meaningful transformative leadership to beat a new path forward. It is for this reason that Shaw and Hanson (2019) argue that Africa needs to leverage digital technologies to become a disruptor itself, advancing its own variety of development in which its AI, IoT innovations and related services such as design, drones, fashion, film, foods, mobile finance, crowdsourcing (IDS 2016) and music facilitate its global role beyond commodities. PwC's (2016:42) report *Disrupting Africa: Riding the Wave of the Digital Revolution* similarly notes the transformative effect of digitization and disruptive innovations for Africa's economic potential while cautioning that to maximize the opportunities, businesses and policy makers alike need to be ready to take on the challenges ahead by creating the skills, telecoms and links that will ensure digital disruption has the infrastructure and capacity to be genuinely transformational.

CAPACITY

The role of education cannot be ignored in such an undertaking. While higher education in general requires significant capital investment (Mugo and Puplampu, Chap. 4, this volume), it is a strategic imperative if African countries meaningfully hope to leverage disruptive innovations (Choi et al. 2019). As highlighted in two recent WEF white papers, the 4IR will not only "shape the future of education, gender and work" (WEF 2017a) but also require "accelerating workforce reskilling" (WEF 2017b). To this end, African countries will need to develop the capacity of a critical mass, enhancing their creativity and technical skills on technology innovation and mastery of nuances of human interaction and experience in the digital age.

Currently, too few scientists and engineers in Africa work in sectors that drive economic transformation, a point underscored by the fact that African college graduates with a science, technology, engineering or mathematics (STEM) degree represent only 2 percent of the continent's total university-age population (AfDB 2018). Efforts need to be made to address this imbalance (Puplampu and Mugo, Chap. 7, this volume). Relatedly, countries need to train a cadre "of inventors and entrepreneurs to develop and scale digital technologies to boost the productivity of all workers, especially low-skilled workers in current and new occupations" (Choi et al. 2019:23). Uganda's Makerere University's AI and Data Science research lab offers a useful template in terms of training learners in AI for the future (Harsh et al. 2019; Srinivasan 2019). The lab's focus on building AI applications for localized applications has the potential to avoid some of the inherent biases built into AI algorithms, such as the Google's 2015 fiasco in which its photo applications labeled individuals with dark phenotypes as gorillas (BBC 2015). Thus, enhancing the capacity of local universities will not only augment the quality of learning and learners needed to better position African universities and institutions of higher learning as engines of innovation for sustainable development and transformation (Zeleza 2017), but also promote universal basic digital literacy that will enable broader participation of all segments of the population in the digital economy.

The issue of institutional capacity is another vital issue that demands attention (Hanson and Puplampu 2018), given its link to transformative leadership and capacity development of the regulators, regulatory and enforcement institutions, as well as individuals and institutions tasked with playing an oversight role. Institutions define and offer a framework for broader social development and the ability of any institution to discharge its mandate requires capable and adequate resources. The general lax attitudes of institutions, regardless of the sector, will continue to hinder and undermine the assumed benefits from disruptive technology.

POLICY

Disruptive innovations, digitization and associated growth in app development and utilization, while in themselves not substitutes for capable policy and institutions (Puplampu and Essegbey, Chap. 3, this volume), are valuable in a given context. The importance of having informed policies and functional institutions cannot be downplayed. Policies should have a component on the development of strategies for wider application and dissemination of disruptive energy technologies (Karekezi 2002). Policies that neither stifle innovation nor are reckless in their implementation will be key (Oppong, Chap. 6, this volume), be it in the agricultural, educational, energy, finance or service sector. The key issue then is the dynamics at stake in both policy making and implementation. It is common knowledge that policy making in the contemporary era of globalization is contested and uncertain. That reality calls for African policy makers to be astute and focused in the policy-making imperatives to better enhance and integrate disruptive technology into the broader continental and national agenda. Take the case of financial sector and disruptive technologies.

Technological innovations have informed drastic changes in the financial sector. Indeed, where with the help of mobile technologies, so much innovation is taking place, PwC (2016) flags the need for effective controls over "FinTech businesses that are growing rapidly and operate within systemically critical areas of the economy". Similarly, for purposes of "consumer protection, labor regulation, property rights, taxation …grasping how and when to regulate [disruptive innovation] companies is essential to keep consumers, operators and traditional companies satisfied, innovating and growing" (Hanson and Puplampu 2018:139). One essential ingredient required for a flourishing banking of financial sector is how policies engender trust in the operations of banking institutions (Baidoo and Akoto 2019). When trust is nonexistent or politicized in terms of the supervision of banks, the result in many cases is the collapse of banks, as was the case in Ghana (Osei-Fosu and Osei-Fosu 2017). The issue is that without adequate oversight and enforcement, financial sectors from the global North and the global South are prone to failure. The puzzling issue is how techno-optimists believe technological innovations will forestall or minimize such problems, an assumption that is made without realizing that technology always operates in a social context. A critical prerequisite and necessary element for understanding the social context is leadership, specifically political leadership.

Leadership

Leadership, its nature and type occupies an essential role in the extent to which technological and institutional capacity can shore up innovation in Africa. Indeed, getting "the political leadership equation right would make it possible to refocus on institutional capacity" (Hanson et al. 2018:169). The issue becomes the requirements for "fostering transformative leadership for Africa's Development" (ACBF 2019). According to ACBF (2019:5–6), transformative leadership

> requires developing and persuasively communicating an agenda for long-term success, fostering supportive institutions, and creating short-term opportunities as an additional incentive. Moreover, transformative leadership must inspire and mobilize the population, deploy and empower the best technical capabilities to implement and coordinate the transformation program, and cultivate the necessary political coalition to ensure sustainability. Transformative leadership is less about the leader or chief executive and more about the leadership group, drawn from the political and management segments of the state, the private sector, and civil society, who are capable of directing change toward desired outcomes. Transformative leadership nurtures the institutions and processes that enable the country to take advantage of whatever windows of opportunity are open, building on favorable conditions in the external environment and finding ways to weather and rise above "bad" conditions.

Based on the above, the fundamental question is whether the current crop of African leaders has the attributes of transformative leadership. If the ongoing attempts by leaders in various countries (from Algeria, Cameroon, Equatorial Guinea, Gabon, Guinea, Rwanda and Uganda) to entrench themselves through constitutional means, by engineering movements to abolish presidential term limits, then the paucity of transformative leadership will undermine the requirements for innovation. This is because the emerging environment calls for leaders who are emotionally intelligent, able to model and champion cooperative working, and possess the expertise to harness the collaborative intelligence of their organizations and create agile teams to deal with the incessant disruptions (Schwab 2016; Oosthuizen 2016). Equally important is the need for transformative leadership at the level of policy and decision making. Getting the political leadership equation right will ensure the refocus on capacity, which should in turn fast-track the continental breakthroughs in disruptive innovations (Hanson et al. 2018:168–169).

CONCLUSION

This chapter reiterates the voices of the volume's authors, in concurring with others elsewhere, to argue that disruptive technologies have, in an unimaginable way, changed and impacted various ways of doing things in countries throughout the world. For instance, apart from disruptive technologies shaping trade and investment, increasing access to knowledge, providing employment, impacting labor practices and helping to diversify the export base of African countries, it has also impacted how the nature of governance and political discourse occur. Notwithstanding the extensive research regarding the role and diffusion of technology, and the increasing appreciation of the benefits that have accompanied the use of various disruptive technologies, significant lacunae and challenges exist when it comes to African countries. It is in this vein that this book offers insights on the role of new and emerging technologies in African countries. Adopting a multidimensional analytical approach, the various contributions in this book make a significant contribution to the literature by demonstrating that changes, which have occurred because of disruptive technologies, cannot be underestimated.

Technology has benefits and drawbacks. The challenge is the ability or flexibility required from institutions to manage new disruptive technologies in key areas such as finance, agriculture and health or to transform the political discourse and governance arrangements and reorganize the workforce in many parts of Africa. The need for structural and institutional changes will be necessary and required if desired expectations and results of disruptive technologies are to be realized. It is in this regard that the authors affirm the importance of education and other capacity development measures, transformative leadership, increased investments in telecommunications industry, and a need to have the requisite infrastructure and related industries in place in African countries if the desired benefits of disruptive technologies are to be realized. These recommendations and suggestions, if followed through by African governments and key stakeholders, will have the potential of improving and further enhancing the increasing benefits associated with disruptive technologies.

References

AfDB (African Development Bank Group). (2018). *Africa Economic Outlook 2018*. Abidjan: AfDB.

Africa Capacity Building Foundation (ACBF). (2019). *Africa Capacity Report 2019 – Fostering Transformative Leadership for Africa's Development*. Harare: ACBF.

Baidoo, S. T., & Akoto, L. (2019). Does Trust in Financial Institutions Drive Formal Saving? Empirical Evidence from Ghana. *International Social Science Journal, 69*(231), 63–78. https://doi.org/10.1111/issj.12200.

Besada, H., Xue, J., Mathers, A., & Carey, R. (2016). Advancing African Agency in the New 2030 Transformative Development Agenda. *African Geographical Review*, 1–26. https://doi.org/10.1080/19376812.2016.1138232.

Brass, I., & Hornsby, D. J. (2019). Digital Technological Innovation the IPE. In T. M. Shaw et al. (Eds.), *The Palgrave Handbook of Contemporary IPE* (pp. 615–631). London: Palgrave Macmillan.

British Broadcasting Corporation (BBC). (2015). *Google Apologizes for Photos App's Racist Blunder*. https://www.bbc.com/news/technology-33347866. Accessed 23 Dec 2019.

Choi, J., Dutz, M., & Usman, Z. (2019). *The Future of Work in Africa – Harnessing the Potential of Digital Technologies for All: A Companion to the World Development Report 2019 on the Changing Nature of Work*. Washington, DC: World Bank Group.

Disrupt Africa. (2018). *African Tech Startups Funding Report 2018*. Available at: http://disrupt-africa.com/funding-report/#. Accessed 10 Sept 2019.

Gyampo, R. E. V. (2017). Social Media, Traditional Media and Party Politics in Ghana. *Africa Review, 9*(2), 125–139. https://www.tandfonline.com/doi/full/10.1080/09744053.2017.1329806.

Hanson, K. T., & Puplampu, K. P. (2018). The Internet of Things and the Sharing Economy: Harnessing the Possibilities for Africa's Sustainable Development Goals. In K. T. Hanson, K. P. Puplampu, & T. M. Shaw (Eds.), *From Millennium Development Goals to Sustainable Development Goals: Rethinking African Development* (pp. 133–151). New York: Routledge.

Hanson, K. T., Puplampu, K. P., & Shaw, T. M. (2018). Crystallizing the Africa Rising Narrative with Sustainable Development. In Hanson et al. (Eds.), *From Millennium Development Goals to Sustainable Development Goals: Rethinking African Development* (pp. 167–177). New York: Routledge.

Harsh, M., Holden, K., Wetmore, J., Zachary, G. P., & Bal, R. (2019). Situating Science in Africa: The Dynamics of Computing Research in Nairobi and Kampala. *Social Studies of Science, 49*(1), 52–76. https://doi.org/10.1177/0306312719829595.

Humphreys, A. (2016). *Social Media: Enduring Principles*. New York: Oxford University Press.

IDS. (2016, November). *Ten Frontier Technologies for International Development*. University of Sussex. www.ids.ac.uk

IHub. (2019). *iHub Research Resources*. www.ihub.co.ke. Accessed 13 Dec 2019.

IT News Africa. (2019). *5 Things You Should Know About the New HUAWEI FreeBuds 3*. Available at: https://www.itnewsafrica.com/2019/11/5-things-you-should-know-about-the-new-huawei-freebuds-3/. Accessed 13 Dec 2019.

Kararach, G., Besada, H., & Shaw, T. (2016). African Development, Political Economy and the Road to Agenda 2063. In G. Kararach, H. Besada, & T. Shaw (Eds.), *Development in Africa: Reframing the Lens after the MDGs* (pp. 365–392). Policy: Bristol.

Karekezi, S. (2002). Poverty and Energy in Africa-A Brief Review. *Energy Policy, 30*(11), 915–919.

Liu, A. (2019, September 1). Africa's Future Is Innovation Rather than Industrialization. *WEF* Online. Available at: https://www.weforum.org/agenda/2019/09/africa-innovation-rather-than-industrialization/. Accessed 9 Nov 2019.

Manyika, J., Lund, S., Chui, M., Bughin, J., Woetzel, J., Batra, P., Ko, R., & Sanghvi, S. (2017, November). *Jobs Lost, Jobs Gained: What the Future of Work Will Mean for Jobs, Skills, and Wages*. McKinsey Global Institute. Available at: https://www.mckinsey.com/featured-insights/future-of-work/jobs-lost-jobs-gained-what-the-future-of-work-will-mean-for-jobs-skills-and-wages. Accessed 20 June 2019.

Oosthuizen, J. H. (2016). Entrepreneurial Intelligence: Expanding Schwab's Four-type Intelligence Proposition to Meaningfully Address the Challenges of the 4IR. In *Proceedings of 28th Annual Conference of the Southern African Institute of Management Scientists* (September), University of Pretoria, South Africa (ISBN: 978–0–620-71797-7).

Osei-Fosu, A. K., & Osei-Fosu, A. K. (2017, July 31). The Sustainability of Microfinance Institutions in Ghana: Causes of Proliferation and Frequent Collapse of Savings and Loan Companies. *Africa Development and Resources Research Institute Journal*, Ghana Vol. 26, No. 9(4), 39–58, ISSN-L: 2343–6662.

Partech. (2019, March 22). 2018 Was a Monumental Year for African Tech Start-Ups with US$1.163B Raised in Equity! *Partech Africa*. Available at: https://partechpartners.com/news/2018-was-monumental-year-african-tech-start-ups-us1163b-raised-equity/. Accessed 10 Nov 2019.

PCM (Payments and Cards Network). (2019). *Banking Innovation Africa Forum*. Online. Available at: https://www.teampcn.com/events/2019/11/06/default-calendar/banking-innovation-africa-forum. Accessed 29 Oct 2019.

PwC. (2016). *Disrupting Africa: Riding the Wave of the Digital Revolution*. [Online] Available at: https://www.pwc.com/gx/en/issues/high-growth-markets/assets/disrupting-africa-riding-the-wave-of-the-digital-revolution.pdf. Accessed 29 Oct 2019.

Schwab, K. (2016). *The Fourth Industrial Revolution*. New York: Crown for WEF.

Shaw, T. M., & Hanson, K. T. (2019, April). *Artificial Intelligence & International Relations in Africa: Drivers of sustainable development?* Paper presented at Shanghai Conference, China.

Srinivasan, R. (2019). *Beyond the Valley: How Innovators Around the World Are Overcoming Inequality and Creating the Technologies of Tomorrow*. Cambridge, MA: The MIT Press.

UNFPA. (2019). *GOAL 17 – Partnership: UNFPA's Approach for the Transformation of Africa and the World*.

World Economic Forum. (WEF). (2017a). *Realizing Human Potential in the Fourth Industrial Revolution– An Agenda for Leaders to Shape the Future of Education, Gender and Work* (Paper). Geneva: WEF.

World Economic Forum. (WEF). (2017b). *Accelerating Workforce Reskilling for the Fourth Industrial Revolution: An Agenda for Leaders to Shape the Future of Education, Gender and Work* (Paper). Geneva: WEF.

World Economic Forum. (WEF). (2018). *Readiness for Future Production Report 2018*. Geneva: WEF. Available at: http://www3.weforum.org/docs/FOP_Readiness_Report_2018.pdf

World Economic Forum. (WEF). (2019, September 4–6). *World Economic Forum on Africa – 'Shaping Inclusive Growth and Shared Futures in the Fourth Industrial Revolution.'* Cape Town: WEF. Available at: http://www3.weforum.org/docs/WEF_AF19_Report.pdf

Zeleza, P. T. (2017). Positioning Universities as Engines of Innovation for Sustainable Development and Transformation. *Journal of Higher Education in Africa, 15*(2), 1–22. https://www.jstor.org/stable/10.2307/26640368

INDEX[1]

[1] Note: Page numbers followed by 'n' refer to notes.

© The Author(s) 2020
P. Arthur et al. (eds.), *Disruptive Technologies, Innovation and Development in Africa*, International Political Economy Series, https://doi.org/10.1007/978-3-030-40647-9

CPSIA information can be obtained
at www.ICGtesting.com
Printed in the USA
LVHW021714080621
689564LV00010BA/1132

9 783030 406493